Advance Praise for *Democracy Unchained*

"This courageous book is a timely treatment of our crisis of democracy! The variety of powerful voices and cogency of analytical viewpoints are badly needed in these grim neo-fascist times!"

—Cornel West, Harvard University

"Where do we go from here? In *Democracy Unchained* some of the country's best minds tackle this most urgent of questions. The result is a must-read for anyone interested in—or worried about—the future of our Republic."

—Elizabeth Kolbert, staff writer, *The New Yorker*,
Pulitzer Prize winner for *The Sixth Extinction*

"This collection of essays by preeminent Americans from a wide array of backgrounds and professions, edited by David W. Orr, Andrew Gumbel, Bakari Kitwana, and William S. Becker, may someday be recognized as the twenty-first-century equivalent of the Federalist Papers. Certainly the times are no less perilous than when Hamilton, Madison, and Jay set their pens to paper."

—Richard Louv, author of *The Nature Principle*
and *Our Wild Calling*

"*Democracy Unchained* is an extraordinary compilation of essays on the parlous state of democracy in our country. Irrespective of whether you may disagree with some essays, every voting citizen should make the effort to read them all as they will stimulate serious thinking and make us better stewards of our democracy."

—Theodore Roosevelt IV, managing director and
chairman, Barclays Clean Tech Initiative

"The looming climate catastrophe requires that we disenthrall ourselves from the constructs and assumptions of the past. *Democracy Unchained* presents an urgent opportunity to think anew, and to engage Americans from every part of America."

—Tim Wirth, former U.S. senator from Colorado;
president emeritus, United Nations Foundation

"*Democracy Unchained*, in both spirit and substance, represents a revolutionary collection of voices and ideas imbued with the kind of hard-headed hope of which the country is in desperate need. We've grumbled amongst ourselves and wrung our hands long enough in the face of these issues, and now here comes an array of disparate and visionary thinkers ready to address the uncomfortable truths inherent in our flawed America."

—Eliza Griswold, writer, Pulitzer Prize winner

"Brilliant, provocative, and timely. These superb essays invite us to reimagine and revitalize democratic institutions and practices. The invitation has never been more urgent or more persuasively articulated."

—Mary Evelyn Tucker, Yale University, co-director,
Forum on Religion and Ecology

"The five-alarm fire that is our democracy in the present moment is a conflagration of our own making, but also one that we alone can put out. This book is a warning, a jolt to the system, but also a way out."

—Tim Egan, *The New York Times*

"Whatever your greatest public worry—from the climate emergency to extreme inequality—none can be resolved without democracy. So, here's your tool for getting to the root solution. Let's dig deep together."

—Frances Moore Lappé

Democracy Unchained

HOW TO REBUILD GOVERNMENT
FOR THE PEOPLE

Edited by
David W. Orr,
Andrew Gumbel,
Bakari Kitwana,
and William S. Becker

THE
NEW
PRESS

NEW YORK
LONDON

© 2020 by The New Press
All rights reserved.
No part of this book may be reproduced, in any form, without written permission from
the publisher.

Requests for permission to reproduce selections from this book should be made through
our website: https://thenewpress.com/contact.

Published in the United States by The New Press, New York, 2020
Distributed by Two Rivers Distribution

ISBN 978-1-62097-513-8 (pb)
ISBN 978-1-62097-514-5 (ebook)

CIP data is available

The New Press publishes books that promote and enrich public discussion and
understanding of the issues vital to our democracy and to a more equitable world. These
books are made possible by the enthusiasm of our readers; the support of a committed
group of donors, large and small; the collaboration of our many partners in the
independent media and the not-for-profit sector; booksellers, who often hand-sell
New Press books; librarians; and above all by our authors.

www.thenewpress.com

Composition by Westchester Publishing Services
This book was set in Minion Pro

Printed in the United States of America

10   9   8   7   6   5   4   3   2   1

To John Powers

The Master doesn't talk, he acts.
When his work is done,
The people say, "Amazing:
We did it, all by ourselves!"
                    —Lao Tzu[1]

CONTENTS

PART II. FOUNDATIONS OF DEMOCRACY

PART III. POLICY CHALLENGES

FOREWORD

Democracy Unchained: How to Rebuild Government for the People

Like a house with a leaking roof, sagging floors, broken windows, and a crumbling foundation, American democracy is suffering from decades of disrepair. The challenge of reforming and updating democratic institutions would be difficult enough in "normal" times, but we do not live in normal times. The pace of change is faster than ever, the problems bigger, the corruption deeper, the risks more global, the time to prevent the worst that could happen is short, and the consequences of further delay beyond reckoning.

The election of 2016 exposed how vulnerable our democracy has become to social and economic divisions, foreign influence, and brazen demagoguery. We have stumbled into a "post-truth" world—a house of mirrors in a circus of the bizarre. Porn stars and illicit payments, corruption and emoluments, WikiLeaks and fake news, *Barr v. Mueller*, the alt-right and white supremacists, an unstable and impulsive president with his "base," coal versus solar, an avalanche of mendacity, Russians in the shadows. Up is down, black is white, in is out, truth is fake. Democracy is always at risk to deceit and to those who refuse to abide by the rules and procedures necessary for civil civic discourse. Absent a decent regard for truth and respect for the law, however, democracy dies, and with it "the last best hope of earth."

The conversations that led to this book began at a three-day conference on "The State of American Democracy" at Oberlin College in November 2017. We intended to clarify the historic and institutional origins of the election of 2016 and the growing risk that we are coming unmoored from our history and our highest values. Conservative writer David Frum puts it this way: "We are living through the most dangerous challenge to the free government of the United States that anyone alive has encountered. What happens next is up to you and me."[1]

Democracy is a wager that its citizens have the stamina and wisdom to maintain a government of, by, and for the people. In the words of Harvard University political scientist Michael Sandel: "The hope of our time rests with those who can summon the conviction and restraint to make sense of our condition and repair the civic life on which democracy depends." In that spirit, we are committed to repairing and strengthening democracy and believe it to be a requisite for meeting large challenges ahead including that of a rapidly changing climate.

The title is adapted from Nancy MacLean's book *Democracy in Chains*. We intend this both as an extension of Professor MacLean's brilliant historical analysis and as a statement of our belief that democracy has yet to achieve its full potential. From early conversations in the Athenian agora to the present, its advance has been intermittent and incomplete. The chains to be broken are those of racism, oligarchy, exclusion, militarization, ignorance, complacency, and the lack of imagination about how to rebuild our politics and government for all the people.

David W. Orr
Oberlin, Ohio

INTRODUCTION

Does Democracy Have a Future?

David W. Orr

If we should perish, the ruthlessness of the foe would be only the secondary cause of the disaster. The primary cause would be that the strength of a giant nation was directed by eyes too blind to see all the hazards of the struggle; and the blindness would be induced not by some accident of nature or history but by hatred and vainglory.

—Reinhold Niebuhr[1]

Plato thought democracy a preface to tyranny. Aristotle was not much more sanguine. The founders of our republic were wary of it. John Adams believed that democracies always end by committing suicide. James Madison believed that with luck democracy in America might last a century. Alexis de Tocqueville thought it would evolve into majority tyranny. English writer E.M. Forster could give it only two cheers, H.L. Mencken none at all, believing people incorrigibly stupid. Economist Joseph Schumpeter likewise thought voters became dumber when they entered the political arena. Robert Dahl, perhaps the greatest student of democracy in the twentieth century, described himself as a "pessimist" about its future. Winston Churchill captured our predicament in his oft-quoted observation that democracy was the worst form of government except for all the others ever tried. In short, democracy is always a bet that enough people will know enough, care enough, be tolerant enough, and be informed enough to participate competently in the conduct of the public business. The United States, a representative democracy, is not exempt from the terms of the wager.

Democracy in America did not begin democratically but with a land grab that displaced those who had occupied the continent for thousands of years. Arrogance magnified the sins of conquest. The European conquerors saw little need to consult native peoples about how to live in a place some called "turtle island," with its varied cultures, ecologies, animals, and landforms. The Europeans were armed with superior weaponry, religious certainty, ideas of enlightened progress, an unshakable belief in the legitimacy of acquiring land by fiat, and, not the least, new diseases that killed millions of natives more effectively than bullets. The truth is that those who settled in what they thought was a vast wilderness did not know "what they were doing because they did not know what they were undoing." Most did not care to know because they had come to improve their lot in one way or another and were not overly concerned about the rights and lives of those they had displaced.

The spaciousness and abundance of the frontier made democracy, for those included, more likely, more stable, and, given their devotion to Christianity and the brutality of the conquest, more ironic. The exodus of millions from a crowded Europe to the new world lessened population pressures and a further drift into political chaos. European occupation of the Americas changed the ratios of people to land, soils, minerals, and forests. And for a few centuries, it lessened stresses posed by overpopulation and scarcity of land and resources. It did not alleviate, however, the challenges caused by class, inequality, archaic governance, and the Dickensian ravages of early capitalism.

A constitution that condoned slavery was yet another potentially fatal impediment to democracy. Historians have long argued whether that compromise was necessary in order to create the nation, but, either way, the price exacted was suffering beyond comprehension and eventually a Civil War that in some ways has never ended. The wealth derived from the sweat and blood of slaves in the cotton fields was theft on a grand scale, and the effects, unrequited, linger today in the persistent poverty of their descendants.

Thomas Jefferson, a slave owner, wrote "all men are created equal," but he did not know the full import of those words. From bondage, however, its victims could see a farther horizon and a larger idea of liberty. In due course, the writings, spoken words, and actions of Frederick Douglass, Abraham Lincoln, W.E.B. Du Bois, Langston Hughes, Martin Luther King Jr., James Baldwin, Barbara Jordan, Toni Morrison, and thousands of others gave meaning and power to the larger idea of an inclusive democracy that embraced everyone regardless of race, ethnicity, nationality, gender, religion, or station in life. If the moral arc of the universe does indeed bend toward justice, it will owe to the fierce determination and expansive vision of people at the margins armed only with the ideal of justice and the faith that the long experiment in democracy will not be in vain.

The rise of the modern corporation posed yet another threat to democracy. Although the Constitution made no mention of corporations, they soon multiplied and thrived amidst the many opportunities to accumulate vast fortunes in a frontier economy where legal and cultural restrictions were minimal, labor costs low, and resources cheap and abundant. By the end of the nineteenth century, the "robber barons" and their lawyers had succeeded in promulgating the convenient idea that corporations were "persons" protected by the due process clause of the Fourteenth Amendment, originally intended to protect the rights of former slaves. Labor unions, churches, and civic organizations, by contrast, have no such legal status. Corporations thereby acquired the rights to lie, conceal, patent life, and exercise their freedom of speech by buying elections. Corporate power, thereby, became the scaffolding of our politics and rendered people of mere flesh and blood increasingly subservient to the structure and prerogatives of wealth. The upshot of that legal reasoning run amuck is starkly evident in two Supreme Court decisions. In *Bush v. Gore* (2000), the court intervened to stop Florida from completing a recount of votes in a highly contested and, as it turned out, fateful presidential election. The five majority justices, with no apparent embarrassment, declared its decision not applicable to any future legal disputes. In *Citizens United v. Federal Election Commission* (2010), five conservative members of the court removed restrictions on unaccountable "dark" money in political campaigns, giving permission to the very wealthy to buy elections anonymously and further undermine democracy. Neither decision should come as a surprise. The expansive imperative of corporate capitalism, whether from the boardroom or the bench, causes it to attack the regulatory powers of the state, mislead the public, and corrupt legislatures and courts alike. In short, as political scientist Charles Lindblom once wrote, the problem is that "the large Corporation fits oddly into democratic theory and vision. Indeed, it does not fit."[2]

The problem, however, may have less to do with the malleable abstraction called the corporation than with the uneasy and unequal relationship that exists between democracy and capitalism. The common wisdom is that the two are opposite sides of the same coin of freedom. But freedom for a few to become inordinately rich works against the reasonable levels of economic equality necessary for a true democracy.[3] History shows that democracy can exist with or without capitalism. Capitalism has at times shown itself agreeable to communism and fascism as well.[4] In other words, the supposedly happy marriage of democracy and capitalism has been more like an unhappy and unequal co-habitation. Capitalism, unsupervised, is a bully, expanding, monopolizing, and eventually corrupting democracy. Its *modus operandi*, according to Adam Smith, its founding theoretician, is secrecy, collusion, and conspiracy among the powerful: "People of the same trade seldom meet together, even for merriment and diversion, but the conversation ends in a conspiracy against the public, or in some contrivance to raise prices."[5]

The fact is that concentration of wealth, disrupted only by occasional war and revolution, is baked into the logic of unregulated capital.[6] The corruption of the public business follows. *Laissez-faire* capitalism, as Mark Twain once noted, gave rise not only to the conspicuous extravagance of the Gilded Age but also to the best legislatures money could buy. The same is true of our time—only in a more deodorized and sophisticated manner and without brown bags filled with hundred-dollar bills. The curators of the ideas and theories devised to explain and justify the manifold ways of mammon chose long ago to regard the study of economics narrowly, modeled on disciplines of physics and mathematics. Adam Smith, on the other hand, regarded himself broadly as a "political economist" concerned with moral philosophy as much as with the ways by which nations accumulate wealth. The decision to constrict the study of how humankind earns its keep, otherwise known as economics, left the professors and practitioners of neo-liberal economics indifferent or even blind to looming crises, including rapid climate change, the rights of our descendants, and the limits to material expansion on a finite Earth governed by the laws of entropy and ecology.

There is a silver lining in that, for a time, economic growth fueled by cheap fossil fuels supported the growth of science and technology and

thereby helped to improve human health, extend life spans, reduce drudg-
ery, increase mobility, spread education, and even create the knowledge
necessary to understand how fragile it is. The question, however, is whether
prosperity can be sustained without wrecking its biophysical foundations
or social stability. It is an old question and the answer throughout history has been imperialism in one form or another. In a policy memo written in 1948, diplomat George Kennan put it this way: "We have about
50 percent of the world's wealth but only 6.3 percent of its population . . .
our real task in the coming period is to devise a pattern of relationships
which will permit us to maintain this position of disparity without positive detriment to our national security . . . we will have to dispense with
all sentimentality and day-dreaming."[7] The word "empire" is conspicu-
ously absent.

Kennan's view was hardly new. American democracy has been warped
by the centuries of expanding frontiers, continual war, racism, empire
building, and the rising costs of militarism.[8] Long ago, James Madison
warned that: "A standing military force, with an overgrown Executive will
not long be safe companions to liberty. The means of defence agst. [sic]
Foreign danger, have been always the instruments of tyranny at home."[9]
One hundred and seventy-four years later, Dwight Eisenhower warned
similarly of a military-industrial complex that could, in time, corrupt and
bankrupt our democracy. Six decades and half a dozen wars later, those
words read like an epitaph for a country grown into an empire that spends
more on its military than the next seven countries combined and maintains upward of one thousand bases around the world. Militarism, in other
words, has a tight grip on our politics, treasury, economy, and imagination, with results evident in endless and unwinnable wars overseas and
despair at home.[10]

The prospects for democracy have been rendered still more dubious
in what Harvard professor Shoshana Zuboff calls "the age of surveillance
capitalism."[11] The revolution in social media and the internet came with
promises to connect all of us in the warm embrace of togetherness. What
could go wrong? Well, a short list includes elections corrupted or stolen,
fake news, heightened incivility, detachment from facts and reason,
extensive foreign meddling in our affairs, an easy platform for a bizarre
menagerie of sociopathy, addiction to any device with a screen—what

Oliver Sacks describes as "a neurological catastrophe on a gigantic scale"—and a deeper manipulation of the citizenry than even George Orwell could have foreseen.[12] In Zuboff's words, surveillance capitalism

> [is a] market-driven coup from above . . . a *coup de gens:* an overthrow of the people concealed as the technological Trojan horse that is Big Other. . . . It is a form of tyranny that feeds on people but is not of the people. In a surreal paradox, this coup is celebrated as "personalization," although it defiles, ignores, overrides, and displaces everything about you and me that is personal.[13]

With much secrecy but little subtlety, the moguls behind Google, Facebook, and Amazon long for a world run by algorithms, not by the reasoned deliberations of flesh-and-blood people capable of choosing their future by democratic means. The profits of surveillance capitalism, however, belong to the moguls; the loss of privacy, control, independence, and transparency is the price demanded of the public. It is the most sinister challenge imaginable to the idea of an independent, informed, and engaged citizenry capable of reason, restraint, and empathy.

In summary, America is an incomplete democracy living beyond its means.[14] From its origins, it has incurred debts moral, economic, and ecological to the excluded and the exploited. Our forebears did not pay for the land they seized. Landowners and capitalists did not pay the true costs of the labor required for extracting and processing raw materials. They did not pay the replacement costs for resources used and discarded. They did not pay for the human suffering imposed in the name of progress or consider the intrinsic value of the cultures and creatures driven to extinction. We are leaving our descendants a land less fertile, less bountiful, less healthy, less biologically diverse, and more threatened by a rapidly worsening climate. The fact that many of these costs are incalculable does not make them any less real. Democracy in America, in other words, is in arrears, which is to say that it has failed to live up to its promise.

Under any circumstances, democracy is difficult. It requires partisans to honor the written and unwritten rules that prioritize the public good over lesser interests. It requires respect for differences of opinion, divergent values, fair procedures, the sanctity of voting, honest elections, the peaceful transfer of power, and for facts, evidence, and reason. It requires pragmatism, tolerance, and a mutual desire to find common ground. In fevered times especially, democracy requires decorum, forbearance, and humility. It becomes all but impossible when corrupted by greed or overrun by partisans too certain of their certainties. In the absence of rules, partisan advantage trumps the common good and democracy deteriorates into a barroom brawl that describes our current political predicament all too well.

Among the many reasons for our present malaise, two stand out. In the words of political scientists Steven Levitsky and Daniel Ziblatt, the primary cause is the Republican Party's "twenty-five year march to the right," by which it became "the main driver of the chasm between the parties."[15] The second is the election of Donald J. Trump.[16] In a whirlwind of effrontery, mendacity, incompetence, venality, malice, and possibly worse, his administration has further weakened the capacity of the office of the presidency to lead, of government to govern, of public agencies to protect the public interest, of the press to report the news, and of the public to focus on issues that matter.[17] He exploits old fears and animosities along the primal fault lines of race and ethnicity with no thought for the public consequences. Among other possibilities, the Trump years will be remembered as a long drought of inspiration, wisdom, humor, kindness, and unity. The legacy of President Trump, Senator Mitch McConnell, and their media enablers will be a weaker, more divided, less tolerant, and more violent nation. They have weakened the federal government by reducing taxes on the wealthiest, cutting social programs for the poorest, making remarkably inferior appointments to important positions, eviscerating environmental protections, ignoring ethical standards, lowering morale throughout federal agencies, and endless distractions that wasted years that we did not have to waste.[18] The guiding philosophy is that of the looter—to get all that one can while the getting is good. To that end, President Trump has created a kakistocracy, an ancient Greek word that means government by the worst, least qualified, and most unscrupulous.

The upshot is that, once elected, the forty-sixth president will preside over a diminished federal capacity to respond effectively to domestic problems, the climate emergency, and the growing crisis of global disorder. Consequently, the first priorities of the next president must be to restore the integrity of the office, repair a badly damaged executive branch, and rebuild competence throughout federal departments and agencies. Some of the damage is repairable, but much of it will last for a long time. Replacing blatantly unqualified appointees now scattered throughout the government with qualified personnel dedicated to public service and to the mission of the particular agency is a longer process.[19] There is no fast way to restore respect for a free press, reestablish the integrity of our public words, undo the effects of pervasive corruption, rebuild an unbiased and competent justice system, restore a proper respect for science and logic, or heal wounds inflicted in the years of hyper-partisanship. The vitality of our democracy and our fate as a nation, however, depend on repairing the damage to public institutions and public agencies and the wounds to the national spirit. Whatever the particulars, the path ahead will be strewn with litigation, vexing constitutional questions, continuing political and social divisions, the threat of politically-motivated violence, international disorder, and a greatly weakened U.S. position in world affairs. The reality is that our democratic institutions are failing.[20] What's to be done?

The search for answers might begin by asking why the public in our democracy counts for so little. "The defining political fact of our time," legal scholar Tim Wu writes: "is not polarization. It's the inability of even large bi-partisan majorities to get what they want."[21] In effect, the bridge that should connect public opinion to public policy is now a toll bridge accessible only to the rich. According to Wu, "about seventy-five percent of Americans favor higher taxes for the ultra-wealthy" and "eighty-three percent favor strong net neutrality rules." The same is true of many other issues. Given a choice and accurate information, how many Americans would prefer breathing filthy air, drinking polluted water, eating chemically saturated food, or living in a much hotter and more capricious climate? What the public wants and needs, however, does not matter much.[22] What matters most is what K-Street lobbyists want.

Perhaps rule by experts would be better. The case for democracy, however, does not depend on the efficiency of results, but rather on the recognition that it is "the one idea to have emerged from the long story of human oppression that insists upon a people's inalienable right to rule themselves."[23] Democratically formed governments are the manifestation of the belief that people have inherent dignity and the right to equal treatment under the law. They have the right to choose how and by whom they are governed. The case for democracy does not presume the inherent goodness and wisdom of citizens, as Jean-Jacques Rousseau proposed, but rather the opposite. In James Madison's oft-quoted words: "If men were angels, no government would be necessary. If angels were to govern men, neither external nor internal controls on government would be necessary."[24] C.S. Lewis put it this way: "The real reason for democracy, is that mankind is so fallen that no man can be trusted with unchecked power over his fellows . . . no men [are] fit to be masters."[25] He considered himself undeserving of even "a share in governing a hen-house." In other words, the case for democracy rests, not on our virtues, but in the acknowledgment of our flaws.

Democracy, however, works only under certain conditions. The founding generation singled out two in particular: an educated and discerning citizenry and a free press. Civic education, however, is disappearing from the curriculum to save money. The news once reported by newspapers and broadsheets now comes by print, television, radio, and increasingly by tweet and social media, any of which can enlighten and inform, but also lie and inflame with a straight face. If the state of the free press is a valid indicator of the health of our democracy, we have good reason for concern. The internet has opened the floodgates for increasingly sophisticated misinformation that precisely targets particular segments of the voting public. Protected by both its anonymity and the constitutional right to free speech, it represents a growing mismatch between agrarian-era institutions and the rapidly developing technologies of the twenty-first century.

A related concern has to do with the role of Fox News. Its business strategy is the adroit use of entertainment, misinformation, and fear projected on vulnerable target populations, "because it keeps people watching."[26] The use of television for partisan political purposes or the animosity of a particular news source toward a particular politician is hardly new. What is new is the fusion of Fox with a particular party and specifically with Donald Trump and his war on the press as "the enemy of the people." His persistent charges of "fake news" against legitimate media is an assault on our capacity to discern the truth and on democracy itself. "A free press and democracy," as media expert Marvin Kalb writes, "are tightly intertwined, each sustaining the other. Lose one, and you lose the other."[27]

Finally, the problem of democracy is not that it does not or will not work but rather, as is sometimes said, that we never tried it.[28] The authors of the Constitution were suspicious of "the people," and one way or another we have been living with a limited vision of democratic possibilities ever since.[29] Democracy too often stops at the factory gate, outside the "C" suite, or outside the legislature. It is time to grow a citizenry, not merely smarter consumers; build forums for public deliberation, not silos for ideologues; support competent public agencies defending the public interest, not pander to the interests of K-Street; and it is time to eliminate all outside money for political campaigns and banish purchased politicians once and for all. Most important, it is time to establish and protect a federal right to vote in fair electoral districts.

On such things, we have reason for cautious optimism. The rise of women in politics across the United States, the mobilization of young people around climate change, and the backlash against corporate authoritarianism evident in the midterm elections of 2018 all signal a hopeful change in American politics. H.R. 1, the "For the People Act" passed by the House of Representatives in March 2019, is a blueprint for deep reform in American democracy and perhaps the beginning of a larger movement to establish a more rigorous and robust democracy. In the right settings and with a bit of supervision, people can overcome partisan animosity to deliberate thoughtfully, rationally, and civilly about political issues. The practice of "deliberative democracy" is one way to bring people together across the political spectrum that "promotes considered judgment and counteracts populism."[30] There are others as well suggesting that we have good alternatives to endless partisan warfare. We have been traveling in a horse-and-buggy democracy for too long; it is time to upgrade and build new, robust public institutions and forums for public engagement at all levels.

Can democratic societies rise to the challenge? Can we protect and improve our democracy? Everything we hold dear as people and value as a nation depends on the answer. In some measure, we have done it before, in our founding as a nation, in the Civil War, in the New Deal, and in the civil rights movement. We now face a much larger test of our commitment to protect and enlarge the ideal of democracy and government of, by, and for all of the people.

The pages that follow are organized into four sections beginning with six chapters on the origins of the present crisis of democracy. Those in the second section describe the foundations of a robust and resilient democracy. Chapters in the third section address vexing policy challenges that must be resolved or managed, not the least of which is the growing crisis of rapid climate change, which will complicate and amplify other problems. The final section poses the question of "Who should act?" Beginning with a revised and greatly improved federal government, the answer includes states, cities, foundations, and institutions of higher education. A more complete answer would be everyone, every organization, every corporation, and every institution. For those who believe in democracy, it is all-hands-on-deck time in America—indeed, everywhere.

We do not presume to have covered the complicated terrain of democracy in its entirety. We selected some issues, omitted others, and all deserve more attention than we had time and space to give. Our goals are to clarify what is at stake, describe a better future than what is in prospect, chart a path forward, and get on with the practical work of repairing and strengthening our democracy from precinct to Pennsylvania Avenue.

Whatever else it comes to mean, an improved and more resilient democracy is not a return to an imaginary bygone era, but something new: a more perfect union that includes all Americans regardless of race, religion, and station in life. They, in turn, must learn to be competent citizen-trustees representing humankind past, present, and future in a succession of obligation and affection. This would be an intergenerational democracy of sorts in which the living, a minority, would also consider the well-being of those yet to be born—a large majority.

Achieving that more inclusive and wiser country will also require advances in the art and science of democratic governance. Instead of self-defeating gridlock between warring factions, can we learn to act in concert to protect our common wealth of air, water, lands, biological diversity, and the values of truth, justice, and decency that we hold in common? From a purely technical standpoint, good reasons exist for hope in our expanding capabilities in earth systems science, computing, forecasting, modeling, ecological design, and sustainable management of soils, forests, waters, and wildlife. The more difficult challenges are political and moral. The great work of our time is to create a more competent, just, and resilient democracy with malice toward none and with charity for all.

Part I

THE CRISIS OF DEMOCRACY

POPULISM AND DEMOCRACY

Yascha Mounk

I t is difficult now to recall either the supposed certainties that structured American political discourse before November 8, 2016, or the deep sense of disorientation that enveloped it afterward.

When Donald J. Trump was rewarded for one of the nastiest campaigns in American history by being elected as the country's forty-fifth president, all of the things that political commentators had long told the world, and themselves, were proven to be so much wishful thinking. No, it was not impossible for an extremist like Trump to win a major party presidential nomination. No, Republican voters did not abandon the party en masse when he did. And no, there was no magical safety valve that would kick in to right the system when all the usual mechanisms failed.

In the weeks and months that followed the election, the diffuse sense of horror slowly crystallized into three pressing questions:

1. Would Trump's election prove to be an aberration, or was it part of a much wider trend, both in the United States and around the world?
2. Could Trump inflict real damage on America's institutions, or would the existence of checks and balances contain the carnage?
3. Would Trump's opponents be able to build a broad ideological coalition against him, or would they tear each other apart with ever more elaborate litmus tests of rage and ideological purity?

It remains too early to offer a definitive answer to any one of these questions. When the history of the twenty-first century is written in years to come, Trump could still feature as a curious aberration. Courts, civil society institutions, and a re-energized Congress could yet defend the rule of law against the daily onslaught from the administration. And of course the hope remains that the American people will deliver a stinging rebuke to Trump in 2020, throwing him out of office with a crushing majority.

But three years into the Trump presidency, the most plausible answer to each of these questions is rather more pessimistic.

Trump's Election Is No Aberration

It is a common frailty of the human mind to project past trends far into the future—to think that a stock that has risen precipitously in the last years will continue to soar in value, or that a team that has won the championship for each of the last five seasons will once again vanquish its competitors. And yet, the definition of madness sometimes lies not in expecting that the same action will eventually produce a different result, but rather in assuming that it will keep bringing about the same outcome. When the number of horse carriages in New York rose precipitously in the early twentieth century, a report warned that every inch of the city's streets would soon be covered in manure; then the car was invented.

Reflecting on this all-too-human bias, it is tempting to wonder whether the astounding rise of authoritarian populism we have recently witnessed might soon reverse course. Was the 2016 election owed to the force of Donald Trump's personality, or to a much broader—and longer lasting—trend?

The Republican Party has, in the past, demonstrated a profound ability to transform itself. George W. Bush was in important ways different from John McCain; John McCain was in important ways different from Mitt Romney; and Mitt Romney bears little resemblance to Donald Trump. Whether Trump wins or loses in 2020, the real answer about whether authoritarian populism has become the new mold of Republican politics or merely owes its prominence to the peculiar political talents of a New York real estate mogul and reality television star will only be answered in the 2024 Republican primaries. But though the future of the Republican Party may still be in doubt, events beyond America's borders strongly suggest that Trump is not nearly as unique as the hopeful interpretation of him as an aberration of American politics would imply.

Speaking in Fulton, Missouri, in March of 1946, Winston Churchill lamented the Iron Curtain that was descending across the heart of Europe, from Stettin in the Baltic to Trieste in the Adriatic. In early 2019, it was possible to drive along that historic fault line—starting in Poland

and the Czech Republic, and passing through Hungary and Austria—without ever leaving a country ruled by authoritarian populists.

Take just one example: Thanks to its vibrant civil society, its history of free and fair elections, and its comparatively high GDP, political scientists long ago proclaimed Hungary a "consolidated democracy." Since the election of Viktor Orban in 2010, however, the country has quickly become more autocratic: Orban has packed Hungary's highest court and its powerful electoral commission with his own loyalists, transformed state television channels into propaganda outlets, brought critical newspapers under the control of his allies, and severely damaged the country's voting system. Over the past year, his oppression has become even more crushing. Central European University, perhaps the country's best institution of higher learning, has now been forced to flee Hungary. Orban has reappointed himself prime minister in elections that were somewhat free but barely fair. According to a new report from Freedom House,[1] the country is only "partly free," a historic first for a member state of the European Union.

It would be tempting to put the scary developments in countries like Hungary, Poland, and Romania down to their long legacy of totalitarian rule or the recency of their democratic institutions. But the sad truth is that these same developments are quickly taking root in parts of the continent that have been democratic for much longer. In Italy, for example, populists took nearly two-thirds of the vote in last year's elections; the Five Star Movement and the League then formed a left–right populist government that recalls the tradition of the red–brown pacts.

The attack on liberal democracy has been even more concerted in other parts of the world. In the Philippines, Rodrigo Duterte has quickly transformed a longstanding democracy into a personalistic autocracy ruled by his whim. In Turkey, Recep Tayyip Erdoğan has jailed a record number of journalists, fired thousands of independent-minded civil servants, and resorted to canceling elections whose outcome he disliked. In Venezuela, years of attacks on democratic institutions have culminated in one of the more ruthless and most dysfunctional dictatorships in the world. Meanwhile, a prime minister in India and a president in Brazil are doing their best to follow suit.

These developments are part of a broader pattern: across the globe, democracy is retreating. According to the Freedom House report, we are now entering the thirteenth year of a "democratic recession": for over a decade, more countries have moved away from democracy than have moved toward it.[2] Three of the four most populous democracies in the world are now ruled by authoritarian populists.

It is, as I have pointed out, perfectly possible that this trend will eventually go into reverse. Just as the reasons for the global rise of authoritarian populism are not yet fully understood, so too its appeal could start to sag for reasons that still lie beyond our grasp. But for now, the evidence suggests a much more pessimistic conclusion: whereas it was still possible to treat Trump's election as a bizarre aberration in the fall of 2016, it now looks like no more than the most mesmerizing part of a much broader story.

Trump Has Severely Damaged Democratic Institutions

In the fall of 2016, optimists and pessimists passionately debated the future of the Republican Party.

Optimists pointed to the large ideological differences between Trump and traditional conservatives, predicting that the Republican Party would be able to curtail his most destructive instincts. Pessimists pointed out that Trump had been able to win his party's nomination in good part because the ideology he supplanted had long since run out of steam, predicting that he would slowly be able to reshape the party in his own image through a series of primary challenges.

The optimists were far too naive. But so, it turns out, were pessimists like me. For in the end, most Republican congressmen and senators simply turned on a dime. Once he was in office, some of Trump's most eloquent critics quickly reinvented themselves as some of his most shameless toadies. (See: Graham, Lindsey.)

Trump's capture of the Republican Party has allowed him to govern with few restraints. The American public has long since ceased to expect that his outrageous utterances might be refuted by senior members of his own party. Whether Trump "jokingly" floats the idea of staying in office beyond his second term, states that his opponents should not enjoy freedom of speech, or lauds some of history's most brutal dictators as honorable statesmen, the response from his congressional allies is a deafeningly shameful silence.

But the complicity extends well beyond pretending not to hear (or read) what he says. The failure of Republicans in Congress to exercise any serious check on the president is only the most visible manifestation of a system of checks and balances that has proven to be much less muscular than most people predicted. After threatening to jail his main opponent and calling into doubt whether he would respect the outcome of the election during the campaign, Trump has, while in office, undermined the independence of law enforcement institutions and threatened to impose a national state of emergency to build a wall on the southern border.

In each case, the people who were supposed to oppose Trump mostly failed to do their job. Attorney General William Barr seems to conceive of his role as serving the interests of his boss, rather than those of the United States. It is no longer unimaginable that the Department of Justice might run a spurious investigation into the Democratic presidential candidate in 2020. However justified they might be on substantive grounds, impeachment proceedings are a fool's errand because it seems exceedingly unlikely that a significant number of Senate Republicans could turn against Trump.

It takes a long time to dismantle a democracy. Even in less affluent or consolidated democracies like Turkey and Venezuela, it took multiple stints in office for aspiring dictators to eliminate institutional obstacles to their power. So the American Republic is not lost yet, and it is very likely that its institutions will prove sufficiently strong to give Democrats a real chance to take back the executive at the ballot box in upcoming elections.

But even if Trump should lose the upcoming elections and leave the White House in ignominy, his presidency will have exposed the brittleness of the world's oldest democracy. For despite his open disdain for democratic traditions, and the constant scandals that have plagued his administration, he has consolidated his hold of the Republican Party, evaded accountability in Congress, and perilously expanded the powers of the presidency.

We Are Failing to Build a Broad Coalition

A few months ago, my colleague Jordan Kyle and I set out to construct the first systematic study of the impact populists around the world have had on their countries' democratic institutions over the past three decades.[3] Our findings are sobering. Looking at all populists who have taken power in their countries since the 1990s, we found they were four times as likely as other elected governments to do lasting damage to the extent to which their country can be considered democratic. Only a third of populist presidents and prime ministers leave office because they lose free and fair elections, or respect their term limits. About half of them succeed in changing the constitution to give themselves expanded powers. Many significantly curtail the civil and political liberties enjoyed by those subject to their rule. And while they frequently campaign on a promise to root out corruption, the countries they govern have, on average, become significantly *more* corrupt.

But despite these pieces of bad news, the main takeaway is far from fatalistic. After all, our study demonstrated that there are also plenty of cases in which a disciplined and energized opposition has managed to withstand the government's attempts to expand its own powers. Just as there are authoritarian populists who have managed to concentrate power in their own hands and destroy the liberties of their subjects, so too there are citizens who have removed aspiring autocrats from office by winning a resounding victory at the polls or impeaching them for massive malfeasance.

What, then, can we do to resist Trump's attacks on democratic institutions?

The experience of other countries suggests three primary lessons. First, the opposition virtually always underestimates the populist, failing to see the shrewdness that lurks beneath his bluster. From upper-class Venezuelans who were convinced that Hugo Chavez could not possibly have the skills to stay in power to educated Italians who just knew that their compatriots would soon recognize Silvio Berlusconi as a cartoonish charlatan, they sneered all the way to the slaughterhouse. All too often, this disdain for the populist figurehead was accompanied by a palpable denigration of his supporters.

Second, opponents of populists often fail to work together until they are united in powerlessness. In most countries, populists only ascend to high office because their adversaries fail to conclude an electoral pact. And though it would be natural to assume that an authoritarian threat would help to focus the mind, the opposite often proves true: feeling anguished and afraid, the populist's opponents start to play the politics of purity, imposing ever more demanding litmus tests on potential partners and refusing to embrace former allies of the populist who are willing to turn their back on him.

Third, opponents of populists often fail to set out a positive vision for a better country. Instead of trying to convince their fellow citizens that they can deliver tangible benefits, they get fixated on the ample failings of their enemy. If only they draw enough attention to his lies, his bigotry, and his bad taste, they seem to think, the country is finally going to wake from its nightmare with a bewildered start.

But most of the supporters of populists are fully aware that their champion lies, that he hates, and that he is boorish. Convinced that traditional politicians have nothing to offer them, this is precisely what they like about him. There's always the chance, they tell themselves, that the populist will deliver on a fraction of his unrealistic promises. And at the very least, he will spare them the preening hypocrisy of the old guard. It is never easy for the opposition to displace a populist. But these three lessons help to guide the way toward the right course of action: if defenders of democracy take the populist threat seriously, work together across traditional ideological divides, and offer a constructive alternative, they will maximize their chance to defend their institutions.

In Turkey, a new charismatic opposition leader has just demonstrated how big a transformation this strategy can effect. For years, the country's main opposition party simply tried to mobilize its base to oppose Erdoğan. Strongly committed to a form of secularism that could, at times, turn into disdain for devout Muslims, the leaders of the Republican People's Party made few inroads among that key demographic.

This only began to change when Ekrem İmamoğlu rose to prominence as the party's candidate for the mayoralty of Istanbul. Unlike his predecessors, İmamoğlu emphasized love rather than hate, and reconciliation rather than recrimination. Though he never shied away from criticizing Erdoğan for his oppressive policies, he deliberately set out to show Erdoğan's erstwhile supporters that they were welcome in his own coalition. Breaking with the precedent in the party, he even went to tour the mosques of Istanbul in the run-up to his election, talking about the practical needs of his would-be constituents and pointing to his past record as an indication that he would deliver the goods.

The impact of İmamoğlu's change in tone has been immediate. Thanks to his immense popularity, Erdoğan has now lost control of the country's most important city for the first time in decades—and the opposition can finally mount a credible challenge to the regime at the next presidential election. But are we, here in the United States, about to heed those same lessons?

When the Black Death ravaged medieval Europe, it was powerlessness, as much as fear, that drove people to the brink of insanity. With little sense of what might have caused the deadly epidemic, and no knowledge of how to respond, it was all the more tempting for people to focus on those few things that were under their control. And so it is, in hindsight, hardly surprising that periods of especially high mortality coincided with especially vicious pogroms. Beaten by an invisible pathogen, its would-be victims turned to scape the one goat they had enough power to victimize in turn: the Jews who had supposedly poisoned the well.

Faced with a terrifying administration they feel powerless to check or control, many members of the resistance have fallen prey to the same all-too-human instinct. Instead of welcoming any principled opponent of Trump's into their fold, they have focused a depressing portion of their energies on casting supposed pollutants out of the tribe. And instead of assembling the broadest possible coalition, we are in the middle of scrutinizing the purity of those who are already on our side.

The sorry fate of the much-heralded Never Trump Conservatives is the most obvious sign of this failure to build a broad coalition. Many conservatives who looked steadfast and courageous during the 2016 campaign have since scurried back into the oppressively tight embrace of Trumpism. Some have fully joined the liberal side, swelling the ranks of MSNBC contributors, but doing little to counter Trump's appeal among right-of-center Americans. The rest of the dwindling band looks more lonely than ever, viciously vilified by the right and disdainfully dismissed by the left.

Amidst the daily outrages of the Trump administration, the fate of the Never Trumpers may seem thoroughly irrelevant. But what is at stake in our collective inability to create a viable space for the center-right in American life goes well beyond those few individuals. For even those who are, like me, proudly on the left should recognize that a democracy that contains many right-of-center voters can only function when it has a right-of-center party with a real commitment to democratic institutions. Unless the Democratic Party will somehow pull off the feat of winning every single election for the next three decades, or we want to resign ourselves to handing over power to authoritarian populists in the Trumpian mold every four to eight years, the reestablishment of a viable conservative movement that has freed itself from Trumpism is in the interest of all of us.

In 2016, Donald Trump won about 63 million votes. Shocked as we may—and should—be by that fact, it obviously implies that any attractive vision for the future of this country needs to tell some story about how his erstwhile supporters will come to embrace it. But very little serious intellectual energy has, in the past years, gone into grappling with this crucial challenge. Instead, Trump's most vocal opponents appear to hold fast to a thesis that first gained wider currency in the heady days after Barack Obama's election. The liberal attitudes of the young, coupled with the rising share of the electorate made up by ethnic minorities, is meant to deliver Democrats their long-awaited dominance.

What I am most struck by in this vision is not so much how disastrously wrong such predictions have turned out to be in the past, or even how flimsy the underlying assumptions are. (Try predicting the politics of 2019 by looking at how Irish Americans and Italian Americans voted in 1969.) Rather, it is how dystopian the future it promises looks.

Martin Luther King Jr. had the audacity to dream of a future in which "little black boys and girls will be holding hands with little white boys and girls."[4] Barack Obama had the audacity to hope that "the union could and should be perfected over time . . . to provide men and women of every color and creed their full rights and obligations as citizens of the United States."[5] Given the bitter experience of the past few years, it is perfectly understandable that many good people now consider such ideals of interracial harmony laughably naive. But all they have, for now, put in the place of these older aspirations is an overconfident insistence on total victory. If their most audacious dream came true, the 63 million people who put Trump into the White House would be, not transformed or convinced of a more constructive political vision, but rather voted into oblivion.

Trump is deeply unpopular. Those pessimists on the left who confidently predict that he is sure to win re-election in 2020 are no more sophisticated than the naive optimists who just knew that Hillary Clinton would prove to be unbeatable in 2016. Even if Trump's administration survives the next months without enormous scandals or a serious economic slowdown, Democrats have a good shot at winning in 2020.

This has emboldened a big part of the Democratic base to go for broke. For them, nothing short of complete ideological purity will suffice. Faced with an eminently beatable opponent, and convinced that the tide of history is on their side, they are in no mood for compromise.

I wish that I, too, could be that sanguine. But while only about 43 percent of likely voters approve of Trump's performance in office, it has so far proven surprisingly difficult to find a Democratic candidate who isn't similarly unpopular. In early head-to-head polls, most frontrunners beat Trump by, at best, a disconcertingly slim margin. And while early polls may say little about the ultimate outcome, I fear that they are at least as likely to under- as to overstate Trump's ultimate performance. After all, it is difficult to think of the shocking scandal or novel line of attack that might prompt Trump's remaining loyalists to abandon him en masse. Many of the Democratic candidates, by contrast, have not yet been the subject of the intense scrutiny and hysterical vilification that is shortly coming their way.

More broadly, a narrow victory fought on overwhelmingly partisan lines will do little to protect us against Trumpism in the long run. Unless Trump suffers a crushing defeat at the polls, he is likely to retain tremendous influence on the right. And unless Democrats manage to avoid all scandals, consistently deliver on their ambitious promises, nominate a long line of charismatic candidates, and finally figure out how to make economic recessions vanish from the face of the Earth, they will eventually lose the White House to a Republican. If we do not manage to broker a meaningful civil peace by that date, the depredations of the past years could come to look like a mild foretaste of a much more bitter future.

The stakes we now face remain as serious as ever. We likely have the tools we need to rebuke Donald Trump and save the American Republic. But to do so, we need to learn the lessons of the past years: without a broad coalition, or a vision of America's future that at least attempts to speak to all American citizens, we will at best succeed in winning a Pyrrhic victory against the generational challenge of authoritarian populism.

RECONSTRUCTING OUR CONSTITUTIONAL DEMOCRACY

K. Sabeel Rahman

Beginning with Donald Trump's inauguration, concerns about an emerging constitutional crisis exploded into the public consciousness and have only accelerated since. From clashes between the executive branch, the courts, and the legislature, to questions about a special counsel, emoluments, and foreign interference in the 2016 election, there has been a growing concern about the damage the Trump administration has wrought to constitutional law and basic norms of governance. But the conflicts of the Trump era are themselves products of a deeper set of challenges facing twenty-first-century American democracy.

For decades, growing economic inequality has concentrated wealth and opportunity and widened the gap in political influence between rich and poor. The basic constitutional structure of American democracy, from voting rights to redistricting to campaign financing, has eroded over time, creating an increasingly fraught electoral system in which too many Americans are not heard. Technological change has altered the media and communications landscape such that "fake news," misinformation, and weaponized racism are now even more virulent, corroding the capacity for public dialogue and debate.

This is not the first time American democracy has faced an existential and deeply self-critical moment in its history. The contradictions of a slavery-based democracy, laid bare in the Civil War, sparked a moment of radical, democratic revolution as freedpersons and nineteenth-century Republican abolitionists remade the Constitution and the fabric of the country in an attempt to uproot the vestiges of slavery. The economic upheavals of industrialization a few decades later sparked the rise of the labor movement and bold new experiments with economic regulation and the modern social safety net, culminating in the transformations of the New Deal era. In the 1960s, the civil rights movement revived the unfulfilled aspirations of Reconstruction and the New Deal, challenging the racial caste system that was Jim Crow, winning transformative changes to civil rights and voting rights. Fights for gender equality expanded protections and membership.

Today we live in a similarly transformative moment. And the stakes of this crisis are nothing less than the realization of a truly inclusive, multiracial democracy—the likes of which America has often proclaimed, but never fully realized.

A key part of this fight for a new democracy lies with the Constitution itself and the basic structure of our political, social, and economic life. While the original Constitution enabled basic democratic politics, it also encoded political, economic, and racial hierarchies that cut against the Constitution's own radical vision of a government built to serve "we the people." So the point here is not to venerate the original founding, but instead the most foundational moral values that we seek to live by—and the underlying institutional structures we need in order to make those values real.

Think of constitutionalism as the underlying architecture, or infrastructure, of our shared political, economic, and social life. A solid structure does not mean that every day-to-day problem is fully resolved. But if that underlying structure is unsound—or if it is built where some inhabitants are stuck in worse conditions than others—surface-level changes can only mitigate, but never fully resolve, these pathologies. A constitutional structure also encompasses more than the formal boundaries of the constitutional text itself; like any form of architecture or infrastructure, there is a range of conditions needed for the system to work. Thus, in order to function, a written constitution also requires a range of critical quasi-constitutional statutes (think of the Civil Rights Act or the Voting Rights Act), background conditions (like basic social and economic equality, the ability to communicate across divides), and norms and values (like aspirations to freedom, equality, democracy).

At its core, a better constitutional system must accomplish three things.

First, it must structure the allocation of political power in a way that manages to contain and channel political conflict productively. As the framers of the American Constitution understood in the eighteenth century, disagreement and political conflict are endemic; the task of constitutional design is in part to ensure that political disagreements do not become explosive or fracturing—and that, instead, political interests are channeled in ways that promote the common good.[1] That in turn means political institutions must strike a balance between *constraining* the coercive powers of government (holding political leaders to account) and *catalyzing* government action (ensuring that those same political leaders are responsive to the needs of we the people). Constitutional structures— like the separation of powers and checks and balances between the presidency, the legislature, and the judiciary, or the system of federalism and decentralization, and the extensive architecture around voting, districting, and elections—are all part of this basic function. Many of the key challenges facing American democracy in the twenty-first century stem from the basic fact that this political infrastructure does not work. It is too warped by concentrations of economic and political power, by technological change, and by the hijacking of powerful interests that are increasingly able to co-opt the operations of government for their own ends. We need a revised political infrastructure to make this kind of responsive, accountable democracy real.

Second, a constitutional system must ensure equality and inclusion for all members of the polity, securing what the Fourteenth Amendment calls the "privileges and immunities of citizenship" for all residents. One of the driving moral values of our constitutional democracy is the vision that a constitutional structure ought to secure the freedom to thrive as individuals and communities. This vision of economic and social flourishing—and of membership and inclusion—requires more than the formal protections of constitutional rights. It also requires a larger economic and social infrastructure built to rebalance the terms of economic power and inclusion.

Third, a constitutional system must also create a social infrastructure that protects against structural forms of discrimination and exclusion. Racial and gender divisions have been a key fault line where membership in the American polity has been systematically restricted. Race and gender have been a central fault line upon which modern and historical aspirations for American democracy have so often collapsed. For example, in the effort to preserve white supremacy after the Civil War, the radically inclusive vision of civil rights, economic redistribution, and political equality seen in Reconstruction was violently suppressed. Likewise, the threat to traditions of patriarchal rule posed by women's equality—and the

further destabilization of traditional roles of membership and power resulting from movements for LGBTQIA inclusion—sparked powerful
political backlashes. The immigration fights of recent decades turn more
on racialized fears of displacement than on matters of policy. The ability
to ensure inclusion in a multiracial, multifaith democracy requires a particular political, economic, and social architecture that resists efforts to
restore old hierarchies—and on the efficacy of government itself, defends
rights and inclusion. Dismantling these structural forms of exclusion requires the (re)building of a civil rights infrastructure that affirmatively
promotes inclusion and belonging.

Reforming Our Political Infrastructure

The first big area for constitutional and structural reform requires us to
remake our political institutions. Achieving a functional and accountable
government in the modern era means we must expand the franchise and
ensure fair, equal, and responsive representation for a diverse electorate.
Key areas include voting rights, redistricting, campaign finance reform,
equal representation, ensuring a fair balance of power, and governing new
media's influence on public debate.

Voting Rights

We need to update our voting infrastructure to resist the strategic (and
often racialized) deployment of voter-suppression tactics to skew political outcomes. Despite frequent claims of "voter fraud" and fears of un-
registered voters tainting election results, the actual incidence of voter
fraud is vanishingly small, less than a hundredth of a percent.[2] But in the
name of combating voter fraud, political actors have constructed a
system to suppress votes, particularly those of young people, working
families, and communities of color. Through draconian voter ID laws,
systematic under-resourcing of election administration commissions, and
the mechanisms of voting machines and polling places, we have a democracy that functions for some, but is largely illusory for others. These tactics have had real and decisive consequences on voter turnout.[3] Recent
studies examining the implementation of strict voter ID laws in places like
Texas and Michigan suggest that these restrictions can preclude tens of
thousands of voters from actually casting a ballot. Furthermore, these

voters are disproportionately voters of color, meaning that these restrictions have a racially disparate impact on the voting public.[4]

Redistricting

Restrictive voter ID laws have emerged against a backdrop of Supreme Court decisions that have dismantled protections long established under the Voting Rights Act and reviewed voter ID laws deferentially. Most famously in *Shelby County v. Holder*, the court effectively made federal review of changes to voting regimes in specified jurisdictions unenforceable. In an opinion by Chief Justice John Roberts, the court held that Section 4's preclearance formula was unconstitutional, adding that "history did not end in 1965." And in an earlier case, *Crawford v. Marion County Election Board*, the court upheld an Indiana voter ID law, recognizing state interests in "election modernization," limiting voter fraud, and safeguarding voter confidence. These cases have thus emboldened states in the Old South and elsewhere to suppress votes through voter ID laws that allegedly protect the integrity of elections.

Gerrymandering, in particular highly partisan redistricting, is a practice that dates back to the very beginnings of the republic and involves the strategic crafting of district lines for political advantage.[5] When done effectively—and with the advent of street-level data and redistricting technology it is easy to do so—gerrymandered districts can result in electoral maps that systematically give rise to one-party rule, blunting majoritarian democracy. Although both parties, in theory, could gerrymander, in practice, Republicans have engaged in and benefited from gerrymandering more than Democrats.[6] In a particularly flagrant recent example, a gerrymandered map in Wisconsin led to Republicans winning 60.6 percent of state assembly seats with only 48.3 percent of the vote.[7]

Supreme Court constitutional doctrine, however, has had divergent and at times conflicting responses to the issue. On the one hand, the court has drawn on both the Equal Protection Clause and the Voting Rights Act to police racial gerrymandering—redistricting on the basis of racial demographics.[8] On the other hand, the court has recently held that partisan gerrymanders—drawing district lines on the basis of the party affiliations of voters—are non-justiciable, effectively blessing the practice.[9] By permitting partisan gerrymanders, however, the court has opened the door to racial gerrymandering. Given the enormous overlap between race and party affiliation in America, legislators can now de facto racially gerrymander—so long as they claim that they are redistricting according to party ties.[10]

Campaign Reform

Just as gerrymandering and voter suppression threaten equality at the ballot box, the current state of campaign finance undermines equal representation in everyday democracy. Ever since the court's decision in *Buckley v. Valeo* to invalidate individual political expenditure limits on First Amendment grounds, the law of campaign finance kept the door open to unlimited corporate spending.[11] And in 2010, the court realized that very possibility, ruling that the expenditure limits on corporate spending in the Bipartisan Campaign Reform Act violated the First Amendment.[12] Significantly, Justice Anthony Kennedy dismissed the idea that corporate spending either counted as, or gave the appearance of, corruption. A subsequent case confirmed that corruption, according to the Supreme Court, only involved quid-pro-quos of money for discrete political favors.[13]

Citizens United v. Federal Election Commission and its view of money in politics have attracted public and scholarly criticism alike. In an age of intense polarization, *Citizens United* is a rare point of agreement, as large majorities of Republican and Democratic voters support a constitutional amendment overturning the decision.[14] Academics have similarly taken issue with the decision, attacking every element of Kennedy's argument—from his views on equality[15] to the entire democratic theory animating its holding.[16] In particular, legal scholars have underlined how Kennedy's narrow view of corruption is unmoored from the historical obsession with the corrupting influence of money in American politics.[17] The court's embrace of lobbying as constitutional, these scholars remind us, represents a break from more than two centuries of institutional design and history aimed at limiting the influence of moneyed interests in democracy. The subsequent flood of dark money via "super political action committees" (PACs)[18] and political science highlighting the overrepresentation of elite interests in public policy[19] suggest current law takes an overly narrow and dangerous view of corruption.

If political equality and public faith in American democracy are going to survive, then voter suppression, redistricting, and campaign finance need serious reform. Reforms would involve fundamentally restructuring American democracy through the creation of new institutions and mechanisms for ensuring political equality and inclusion. Thankfully, models for change are available at the state and federal levels. At least fifteen states provide a clear way forward against voter suppression through automatic voter registration.[20] Moreover, a majority of states allow electronic registration at DMVs, and sixteen states offer portable registration for voters who have moved, as well as Election Day registration.[21] At the federal level, the proposed Automatic Voter Registration Act (H.R. 2840) builds on these efforts to require state DMVs to automatically register voters.[22] In addition, the For the People Act of 2019 (H.R. 1) seeks to help restore voting rights to formerly incarcerated voters, as do recent state-level reforms in places like Florida—a substantial shift, given the number of Americans and in particular people of color who fall subject to the expanding reach of a mass incarceration criminal justice system.[23]

Similarly, states have charted a path forward on gerrymandering through the use of independent redistricting commissions. Currently eight states use independent commissions to draw congressional and state district lines,[24] and another nine states either currently or soon will deploy similar commissions.[25] Through partisan balance requirements, nonpartisan experts, judicial involvement, or a combination of these features, independent redistricting commissions take political structure out of the political process itself, insulating decisions over underlying structure from self-interested and compromising political involvement. Here too, H.R. 1 proposes independent redistricting commissions on the state level that would be responsible for crafting fair congressional lines.[26] Finally, H.R. 1 currently in the Congress also introduces campaign finance reforms intended to improve transparency and bolster political equality. Given the scope of *Citizens United*'s central holding, H.R. 1 instead homes in on stronger disclosure requirements for Super PACs, 6:1 small-donation matching, and reducing the size and changing the composition of the FEC to enable it to act more effectively in enforcing campaign finance laws.[27]

Equal Representation

Looming behind important changes to the constitution of critical democracy statutes, however, are urgent problems with the constitutional structure itself.

- The Senate is undemocratic. In assigning two senators to each state, regardless of its population, the Constitution reproduces at the state level the very problem *Baker v. Carr*[28] and *Reynolds v. Sims*[29] solved at the district level: enormous differences in the weight of individual votes. For instance, a voter in Wyoming has 67 times the voting power of a voter in California.[30]

- Additionally, the Electoral College threatens majority rule—a central principle of democracy. President Trump's victory in 2016 marked the second time in twenty years that a candidate won the election while losing the popular vote. The risks of minority rule in the Senate and the presidency only figure to get worse as Democratic voters cluster along the coasts, leaving vast swaths of America sparsely populated but politically influential.[31]

- Finally, democratic experimentation with district design is limited. While the Supreme Court has held that "under our cases, MMDs [multi-member districts] are not per se unconstitutional, nor are they necessarily unconstitutional when used in combination with SMDs [single-member districts] in other parts of the State," proportional representation is not a constitutional requirement.[32] Experimenting with multi-member districts or guaranteed minority representation, however, would allow for potentially more representative and responsive government by allowing for more parties and more inclusive participation.[33] Similarly, rank-choice voting, when allied with concerted civic education, could allow for more sophisticated and precise accounting of voter preferences.

Balance of Power

Our constitution is partly premised on the idea that the separation of powers—dividing authority between executive, legislative, and judicial branches—can prevent tyrannical government and ensure responsiveness to the public will. However, the separation of powers in practice has operated as a system of increasingly polarized, scorched-earth politics. Gamesmanship and hardball partisan politics have undermined the legitimacy of the executive, legislative, and judicial branches. Consider, for example, the Republican blockade of President Barack Obama's Supreme Court nominee Merrick Garland in 2016, or how presidents of both parties have increasingly deployed executive orders and other administrative

efforts to bypass a hostile or gridlocked Congress in order to advance budgetary and policy positions on everything from immigration to environmental protection. We might consider restructuring the balance of power
between the three branches of government to ensure greater accountability. For example, Congress could be made more dynamic and responsive
in part by rule changes to prevent majority parties from blocking votes
on legislation in either house. Supreme Court terms might be shifted by
constitutional amendment to be fixed, eighteen-year terms that vacate on
a staggered basis so that each presidential term is set to have one Supreme
Court appointment, ensuring a greater degree of responsiveness, representativeness, and de-escalation of the judicial appointment process. Similarly, the executive branch appointments process should be reformed to
prevent the executive from bypassing congressional approval through use
of "acting" cabinet members or informal advisors, while also reining in
Congress's ability to block executive appointments indefinitely by requiring up-or-down votes on appointees in the Senate within a specified time
limit.

New Media's Influence on Public Debate

Finally, a working and responsive democracy requires a media infrastructure that facilitates public debate and deliberation. From the print pam-
phlets of the eighteenth and nineteenth centuries to the rise of the
telegraph, radio, and broadcast television in the last century, technological changes to our media ecosystem have had major implications for the
state of our democracy. Communications technologies enable new forms
of association, debate, and civil-society organization. But as these new
technologies arise, they also create dangerous concentrations of power
among the firms and individuals that own and govern them. And they
create new possibilities for propaganda, misinformation, and weaponized
extreme political ideologies. These are not just new concerns for the era
of online misinformation and "fake news"; similar concerns arose in context of the rise of the telegraph and of radio over a century ago.[34] Today
the key challenge to our digitized media ecosystem is two-fold: online
communication through platforms like YouTube, Facebook, and Twitter
create "epistemic bubbles," where groups systematically are constrained
in interacting only with like-minded views, leading to greater insulation
and even radicalization and where the business model of these platforms

monetizes user interaction through selling ads, creating incentives to feed users ever-more extreme content so as to maximize user time on the platform.[35] The result is an online public sphere essentially optimized for misinformation, disinformation, and polarization.[36] Just as the New Deal created a Federal Communications Commission and a suite of statutory and regulatory requirements for broadcast media to ensure that new technologies and free speech facilitated, rather than tainted, modern democracy, so too will this digital era require a governing regime of public law that addresses these concerns, consistent with First Amendment protections for speech and association.

These reforms, while far-reaching, would not by themselves succeed in securing an inclusive, responsive, multiracial democracy. The reality is that our politics is distorted not just by limitations to our political infrastructure, but also by the increasingly stratified and unequal social and economic order. The next two sections explore these other dimensions of democratic inclusion. The history of American democracy has been one of a recurring clash between reform movements that transform our underlying constitutional structure to advance a more inclusive vision of "we the people"—think of the moral and legal transformations resulting from the civil rights movement, fights for gender equity, and more—and attempts to reassert pre-existing economic, racial, and gender hierarchies against these efforts. The latter has undermined the nation's attempts to fulfill its promise. This moment of possibility will be no different if wealth inequality persists and assurances of inclusion remain illusory.

Economic Reform and the Foundations for Democracy

As we enter the twenty-first century, our vision for an inclusive democracy is threatened by escalating income and wealth inequality.[37] These disparities undermine political equality: wealthier constituencies and economically powerful interests have systematically exercised outsized political influence, which in turn has helped accelerate policy shifts that further concentrate economic wealth.[38] These distinctions are inextricably intertwined with race and gender, exacerbating inequities across multiple dimensions.

We cannot fully realize the promise of equal membership, dignity, and inclusion in an economy premised on such discrepancies. But just like the imbalance of political voice and power described above, these economic conditions are not "natural"; rather, they are the product of background policies and rules. And those rules need to be radically remade in order to make real the kind of economic and social inclusion that a genuine democracy requires. Achieving this level of inclusion requires a rebuilt constitutional infrastructure encompassing not only changed Supreme Court doctrines, but also new quasi-constitutional commitments in the forms of foundational legislation and renewed administrative agencies. The challenge here is to restructure the background rules of the modern economy to rebalance economic power in more democratic terms. Without such a rebalancing, corporations and wealthy elites will continue to have outsized political power.

Part of this task involves the rebuilding of organized labor and worker power. Today's workers find themselves in a dynamic, precarious, and increasingly extractive system of work. From outsourcing and "gig"-based models of work to more traditional, once-secured, professionalized jobs, workers have been particularly squeezed by the modern economy.[39] While productivity has increased in the last forty years, wages have stagnated—a problem that stems in part from the decline of organized labor. Furthermore, even as social justice membership organizations fighting for the interests of young people, working families, and communities of color have struggled to be heard, policymakers have been more responsive to organizations representing wealthier constituencies and business interests.

At the same time, the task of organizing workers in civil society has been made more difficult by deliberate legal, policy, and constitutional choices. While a central pillar of the New Deal revolution was the establishment of labor rights through the 1935 Wagner Act, the position of organized labor has always been fraught, bitterly opposed by business interests, with legal protections through federal regulation and oversight often swinging wildly depending on which party controls the White House. In recent years, statutory changes have further eroded the legal protections for worker voice, while constitutional jurisprudence has increasingly leveraged the First Amendment as a weapon to undermine worker collective bargaining.[40]

A key front line for building an inclusive economy and democracy, then, requires the reinvention of labor law. For workers like those behind the successful Fight for Fifteen campaign to more recent bursts of labor activism among domestic workers, public school teachers, tech workers, and gig-economy participants, we see the beginnings of a potential labor law premised on wider bargaining at the regional level, rather than the traditional employer–employee model. We also see important new approaches to rethinking policy that leverage worker organizing as part of a broader political push for racial and economic justice beyond the workplace.[41] Codifying this new model of labor power, or some variation of it, will be critical to restoring an economic and political voice for workers, and in so doing rebalancing the terms of economic and political power.

Similarly, we need a revision of the background legal rules that govern corporate power and corporate concentration. A century ago, Progressive Era reformers saw the rise of industrial-era conglomerates and mega-corporations, from J.P. Morgan's financial empire to the Vanderbilts' control of the railroads, to Standard Oil's dominance over fuel, and the monopolistic control of information by Jay Gould's telegraph empire. These corporate titans had so much control over the economy that they held the fates of whole communities in their hands—and their economic power and wealth gave them incredible political influence over government officials. Reformers of this period knew that democracy could not survive such concentrated economic and political power. They saw measures like the Sherman Antitrust Act as a critical, quasi-constitutional shift needed to preserve economic liberty and ensure a constitutional democracy.

Today, we are at a similar point of corporate concentration and power, fueling a new interest in reviving robust antitrust laws aimed at dismantling monopolistic control over markets in order to both spur economic competition and innovation and protect against the political influence.[42] Rebalancing economic power to protect an equitable and inclusive democracy thus requires a revived commitment to anti-monopoly regulations, from antitrust laws that prevent excessive corporate mergers to greater federal oversight of the political influence that corporations exercise.

Administering Inclusion

An inclusive democracy also requires a background legal and institutional structure that facilitates the administration, enforcement, and defense of inclusion, protecting marginalized communities and dismantling systematic forms of discrimination, exclusion, and inequality. This institutional apparatus represents another essential underlying infrastructure for an inclusive democracy, one that is easily overlooked. Yet this is where some of the most pitched, high-stakes battles over democracy, inclusion, and equality have taken place throughout U.S. history.

Consider how communities of color have—despite the passage of the Fourteenth Amendment, the desegregation of schools in *Brown v. Board of Education*, the Civil Rights Act, and numerous other legal efforts to dismantle systemic racial exclusion—continued to face conditions of exclusion, exploitation, and subordination. Communities of color have continued to be geographically segregated, first formally through the explicit policies of the Jim Crow and New Deal eras, then informally through the operation of zoning rules and urban planning decisions that have produced persistent forms of economic and racial segregation.[43] This segregation in turn has intergenerational effects on health, income, and well-being.[44] Similarly, many safety net and social insurance programs like welfare, food stamps, or health care are provided in ways that magnify racial and economic inequities. By imposing difficult barriers to entry and enrollment or other frictions, governments can often make it harder for low-income Americans and particularly communities of color to access these basic goods.[45] These systemic forms of exclusion and inequality are facilitated by the silence—or in some cases, active participation—of state actors.

Advances for membership, inclusion, and equity, on the other hand, have often depended on the creation of administrative systems to enforce civil rights and economic and racial justice against precisely these types of systemic and structural forms of exclusion. The modern administrative state has its origins in nineteenth- and early-twentieth-century efforts to redress economic inequities by creating regulatory oversight to protect the safety and quality of and access to basic necessities like food, water, milk, transportation, pharmaceuticals, and much more.[46] Indeed, while we think of rights guaranteeing equality and inclusion as being "constitutional," they very much depend not just on the formal text of the Constitution itself but also on the administrative apparatus that interprets broad constitutional values and makes possible the day-to-day experience of inclusion.[47] Labor protections and antidiscrimination law depended on the formation of administrative agencies to monitor and enforce these provisions.[48] Welfare rights and social insurance systems grew in large part thanks to (often fraught) efforts by bureaucrats and new state and federal agencies to shift welfare to a system based on norms of economic rights rather than on charity.[49] The attempted desegregation of hospitals, health care, and cities required the formation of civil rights strategies and policies by federal administrative agencies, incentivizing desegregation and monitoring localities and private actors for problematic discriminatory practices.[50]

Administrative agencies have thus been a key legal-institutional "technology" for addressing these systemic forms of economic, racial, and gender inequity. Whether at the state or federal level, the ability for legislatures to create administrative bodies to make rules, monitor compliance, and enforce social, civil, and economic rights is critical to making real the promise of the constitutional rights of equal protection and due process—and to the broader moral vision of a country committed to constituting itself on the basis of equality, dignity, and membership.

A future constitutional structure will have to respond to the current assault on this administrative apparatus. While legal and political battles over administrative power and state regulation are often framed in terms of "big government" against "free markets" or "individual liberty," the reality is that opposition to economic and social regulation has too often been animated by a lurking hostility to the equalizing and inclusionary force of these agencies. Thus the political movements for dismantling the modern administrative state—while encompassing some good-faith critiques of governmental power and desire for accountability—have often fused with movements and interest groups aimed at dismantling restraints on economic power (in the case of the business lobby)[51] or at resisting the advances of racial justice (in the case of persisting mobilization by white communities in opposition to ensuring civil rights across race).[52]

Responding to these attacks on the basic infrastructure of inclusion will require legal, institutional, and constitutional change. Just as the Supreme Court has shifted the legal landscape in problematic ways on democracy, so too has it narrowed the scope for equality-advancing regulation in recent years. Judicial deference to regulatory policy decisions has become more fraught as the court has expressed a greater willingness to reconsider the policymaking latitude afforded to regulatory agencies.[53] More troublingly, the court has increasingly used claims of First Amendment speech protections and trade-secrets rules for corporations as a way to "protect" corporations from economic and social regulations— effectively neutering many critical forms of equality-enhancing regulation.[54] Furthermore, the recent weakening and dismantling of regulatory agencies like the Consumer Financial Protection Bureau, the Office of Environmental Justice, and others has further limited the government's capacity to address such systemic economic and racial inequities. An affirmative agenda creating an inclusive democratic constitutional infrastructure will require a rebuilding of the administrative state, particularly focusing on building the institutions and authorities needed to tackle twenty-first-century forms of civil rights, racial justice, and economic justice.

For a country that takes democracy as its birthright, the reality is that our foundational political, economic, and social structures do not live up to the aspiration of being an inclusive, multiracial democracy that protects each person's freedom to thrive and flourish. Remaking our constitutional order will not be easy. This transformative alternate constitutional vision will require more than legal expertise. The changes will have to be driven by we the people, by grassroots social movements that mobilize, organize, and advance a bold vision of the kind of democracy we can and ought to be. It is this kind of bottom-up mobilization and big ideas that have in previous eras driven the big expansions of our democratic order. If we are successful, we can bring our constitutional system closer to our aspirations for a truly inclusive and equitable multiracial democracy of, for, and by the people.

RESTORING HEALTHY PARTY COMPETITION

Jacob S. Hacker and Paul Pierson

For a generation, the capacity of the United States to harness government authority for broad public purposes has been in steep decline, even as the need for effective governance in a complex, interdependent world has grown. Whether the challenge is climate change, a broken immigration policy, or rising economic insecurity and inequality, America's national leaders have proved all but incapable of reasonably updating federal laws.

The transformation of our two-party system is a principal cause of this crisis. With brief and unpleasant historical exceptions, the United States has never had two nationalized parties that are as closely balanced and territorially distinct as the current Republican and Democratic parties. Nor have we seen two major parties with so few of the cross-cutting regional and ideological cleavages that have marked major U.S. parties in the past. Although partisanship has always been part of American government, today's hyperpolarization fundamentally undermines the effective operation of the nation's "Madisonian" constitutional framework. Moreover, this mismatch was fostering a range of political pathologies well before the arrival of a race-baiting demagogue in the White House.

At the same time, efforts to build a constructive version of party politics must be clear-eyed. We cannot afford to fall back on generalized laments about "the parties," as if both are equally responsible for our present plight. The parties have not raced away from each other at equal speeds; instead, it is primarily the radicalization of the Republican Party that has brought us to this dangerous juncture. If we are to repair the lost legitimacy of our national institutions and empower the federal government to play its essential role, this cycle of increasing GOP extremism will have to be broken.

* * *

Most Americans don't realize just how unusual our political system, with its separate branches of government sharing powers, is among modern democracies. A crucial distinguishing feature is the presence of many barriers ("veto points") that must be surmounted if political authority is to be harnessed to address public problems. This is often referred to as a "Madisonian" system—a bit of a misnomer, because while he is remembered as the principal architect (and most sophisticated defender) of the Constitutional Convention's work, he was at the time in favor of a system with far fewer veto points.

To operate well, the Madisonian system requires the major political parties to exhibit a significant capacity for cooperation and tolerance. That the need for this cooperation was rarely noticed reflected the fact that usually the system managed to produce it. The dominant (conservative) coalition of the 1940s and 1950s was bipartisan. So was the liberal coalition of the mid-1960s and early 1970s. Every two years the parties planted their electoral flags. Those contests garnered much attention, and they mattered. In between campaigns, however, government rested on fluid majorities that encapsulated elements of both parties and shifted from issue to issue.

If this system mostly worked reasonably well, managing to generate the degree of consensus needed to govern, it did so in large part because parties played only a modest role in organizing our politics. In the language of political scientists, they were "weak." Our institutions promoted a proliferation of distinct political contexts and interests. In turn, this proliferation yielded cross-cutting cleavages and pluralism. Adages like "where you stand depends on where you sit" or Tip O'Neill's "all politics is local" were broadly accurate portrayals of the political system. Within it, coalitions were loose and fluid, reflecting not only national partisan battles but also the multiple pulls of geographic, sectoral, and cultural constituencies that divided as well as unified partisans.

Thus, even as the American political system *necessitated* compromise, it also *facilitated* it through electoral and governing incentives that cross-cut party lines. Most of the time prior to 1990, major legislation in the United States was bipartisan. As a result, even periods of divided government—with each party controlling part of the national government and thus hypothetically exercising an effective veto over legislation—did not prevent action on pressing public issues.

No more. Over the past few decades, the political fluidity of the Madisonian system has given way to an increasingly entrenched partisan divide. In part because of the massive growth of policy activity in Washington, major aspects of American politics—from media environments and interest group structures to party organizations and even state-specific policy battles—have nationalized.[1]

These trends both reflect and have reinforced the shifting incentives and activities of political elites. Individual politicians, beholden to national organizations, are less free to defect on issues based on local conditions. Most powerful interest groups have also chosen sides. They too operate on a national level, and for understandable reasons they often see one party or the other as far more responsive to their demands. As partisan battle lines have hardened, these groups face incentives to offer political loyalty in return for policy favors.

Even voters—relatively late and sometimes reluctant enlistees in the polarization wars—are increasingly attached to national partisan identities and outlooks. They are also increasingly antagonistic toward politicians, groups, and citizens on the other side of the aisle. Mass and elite polarization generally work in tandem—for example, the polarization of voters makes it harder for politicians to moderate, and the strategies of elite organizations often hinge on creating clear "litmus tests" for pivotal constituencies.

Combined, these shifts have created a new kind of partisanship: one that is more cohesive, more consistent, more homogenous, and much, much more intense. The nationalization of American politics in recent decades has eroded the cross-cutting cleavages that our institutions silently relied upon. The forces pushing for consensus have weakened. The electoral incentives for cooperation have evaporated. Norms supporting compromise and partisan restraint have crumbled. Under the weight of these trends, the federal government's capacity to address collective problems— from climate change to rising health care costs to skyrocketing inequality—has virtually collapsed. That collapse, in turn, has helped propel us to our current crisis of governance, fueling voter discontent, alienation, and a search for scapegoats. We face a real threat of a downward spiral, in which failed governance undercuts political legitimacy, further diminishing the capacity to govern and throwing open the doors of government to demagogues.

* * *

There is a common diagnosis of this problem: "partisan polarization." The two parties, in this view, have moved away from the center, creating a yawning gulf and intensifying mistrust. This polarization makes shared governance impossible. This common framing of the problem leads to a particular list of possible solutions. Some—typically pundits or political amateurs—argue (wish?) for a new, moderate party to represent sensible, centrist opinion. More grounded reformers seek political steps to strengthen moderate forces within the existing parties. Some emphasize the need to change the rules of political contestation, targeting gerrymandering or the existing primary system. Others argue that the goal should be to limit the sway of activists, whom they see as carriers of extremism, and strengthen the hands of traditional party elites, whom they see as more open to compromise.

If we are skeptical of most of these suggestions, it is because we see this basic diagnosis as seriously flawed. Years before Donald Trump became the GOP's champion, two longtime moderate observers of Washington politics, Tom Mann and Norm Ornstein, reluctantly reached this stark conclusion:

> Today's Republican Party . . . is an insurgent outlier. It has become ideologically extreme; contemptuous of the inherited social and economic policy regime; scornful of compromise; unpersuaded by conventional understanding of facts, evidence, and science; and dismissive of the legitimacy of its political opposition, all but declaring war on the government. The Democratic Party, while no paragon of civic virtue, is more ideologically centered and diverse, protective of the government's role as it developed over the course of the last century, open to incremental changes in policy fashioned through bargaining with the Republicans, and less disposed to or adept at take-no-prisoners conflict between the parties. This asymmetry between the parties, which journalists and scholars often brush aside or whitewash in a quest for "balance," constitutes a huge obstacle to effective governance.[2]

If anything, these words of less than a decade ago seem too mild as we watch the GOP—its core voters, its activist groups, and its political class—rally around a man who engages in relentless race-baiting, assaults on the press, and denigration of the rule of law.

As Mann and Ornstein emphasized, we must resist the temptation to avert our eyes from this reality in the effort to maintain a *posture* of even-handedness. Neutrality does not mean positioning oneself midway between the two parties, wherever they may be at the moment, and pointing one finger in each direction. Neutrality means weighing the evidence and following where it leads. And with ever-greater clarity that evidence leads to a basic conclusion: the main challenge we face is not polarization but *asymmetric* polarization. The GOP has not only moved much further right than Democrats have moved left; it has embraced positions that undermine longstanding governing institutions and norms, limit or subvert electoral competition, and incite us-versus-them tribalism among both political elites and supporters. In the language of comparative politics, Republicans are now an "anti-system" party—one that challenges not just its opponents but the legitimacy of the system itself.

Worse still, these tendencies have been getting stronger and stronger. Although he has worked relentlessly to stoke the worst forms of tribalism, this transformation began well before President Trump's election. The problem, in other words, is structural. And while Democrats have faced some pressures to move left while Republicans have moved right, they have not embraced either extreme anti-system strategies or intense us-versus-them mobilization. Any effective approach to rebuilding healthy two-party competition must begin with this central reality.

We start, therefore, by trying to get the diagnosis right. We identify the main causes of Republican radicalization, which stem ultimately from profound economic, demographic, and technological changes in American society. Moreover, we note that asymmetric polarization has been *self-reinforcing*. Rather than provoking a moderating reaction, extremism on the right has grown. Positions that were once on the fringe of our politics have become first acceptable and then Republican orthodoxy. It is not just that GOP elites have become more conservative as the party's foundations of geographic and financial support have shifted. It is that key causes of polarization—such as the changing media landscape on the right, the rise of organized conservative groups within an increasingly unequal economy, and the shifting geographic base of the party—feed on themselves, and will almost certainly continue to do so, even if Republicans are electorally rebuked (absent the unlikely outcome of electoral decimation). In short, successful reforms must break the doom loop of GOP extremism.

After exploring these issues, we propose a series of institutional changes and political strategies that would specifically tackle these self-reinforcing dynamics, not just try to draw particular Republicans toward the center on particular issues. Some of these efforts, we argue, should focus on larger political reforms (for example, changes in electoral systems and the role of money in politics) that will increase the sway of voters and increase the capacity for the American government to act even when anti-system strategies are deployed. Many of the reforms that are most essential, however, will have to focus on the specific dynamics within the conservative coalition that have fostered extremism. In particular, they will need to focus on weakening or counteracting what might be called "meso-institutions," such as conservative media and donor networks.

Elite discourse—in journalism and academia and among foundations— is intensely resistant to the very strong evidence that polarization is primarily about steadily increasing GOP extremism. Regardless of what the evidence may show, to argue that one party is more responsible than another for political dysfunction is seen as itself evidence of bias, not to mention bad manners. But the evidence *is* clear: the dramatic polarization of political elites (and, increasingly, voters) over the last generation has not been symmetrical.[3] Republicans have moved much further right than Democrats have moved left. This asymmetry can be seen in congressional voting patterns. It can be seen in the relative positions on the issues (and, for those who have served in Congress, on their roll-call votes) of the two parties' presidential and vice-presidential nominees. It is evident in the relative positions of each party's judicial nominees. It can also be seen, to a lesser extent, in the polarization of state-level elected officials and when comparing the policy conservatism or liberalism of Republican and Democratic "trifectas" (when one party controls both houses of the state legislature as well as the governor's office).[4]

In addition to moving right, Republicans have become much more confrontational—willing to use aggressive tactics that, while technically legal in most cases, had previously been shunned as un-civil or anti-democratic. Crucial figures in developing these tactics—again, predating Trump—were congressional leaders Newt Gingrich and Mitch McConnell, among others. Recent political history at both the national and state levels is replete with instances of GOP "constitutional hardball."[5] At the national level, Republicans have led the way and deserve exclusive or primary responsibility for

- routinized use of the filibuster to block virtually all initiatives of the majority party;
- repeated government shutdowns;
- using the periodic raising of the authorized ceiling on federal debt (to finance spending *already appropriated* by Congress) to extract concessions from Democrats—in effect, taking the full faith and credit of the federal government hostage so as to ransom it for favored GOP policies;
- refusal to accept *any* Democratic appointment to key positions, most dramatically in the case of Merrick Garland's nomination to the U.S. Supreme Court; and
- the use of congressional oversight as a weapon designed to foster distrust and alienation.

Initiatives at the state level where Republicans have gained control have been equally troublesome:

- Resorting to mid-decade reapportionments (which are traditionally done following the census counts that occur once every ten years) in order to gerrymander house seats.
- Post-election efforts to remove political authority from offices when voters have chosen to select Democratic Party candidates.
- Repeated legislative reversals of voter-passed initiatives on issues from expansion of Medicaid to the disenfranchisement of ex-felons.
- Systematic efforts to disenfranchise younger, lower-income, and non-white voters viewed as unlikely to support the GOP.

The list is not short, nor are the items trivial. Efforts like these are what led Mann and Ornstein to call the GOP "an insurgent outlier" in 2012. Of course, the intensity of that insurgency has only grown in the years since. The Trump presidency has launched attacks on the infrastructure of democracy—the press, the courts, law enforcement, the political opposition—that would have been unthinkable only a few years ago. Yet these norm-exploding stances have faced little to no resistance within the GOP. With right-wing media, powerful conservative interest groups, and the party's electoral base lining up behind the president, Republican-elected officials have fallen dutifully in line.

In short, it is now polarization all the way down. GOP legislators, whom the Madisonian framework counts on to help protect a co-equal branch of government, back the president even as he takes unprecedented swipes at the constitutional prerogatives of Congress. Such startling developments have rightly led prominent analysts to highlight the risks of "democratic backsliding" in the United States.[6]

Three developing features of the American polity have facilitated this transformation of the Republican Party: the rising role of powerful and extreme groups within its coalition, the increasingly formidable presence of right-wing media, and the growing electoral advantages for the GOP as the country splits on rural–urban lines. These trends have fed on each other, creating a dynamic in which the party has moved steadily rightward and raising the prospect of a downward spiral of intensifying extremism, in which politicians radicalize voters, who in turn place increasing electoral pressure on politicians to eschew compromise and seek confrontation.

The role of groups of "intense policy demanders"[7] has been especially evident over the past generation. Examining the party's organized supporters—many large corporations and wealthy individuals, conservative Christian organizations, the National Rifle Association—is crucial to understanding the GOP's transformation because the organized typically play an outsized role in influencing governance.[8] They have the knowledge, long-time horizons, and financial resources to monitor and apply pressure on policymakers.

A sharp shift in economic and political resources toward corporations and the very wealthy has taken place in the United States. The scale of this shift toward "top-end inequality" is without parallel in affluent democracies.[9] And it has carried over into politics. The top .01 percent of campaign contributors accounted for 10 to 15 percent of donations to federal campaigns in the early 1980s; by 2018 that figure was almost 50 percent, and it would almost certainly be much higher if indirect "dark money" contributions were included.[10]

The network of powerful conservative interests aligned with the Republican Party includes those focused on restricting abortion and battling against gun control. Yet economics remains central. The "Koch network" of multi-millionaires and billionaires has devoted unprecedented resources to building a virtual shadow party. That network is dedicated, above all, to extremely conservative economic policies.[11] The powerful U.S. Chamber of Commerce has undergone a massive expansion, moved far to the right, and become an increasingly integrated part of the Republican Party network.[12]

As inequality has skyrocketed in the United States, Republican elites have chosen to embrace that trend and ally with the economy's big winners. It is impossible to make sense of our current politics without wrestling with this central fact of the past twenty-five years of Republican governance. This deepening alliance has fed Republican extremism in two ways. Directly, it has committed the party to positions on vital issues that lack mass popular support. On the contrary, they are massively unpopular. Among ordinary Republicans the biggest complaint about taxes has long been consistent: *the rich and corporations do not pay their fair share*. Republican officials have indeed fixated on taxes, but only to demand that these increasingly wealthy groups pay less and less. Indirectly, it has encouraged the party to make up for the lack of support it receives on these positions by playing up and intensifying conflict on other issues— especially matters touching on race—that generate highly polarized politics. In this sense, the "plutocratic" and "populist" faces of the contemporary GOP are really two sides of the same coin.

A second factor feeding this anti-system shift in the GOP has been a large and growing partisan media presence in cable television and talk radio. The incentives created by the fragmentation of news media have fueled the growth of an "outrage industry" that harnesses partisan intensity for profit.[13] Although not unique to the right, these forces are much larger and far more influential on the conservative end of the spectrum.

The growth of conservative media has played a central role in isolating conservative voters and intensifying their hostility toward traditional governance. A distinctive feature of conservative media is the extent to which it aims to discredit alternative sources of information. This effort has been remarkably successful. Over time, the "center-right" media space has completely emptied; the core GOP audience now typically limits itself to a handful of ideologically convivial sources of information. Neither of these characteristics is true on the left. Right-wing media has helped draw Republican voters to confrontational, tribal politics.[14] It has helped create a GOP electorate that is motivated primarily by "negative partisanship"—i.e., hatred of the other side.

The third key contributor to and enabler of the GOP's radicalization has been the distinctive character of American electoral geography. Over the last quarter-century, rural areas have grown more Republican and urban areas more Democratic. This has gone hand in hand with the growing concentration of prosperity in urban and coastal areas. Notwithstanding the longstanding and continuing issues of concentrated poverty in much of urban America, the most affluent regions of the country are increasingly Democratic; the most depressed areas distant from city centers are increasingly Republican.

These hardening geographic political cleavages are highly consequential. That's because America's electoral system—its malapportioned Senate; its single-member, winner-take-all districts; and to some extent the Electoral College—rewards parties that are broadly distributed across large swaths of sparsely populated territory.[15] Nowhere is this clearer than in the Senate, with its huge bonus for people living in low-population states (a bonus that partly carries over to the Electoral College). The anti-tax activist Grover Norquist explained the math to attendees at the Conservative Action Conference a few years back: "While you do not redistrict states, the nice people who drew the map of the United States districted in such a way that we have all those lovely square states out West with three people who live in them—two are Republican senators and one's a Republican congressman." The conference ballroom erupted in laughter. Three of the party's recent Supreme Court nominees and all of its major legislative successes in 2017 and 2018 relied on Republican Senate majorities that collectively represented well less than half the population.

Although less obvious, the problem carries over to the House of Representatives, where Democratic votes are concentrated ("wasted") in urban districts, while Republican voters are spread more efficiently across seats. The GOP has been distinctly shaped by the party's increasingly strong performance in rural areas and sparsely populated states. Republicans can capture a larger share of House seats than their share of the overall vote in House elections. And bias feeds on bias—the same advantage of "packed" Democrats plays out at the state level, giving Republicans an edge that they have accentuated by partisan gerrymandering—for both state legislatures and the House of Representatives. In Wisconsin, for instance, Democrats won the majority of the two-party vote in state legislative races in 2018, but little more than one-third of the seats in the state legislature.

Minority support but political control is becoming an increasingly common pattern far beyond the Senate. With growing regularity, Republicans have lost the popular vote in Congress while gaining a majority of seats. Republicans have also lost the popular vote for president in six of the past seven elections. Despite all those losses, conservative Republicans now have a majority on the Supreme Court. In short, the antiquated and spatially biased structure of American electoral institutions has allowed the GOP to forego the search for majority support while sustaining, or even expanding, its political power.

All of these developments have pulled the GOP away from conventional politics. And they have fed on each other. The growth of inequality, for instance, has both empowered economic elites and given their political allies an incentive to substitute populist, anti-system cultural appeals for the commitment to economic opportunity and security for average Americans that the party can no longer offer. The growing clustering of Republican voters in parts of the United States "left behind" by both demographic shifts and the rise of the Knowledge Economy has created increasingly fertile terrain for the fear-mongering of the right-wing media. Many of these voters live in cultural environments where conservative politicians and media dominate political discourse. We know that voters rely heavily on elite cues to form judgments about policies. Mass polarization is increasingly overlaid onto geographic divisions between cities and rural areas, thriving metro centers and declining industrial towns, and red and blue states. Taking their cues from conservative elites and plied with hostile framing in the media, the Republican base has become highly resistant to calls for compromise and bipartisanship, and worryingly open to extremist appeals.

Sadly, our unusual political institutions, whose designers hoped to avoid the emergence of organized parties and certainly were not imagining this kind of intense partisan division, are only compounding the problems.

* * *

As these forces have intensified within the GOP, the party has adopted an unusual strategy.[16] Once again, Madisonian institutions—which fracture authority and blur accountability—have been turned to un-Madisonian ends. Our institutions allow the GOP to combine its substantial political power within the national government (which can be used to generate gridlock and dysfunction) with many of the trappings traditionally associated with "anti-system" parties. Employing strategies developed by House Speaker Newt Gingrich in the 1990s and Senate Majority Leader Mitch McConnell a decade later, the GOP increasingly resorted to brutal attacks on national institutions and mainstream politics, conspiracy-mongering and extreme vilification of opponents, and apocalyptic rhetoric suggesting that politics as usual—such as the Affordable Care Act (ACA), which built on prior *Republican* proposals—represented some kind of existential threat.

These strategies have facilitated the GOP's transformation into what can fairly be called a "counter-majoritarian" party. At the state level, GOP legislators have preemptively curtailed the power of statewide elected offices when Democrats win those posts, in effect rewriting the rules of the game after they have lost. In Wisconsin, for example, Republicans held a lame-duck session after the 2018 election to take away many of the incoming Democratic governor's powers. One Wisconsin GOP leader explained the logic, "If you took Madison and Milwaukee out of the state election formula, we would have a clear majority."

This disrespect for one-person-one-vote is now deeply embedded in GOP tactics. Increasingly, the party's ability to rewrite policy depends on rigging state-level rules and exploiting its Senate edge to lock in far-right policy achievements. More and more, it depends on creating and protecting deeply biased electoral systems at both the state and national levels. It depends not just on turning out its own voters (now armed for bear every election day), but also on keeping its opponents (often, among the most disadvantaged members of our society) from voting.

In the long run, the developing political alliances on the right and the strategies they have evolved place the American polity at considerable risk. At a minimum, they have made it almost impossible to govern effectively—to use political authority to address the kinds of collective challenges that every prosperous society must at least try to address. Republicans have tried to shackle that collective capacity—a stance that benefits the powerful economic interests that have dominated their thinking on most domestic policy issues. At a maximum, the reliance on divisive politics, including ethno-nationalist appeals, combined with the embrace of counter-majoritarian initiatives, opens up the real prospect of democratic backsliding. Restoring a healthy party politics requires that something be done to disrupt this dangerous spiral.

We have developed our diagnosis of the challenge at some length because prescriptions must be based on the right diagnosis. Many analyses of our politics botch the diagnosis. They decry political polarization without recognizing either the asymmetric quality of that process or how it (in combination with our constitutional design) has allowed the GOP to build obstruction and, increasingly, counter-majoritarian initiatives into our politics.

Many ostensibly moderate or centrist proposals fail this fundamental test. To begin with an idea often floated by casual observers, the effort to construct a third party in the "middle" of the electorate would either fail to take off or backfire if it did. There is a reason the United States has not had a really influential third party in a century—our first-past-the-post electoral system is punitive toward third parties. Given the intensity and organizational resources of powerful forces on the right, moreover, a party that was able to gain a toehold in the center would be much more likely to *strengthen* the GOP's electoral position, allowing more extremism, than to force it to make a moderating course correction.

Other proposals to encourage moderation are also likely to misfire, if perhaps not so spectacularly. In principle, some reforms, if applied across the country, could encourage the election of a greater number of moderate candidates and create more incentives to pay attention to moderate voters. Ranked-choice voting and reforms to limit gerrymandering are good examples. Yet political scientists have generally concluded that these initiatives would likely have only modest effects. Moreover, there is a risk that these changes would be adopted primarily in Democratic-leaning states, which again might have the effect of strengthening Republicans (who seem uninterested in such reforms and would continue to gerrymander where it helps them) nationwide.

Sadly, many proposals for reform are a bit like the joke about the so-cial scientists stuck on a desert island with nothing but canned food—the economist suggests "assume we have a can opener." Proposals that might encourage our political system to be more responsive to ordinary voters, such as efforts to ease voting or reduce the role of big money, are very un-likely to proceed with Republicans holding the counter-majoritarian ramparts of the Supreme Court and the Senate filibuster. Valuable as these reforms might be, we think the pragmatic step is to think about what, in their absence, might prod the Republican Party back toward its tradi-tional role as a constructive participant in the responsibilities of shared governance.

Finding solutions to our current challenges requires recognition that the two parties are not mirror images and are not equally responsible for ris-ing polarization. The interaction between the nature of its electoral base, the organizational forces within the Republican Party, and the skewed op-portunities of our system of representation create much stronger incen-tives for extremism than exist within the contemporary Democratic Party. The fateful concentration of Republican supporters in declining rural ar-eas favored by our electoral institutions creates the motive and opportu-nity to renounce appeals to the center of American public opinion and pursue counter-majoritarian strategies. To effectively tackle polarization and the growing risks of democratic backsliding, we must recognize this basic difference between our major political parties and tailor our pro-posals accordingly.

We need to start, also, from an appreciation that our political system cannot function if one of the two parties behaves like an anti-system party. Our institutions grant a major party the capacity to block or sabotage pol-icy initiatives and fuel alienation. Although certain general political re-forms might help the situation, as noted, these approaches suffer from a catch-22: designed to overcome polarization and obstruction, they are likely to fall victim to polarization and obstruction.

We think a more direct and useful way to think about the challenge is simply to ask what might change the Republican Party to make it once again a contributor to a healthy polity, capable of addressing pressing pub-lic problems. It is worth noting that the journey of the Republican Party to its current anti-system, anti-majoritarian posture has been uneven and contested rather than a steady march. On occasion, figures within the party have argued for a different course—one that would diminish the GOP's responsiveness to the wealthy and expand its appeal to those of more limited means, including racial minorities. Indeed, as late as 2013, there were significant calls within the party—the so-called autopsy report prepared by the Republican National Committee following its fifth loss of the presidential vote in six chances—to chart a more inclusive course. The challenge is to resurrect those calls and strengthen the forces working for them.

At the same time, the marginalization of such figures in the contemporary GOP provides perhaps the clearest evidence of how completely the growing forces on the right have come to dominate the party's inner circles. A telling feature of contemporary politics is the virtual absence of serious *organized* effort among GOP moderates, whether in or out of office, over the last two decades.[17] If modern American government needs a capacity for bipartisanship to function—and it does—then we desperately need the Republican equivalent of the Democratic Leadership Council, which became an organized and influential force for moderation within the Democratic Party in the 1980s.

No single direct initiative is likely to bring this about. Instead, it will require a number of developments that shift the cost-benefit calculations of some subset of ambitious Republican politicians. Asymmetric polarization stems not simply from rules but also from the interaction of rules (many of which can't or shouldn't be altered) with changes in social structure. As we have stressed, social transformations have created a large and intense Republican base, reinforced by well-resourced organizations and an extremist media. Can those forces be weakened?

Some hold out hope that the business community will emerge as a moderating force. Indeed, the development of such pressures over time would more likely make a considerable difference, as they did in nurturing the Democratic Leadership Council. Yet although the emergence of such organized action in the GOP might matter a lot, we are not optimistic about the prospects. Large business organizations such as the Chamber of Commerce have been a driving force encouraging the GOP's long rightward march.[18] Even as some business leaders decry the vulgarities and authoritarian impulses of Donald Trump, the wealthy Americans who finance such organizations have benefited enormously from the GOP's increasingly aggressive stances on taxes, government spending, and deregulation. Equally beneficial for economic elites is the flow of pro-business appointments into the courts, as well as the GOP's embrace of gridlock as an essential tool for constraining government activism. As in the past—the New Deal is probably the clearest example—moderation from the most economically privileged sectors of American society is most likely to emerge as a response to growing pressure from below rather than an exercise of enlightened self-interest.

A healthier media market would undoubtedly help. Here as well it is hard to find reason for optimism. Technological change and the relentless pursuit of profit have simultaneously nationalized conversations and created lucrative niches for those hawking intensity and division. Neither of those tendencies will be easy to undo, although efforts to promote or subsidize local, independent sources of news are of vital importance.

More broadly, any efforts that increase pluralism in our politics, that diminish the tendency to "stack" one cultural divide on top of another, would help enormously. Again, our political system was designed to promote diversity of views and interests. That diversity should in turn create the basis for compromise and collective capacity: *e pluribus unum*, out of many, one.

It is worth emphasizing that what looks more and more like a monolithic "red state" coalition in fact masks considerable underlying heterogeneity. There are extraordinary differences in the circumstances of the Deep South, the mountain West, the sparsely populated plains states, the deindustrializing Midwest, and the "sunbelt" areas that combine large and growing Latino populations and significant outposts of the high-tech "knowledge economy." Such a diversity of interests would be a challenge to hold together under any circumstances. It becomes especially so in a context where the GOP's intense commitments to economic elites—nakedly displayed in their astonishingly regressive tax bill and punitive efforts to repeal the ACA—leave them hard-pressed to address the aspirations of ordinary citizens in *any* of these settings. There are opportunities to chip away at the supposedly homogeneous Republican coalition with more inclusive appeals and policies.

Arguably, this will become only more likely over time. The radical GOP strategy is a bet against the future. The current Republican voting base—old, white, rural—is on the losing side of the major demographic trends in American society. Although the biases of American political institutions offer some protections, they are unlikely to provide a basis for long-term competitive success in a relatively open political system. Eventually, if our polity can hold together in the meantime, the argument of the 2013 "autopsy report" will be proven right: absent a total breakdown of our electoral arrangements, Republicans *must* adapt to the country's growing diversity.

Successful experiences with truly multiracial democracy are rare. Demographically, the country is replicating the experience of California, transitioning to a majority-minority polity. This transition is fraught,[19] and there is no reason to be sanguine about the prospects. Just as is now happening nationally, a majority that saw its dominant position slipping away in California initially reacted with a backlash. Over time, however, this stance became less and less viable. Indeed, in California it has led to the virtual collapse of the state GOP, as it turned inward on itself. But in the short run, a declining state party, caught up in the national configuration of media and interest groups that has fed GOP extremism, has chosen to retain allegiance to the party's national brand (and standard bearer). Within California—a state that much more closely resembles the economic and demographic trends of American society than core areas of Republican strength—this increasingly toxic brand of politics has obliterated the GOP's prospects to be competitive.

Effective party competition is essential to maintaining a vital democracy. Thus we do not regard the current dominance of California Democrats as particularly healthy. Yet parties want to win elections, and in time, California Republicans are likely to face mounting pressures to adapt. In practice, that means mounting pressure to become a truly multiracial party. Of course, reaching out to minority communities would require it to back away from its current embrace of white ethno-nationalist appeals. It would have to appeal less to prejudice and more to the felt needs of ordinary citizens for plausible solutions to their problems. Similarly, once a demographic tipping point is reached nationally there will be strong pressure on the GOP to adapt—indeed to do so much more quickly.

In short, the hope—a realistic if highly uncertain one—is not for the GOP to be permanently relegated to minority status. It is instead that Republicans will face growing incentives to turn toward the future rather than the past, becoming a more inclusive and multiracial coalition. This would not end partisan conflict—an unreachable and in any case undesirable goal for a healthy democracy. It would, however, diminish the incentives to engage in irresponsible, anti-system partisan conflict. And it would restore the prospect that areas of cross-party consensus and compromise could once again emerge. Under our peculiar constitution, such conditions remain a prerequisite for effective national efforts to address urgent challenges.

WHEN DEMOCRACY
BECOMES SOMETHING ELSE:
THE PROBLEM OF ELECTIONS AND
WHAT TO DO ABOUT IT

Andrew Gumbel

I n the spring of 2018, as a fretful country plunged into a bitter midterm election campaign, Crystal Mason of Fort Worth, Texas, was sentenced to five years in prison for the crime of voting.

It was, by any measure, an unusual prosecution. Mason had not participated in a scheme to change the outcome of any race on the November 2016 ballot. Her prosecutors presented no evidence that she had intentionally defrauded anyone. Rather, her mistake was to fail to understand that, as an ex-felon still on probation from a tax fraud case, she had not recovered her right to vote under state law. It was a mistake without consequence, because the provisional ballot she cast—with the help of a poll worker to whom she willingly gave her name and picture ID—was never counted. That made no difference to the Tarrant County district attorney, who threw the book at her for failing to read the fine print on her ballot form. And it made no difference to Ken Paxton, the Texas attorney general, who was all too happy to find a case, however flimsy, to uphold the contention, however dubious, that the state electoral system was rife with fraud and demanded the severest possible response.

Why would Paxton make such a contention? For the same reasons that Texas Republicans have been crying fraud for more than a decade: to cast a pall of illegitimacy over their Democratic opponents and to play to the Trump-supporting Republican base, who lap up stories, true or untrue, about felons and noncitizens overwhelming the polls on Election Day. The rules applied to Crystal Mason emphatically did not extend to Russ Casey, a Republican justice of the peace in Fort Worth who, just a month after Mason's case, admitted to submitting a re-election form filled with forged petition signatures. Here was a proven instance of actual fraud, but Paxton, strangely, had nothing to say about it. Casey was sentenced to probation only.

Mason, a divorced mother of three, was an African American in a city and a state with a tawdry history of racial discrimination that has persisted well past the advent of civil rights. On top of that, she ran smack into a buzz saw of Trump-era hyperpartisan politics. She was, in the profoundest sense of the term, a political prisoner, whose confinement served a specific political purpose. "Black people in Fort Worth hear about her case," her lawyer, Alison Grinter, said, "and they understand that they are not welcome in the voting booth."[1]

A similarly dispiriting story surfaced later in 2018, on the first day of in-person early voting in the midterms in Georgia. About forty black residents of a county-operated senior center near Augusta climbed into a bus to head to the polls, only to be told by the center's senior director that they were engaging in illicit "political activity" and needed to climb out again. The bus was provided by Black Voters Matter, a nonpartisan group that works to encourage African American participation, and the day's activities had been cleared with the center in advance. Somewhere along the line, though, a county clerk got cold feet and intervened, for reasons that may or may not have had to do with the fact that black voters across the state were rallying in support of Stacey Abrams, the Democratic candidate for governor, and against her Republican opponent, Brian Kemp, who was widely seen as an apologist for minority voter suppression. The Jefferson County authorities said only that they were concerned the local Democratic Party was putting its thumb on the scale. The county administrator said he "felt uncomfortable with allowing senior center patrons to leave the facility with an unknown third party."[2]

Such episodes ineluctably recall the brute political tactics of the segregation era, and in 2018 they were far from isolated—or restricted to the South. "The range of voter suppression efforts," two experts from the Brennan Center for Justice declared on the eve of the midterms, "has been more widespread, intense, and brazen this cycle than in any other since the modern-day assault on voting began."[3] Those efforts ran the gamut: overzealous purging of the voter rolls; capricious restrictions on registration requirements; elimination of early voting days; intolerable delays and omissions in sending out absentee ballots, excessively long lines at polling stations; aggressive gerrymandering of state and congressional districts; barrages of deceptive, negative advertising to confuse or deter voters; and, perhaps most insidious, the insistence in many states that voters present valid government ID, a policy that seemed incontrovertible on its face but in practice penalizes the poor, the elderly, the transient—many of them racial minorities—and large numbers of out-of-state students who do not have the documentation and, in many cases, face obstacles if they try to obtain it. To what end? All evidence suggests that the old system of checking signatures was more than sufficient to police individual voter fraud, a passingly rare crime for which the potential consequences (years in prison) far outweigh the potential rewards (adding just one vote to a desired candidate's total). As acknowledged in a number of district and federal appeals court rulings, voter ID laws are, at best, a solution to a nonexistent problem and, at worst, a blunt instrument with which to prevent eligible voters, particularly minority voters, from exercising their rights.

Yet they continue to proliferate. One of the reasons the 2018 election cycle was so grim for voting rights was that six states—including the key presidential battlegrounds of Georgia and Iowa—passed new legislation to make it more difficult to register, or to vote, or both.[4] On Election Day, a staggering thirty-five states implemented ID laws of varying degrees of strictness; the first of these laws was enacted only in 2005.[5]

Behind all these maneuvers was a concerted effort by the Republican Party across multiple states to secure a political advantage, not by winning the policy argument or by appealing to a more diverse electorate, but by waging legislative and bureaucratic warfare in the hope of clawing a few percentage points from its adversaries and thus clinging to power by fair means or foul. A Government Accounting Office study concluded in 2015 that voter ID laws were worth two to three extra percentage points to the GOP in any given race.[6] Reversing that advantage would have transformed the Republicans' clean sweep of statewide offices in Georgia in 2018 into a clean sweep by the Democrats. It would have similarly upended the results of the high-profile, razor-close races for governor and Senate in Florida.

Usually, Republicans deny up and down that voter ID has anything to do with restricting ballot access or eligibility. They argue, rather, that it is about basic nuts-and-bolts ballot security. Just occasionally, though, they let the façade drop. Dick Armey, the former House majority leader told party supporters in California in 2010 he saw voter ID laws as a way of taking three percentage points back from the Democrats.[7] And in 2016, the Wisconsin congressman Glenn Grothman predicted, correctly, that the GOP would prevail in the upcoming presidential election in his state with the help of a newly introduced photo ID requirement.[8]

It is important to point out that there is nothing *inherently* undemocratic in the ideology of mainstream Republicans. The laws they have passed are a partisan choice that go beyond labels one can readily identify as conservative or neo-liberal or libertarian. It is also important to remember that the Republicans' behavior over the past fifteen years, while shocking, is not unprecedented in American history—or restricted to just one side of the aisle. Far from it: the late nineteenth century saw a proliferation of arguments similar to the ones touted today about the need for common-sense policing of corruption and fraud, all the better to curtail the rights of black voters in the South and of working-class voters across the country. The Democrats, throughout their history, have proved capable of playing just as dirty as their rivals, given circumstances in which the stakes are high, the electoral competition is intense, and the opportunity exists, either through legislation or bureaucratic maneuvering, to bend or break the rules. Not only have Democrats gerrymandered as enthusiastically as Republicans, but they still do it, in states like Maryland, where they control the legislature, and the legislature controls redistricting.

This is about raw politics, not ideology. Time and again over the past two decades, the Republicans have considered their electoral prospects and chosen an undemocratic path. In the wake of the meltdown in Florida in 2000, the GOP *could* have made common cause with the Democrats to institute comprehensive electoral reform, as indicated, albeit imperfectly, by the bipartisan commission headed by Jimmy Carter and James Baker in 2005.[9] In 2013, the party *could* have listened to its own internal critics after losing the popular vote in five of the previous six presidential elections and fashioned a platform to appeal more broadly to minority voters as well as its shrinking white base.[10] Each time, though, the lure of short-term advantage won out over long-term coalition-building.

The party's anti-democratic inclinations went into overdrive after 2010, a year in which the Supreme Court's *Citizens United* decision sanctioned the use of almost unlimited dark money to fund political campaigns. The GOP used that money to deliver an outsized thumping to the Democrats in that year's midterms, and then used the advantage it gained in key state legislatures, including North Carolina, Pennsylvania, Ohio, and Wisconsin, to redraw district maps. In so doing, it gave itself a lopsided advantage in congressional and state legislative races for the next decade.

The effect was almost magical. In North Carolina, which Barack Obama won in 2008 and lost only narrowly four years later, a 7–6 Democratic advantage in the congressional delegation on the eve of the 2012 election turned into a 9–4 Republican advantage after, *even though the Democrats won more votes*. The Republicans also won supermajorities in the state legislature and embarked on a radical conservative agenda whose tenets included prosecuting children as young as thirteen as adults, imposing a drug-testing requirement on welfare recipients, and making Christianity the state religion. None of this remotely conformed to a reasonable interpretation of the will of the people.

Some of the distorted results of recent years were ones the Republicans didn't work all that hard to secure. They were just quirks of the system, like the Electoral College victory that put Donald Trump in the White House even though he lagged behind Hillary Clinton by more than three million votes, or like the 2018 midterms, which increased the GOP's Senate majority from 51 seats to 53 even though the Democrats won 12 million more votes in national Senate races. Democrats often see their support squandered this way: they generally do better in big states than in small ones, which carry disproportionate weight in the Senate and the Electoral College, and their candidates often win by wide margins in the cities, whereas Republicans in the suburbs elect their candidates more narrowly and thus distribute their support more efficiently.

These structural imbalances are not the whole story, though, because gerrymandering can push them to an intolerable extreme. In Virginia, the Democrats won the governorship by a nine-point margin in 2017, but lost control of the House of Delegates by a coin toss despite a near-identical distribution of state legislative votes. A system where a party needs to be ahead by nine percentage points just to pull even is no longer a democracy; it has become something else.

The push for voter ID laws has been in keeping with these broader distorting trends and has also, in an important sense, driven them. Rank-and-file Republicans love voter ID because it encapsulates their concerns and grievances about a country awash with undocumented immigrants, a country where old certainties seem to be melting away and politicians seem to bestow endless favor on minorities and foreigners while ignoring the needs of *real* Americans, as they like to think of themselves. On talk radio and on Fox News, voter ID is often discussed in the context of fantastical but widely believed stories about Democrats enlisting noncitizens and criminals to vote in overwhelming numbers. Voter ID laws trace their origins, in fact, to just such a story. When Kit Bond, the long-time Missouri senator, and a gaggle of Republican lawyers saw a surge of African American voters in St. Louis as the polls were closing on election night in 2000, they decided that a nefarious scheme was afoot to rob the other Missouri senator, John Ashcroft, of his re-election. No evidence ever emerged of such a scheme, despite extensive investigation, but the episode inspired Bond to push for voter ID anyway. The more Bond talked, the more he noticed the party faithful latching on to his red-meat rhetoric about dead people and dogs finding their way on to the voter rolls, and he understood—as the party as a whole would soon come to understand—that voter ID was an excellent rhetorical tool for driving turnout, particularly of more radical Republicans, who could be induced not only to vote against Democrats but against more moderate Republican incumbents in primary elections for state legislatures and for Congress.[11]

Once Obama was elected, the "otherness" of having a black man in the Oval Office and the suspicions played up by radical Tea Party candidates about the eligibility of nonwhite voters started to blur into one and the same issue. The "birther" movement championed by Donald Trump to challenge Obama's bona fides as an American was one instance of this. The efforts by Kris Kobach, one of the Republican Party's most ardent champions of voter suppression, to push a proof-of-citizenship requirement in Kansas and to cross-check the voter rolls against a database of immigrants enrolled in federal benefits programs, were another.[12]

To pander to the electorate's basest instincts in this way was to play with fire. Not only did the new discourse reopen long-dormant questions of who had the right to vote and what constituted the "real" electorate, questions with a lineage going directly back to the days of slavery; it turned the basic nuts and bolts of representative democracy into partisan fodder, which made the arguments much harder to refute or reverse. One can be cynical about the strength of either party's adherence to bedrock democratic principles even before this erosion of our civic discourse, but at least there had been an understanding, from the time of the civil rights movement, that universal suffrage was a fundamental part of America's civic creed, before which every politician was wise to bow, in word if not always in deed. Now, the rhetoric about America's core values has become more slippery and Orwellian. The worst Republican offenders seem to find entertainment in violating longstanding norms and blaming their opponents for it. Take, as an example, Brian Kemp, whose narrow election as Georgia governor in November 2018 appeared to owe something to the restrictive voting rules he had previously introduced as secretary of state. When the Democrat-controlled House Oversight Committee in Washington initiated an investigation into his actions, including a purge of 1.7 million names from Georgia's voter rolls, about a quarter of the state's total electorate, Kemp turned right around and urged *them* to "quit playing politics."[13] There is no winning such a fight, because the upshot of further sniping could only be *more* voter disgust, and even *lower* turnout, in a country whose participation rates in elections were already dismal enough.

Deterring voters in this way is a tool that both parties have used in the past, the thinking being that they'd prefer to control the electorate they know than to take bets on cultivating a new one. These days, though, the calculus has shifted because both parties believe—not always correctly—that Republicans do better in low-turnout elections, while Democrats stand to gain more from higher registration and higher participation rates. That, too, has put a dangerously partisan spin on the baseline principles of representative democracy. Two days after Kemp's broadside at the oversight committee, a Democrat-sponsored omnibus bill on voting rights came up for a House vote, and not a single Republican supported it. The merits of taking redistricting out of the hands of elected politicians (something state-level Republicans have often endorsed) or standardizing online registration (ditto) were scarcely discussed. Nor were the other particulars of the "For the People" bill, which covered everything from campaign finance to voting machines. It was enough for Mitch McConnell, the Senate majority leader, to highlight a proposal to make Election Day a national holiday, something the public supports in polls, and dismiss the entire bill as a Democratic "power grab."[14]

Donald Trump did not invent most of the rhetorical tropes he has hurled in the direction of voting and voting rights. The notion that the system is corrupt; that Democrats routinely cheat; that the voter rolls are stuffed with dead people, pets, criminals, and foreigners; that when Republicans are ahead in the early count they have already won but when Democrats are ahead they are secretly plotting to prevent all the ballots being counted—these are the talking points that have been rehearsed and honed and trotted out time and again, going back at least as far as the battle over Florida's presidential electoral votes in 2000. Even the idea of adding a citizenship question to the U.S. Census, which the Trump administration sought unsuccessfully for 2020, is not a new one; a top Republican consultant conducted a confidential study in 2015 and concluded that asking respondents for their citizenship would lead to an undercount of minority residents, both citizens and noncitizens, and thus give Republicans opportunities to draw district maps more heavily tilted in their favor.[15]

What Trump has done, through sheer force of personality and a tsunami of media attention, is to vulgarize the controversies surrounding elections and expand what had been largely a state-by-state field of combat into a raging national battle. Paradoxically, this has not been an entirely bad thing, because Trump has jump-started a conversation that should have taken place a long time ago. The toxicity, dishonesty, and partisan rancor he brings to just about any conversation have inadvertently exposed the hollowness of the arguments in defense of voter suppression and thus provided the basis of an answer to them.

The pushback against Trump began days after his inauguration when he claimed that the only reason he had lagged so far behind Clinton in the popular vote was that millions of noncitizens had voted illegally. Right away, the National Association of Secretaries of State, which is majority Republican, insisted it was "not aware of any evidence that supports the voter fraud claims made by President Trump."[16] Party allegiance was one thing, but Trump was accusing the country's election managers of gross incompetence, and that they could not tolerate.

The pattern was similar a few months later when Trump installed Kris Kobach as the driving force of a Presidential Advisory Committee on Election Integrity, whose purpose—to substantiate his bogus claims of fraudulent voting—was as Orwellian as its name. When Kobach petitioned the states to provide voters' Social Security numbers, military status, and voting histories, among many other data points, many saw the request as an unjustifiable violation of privacy, or a prelude to wide-scale voter suppression, or both, and they refused to comply. The Republican secretary of state in Mississippi told Kobach to "go jump in the Gulf of Mexico."

The commission was packed with notorious voter suppression advocates, one of whom freely acknowledged that he didn't want Democrats or mainstream Republicans involved for fear that they would "guarantee its failure."[17] Kobach and his staff resisted making their documentation public, as required by federal law, and were eventually sued by one of the rare Democrats on the panel who said he too was being denied access. Soon, even White House insiders were calling the commission a "shit show," and they pulled the plug after just seven months.

It became increasingly obvious that Trump and his allies had no interest in fixing the actual problems besetting American elections; the more they talked about cheating and corruption, the more apparent it became that they were stirring anger and division for partisan purposes without the slightest concern that their words and actions might in themselves undermine the integrity of the system. Both national security and the cybersecurity experts found this alarming, because Trump was, in essence, doing to America exactly what the Russians had set out to do in 2016—that is, to delegitimize everything in sight.[18] That alarm, in turn, created pressure from outside the party political system to address what Trump would not—everything from the security of registration and voting systems to the penetration of social media networks by Russian bots and paid disinformation specialists.

Where Trump started sounding alarm bells, others soon followed. One of the reasons the 2018 governor's race in Georgia attracted such broad national attention was the fury the president had stirred up about voter fraud, real or imagined, and the provocative language he had introduced into public debate about it. Kemp's Democratic challenger, Stacey Abrams, was an ardent voting rights activist who had set out to register hundreds of thousands of new voters even before launching her candidacy. As the campaign gathered pace, the question of who should be Georgia's next leader frequently took a back seat to a furious secondary debate about who was able to register to vote, who stayed registered, who got to cast a ballot, and how. The country learned all about Kemp's voter roll purges and about his "exact match" law, under which any inconsistency between a voter registration form and a government ID—even something as inconsequential as a missing hyphen or middle initial—was grounds to put a registration on hold. To the shock of absolutely nobody, this law had the greatest impact on African American voters, tens of thousands of whom were told they could cast a provisional ballot only while their identities were subject to further checks.

The country also learned about Georgia's inauditable all-electronic voting machines, which had not worked properly since they were first introduced in 2002 and were now deemed pitifully insecure because the roadmap to their internal security workings had been left on an open internet site for seven months in 2016–17. Kemp's response to this breach was not to replace the machines with a verifiable paper system, as security experts urged, but to take direct control of the infrastructure himself, where previously it had been overseen by an outside agency. He thus had the luxury not only to set the rules for his own election, but also to monitor the internal workings of the voting machines. It was not until after the election, when he risked being in charge of his own recount too, that he acknowledged a possible conflict of interest and resigned as secretary of state.

None of these circumstances—a partisan election manager, lousy machines, rules that risked disenfranchising minority voters, long lines on Election Day, malfunctioning machines, and a woefully short supply of provisional ballots—was unprecedented. The same broad pattern has arisen in controversial close races again and again, going back to the days before machines and, in the South, before minority voters. Unlike many of those contests, though, this circus was on full public view. And the public was primed both to hope for the best and to expect the worst, because they understood this was a battle for Georgia's soul, pitting the vestiges of a fast-disappearing world of plantations and genteel good-ol'-boy manners against an emerging new South that was multicultural, globally-minded, tech-driven, and economically dynamic. Seen in these terms, the race wasn't simply about Republicans and Democrats. It was about how long the old order could cling on before it gave way to the inevitable. And that, too, suggested some sort of answer to America's voter suppression frenzy. The Republicans could mount all the rearguard actions they wanted, but sooner or later the sheer number of their opponents would overwhelm the efforts to contain them.

*   *   *

The problem with seeking to repair America's electoral system in the midst of a crisis is that it was never fully functional in the first place. This is not the same as saying that the system *can't* function, or never has. On the contrary: since the early nineteenth century, the United States has been a living experiment in the exercise and expansion of suffrage rights as much as it has been a laboratory for eye-popping voter suppression techniques. The progressive side of its dual nature is evident in many jurisdictions, across many states, where elections are generally well run and administrators open to new ideas. But there is also a reason for the constant back-and-forth between champions of electoral democracy and their antagonists; the United States, unlike every other advanced Western democracy, has never had a set of clear, uniform rules for the conduct of elections, and that has left the country perennially vulnerable to unscrupulous party managers, corrupted bureaucrats, and outside interests who have seized the opportunity to make up their own rules as they go along.

America's unfortunate exceptionalism in this respect is largely the result of its unique history. The country's institutions were conceived in an age before democracy, and the ideal of coequal citizenship was blighted from the outset. The founders not only accepted slavery but also baked it into the architecture of the House of Representatives, the Senate, and the Electoral College by giving disproportionate weight to slaveowners and the states they represented. Idealists and reformers have struggled mightily over the past two centuries to overcome this deep structural flaw and enshrine a universal definition of citizenship and voting rights, but the definition has never quite stuck, and the legacy of slavery has, in one way or another, lingered on. The Fourteenth and Fifteenth Amendments, passed in the wake of abolition at the end of the Civil War, fell crucially short of protecting the rights of Southern blacks and could not prevent the former Confederate states from establishing a system of institutionalized apartheid—and indeed the disenfranchisement of large swaths of the working class more generally. Likewise, the landmark civil rights legislation of the 1960s could not prevent a decades-long backlash that culminated in a conservative-majority Supreme Court eviscerating a key provision of the Voting Rights Act in 2013 and opening the door to a flurry of new voter suppression laws in states where the civil rights division of the Department of Justice had previously held veto power.

It is often said that the devolution of election management to the states and to individual counties is a sign of the strength and adaptability of the American system, but really it is another symptom of America's underlying failure, willed or otherwise, to settle the most fundamental questions about the rights of citizenship. Every other advanced democracy has an apolitical central electoral commission that sets rules and standards for everything from registration and polling-place management to voting machines and recount procedures. If the United States had a similar body, the vast majority of the problems plaguing the system would disappear overnight. Secretaries of state would have no discretion to impose capricious rules on, say, the minimum thickness deemed acceptable for a voter registration form, or the availability of Sunday early voting in areas where African Americans are habitually bused to the polls after church.[19] Counties would not be able to buy expensive, inauditable, bug-ridden voting machines, because the central authority would have more scrupulous certification standards and could negotiate a more favorable bulk-purchase price.

A central electoral commission wouldn't just eliminate the problem of discriminatory laws in parts of the country with a history of hostility toward minority groups; it would in effect extend the reach of the Voting Rights Act to all jurisdictions and all aspects of election management. It says much about the lapsed state of American democracy that establishing such a commission and guaranteeing its political independence remains as inconceivable now as it would have been at the height of Jim Crow. The tools of democracy we have are unable to deliver the strong system most of us want.

What, then, is the answer? Much of the pushback against voter ID laws and other forms of voter suppression has played out in the federal courts, which have issued a flurry of mostly favorable rulings. But legal cases move at a glacial pace and not always in a straight line. A federal judge declared Texas's strict ID requirement to be discriminatory and "an unconstitutional burden on the right to vote," but only in 2014, three years after it became law. And, even then, it stayed on the books while the legal wrangling continued and ended up surviving following a light rewrite endorsed by the Fifth Circuit Court of Appeals.[20] Courts are, of course, capable of upholding unjust and discriminatory electoral practices as well as striking them down, and the risk may be deepening now that Trump has filled two Supreme Court vacancies and hundreds of other federal judgeships.

More promising are the developments in the states, particularly those that are not competitive in statewide federal elections and thus find themselves out of the national spotlight. Provisional balloting, early voting, and same-day registration have all become common in the years since the Florida debacle of 2000. Close to a dozen states have now moved to take the redistricting process out of the hands of elected politicians. Oregon and California have started a national movement to make voter registration an opt-out rather than an opt-in process, Maine has elected its first member of Congress via ranked-choice voting, and Florida has at least attempted to restore voting rights to felons after they have completed their sentences. (The voters approved it at the ballot box, only for the Florida legislature to push back with a bill that all but neutered the will of the people.[21])

When the Democrats took control the House of Representatives in 2019, one of their first moves was to seek to nationalize the best of these initiatives. They knew, going in, that the omnibus bill they wrote, known variously as the "For the People" act or H.R. 1, stood no chance of passing as long as the Republicans controlled the Senate and the White House. Still, it was significant that Congress was giving serious consideration to a subject that had commanded little or no attention since the civil rights era. The ideas in the law were overwhelmingly good ones: to standardize early voting, provisional balloting, and automatic voter registration; to restore the Voting Rights Act; to reinstate the voting rights of ex-felons as a matter of course; to create independent redistricting commissions in every state; to establish a federal matching fund for political candidates who attract large numbers of small-dollar donors and to impose disclosure and transparency rules on "independent expenditure" organizations active in campaigns; to mandate auditable voting machines; and, finally, to reform an increasingly toothless Federal Electoral Commission to enhance both its effectiveness and its political independence. Just as Trump was nationalizing right-wing paranoia about noncitizens and criminals taking over the system, his opponents in Congress were now offering a national response.

The biggest obstacle to progress on any of these issues remains the deep, insidious hyperpartisanship gripping Washington and the rest of the country. We can never have a fully functioning democracy until *both* parties embrace the idea of free and fair elections and agree to an oversight system to ensure they practice what they preach. That, in turn, almost certainly means creating a world with a more reasonable breed of politician, and a more reasonable form of public discourse. And that's a tall order, no question, particularly in a world of tribal allegiances reinforced by relentless social media memes, and by an election industry that spends billions every cycle to deepen division for partisan gain.

The good news, though, is that while voters may *start* from the position that the other side is irredeemably corrupt and hell-bent on cheating, they also generally support the notion that control of the electoral process should be taken out of the parties' hands and made fair and uniform for all. They like early voting and other conveniences, regardless of party. In a number of ballot initiatives around the country, in red states as well as blue, they have voted to curtail the power of big money and end gerrymandering, and they have voted, too, in favor of ranked-choice voting, which tends to favor moderate, consensus-seeking candidates over hyperpartisan ones.[22] And, yes, they'd be happy to make Election Day a federal holiday.

How can those voter preferences be harnessed into a national movement? How can rank-and-file Republicans and Democrats set aside their differences and band together to demand better of their election officials? One starting point may be to identify those elected officials most egregiously hostile to the cause of representative democracy and to organize campaigns to vote them out of office. It can't matter if the offending parties are Republicans or Democrats. We saw the beginnings of such a campaign in Georgia in 2018, even if the result was not the one that voting rights activists behind the Abrams campaign had hoped to see. One bad election, though, doesn't have to kill a movement.

If anything, the Georgia race and its manifest imperfections have deepened the sense of injustice and further galvanized support for comprehensive change. Abrams's response to defeat was not to concede, but to start a new organization, Fair Fight Action, which has pushed for greater accountability and for answers to the questions that Kemp refused to address on the campaign trail. The effort has brought her national attention, and the respect of political figures on both sides of the aisle—a step, surely, in the right direction.

THE BEST ANSWER TO MONEY IN POLITICS AFTER *CITIZENS UNITED*: PUBLIC CAMPAIGN FINANCING IN THE EMPIRE STATE AND BEYOND

Chisun Lee[1]

T he 2016 presidential election slammed the door on any near-term hope of overturning *Citizens United*. The candidate who won seemed more than unlikely to appoint a Supreme Court majority that would reverse the 2010 decision setting off unlimited corporate spending in politics. But the elections of 2018 opened a window. Americans delivered a majority to the U.S. House of Representatives that not only talked the talk of campaign finance reform, but also, in some critical wins, credited victory itself to the collective power of so-called small donors.[2]

The same occurred in New York, except that the progressive wave did not just take one house. By flipping the state Senate, challengers succeeded in turning a divided government into a liberal trifecta. After years of seeing one election reform bill after another wither, the Empire State suddenly was in a position to get big things done for democracy. Chief among them was the goal of disrupting a state power structure built on massive special-interest donations, by reviving a longtime effort to enact public financing of campaigns for elected office.[3]

The problem was unquestionably dire. In 2018, the biggest one hundred individual donors gave more to New York candidates than all 137,000 estimated small donors (who gave $200 or less) combined.[4] That was not counting the much greater giving done by corporations and PACs. Small donors made up just 5 percent of money raised by state candidates—far less than the 19 percent raised by federal candidates, which is also not much.[5] Simply put, the vast majority of New Yorkers had no financial influence in electing candidates to state office.

The outsized influence of wealth in American politics takes many forms. But in the category of campaign finance, the boldest solution is as clear as the problem. *Citizens United* had, of course, closed off any possibility of limiting special interest spending. But amplifying the voices of people who cannot afford to spend a lot of money on politics remains constitutional.[6] The most popular approach for doing so is small donor public financing (also known as the matching funds model). The way it works is simple. Constituents who give small amounts to participating candidates will see their contributions matched by public money. The system is voluntary: candidates opt in by raising enough small initial donations from constituents to qualify for public matching funds and accepting conditions, including lower contribution limits.

New York's newly progressive state majority happened to have the nation's best example of small donor public financing in its backyard. New York City's matching funds program, over the course of three decades, has transformed the political participation of non-wealthy residents—both as donors and as candidates. The vast majority of candidates who run for district or citywide office participate in the program.[7] It has made residents, even of the city's poorest districts, agents in electoral politics—as modest contributions are made greater and thus more important by public funds.[8] In the past few years alone, eight local governments, including Washington, DC, and Suffolk County, New York, have adopted similar reforms.[9]

What has happened with public financing in New York state since Election Day 2018 is both a story of progress and a cautionary tale. The progress has been too incremental for some, particularly newer activists, yet astounding to many who had advocated fruitlessly for years in the face of a powerful establishment. An overview of the months-long campaign to achieve this progress shows the daunting scope of the alliances and actions necessary to begin changing the status quo. This progress could culminate in a huge win—a reform that enables non-wealthy New Yorkers to hold a significant stake in who is able to win elected office. Whether it does will depend on the agility and stamina of a broad, diverse coalition of advocates to parry the relentless arguments of incumbents who see public financing as an existential threat.

On September 14, 2018, a secret meeting took place in the Manhattan headquarters of one of New York's most powerful unions. The twenty or so people who gathered included leaders of organized labor, a politically active grassroots group with members throughout the state, a prominent third party, and the Brennan Center for Justice, the nonpartisan public policy think tank where I work.

Everyone was bleary-eyed from staying up late and then waking up early. The evening before, progressive challengers had upset a critical number of centrist incumbents in the state Senate's Democratic primaries. Now, the idea that had percolated for weeks in calls and emails seemed worth taking more seriously. For the next few hours, the group plotted a campaign to finally bring public financing of elections to New York state, depending on what happened in the November general election.

November 6 exceeded even the most optimistic hopes of progressives. As official counts in close contests solidified, it turned out that reform-touting challengers had won not just a majority for liberals in the state Senate, but the biggest liberal majority since 1912.[10] New Yorkers were fed up with the dysfunctional status quo, where an alliance of conservatives and a few independents in one chamber of the legislature had managed to stymie campaign finance reform (and voting reform, and environmental reform, and housing reform, and more) for years.[11]

The Fair Elections for New York campaign took off. The *Daily News* announced the campaign's launch on November 26.[12] In a matter of weeks, more than two hundred groups from across the state and the nation had signed on to "tackle the crises we face in housing, living wage jobs, criminal justice, affordable health care, transportation, climate, fair taxes, and more" through small donor public financing.[13] The reform would "amplify the voices of women; of people of color; of the working and middle classes; and of any and all under-represented New Yorkers in the political process," the groups agreed. Campaign members range from nationally known names such as the Natural Resources Defense Council, the Service Employees International Union, National Association for the Advancement of Colored People, and the state's Planned Parenthood chapter, to local grassroots groups of tenants, immigrant workers, and criminal justice activists. Some twenty New York chapters of Indivisible— the national advocacy network created after the 2016 presidential election to elect progressive leaders, which had played a significant role in flipping state Senate seats—were all in.

The draw for many was the prospect that New York would be a critical test case for the nation. Public financing, particularly the small donor matching funds model the New York campaign would pursue, had in the years since *Citizens United* gained popularity in cities and counties across the country.[14] Then no less than Rep. Nancy Pelosi declared, in an op-ed in the *Washington Post* days after the midterm election, that the reform would be a cornerstone of the new House majority's first legislative package, an omnibus bill to "restore democracy."[15]

In the first days of the new congressional session, the House indeed introduced—and eventually passed—its proposal to take small donor public financing nationwide.[16] But the U.S. Senate's leadership was adamant in its opposition, giving the federal bill practically no chance of enactment in the near future.[17] If the reform could make it in New York—dominated by the real estate, finance, and health care industries, and home to the highest number of federal public corruption convictions in the nation—it might just make it anywhere.[18]

Conditions for passage of public financing in New York seemed unusually favorable. The governor and the leader of each legislative chamber had all introduced strong small donor public financing bills in recent years. Never had grassroots demand for the reform been as strong or as diverse across issue groups, nor the tools to rapidly organize and call out politicians as immediate and far-reaching as social media had been during the recent election. New York could lead the nation. It could be the first to enact a robust small donor matching program statewide. Passage would send a message to Americans that, even in the age of *Citizens United*, transformative change to take back democracy for working people was still possible.

The growing popularity of public financing reflects a growing awareness of, and impatience with, the status quo of money in U.S. elections. The problems of this status quo are by now well known. A handful of megadonors dominate political giving and spending at every level of election.[19] Often they do so in close cooperation with candidates, operating in effect as shadow campaigns that are unfettered by the contribution limits and transparency rules that campaigns proper face. Often they do so through vehicles that hide their identities and true interests from voters, obscuring accountability for negative or misleading election ads.[20] Though the social science on causality is mixed, common sense (and the occasional investigative news story) says that this overwhelming influence of the wealthiest donors on campaigns for elected office affects the policy decisions of those elected.[21] That leaves millions of Americans excluded from their own political process.

This status quo includes the reality of a Supreme Court that is unlikely to reverse course soon on a spate of cases from the 2000s that enable and protect unlimited corporate spending in elections.[22] Nor is the effort to create a constitutional amendment to overturn *Citizens United* likely to succeed in the near future. Public financing remains the only immediate solution to increase the relative influence of non-wealthy Americans in campaign finance within current legal constraints.

National polls in 2018 showed these realities sinking in across the country—and the demand for public financing as a solution rising. Global Strategy Group's poll in August, for End Citizens United, a political action committee devoted to electing campaign finance reformers to Congress, showed 81 percent support for public financing—across gender, race, age, education, and party.[23] In April, Pew found that 74 percent of Americans believe it is "very important" that "people who give a lot of money to elected officials do not have more political influence than other people."[24] Freedom House, the George W. Bush Institute, and the Penn Biden Center for Diplomacy and Global Engagement together published a poll that June (The Democracy Project Report) showing "the influence of money in politics" tying with racism as the top issue causing Americans to worry about our democracy.[25]

The wave of local governments passing small donor match systems in recent years underscores the growing national interest in this public financing model.[26] Portland, Oregon, and Berkeley, California, both enacted the reform in 2016. Last year, candidates in Berkeley tested out the system for the first time—twelve of the fourteen city council candidates participated, with several observing that the system was already making it easier to raise campaign funds and increasing participation from the community.[27] In Maryland, Montgomery, Howard, and Prince George's counties have all passed small donor match public financing in the last five years. First-time candidates have already emerged in Washington, DC, saying the city's enactment of a matching funds program last year has given them hope of competing with well-heeled incumbents.[28] Suffolk County, New York, is building out its system to launch in 2021. And Denver, Colorado, recently joined this growing list after residents approved a ballot measure in November 2018. To be sure, several other forms of

public financing exist elsewhere.[29] However, after *Citizens United*, jurisdictions enacting public financing have largely gravitated toward small
donor match because the model multiplies the importance of small donations and thus enables candidates to seek support from non-wealthy
constituents while still raising competitive sums.

Nothing seems more indicative of public financing's graduation from
niche "good government" concept to broadly sought empowerment tool
than its inclusion in the Movement for Black Lives policy platform.[30] As
Movement policy leaders Monifa Bandele and Richard Wallace wrote in
their op-ed urging New York lawmakers to enact small donor public
financing:

> We can't truly build Black political power and combat racism and op-
> pression if wealthy donors continue to hold outsized influence. While
> Black representatives may be gaining in number and power, without
> systemic campaign finance reforms these gains will be fleeting. This is
> true here in New York, where we celebrate a historic occurrence—leaders
> of both chambers in the state Legislature are Black.... To get true
> democracy—especially for historically oppressed people—you need to
> have fair elections. That includes both public financing and easier access
> to the polls.[31]

Mid-January loomed as a critical milestone for the New York public
financing effort. That was when Governor Andrew Cuomo typically
announced his annual legislative priorities, in the form of a budget proposal for the state's next fiscal year. In New York's eccentric lawmaking
process, the governor's office wields enormous power to create policy by
putting ideas into its budget proposal, which the legislature is able only to
react to and must pass by April 1. Conversely, the governor also signals
near-certain doom for any policy proposal by not including it in the executive budget. Each year, the Albany press corps, special interests and
their lobbyists, and community advocates across the state hold their
breath for the governor's budget announcement.

Cuomo had put small donor public financing in many prior budget
proposals.[32] But 2019 would be the first year the state's legislative majority was progressive enough to pass it. Fair Elections advocates worried
that the prospect of actual passage, and of disturbing a campaign finance

regime dominated by the wealthy corporate donors who support him, would give the governor cold feet.

Election Day kicked off weeks of advocacy, much of it behind the scenes, to persuade the governor to come through. Then presumed to be a presidential aspirant, Cuomo bore reminding of America's hunger for a response to *Citizens United*. Heads of the most prominent national groups in the Fair Elections campaign, who were also lobbying the U.S. House majority to take similar steps, wrote to urge Cuomo to set an inspiring example for the country. The Brennan Center convened a roster of nearly one hundred business, civic, and culture leaders—including many large donors—as NY LEAD (New York Leadership for Accountable Government) to persuade the governor that reducing Albany's culture of cronyism and enabling more fair and efficient government would be as good for business as it was for working people.

On January 4, the House introduced H.R.1, the sweeping democracy reform bill Speaker Pelosi had promised in her op-ed after Election Day that included small donor public financing.[33] On January 13, the *Wall Street Journal* reported that NY LEAD—including Facebook co-founder Chris Hughes, Craigslist founder Craig Newmark, and hedge-fund manager Jonathan Soros—had written Cuomo, urging him to "cut a path the nation can follow."[34] On January 15, in a livestreamed announcement that Fair Elections campaign members watched with bated breath, Cuomo announced that his budget would "overhaul the campaign financing system. . . . Create a public financing system with a $6-to-$1 match."[35]

The fight for public campaign financing in New York State was officially on.

The Fair Elections campaign's next challenge was to persuade legislators to transform a campaign finance system they had just used to win office. In mid-March the state Assembly and Senate would announce their reactions to the governor's budget. They could echo, or they could reject, his proposal for small donor public financing.

The reform is more complex to understand than many democracy reforms. Its mechanics and benefits are not as obvious as those of, say, early voting. To persuade lawmakers, their constituents, and the press, advocates had to execute a strong public education campaign in the space of two months. They had to make the case that New York urgently needed small donor public financing.

The first step was to present evidence of the problem. Plenty of corruption trials and investigative news stories over the years had produced anecdotal evidence that big donors wielded too much influence in Albany.[36] But just how badly did big donors outweigh ordinary New Yorkers?

The dominance of big donors in New York was, it turned out, much worse than people realized. When the Brennan Center analyzed 2018 state campaign finance records, we were surprised to arrive at the data point that would appear in countless op-eds, tweets, press conferences, and speeches by advocates and supportive lawmakers over the next months. In 2018, the biggest one hundred individual donors gave more money to New York candidates than all 137,000 estimated small donors combined. (Nearly $2 million more. And that was not even counting contributions from corporations, which would tip the scales even further toward the wealthiest donors.)[37]

Our study, *The Case for Small Donor Public Financing in New York State*, concluded that most New Yorkers had not just too little, but practically no financial influence at all in sending candidates to office.[38] Small donations made up less than 5 percent of money raised by state candidates. Most donors to New York state candidates gave more than $10,000—they were not just big donors, but megadonors. (New York's contribution limits are sky high.[39] Individuals can give as much as $69,700 to a candidate for statewide office, $19,300 to a state Senate candidate, and $9,400 to a state Assembly candidate in an election cycle. That's much higher than federal contribution limits or those in most states.) Big donors tended to come from areas that were whiter, wealthier, and had higher education and employment levels than where small donors lived. If money talked—and considerable research establishes that it does, in the lawmaking context—New York's elected officials were hearing from a deeply underrepresentative and highly privileged minority of people and corporate interests as they set about making policy decisions.[40]

But would small donor public financing—specifically, the $6-to-$1 matching funds model Cuomo proposed in his budget bill—be an effective remedy to the stark disparities of financial influence in New York elections? After all, the matching funds model is not the only approach to public financing. Several states, including Connecticut, Maine, and Arizona, provide block grants to qualifying candidates. Meanwhile, Seattle has implemented the country's first "Democracy Voucher" program, in which residents receive government-funded vouchers that they can contribute to eligible candidates.[41]

But multiple-match public financing is the most well-established approach, and thus offers the most evidence of public benefits, particularly in New York City, where it is widely used. Following the establishment of the city's small donor match, candidates now rely more on small donors to finance their campaigns.[42] The number and diversity of New Yorkers participating in elections as donors has also increased.[43] The city's small donor match was designed and continues to be expanded, with the goal of increasing civic participation.[44]

Ultimately, a combination of data-based analyses and testimonials from elected officials who had used the city's matching funds program made for a strong case in favor of enacting $6-to-$1 public financing at the state level. The reform proposed by the governor, if adopted and used, would dramatically increase the relative influence of small donors in New York electoral campaigns.

First, the Brennan Center wanted to show what effect the reform could have had on the overwhelming dominance of megadonors in the 2018 state election cycle. We projected the governor's campaign finance reform package—a $6-to-$1 match on up to $175 of donations, lower contribution limits for publicly financed candidates, and a ban on corporate contributions—onto the state's 2018 fundraising numbers. The effect was dramatic. The proportion of money candidates would have raised from small donors rose from less than 5 percent to 30 percent. The share of money raised from donations of $2,000 or less rose from 16 percent to 60 percent.[45]

Next, we sought to demonstrate that, beyond shifting the balance between large and small donors, small donor public financing would yield benefits in terms of increasing civic engagement. It would bring more New Yorkers into the political process as donors, which research shows can be a gateway to other acts of democratic participation, such as voter canvassing.[46] The key advantage of a public matching funds model is the incentive it gives candidates to go out and engage as many people as possible in elections, knowing that even with modest private dollars their campaigns will be able to raise competitive sums. The reform, in essence, can transform candidates into agents of civic participation.[47]

Indeed, one of the most remarkable trends the data showed was that many more New Yorkers had participated as donors in city elections than in state elections, even in the poorest neighborhoods. We compared donors in 2017 New York City Council elections (with $6-to-$1 small donor public financing) with donors in 2018 state Assembly elections (without public financing), because the two types of districts roughly overlap in size and boundaries. It turned out that, even in neighborhoods with relatively high rates of poverty, nearly seven times more residents had donated to City Council campaigns than to Assembly campaigns.[48] These residents gave nearly five times more of their own money to City Council campaigns than to Assembly campaigns.[49] When public matching funds were included, small donations to City Council candidates from these neighborhoods yielded nearly twenty-seven times more money than Assembly campaigns were able to raise in the same neighborhoods.[50]

Residents in these relatively poor neighborhoods engaged more often, and were more financially valuable, in elections that matched their modest dollars with public funds than in elections that did not. Our conclusions lined up with previous research by the nonpartisan Campaign Finance Institute, which found that New York City's small donor public financing program had "brought more low-dollar donors into the system," leading to a "substantial increase not only in the proportional role of small donors but in their absolute numbers per candidate."[51]

Finally, we sought to highlight the benefits of small donor public financing for candidates, not just constituents, as that was the likely mindset of state legislators considering the reform. Numerous elected officials attested to the relative freedom of running for office using New York City's $6-to-$1 small donor matching system—freedom from courting megadonors, and freedom to spend that time instead engaging with voters and constituents—and to their ability to win using that system.[52] Few were as significant as Letitia James, who had just become the first Black and the first female candidate to win election to be the state's attorney general.

James had long been a vocal proponent of small donor public financing. She credited her previous historic win, as the first Black woman elected to citywide office in the New York City public advocate election of 2013, to her ability to use the city's matching funds program. She said in an interview as public advocate that she "would not be in this position but for campaign finance reform and the support of working-class people."[53] At a national event called Unrig the System, in 2018, she said that "every elected official in this country needs the freedom to represent the interest of Americans. And it is through public financing that we will get one step closer to ensuring that our elected representatives are representatives of our electorate."[54]

In her campaign to become state attorney general, James faced criticism for raising large checks from industry donors. She responded that she needed to raise funds in that way in order to compete for state office. The state lacked a matching funds program that would enable her to rely on constituents' support as she had as a candidate in the New York City public financing system.[55]

Research backs up James's remarks on improved representation. Public financing allows candidates to spend more time with residents on the campaign trail, which enables eventual winners to govern with a deeper understanding of the issues and closer relationships with their constituents.[56]

Along with offering testimonials of candidates who had successfully used public financing, we advocates more quietly offered state legislators data that went straight to the core of their self-interest. The Campaign Finance Institute ran projections showing that, if sitting legislators had been able to opt in to the governor's proposed matching funds program in 2018, nearly every one of them could have raised as much money as they had raised in traditional, mostly large donations.[57]

This body of evidence of the benefits of small donor public financing, both data-based and anecdotal, formed the basis for numerous closed-door briefings for Albany legislators and a first-ever legislative hearing on public financing for the state. The evidence emerged in twenty-seven op-eds.[58] Voices from Jesse Jackson to the state's fiscal watchdog, State Comptroller Thomas DiNapoli, urged legislators that this reform was a worthy investment for the public good.

On March 12, the state's Senate and Assembly issued their reactions to the governor's budget proposal. In broad strokes, they expressed support for small donor public financing.[59] The Fair Elections for New York campaign had cleared one more hurdle.

And yet. Legislative support in the aggregate, aside from a few progressive proponents, remained lukewarm at best. In the remaining two weeks

before the deadline to pass the budget with its public financing compo-
nent, the Fair Elections campaign intensified both its "inside" and "outside" advocacy, fielding one concern after another in private meetings with
legislators and ramping up public pressure on them to vote yes.

New York being a left-leaning state, most legislators did not express
outright opposition to the reform. Rather, they raised a slew of concerns
about its feasibility and efficacy.

One major worry they expressed was cost. The state faced a budget
shortfall for the coming year. The estimated price of public financing for
all statewide and state legislative offices—assuming an unrealistically generous opt-in rate of 100 percent of all candidates who had run in 2018—
was $60 million per year, less than one-tenth of one percent of New York's
$175 billion budget.[60] Yet with a flood of populist demands hitting the
capital after the election's progressive wave, it was difficult for campaign
finance reform to compete with urgent demands to spend on education,
health care, immigrant defense, and transit infrastructure.

To answer the cost worry, the New York Fair Elections campaign took
a page from the small donor public financing push in Congress and proposed that the state place a surcharge on penalties paid by corporations
for securities and consumer fraud.[61] Multinational banks and large insurance companies had paid hundreds of millions of dollars in fines for violating New York antifraud laws in recent years.

Another worry some legislators brought up was that a candidate who
participated in public financing would not be able to compete in this era
of unlimited independent spending, because, they claimed, the program
would require candidates to limit their spending.[62] But the governor's public financing bill, and the policy demands of advocates, required no such
thing.

We knew that caps on total fundraising or spending would turn off
too many candidates from opting in to public financing post–*Citizens
United*, as they would need the flexibility to respond to heavy super-PAC
spending in competitive races. And we knew that, even without such caps,
a well-designed public financing system would still incentivize candidates
to spend time soliciting support from a large number of constituents rather
than from a few large donors. Projections showed that candidates could
raise competitive sums through matching funds, which they would be free
to supplement—by raising an unlimited number of private donations

subject only to individual per-donor caps—and spend without limit.[63] The proposed public financing bill simply did not impose spending caps on candidates, contrary to skeptics' claims.

It was hard to tell if their claims were simply misguided, based on a sincere misreading of the bill, or deliberately disingenuous. For incumbents who did not want to rock the big-money boat they had ridden to power, it was easy to brandish *Citizens United* and the unlimited spending it triggered as the reason campaign finance reform was impractical. That's an argument the press and public have grown used to hearing.

Other legislators' concerns were more difficult to refute, not because their underlying motives were necessarily sincere—political intel often told advocates the opposite—but because the concerns themselves had merit. Chief among these was the worry that candidates running in relatively low-income districts would have trouble raising the threshold number of donations from residents to qualify for public matching funds. A related worry was that the poorest New Yorkers, who cannot afford to contribute ten dollars, would be excluded from the opportunity to see their influence with candidates multiplied by public funds. Whether small donor public financing sufficiently includes the least socioeconomically privileged constituents is an important question.

We offered a number of responses to these concerns as part of the Fair Elections campaign's "inside" advocacy. The number of donations required to come from inside a district could be reduced without diminishing candidates' incentives to turn to regular New Yorkers for support. There were some novel options for including impoverished constituents in small donor public financing, once the state enacted and implemented the well-established framework of a $6-to-$1 matching funds program. These answers rarely seemed to satisfy our questioners, perhaps because the questioners' true worry was disrupting a campaign finance status quo that they knew they could use to win.

The campaign's "outside" advocacy became more aggressive as the budget clock counted down. Grassroots groups visited legislators' offices, documenting their presence and legislators' reactions on Twitter. They tweeted fundraising records of individual legislators, showing the minuscule share most had raised from small donors and demanding their support for public financing. They staged rallies and press conferences, connecting the demand for small donor public financing to campaigns for affordable housing, living wages, and criminal justice reform. Media coverage multiplied.

But the vote count remained uncertain. Many veteran legislators had been raising money the old-fashioned way—by collecting a few huge checks—for a long time. They also were used to facing almost no competition, cycle after cycle.[64] That small donor public financing requires a fundraising strategy that appeals to as many constituents as possible, and offers a pathway for candidates who do not already have big-donor networks, worried the old guard. They did not have the confidence of their newest and more progressive colleagues, who had beat incumbents in 2018 on a wave of grassroots support, that they could win in a world with public financing. And it was the veterans who held leadership positions and thus most of the power. On the eve of the budget deadline, the fate of small donor public financing for New York state was far from clear.

Few with a stake in state policy are able to sleep well the night New York's budget is due. Sunday, March 31, 2019, was no exception. Reporters, advocates, and lawmakers and their caffeine-soaked staffers were up until dawn. Negotiations between the governor, Senate majority leader, and Assembly speaker had continued all weekend behind closed doors on the most controversial issues. Public financing lingered on that list. Intel trickled out in the wee hours that the leaders had struck a deal on the reform. But the final version was not published until later the next day.

It began with a sweeping and historic pronouncement. "The state shall establish a system of voluntary public campaign financing for state and state legislative public offices."[65] Shall establish—not *may* establish or shall *consider.* The statement of law was clear and definitive. Considering the unrelenting anxiety of veteran legislators that seemed to spell doom for the reform, this statement was a huge win for the Fair Elections for New York campaign.

But the text that followed did not lay out what that system of public financing would look like. Instead, it left the details to be decided before the end of the year by a nine-member commission, with two appointments each by the governor and majority leaders of both legislative chambers, one each by the minority leaders of the chambers, and one by agreement of the governor and the two majority leaders. There was no pretense of independence. Whoever served on the commission would be unlikely to create a system that displeased the politicians who selected them.

News that the budget law had created a politically controlled commission, rather than enacting a $6-to-$1 matching funds program outright, devastated parts of the Fair Elections coalition. Members accused the governor and legislative leaders of "punting" to a commission destined to produce anemic reform while giving the politicians themselves cover.

It did seem unlikely that the commission would decide on the robust small donor matching funds model that reformers had spent months advocating. That model would enable candidates to compete with enough constituent support, and even without the blessing of establishment donors and political leaders—precisely the pro-democracy quality that had unnerved veteran lawmakers.

Unlikely, but not impossible. The commission unquestionably would be seen as the creature of the elected officials who appointed it. Though the commissioners might not be accountable to the public, their appointers would continue to be. In the Brennan Center's view, as I wrote with a colleague in an op-ed in the *Daily News*, enactment of public financing to be designed by this commission was hardly everything that we had fought for—but it was a good start, with the potential for advocacy over the next eight months to make a real difference. "We're cynics about Albany, too," we wrote, "but the weeks before the budget vote showed that the press, New Yorkers and Washington policymakers are watching what happens with public financing. As long as that attention remains, our elected officials will find it difficult not to follow through."[66]

The advocacy campaign had already pushed the reform further than it had ever gotten before. Lawmakers could have enacted the budget without any mention of public financing. But the relentless fighting of a massive and diverse campaign—grassroots, grasstops, across every social justice issue area—made them decide they had better include it in the end.

It remains to be seen whether the commission will create a public financing system that will empower the majority of New Yorkers to have significant influence in their elections and enable otherwise qualified candidates to compete for office, even if they lack ties to wealthy donors. Certainly that will not happen unless a broad and diverse movement keeps fighting. But this is the challenge for preserving democracy in the new landscape of money in politics in New York state and across the nation.

REMAKING THE PRESIDENCY AFTER TRUMP

Jeremi Suri

It is difficult to make the people participate in government. It is still more dif-
ficult to provide them with the experience and inspire in them the feelings
they would need to govern well. The will of a democracy is changeable; its
agents are and its laws are imperfect.

—*Alexis de Tocqueville, 1835*[1]

The American presidency has always displayed the best and worst of American democracy. Respected figures with distinguished careers in public service—including George Washington and Dwight Eisenhower—have united citizens for common purpose. Men of eloquence and charisma—especially Thomas Jefferson and Theodore Roosevelt—have motivated Americans for reform. Leaders of extraordinary courage and empathy—particularly Abraham Lincoln and Franklin Roosevelt—have inspired citizens to sacrifice and expand the reach of democracy. The best presidents used their power to bring out the "better angels of our nature."[2]

Other presidents did not do the same in their time. Andrew Jackson promoted genocidal violence against Native Americans, often despite Supreme Court restrictions, and he defended slavery. Woodrow Wilson re-segregated the federal civil service and refused to prohibit the most violent elements of Jim Crow, especially the frequent lynching of African Americans and others. Warren Harding and Calvin Coolidge encouraged American isolationism and xenophobia, including some of the strictest restrictions on immigration in the nation's history. Even Franklin Roosevelt incarcerated over 100,000 citizens of Japanese descent without due process. As Tocqueville witnessed in Jackson's time, American presidents often pandered to the worst forms of public hatred and ignorance. They added power and prestige to the ugliest prejudices.

Winston Churchill famously quipped that democracy is the worst form of government, except for all the others.[3] In this context, American

democracy manifests many of the frustrating and inefficient qualities implied by Churchill's comment. The American presidency, in particular, is
overloaded with domestic and international responsibilities, but severely
constrained in direct capability for action. Presidents cannot, in fact,
spend a dollar without the approval of Congress. The Supreme Court can
reverse presidential actions on constitutional grounds. State and local governments can resist, and they frequently refuse to follow the president's
lead. Since the early twentieth century, a large administrative state filled
with career civil servants can redefine presidential orders in their implementation. And presidents cannot control their image in a free-for-all
marketplace of politicized and profit-making media.

Presidents are often overwhelmed. The expectations surrounding their
power always exceed their daily leverage over the nation's actual governance. As the scholar Richard Neustadt observed more than fifty years
ago, presidents have to negotiate with countless stakeholders, and they
must compromise, often at the cost of their most treasured goals. They
are pulled in numerous directions, and they must pursue balance over
perfection, lesser evils rather than outright victories. This has always been
an ugly, sometimes dirty, process.[4]

The difficulties of negotiating presidential power have made the office
unstable. Every period in American history poses new challenges for presidents. Each president seeks new sources of leverage over Congress and
other institutions to pursue his or her goals. Each president experiments
with new ways to shape the public narrative. The ambitions, obstacles, and
vagueness of presidential authority make each era of American history
one where the role of the president is up for grabs. Past precedent matters,
but it rarely defines what presidential leadership becomes. The leadership
of American democracy is made, destroyed, and remade with each generation. Even the mid-twentieth-century presidents would hardly recognize the office in its scale, scope, and speed today.[5]

Donald Trump represents a transitional moment in the presidency. He
rode to power on a cacophonous wave of public discontent and uncertainty. With rising inequality and foreign competition looming, many
American citizens worried that established leaders were too timid and too
predictable. With the growing complexity of technology and governance,
many voters wanted a candidate who promised to cut through the chaos
and make things simple.

Trump appealed to citizens who feared a more difficult future with current socioeconomic trends. He has remained consistent with this message, and he has unhinged the internationalist, inclusive, and dignified assumptions about the presidency that he inherited from predecessors. He has adopted a self-consciously disruptive posture.

His aggressive rhetoric notwithstanding, the Trump presidency has not offered citizens—whether they voted for him or not—hope for the future. In fact, Trump's continued appeal for some is the continued presence of fear, which he exploits whenever possible. Trump has attacked the office of the presidency as he inherited it, but he has not redesigned the office in any way to build promise for long-term changes that will address popular concerns about inequality, complexity, and socioeconomic difficulties. Health policy is perhaps the best example. Trump continues to attack the Affordable Care Act, but he and his allies have not proposed an alternative framework for the millions who will lose access to health insurance. His presidency is transitional because it is destroying the old office without anything substantive to replace it.

In this sense, Trump is what Tocqueville predicted: an imperfect agent of change for institutions and practices that no longer serve the nation well. Trump exploits the current alienation of citizens from government, and he forces millions—his opponents and his supporters—to rethink the contours of democratic leadership in the twenty-first century. He is the opening to a new presidency that will not look anything like him, but will not resemble his predecessors either.

Opening Up the Presidency

After Trump, anyone can be president. Running for office requires money, organization, and name recognition—perhaps more than ever before—but the expectations of previous partisan ties have been shattered. Trump is not just an "outsider," but an adversary to both parties. He succeeded in forcing one of them (the Republican Party) to bend to his personal popularity. He used media and populist rhetoric to appeal to voters over the heads of partisan and media gatekeepers, and he mobilized voters to make the established party institutions follow him—not vice versa. He now personally controls the mainstream of the Republican Party as few other presidents have before.

This dynamic does not make parties unimportant—they remain essential for mobilizing voters and holding other elected officials in line. What Trump has done is put the presidential candidate in the driver's seat more so than in the recent past. Candidates will choose the party, more than the party will choose the candidate. And candidates will tell the party what to think, and then punish defectors, as Trump has done so effectively.

In the short run, Trump's dominance of his party has limited checks on his abuses of power; Republicans in Congress defend him at almost all costs. In the long run, however, presidential figures that can dominate their parties will bring the potential for new ideas and policies into what has been a largely stagnant modern American partisan system. The dominant parties locked out many radical ideas for economic and political reform in prior decades, but that will be more difficult when popular candidates can move the parties based on direct connections with their voters. Reduced partisan gatekeeping opens opportunities for wider policy debate.

Trump has shown that more open debate can be ugly and irresponsible; it need not be so. Although the exploitation of hate and fear will remain powerful, new presidential candidates have the opportunity to mobilize voters by giving attention to major issues and innovative solutions. Public opinion is divided, but also susceptible to major shifts behind charismatic personalities and attractive ideas, as Trump has exemplified on topics from Russia to free trade and deficit spending.

Progressive shifts might be occurring among the many candidates running (or planning to run) against Trump in 2020. Each is trying to differentiate him- or herself by emphasizing one of a number of issues, including climate change, economic inequality, antitrust regulation of technology monopolies, health care, and education, among others. Issue and personality campaigning can mobilize voters for real policy change, pulling the Democratic Party further away from its traditional and somewhat stagnant center. The risk is a splintering of voters, but the opportunity is for a very real realignment of citizens behind serious policy changes, on a scale not seen in a presidential transition for decades.

The serious discussion since the 2018 midterm elections of reform to the Electoral College, break-up of major technology companies, Puerto Rican statehood, and even a guaranteed income for all citizens is evidence of the issue- and candidate-led dynamic. Party gatekeeping has broken down. The range of possible presidential candidates is wider than it has been in at least fifty years. The possibility for mobilizing voters to embrace major reforms, and force parties to follow, is greater than it has been since the New Deal. Less partisan moderation reduces resistance to big policy changes for candidates with serious ideas.

As of 2019, millennials will outnumber baby boomers in American society. Within a decade they will compose a majority of the workforce. They will be the largest likely voting group soon thereafter. They are less partisan than their parents, and less susceptible to the racialized fear-mongering of figures like Trump. Millennials are likely to exploit a more open system by boosting younger, more innovative presidential candidates. They are also likely to demand that these candidates embrace serious reforms for the environment, health care, economic fairness, and electoral processes. A less party-controlled presidential-selection system will be more responsive to the young and innovative citizens who have previously been locked out by older, established figures. This will apply to congressional elections as well as to presidential elections—all of which have been dominated by older, partisan voters in recent decades.[6]

Reducing Presidential Power

The history of the United States, particularly since the Great Depression, has involved almost steady growth in presidential power. Beginning with Franklin Roosevelt, presidents have spoken directly and frequently to the American public through radio, television, and, most recently, social media. They have used the modern "bully pulpit" to set the nation's legislative agenda, define threats (at home and abroad), and demand policy action. Through executive orders, they have taken on de facto legislative authority to manage national security, immigration, and many other issues formerly left to Congress.

Presidents have also become global leaders, as never envisioned by the founding fathers. They participate actively in foreign alliances, international organizations, and trade relationships that shape economy and society. Presidents have enormous discretion to distribute aid and arms, and they can institute sanctions and other penalties to alter international relationships. They not only dominate foreign policymaking; they also use it as a justification for deepening their reach at home through "national security" measures that allow closer coordination with domestic policing and military agencies, increased surveillance of citizens, and reduced transparency for policy matters deemed sensitive. Global engagement has contributed to domestic influence for presidents since the start of the Cold War.

The best evidence for the growth of presidential power is, of course, the metastasizing of the executive branch bureaucracy since the mid-twentieth century. The process began with Franklin Roosevelt's alphabet soup of New Deal agencies during the Great Depression, followed by the creation of the "warfare" state during the Second World War, and then what Dwight Eisenhower called the "military-industrial complex" in the Cold War. In each of these settings, the number of professional and po-litical administrators working for the president grew exponentially. They did the work of new agencies charged to regulate a larger, more complex, and more global American society. They also established close working relation-ships with powerful private and semi-private organizations, including businesses and universities. The late-twentieth-century administrative state ensured remarkable stability in American society, and it empowered the federal executive to influence daily behavior more than ever before. From the food we eat to the air we breathe, civil servants working for the president define our daily existence.[7]

Trump campaigned for office, alleging that the growing tentacles of the executive bureaucracy constituted a conspiratorial "deep state" that denied the preferences of the president and his voters. Nothing could be further from the truth. The modern executive bureaucracy ensures the high levels of safety, stability, and predictability that citizens demand above all. It keeps the planes flying, pays the Social Security checks, and patrols the borders and high seas. Trump's frustration is that the bureau-cracy follows established rules and procedures, not his whims. He has worked during his presidency to reshape the bureaucracy in his image through appointments of personal loyalists and targeted defunding efforts.

Although Trump seeks to increase his personal authority, his attacks on executive power diminish the presidency—denying him and his suc-cessors much of the legitimacy and bureaucratic reach accumulated in prior decades. Trump inspires other branches of government—as well as allies abroad, and states and cities at home—to seize back powers taken by recent American executives. He encourages professional civil servants to resist his authority, or to resign and bring their skills and experiences to other governing bodies. Most of all, Trump's budgets have starved entire agencies, especially the Department of State, causing a reduction in American government activities.

These terrible circumstances, which hurt vulnerable Americans and allies most of all, have forced a fundamental rethinking of presidential power and its place in a constitutional democracy. Federal courts have been the front line for this public conversation, reversing and rewriting many of Trump's executive decisions on immigration, health care, and the environment. The courts are using the law to limit presidential discretion, and they are asserting a powerful role of their own in the enforcement of the law. The same is true for Congress, where both houses have taken unprecedented action to enforce sanctions against Russia for its invasion of Crimea and its interference in the 2016 presidential election. Although Trump has opposed these efforts, members of the Senate and House of Representatives, especially since 2018, have pushed forward to replace presidential decisions with their own. Congress has also asserted more direct supervision of budgets, appointments, and actions by various agencies, including the Departments of State, Interior, Justice, and Defense. State governments, particularly California, have directly challenged presidential authority on immigration, health, and environmental issues, among many others.

We should expect these challenges to presidential authority to continue and expand in coming years, even after Trump leaves the White House. He has exposed the dangers and dysfunctions of excessive presidential power—what Arthur Schlesinger Jr. famously lamented as the "imperial presidency." Trump has also shown other parts of the government (as well as allies abroad) that they can, in fact, function more effectively when challenging the federal executive. Although presidents will remain powerful, the decades-long process of increasing reach and influence has reversed.[8]

A less powerful and more frequently challenged executive will inspire a productive reordering of American democratic governance, with new openings for innovative leadership. Future presidents will have to be more collaborative with other institutions and partners. Future presidents will also have to focus on fewer big issues where they can persuade, rather than force matters through by order, secrecy, or bureaucratic legerdemain. Presidents will need to build a resilient consensus across regions, more than appeal to partisan prejudices.

In this sense, the presidents of the twenty-first century might return to the earlier history of the office, when the president was more of a skilled and restrained consensus-builder, not a ubiquitous communicator or dominant policy actor. Successful presidents will be less ideological and more pragmatic. They will create new stories to bring the country together to address major problems. That will be their main role, hewing perhaps most closely to what the founders intended for an office heavily constrained by Congress, the courts, and the states.[9]

Communicating with the Public

Every generation of leaders invents a new way to communicate with the public. Presidents need to inform, educate, and mobilize citizens behind their chosen policies. As the country grows, and the sources of information multiply, the challenges of communicating effectively become more difficult. Presidents have always struggled to control their narrative, and that is surely the case today.[10]

President Trump's outlandish remarks and Twitter trolling are part of a simple strategy to attract attention through shock and drama. He does not have a coherent popular narrative for how he will "make America great again," but he can use his prominence to fuel anger and resentment among listeners. He exploits mass communication to divide and antagonize. He seeks to provoke rather than educate the public.

This pattern of communication is unprecedented in its rapid spread of hate and false information, but it is not unique. In each generation, new communications technologies have initially promoted divisive and hateful messages because these messages are easiest to circulate. They are simple and visceral, and they bring immediate satisfaction. They puncture standard narratives, create useful adversaries, and elicit emotional reactions. Presidential self-promotion often encourages gutter-like communications designed to appeal to the worst instincts of citizens without educating or improving their condition. Donald Trump has mastered this form of demagoguery.

The historical pattern is that after the first generation of politicians uses a new communications medium for hate (Father Coughlin on the radio, Joseph McCarthy on television, and Trump on social media), a second generation finds ways to use it for unity and creativity (Franklin Roosevelt on the radio, John F. Kennedy and Ronald Reagan on television). Seeing how words can hurt and divide, younger leaders develop new arguments and stories that lend themselves to the contemporary media in positive ways. Roosevelt beamed the hope of his New Deal by radio, and Kennedy extolled muscular New Frontiers on television, followed by Reagan's evocative "Morning in America."

A younger generation of social media users will replace Trump's hateful tweets and his defense of white supremacy with a widely communicated narrative of unity and democratic renewal. They will surely emphasize the possibilities in American and international society, and the urgency of reform. They will bring a passion and an eloquence that will motivate readers well beyond the jolt from a Trump tweet.

Although the current president has opened a new mechanism for direct communications between the White House and citizens around the world, his language and message will not dominate social media for long. After three years of his presidency we are already seeing slippage in his effectiveness from listener fatigue and competition. Other candidates and countless citizens are offering alternative messages with hope, tolerance, and scientific rigor at their core.

Beto O'Rourke, Pete Buttigieg, and Alexandria Ocasio-Cortez are three of the many youthful figures who have turned social media into a forum for idealism, connection, and creative policy ideas. They engage citizens and encourage them to participate. They offer hope and a sense of possibility. Most of all, they use social media primarily to mobilize people for reform, not attacks on the other side. Their Twitter feeds build social capital and circulate images of politics as a noble and higher calling. They are writing a new story of American political reform, and they are just the beginning.

In coming years, politicians will build on these experiments in leadership from the second generation of social media users. The new presidency will indeed communicate more often and directly with citizens. And that will become a great unifying, progressive asset for the country.

Aspiring leaders must commit themselves to experimentation and trial-and-error in this area. They must innovate. They must bring creativity, artistry, and authenticity.

These qualities are in abundance among younger citizens. We have every reason to believe the historical pattern of communications technologies improving our national and international narratives after initial disruptions will hold. Instead of denying the importance of how Trump communicates, rising leaders must reorient social media for reform purposes. This is a promising field for young future presidents and their teams.

A Pivotal Decade

The decade after Trump's presidency will be pivotal for the national executive. Reformers would do well to find new ways of building legitimacy for presidential power. The presidency was not designed to represent a part of the nation or to cater to "the base." Trump's presidency is the culmination of a long line of distortions that have trivialized democratic accountability as goods delivered to mobilized followers. The Trump presidency has squeezed out the interests of the government as a whole and service to the nation at large. Narrow instrumentalism of this sort strains constitutional relationships and ultimately threatens the rule of law.

To put presidential power on a firmer foundation, citizens will have to create institutions that promote personal integrity (virtue), diversity (representativeness), and transparency (communication.) A more virtuous, representative, and transparent presidency will be less enamored with great disruptions. It will focus more naturally on a few big issues and implement targeted reforms. It will seek out new ways to persuade and credibly explain its actions. Needless to say, these goals cut against the grain of recent developments. A presidency better attuned for American democracy in the twenty-first century will be neither "imperial" nor "impossible." The goals of greater citizen accountability and more creative problem solving will be well-served by a smaller and humbler presidency, one focused on fewer promises and tethered more closely to ethical limitations.

The hope is that the excesses of the Trump presidency will prompt a more cautious nation to support constructive changes along these lines. The evolution will be painful but productive. It fits with the broader pattern of democratic evolution that Tocqueville described so well. Change in American politics happens fast, after long periods of stasis, and it follows clear evidence of the ugly and imperfect undersides of American leaders and institutions. The most innovative and successful presidents have always followed the worst.

THE PROBLEM OF PRESIDENTIALISM

Stephen Skowronek

In the early decades of the twentieth century, when progressive reformers were thinking about how to craft a more efficacious democracy, the presidency was full of promise. It held out hopes for getting things done more expeditiously, for overcoming the cumbersome constitutional constraints that thwarted concerted national action. The idea was to relax formal arrangements that served to protect entrenched interests and to embrace change. Building up the presidency was, in the words of progressive historian Henry Jones Ford, "the work of the people breaking through the constitutional form."

Today, the progressives' solution stands as a monumental problem in its own right. Presidentialism has become a threat to constitutional government and democratic politics alike. Those of us hoping to build a more efficacious democracy for the twenty-first century would do well to break with our progressive forebears. It is time to end our fixation on the presidential office and look elsewhere for revitalization.

That will not be easy. Over the course of its development, presidentialism has gradually drawn everything else into its orbit. It has weakened competing sources of authority and become, in effect, the only game in town. In these circumstances, reformers will always be tempted just to capture the office for themselves. They will want to leverage the powers of the presidency, flexing its muscles aggressively in pursuit of their own chosen purposes. That feeds the beast. It is our collective entrapment.

Twentieth-century reformers built the "modern" presidency by reworking the two main pillars of its power: political mobilization and governmental management. They did so with the best of intentions. In the first instance, they sought to liberate the president from control by the local party bosses. Progressives promoted preference primaries to encourage candidates for a party nomination to make their appeal directly to the people. Primary elections allowed candidates to articulate their own agendas, to create their own organizations, to fashion a personal following. This eased the bosses' grip over the proceedings of national party conventions and bolstered the democratic credentials of the nominee. Concomitantly, progressives reimagined governmental management. Dismayed by the localism and logrolling of "congressional government," they sought to shift the locus of national planning and policy development out of the legislature and to lodge it instead in the offices of the chief executive. Their new Executive Office of the President became the fulcrum of agenda setting, coordination, and direction for the entire federal government. All told, the progressives' vision of a new presidency-centered democracy was comprehensive, even architectonic. Through their reconstruction of national political mobilization and federal governmental management, progressives turned a constitutional system weighed down by localism and fragmented power into a presidential system prioritizing energy and productivity.

But not all at once. The progressives' new governing arrangements took hold gradually, and during the middle decades of the twentieth century, they mingled in interesting ways with the older arrangements they were meant to displace. It is notable that America's love affair with the presidency blossomed in that murky amalgam. Presidents assumed their place at the center of national action, but incumbents were not yet free agents, and for all practical purposes, the exercise of governmental power remained a collaborative proposition. Presidents still had to deal seriously with other authorities, the leaders of Congress and of the parties in particular. When Richard Neustadt examined the emergent system at mid-century, he described bargaining and persuasion as the hallmarks of power in the modern presidency. The tipping point came in the 1970s. That is when developments in both mobilization and management brought the implications of presidentialism into starker relief.

It was in the 1970s that primary elections for the selection of convention delegates finally displaced the old system of delegate selection by local party organizations. In effect, the traditional parties lost their mediating role. The new candidate-centered parties—what we now call "presidential parties"—took charge of mobilizing the electorate and determining the party nominee. Collective responsibility gave way to a personal claim on power. It was also in the 1970s that collaboration in presidential management gave way to more aggressive assertions of presidential control. The change was signaled institutionally by President Richard Nixon's reorganization of the progressives' Bureau of the Budget into an Office of Management and Budget, the latter meant to be more directly concerned with subordinating the administrative agencies to the political priorities of the presidential party. A subtle intellectual shift occurred at this time as well. Advocates of presidential power began elaborating a theory of "the unitary executive," a theory that defended the president's new bid for control on constitutional grounds. By the 1980s, Henry Jones Ford's earlier image of a heady, vibrant democracy playing fast and loose with formal constitutional constraints had hardened into a set of formal constitutional arguments for the president's exclusive control over the now vastly expanded powers of the executive branch.

The independent mobilizing power generated by presidential parties and the pretenses of management under a unitary executive have proven mutually reinforcing. Together they make for a perverse and volatile brew. Presidents, whether on the left or the right, now routinely proclaim their superiority to Congress in representing the interests of the nation. Bargaining and collaboration have fallen by the wayside. The Executive Office of the President has become a springboard for unilateral action. As presidentialism maximizes the authority of chief mobilizer and chief manager, it squeezes out the authority of all rival claimants. The presidents of our day are not rewarded for balance or synthesis or prudence. They are expected to deliver the goods demanded by the particular interests mobilized behind them. Barack Obama justified unilateral action by reaching out to his supporters and telling the nation "We can't wait."

The Trump administration is no aberration in this regard. It is more properly understood as a culmination. What began as a democratic idea for overcoming the perceived limits of the Constitution is now a winner-take-all proposition, one that defies progressive notions of national stewardship and undermines the constitutional sanctions available to those who dare rein the presidency in. A political outlier with no prior experience in government, Trump used the primary election system to mobilize his own following and effect a hostile takeover of the Republican party. The Trump party has since turned national stewardship on its head. Its leader is unabashed in his determination to run the federal government as political service to his "base." Management has followed suit, with the dictates of the presidential party running roughshod over the norms of best practice. Trump has used the claims of the unitary executive against all rival assertions of authority. He has called into question Congress's authority to investigate and the authority of judges to say what the law is. He has dismissed administrators for challenging the legality of his chosen course, and he has taken aim at the "deep state," gutting the institutional infrastructure of the federal government. Deploying interim appointments, he has bypassed Senate confirmation, the key constitutional provision for collaboration in management. Scores of offices where legal authority might interfere with the president's preferences are simply left vacant.

If nothing else, the Trump administration has laid bare the perils of sticking to the present course. Presidentialism breeds instability and division. It is intolerant of disagreement and meets criticism with belligerence. It politicizes all aspects of administration. It is the victor's imposition, a perversion of democracy.

Unfortunately, with the genie out of the bottle, no alternative means of containment are readily at hand. The old conceit that our constitutional system is self-correcting is belied by developments that have invested so heavily in executive power as to hollow out all balancing provisions. There is no quick fix for that. We might look to the courts to do the hard work of restoration, but it seems doubtful that they are up to the task. Presidents are not known for appointing judges who are hostile to executive power. The long expansion of presidential power has, after all, taken place under judicial supervision. Back in the 1970s, when fears of an "imperial presidency" were running high, Congress did some symbolic trimming of its own. Its widely touted "resurgence" promised to redress the most glaring imbalances. But the correction was short lived; the aggrandizement soon resumed. Developments since that time suggest that an effective, durable response will entail a more fundamental reworking, one that rivals in scale and imagination the work of the reformers who initially set us on our current path.

There are today serious observers who still believe that, with a bit more power, presidents could make things a lot better. But arguments like that, familiar as they are, are harder now to mount convincingly. It seems plain that our long history of investing in this office has run amuck, that the foundations are no longer holding things together. Far from making American government work better, the presidency's enhanced capacity for mobilization and management is pulling it apart.

Whatever the shortcoming in their designs, those early-twentieth-century progressives were masters of redirection. So there may be a few things to be learned from them even as we search for an alternative response to the problems that they bequeathed to us. One is that redirection is a long-term proposition. It does not happen overnight. It is not secured by any single election. Redirection requires steady adherence to a clear vision of a new ordering, and for that it draws on a lot of prior intellectual spadework. Concomitantly, the new thinking must be comprehensive, attacking current maladies from different angles and penetrating to their core. It is unlikely that a more efficacious democracy will be built on ad hoc responses to problems as they appear. Campaign finance reform is a good idea. It is, in fact, one of the progressives' original ideas. But it is not a magic bullet. If we are to redirect the system in a sustainable way, we will need more systemic thinking about how different elements of reform will fit together and refigure the whole. Finally, and most important, we might take a cue from the middle years of the twentieth century when presidentialism was still only half-baked. The reformers' vision proved most attractive when it competed for supremacy and when other authorities were not so easily sidelined. Though there is no going back to those days, we might want to follow that lead, thinking less about the presidency per se and more about the kinds of authority that surround it and might compete with it effectively again.

The task is a daunting one, and it is easily trivialized. What made progressivism effective as a reconstructive movement was not a top ten list of reforms popular with discrete constituencies but rather the collective voice of a common carrier. Progressivism was the intellectual movement of a reform vanguard, and that will be difficult to replicate in the more fragmented intellectual environment of our day. It should not be difficult, however, to identify a productive focus for this work. A constructive discussion should now ensue about new—specifically non-presidential—forms of political mobilization and governmental management.

The Trump administration should have a liberating effect in this regard, freeing us to think anew about ideas that the promise of presidentialism discredited. So, for example, Trumpism has exposed the dangerous downsides of the current presidential nominating system and the presidential parties that it breeds. That might free us to reconsider the value of robust party organizations as independent sources of collective control, and to think about how to tap that potential without recreating some new version of bossism. Trumpism might also persuade us to rethink our mindless attacks on the authority of bureaucrats. It might finally dispel the dangerous delusions of the unitary executive and prompt us to think about new ways to support professional authority, neutral competence in administration, and knowledge-based government. More often than not, the biases of the so-called deep state are just good-faith efforts by administrators to abide by their authorizing statutes in the face of hostile presidential appointees. The challenge of reconstruction will be to restore rule-of-law values while still providing credible protections against bureaucratic overreach.

These are just the most obvious targets for rebuilding. They may, in fact, be too obvious, too reflexive for the challenges at hand. A new, more vibrant democracy may require more novel forms of mobilization and management for its full expression. The point of this exercise is not to close off that discussion. It is to suggest that presidentialism has run its course, that its constructive work lies in the past. In the current environment of mobilization and counter-mobilization, all creative energy is absorbed in efforts to replace one president with another. For the "outs" the main chance is to reverse the achievements of the "ins" and impose its own priorities. That is not a solution to our problems. It is ultimately self-defeating. The problem is presidentialism itself. The hope now lies in building up decidedly non-presidential forms of political and institutional authority.

Part II

FOUNDATIONS OF DEMOCRACY

RENEWING THE AMERICAN DEMOCRATIC FAITH

Steven C. Rockefeller

We hold these truths to be self-evident, that all men are created equal, that they are endowed by their Creator with certain unalienable Rights, that among these are Life, Liberty and the pursuit of Happiness.—That to secure these rights, Governments are instituted among Men, deriving their just powers from the consent of the governed.

—Declaration of Independence, 1776

We the People of the United States, in Order to form a more perfect Union, establish Justice, insure domestic Tranquility, provide for the common defence, promote the general Welfare, and secure the Blessings of Liberty to ourselves and our Posterity, do ordain and establish this Constitution for the United States of America.

—Preamble, U.S. Constitution, 1787

The founders of the United States of America embarked on an audacious experiment. Could a diverse people given individual freedom and political sovereignty work together to build a unified nation that promotes freedom and advances equality, justice, and the common good? Aware of the fallibility of human nature, many of the founders had serious doubts. They knew that freedom and self-interest would always exist in tension with the ideals of justice and the common good. Nevertheless, they had the faith and courage to persist. Their hopes rested on the possibility of establishing an innovative constitution with checks and balances that recognized certain inalienable human rights. They also believed that if the American experiment was to succeed, it would require a moral and spiritual foundation. Essential to the flourishing of a free society, they argued, are shared moral and political ideals, leading to a way of life that involves a strong sense of national solidarity, social responsibility, and engaged citizenship. Even though the founders lived in a very different world from ours, their thinking in this regard is one key to rectifying the deficits in twenty-first-century democratic practice.

In recent decades, the United States has become a deeply divided and fragmented nation unable to address pressing social, economic, and environmental challenges. There is an urgent need to reawaken a shared faith in unifying democratic ideals and values that can provide the nation's people, in all of their cultural diversity, with an inspiring sense of a national identity and common destiny. From the beginning, what has defined the American people as Americans has been their shared moral and political ideals, which is not to deny the history of repeated attempts by some Americans to marginalize others on the basis of race, religion, or ethnic origin. This essay explores the ideals and values that formed the early moral and spiritual foundations of the nation and offers reflections on pathways to a renewal of American democracy and the advancement of social justice and the common good.

When describing America's moral and spiritual foundations, historians, sociologists, and philosophers refer to the American creed, the American Covenant, American civil religion, Americanism, the democratic faith, moral democracy, spiritual democracy, and a public moral philosophy. Walt Whitman, John Dewey, Jane Addams, and Martin Luther King, Jr. get to the heart of the matter when they conceive of democracy as first and foremost a great moral ideal. It is with this understanding that this chapter identifies the nation's deepest foundations with a faith in shared ideals and a personal way of life along the lines envisioned in Dewey's *A Common Faith*. When the American democratic faith possesses a person's mind and heart, it becomes a relational spirituality that integrates spiritual life and everyday life.

The Ideal and the Real

In the midst of significant ethnic and religious diversity there emerged with the American Revolution of 1776 and the subsequent founding of the republic a set of shared moral and political ideals, which were set forth in the Declaration of Independence and the Preamble of the Constitution.

Among the ideals affirmed in these documents by "We the people" are freedom, equality, individual rights, the pursuit of happiness, the sovereignty of the people, the rule of law, justice, the common good, peace, unity in the midst of diversity, and intergenerational responsibility. James Madison, credited with being the principal drafter of the Constitution, explained that "the public good, the real welfare of the great body of the people, is the supreme object to be pursued."[1] The Constitution is a secular document that makes no reference to God, prohibits the establishment of religion by the government, and proclaims freedom of religion as a basic right. The Declaration of Independence, however, does affirm the widely held eighteenth-century faith in God as the Creator who has endowed "all men" with equal dignity and inalienable rights.

America's founding ideals were set forth as self-evident truths and universal values that all can know and understand through rational reflection and an awakened conscience. For many, they were sacred truths that promised liberation from the oppression, conflicts, and burdens of life in the Old World. "We have it in our power to begin the world over again," wrote Thomas Paine in *Common Sense*, his widely debated tract in support of revolution. America was the New World. Further, in the spirit of the eighteenth-century Enlightenment movement, many of the founders adopted a cosmopolitan worldview and, like George Washington, saw no conflict between being a patriotic American and identifying as "a citizen of the great republic of humanity at large."[2]

There have, however, always been contradictions between America's aspirational founding vision and the reality that is American society. Moreover, there were complex problems with what the founders succeeded in accomplishing, revealing ways in which the colonists had not left behind the attitudes and practices of the Old World. It would take 150 years of protest by women for the nation to adopt the Nineteenth Amendment, which granted them the right to vote. The 1787 Constitution does not recognize the rights of Native Americans who were driven from their lands, forced onto reservations, and in the process suffered the destruction of their cultures. It was not until 1924 that Native Americans were granted the right to vote. Most egregiously, the Constitution allowed the continuation of slavery. There were many citizens in the new republic, including founders like Benjamin Franklin, president of the Pennsylvania

Society for the Abolition of Slavery, who viewed slavery as the atrocity it was and wanted it outlawed. It was outlawed in the New England states by 1791.

Leaders like George Washington and Thomas Jefferson, who were plantation owners and slaveholders, could not escape the terrible moral dilemma presented by slavery, and they feared the consequences if it were not ended. Washington did grant his slaves their freedom in his will. However, he and Jefferson knew that if faced with abolition, some of the southern states would refuse to join the union. The nation was created deeply divided over slavery, leading tragically to the Civil War (1861–1865) that took the lives of over 600,000 men and left much of the country in ruins. Only then did Congress adopt the Thirteenth, Fourteenth, and Fifteenth Amendments, abolishing slavery, granting African Americans "the equal protection of the laws," and granting African American men the right to vote. It was in many ways a second founding of the nation. However, confronted during the Jim Crow era with brutal systems of racial segregation and discrimination, including denial of education, jobs, and the right to vote, the struggle of African Americans for their freedom and rights was far from over. A hundred years after the Civil War, the civil rights movement would generate massive protests over long-denied justice that would force major change, but in the twenty-first century the persistence of discrimination and the need for healing remain critical issues facing the nation.

The general principles set forth in the Declaration of Independence and the Preamble of the Constitution remain among the most powerful, transformative social and political ideals ever articulated. However, ignorance, narrow self-interest, and the corrupting influence of money and power make the advancement of freedom, equality, and justice a never-ending task. America has always been a work in progress, and its founding ideals express the unfulfilled promise of American life and function as a force driving social change. Langston Hughes, the Harlem Renaissance poet, spoke for all marginalized groups in the nation when in 1935 he wrote: "Let America be America again. Let it be the dream it used to be . . . The land it never has been yet—And yet must be . . ." Each generation faces the challenge of renewing the nation's faith in its founding moral and political ideals and striving to give fresh expression to what that faith and commitment to the common good means.

Freedom, Virtue, and the Common Good

At the time of the founding of the nation, biblical religion, especially the prophetic call for compassion and social justice, was a major source of moral and spiritual inspiration. In the seventeenth century, Puritans, who were Protestant Christian reformers, settled New England, and Puritanism was the most influential religious tradition among those who supported the Revolution.[3] In seeking to understand themselves and their mission, the Puritans drew heavily on biblical narratives and language. America was the new Promised Land. Their destiny was to create a New Israel in America founded on a new Covenant between God and his people. They were especially mindful that in the biblical narrative God's liberation of the Hebrew people from slavery in Egypt is followed by revelation of the law at Mt. Sinai. In their view, freedom must be harnessed and guided to become a force for the good. The Puritans' idealism has had an enduring influence. Most of us want to believe that America is a unique nation with a higher moral purpose. In addition, in their efforts to interpret the meaning of American history and inspire change, many of the nation's political and social leaders return to biblical themes.[4]

Prior to the Revolution there was much discussion in the colonies about republicanism as a form of government and way of life that provided an alternative to British monarchical society with its rigid social hierarchy. A republic is a self-governing society without a king, in which the supreme power resides with those recognized as citizens, who enjoy a certain measure of freedom and equality and elect their own leaders. Many of the founders were influenced by ancient models of republican government, especially Athens and Rome, as well as by more contemporary experiments with republicanism. It was republican ideals that gradually undermined support for monarchical society in the colonies.[5] The goal of those involved in drafting the Constitution was to establish the United States as a modern republic supported by both Christian and classical moral values.

The founders believed that the republic they were creating would require independent, visionary leaders with exceptional intelligence and moral integrity and citizens with a high level of social and moral responsibility. They emphasized the vital importance of virtue as the guide to individual fulfillment and social well-being. In accord with the Socratic tradition, they identified virtue with wisdom, knowledge of the good. The essence of the civic virtue was understood to be devotion to the common good. In short, the founders aspired to create a new, enlightened moral and social order governed by virtuous and wise leaders.

The federal and state constitutions manifest a qualified trust that the citizens of the new republic would have the intelligence and moral responsibility to elect such leaders. The founders did fear that self-interest could generate a divisive factionalism and anarchy. To guard against such a development, they insisted that certain cultural conditions be established including access to a basic education and information on public affairs. The state constitutions limited the vote to tax-paying, male property holders. Further, most of the founders agreed with George Washington when, in his Farewell Address, he asserted, "Of all the dispositions and habits which lead to political prosperity, religion and morality are indispensable supports." Washington understood that shared moral values underlie respect and support for the law, and he believed that religion is necessary to sustaining a commitment to "the national morality."

The founders were realists about human nature. They were well aware of the Christian doctrine of the universality of sin and of the warnings in classical philosophy regarding the corrupting power of the passions. For this reason they crafted a constitution that divided sovereignty between the federal government and the thirteen states, constructed a federal government with a separation of powers and checks and balances, and protected freedom of speech and the press. It was an innovative system of government carefully designed to prevent the centralization of power in the hands of any individual leader or group. Defending the Constitution, Washington declared: "A just estimate of that love of power, and proneness to abuse it, which predominates in the human heart, is sufficient to satisfy us of the truth of this position."

The founders' republicanism emphasized the interrelation between freedom, the cultivation of virtue, and citizen engagement in the process of self-government. It regards humans as social and political beings who thrive as members of communities. People may be born with an inalienable right to liberty, but they are also interdependent. In this tradition, there is no inherent contradiction between freedom and respect for the law. For the revolutionaries, political independence meant living in a society governed by the rule of law as opposed to the arbitrary will of a tyrannical monarch. Further, personal freedom meant more than the absence of restraint. Someone in the grip of delusion and blind passion cannot be considered free. Becoming a truly free person, they argued, requires self-knowledge, self-discipline, and the wisdom and will to pursue what is good and just.

In addition, the founders believed that people realize their full potential as free persons in and through engaged citizenship—working collaboratively with fellow citizens to protect their rights and to advance shared goals. In a republic, active participation in self-government and other forms of public service become the primary way independent citizens acquire a sense of belonging to a community, are educated about public affairs, and develop the virtues and skills needed to deliberate productively and cooperate in promoting the common good.[6]

Equality and the Democratic Way of Life

The result of the Revolution was a far-reaching reconstruction of American society that gave birth to the dream of a new democratic culture. It is the original American dream of what America could be. In this new democratic, moral, and spiritual ethos is found the only sure foundation for the flourishing of the nation's political democracy. Again and again the nation has strayed from this understanding, and it finds itself anew by rediscovering its foundational moral and spiritual ideals, what Alexis de Tocqueville described as those "habits of the heart" that create and sustain authentic community.

The two most powerful American ideals driving revolutionary change are freedom and equality. Freedom has been America's most cherished ideal, "the holy light," celebrated in the nation's statues of liberty and in song, sermons, protests, and political rhetoric. Reduced to a self-centered individualism, however, freedom can undermine equality, the general welfare, and democracy itself. Equality is the most radical ideal unleashed by the Revolution. Freedom and equality, together with the ideals of individual rights, the rule of law, justice, and the common good, are the fundamental values at the heart of the spiritual and ethical vision that expresses the true spirit and deeper meaning of American democracy.

One major influence shaping the thinking that would, over many centuries, lead to the American concept of equality is found in biblical religion. The Book of Genesis proclaims that human beings are created in the image of God, recognizing the immeasurable, intrinsic value and dignity of every person. The basic moral teaching of the ancient Hebrew prophets is the imperative to do what is right, good, and just and to avoid evil. The most concise, general formulation of what this means is set forth in the Bible's Golden Rule. God commands the people of Israel: "Love your neighbor as yourself" (Leviticus 19:18). Jesus's teaching in the Sermon on the Mount summarizes the principle as follows: "In everything do to others as you would have them do to you; for this is the law and the prophets" (Matthew 7:12). This very general ethical principle invites us to identify with the other as a person who shares with us a common humanity and who like us seeks happiness and wants to avoid suffering. It encourages an attitude of empathy and sympathy. It is the imperative to treat all persons, including oneself, as an end and never as a means only.

In the West, the Golden Rule was promoted by the Christian and Jewish traditions, but it is a universal ethical principle that finds expression in many different religions and cultures around the world. Further, it is a very general ethical principle that tells us what to think about when we are trying to decide what to do, but it does not tell us exactly what to do in any specific situation. The principle is interpreted differently by diverse cultures and generations. As the ethical consciousness of a people becomes more tolerant and inclusive, their understanding of the Golden Rule can change dramatically as is evident in contemporary efforts to end discrimination of all kinds.

In the new republic, equality meant that one's worth and social standing are not determined by birth and class. The core notion in the American ideal of equality is the moral principle that all people share a common humanity and are born equal in dignity, and all, therefore, are worthy of respect and moral consideration. Right relationship begins with recognition of the inherent and equal dignity of other persons as human beings like oneself. In the eighteenth century it was, of course, primarily men, and not all men, who were recognized as equal. However, if the American story has a moral meaning, to a large extent it is found in the ongoing, contentious process of working out the full implications of the idea that all human beings are "created equal."

Equality and liberty are interrelated ideals. The principle of equality meant to the revolutionaries that all white male citizens should be independent and autonomous, able to think and decide for themselves. Further, inherent in the ideals of equality and freedom is the belief that all should have the opportunity to develop their abilities and pursue their aspirations. Moreover, it was widely understood that with freedom and opportunity goes an obligation to strive to realize one's potential and to contribute according to one's talents to the life of the nation. Equality of opportunity meant that all careers, including leadership in government, should be open to any white man with the self-discipline, intelligence, and virtue required. The revolutionaries were not interested in leveling society and eliminating all economic inequality. However, they did believe that a large gap between the rich and the poor is a destabilizing force in a republic, and they strongly opposed the development of an aristocracy in America. It was their expectation that equality of opportunity would create more equitable economic conditions, but they did not foresee the dramatic way in which capitalism would increase economic inequality.

Respect for the equal dignity of other persons includes respect for their basic rights. The concept of individual rights had a long history in England, stretching from the thirteenth-century Magna Carta to John Locke's liberal defense of the equality and natural rights of all men in the seventeenth century. Initially, the concept of rights and liberties was developed as a way to secure protection for the people from the arbitrary power of monarchs and the abuse of power by governments. However, as the human rights tradition has developed, the vision of humanity's civil, political, economic, and social rights has also become an essential part of the vision of what constitutes the common good and is necessary for the flourishing of freedom and full human development.

It was the hope of the revolutionaries that the spirit of freedom coupled with cultivation of mutual respect among the American people would open new pathways to authentic community and national unity. The goal was *E Pluribus Unum*—out of many, one. The Enlightenment movement taught that when the inborn moral and spiritual capacities for empathy, sympathy, and love are supported, people are naturally drawn to form friendships, cooperate, and build community. As they abandoned the old monarchical social order and looked for new ways to build "a more perfect Union," many of the revolutionaries envisioned the spirit of freedom and equality as being infused with these natural feelings of sympathy, love, and benevolence, creating the new social ties and bonds needed.[7] George Washington expressed this ideal in his "Farewell Address" when he envisioned a nation "bound together by fraternal affection." With the end of the Civil War in sight, Abraham Lincoln in his Second Inaugural Address endeavored to restore this spirit with his concluding words: "With malice toward none, with charity for all, with firmness in the right as God gives us to see the right, let us strive to finish the work we are in, to bind up the nation's wounds, to care for him who shall have borne the battle and for his widow and his orphan, to do all which may achieve and cherish a just and lasting peace among ourselves and with all nations."

In the late eighteenth and early nineteenth centuries, the newly created republic very rapidly underwent a major democratic transformation. In the midst of an enormous release of creative energy, the franchise was expanded. Men from all walks of life with a host of different interests, not just the highly educated and public spirited, were elected to serve at all levels of government. In this regard, historians describe a transition from the republicanism envisioned by the founders to the kind of fractious democratic republic that has existed ever since. It is not, however, the purpose of this chapter to explore this history. It remains to consider the contemporary relevance of the founders' revolutionary ideals and dreams.

Radical Individualism and the Fraying Moral Fabric of Society

We live in a highly complex industrial-technological society linked with a global civilization that the founders could never have imagined. Nevertheless, we can still benefit from their republican social and political philosophy, especially their understanding of freedom and firm belief that a free society requires a foundation of shared moral and political ideals to hold the nation together at all levels. In recent decades, however, the influence of the founders' republicanism has waned, and, as Michael Sandel, the political philosopher, explains, there is a widespread sense "that from family to neighborhood to nation, the moral fabric of community is unraveling around us."[8] In "A Report to the Nation," the Council on Civil Society states that "the core challenge" facing America is "the moral renewal of our democratic project." The Council Report asks: "What are those ways of life that self-government requires? What are those qualities the Constitution presupposes in the American people? They are precisely those qualities that are currently disappearing from our society."[9] As the bonds of community have frayed, the safety and well-being of children have declined, increasing numbers of people struggle with loneliness, depression, and drug addiction, suicide rates keep climbing, and the nation's politics become ever more abrasive. There are many contributing factors to this moral and spiritual crisis, including economic inequality, the internet, and social media. However, the most fundamental underlying cause is the culture of radical individualism that became widespread in the wake of the 1960s.[10]

Radical individualism involves the notion that the self exists as a separate entity independent of other selves and society. It makes the autonomous self, not the community, the center of the individual's world. Freedom is defined simply as the absence of restraint and the ability to do whatever one desires. Radical individualism emphasizes being faithful to one's own personal values, but it also involves the notion that a person is not bound by any moral obligations or civic duties that the individual has not chosen to embrace. This brand of individualism may lead to a personal spiritual quest, but it also has generated a culture of narcissism and consumerism and a secular moral relativism that considers moral judgments to be just subjective personal preferences. One implication of this outlook is liberal neutrality, the widespread idea that government should be neutral regarding any particular set of moral and spiritual values beyond respect for human rights, tolerance, and fair procedures for resolving conflicts.

The weakening of the bonds of community and the social fragmentation created by radical individualism have been further complicated in recent decades by the rise of identity politics, which divides society into an ever-increasing number of minority groups who feel deep resentment over how they have been marginalized and oppressed. Many in these groups have grown disillusioned with having faith in traditional American ideals. On the one hand, identity politics has focused attention on real injustices suffered by women, Native Americans, African Americans, immigrants, and LGBT people. On the other hand, identity politics is a force generating new forms of tribalism and fragmenting society. This has contributed to a form of multiculturalism that supports a vision of American society as divided into many competing groups with distinct identities and no common national identity.

The most fundamental problem with America's radical individualism is that it is based on a misguided concept of the self and freedom. It involves what Thomas Merton, the American Trappist monk, has called "the illusion of separateness." Everything that exists is both a unique individual and interconnected with the larger universe. People are born interconnected with families, local communities, spiritual traditions, nations, the larger human family, and the greater community of life on Earth. With these interconnections go ethical responsibilities without which human life and development are not possible. Moreover, the individual finds meaning and purpose and realizes true freedom through a sense of belonging, self-mastery, honesty, humility, trustworthiness, courage, caring, compassion, and service. It is love that makes us whole. Centuries ago, Rabbi Hillel said it simply: "If I am not for myself, who will be for me? If I am only for myself, what am I? And if not now, when?"

Renewing and Reconstructing the Democratic Way of Life

The ideal of building a cohesive pluralistic society guided by reason and experience and inspired by a love of freedom coupled with a compassionate spirit of respect for the equal dignity of all persons is the meaning of spiritual democracy. A commitment to human rights, justice, and the common good flows from respect for the freedom and equality of the other. In the world's great spiritual traditions, spiritual development is centrally concerned with nurturing a sense of meaning and purpose and the spirit of understanding, compassion, and love. It is in this regard that one can talk about democracy as a spiritual practice. For many, spiritual democracy is a way of being and living together inspired by a religious faith, but for others it springs from an open-hearted ethical humanism. Whatever its source, it is both a demanding and a rewarding spiritual and moral discipline that never forgets there is a tendency toward injustice as well as goodness in all of us. In these troubled times, those seeking the soul of America, the animating spirit of the nation, will find it here.

Paula Winkler, who promoted the role of women in Judaism, in a letter to her soulmate and future husband, Martin Buber, sharpens the focus on the spiritual dimension of respect for the dignity of the other that is at the heart of the democratic faith. She writes: "Our attitude toward each other ought above all to be person to person—not 'Frenchman to

German,' not 'Jew to Christian,' and perhaps less of 'man to woman.'"[11] Had Winkler been writing in America today, she might have added "black to white, Democrat to Republican, and established citizen to immigrant." One ideally encounters the other first and foremost simply as a fellow human being. As Paula Winkler makes clear, embracing this attitude should not be confused with an attempt to deny the importance of difference and to blur the distinctions between cultures and religions. It is, however, a corrective to a one-sided emphasis on difference that generates separatism and fails to perceive what can bring people together in the midst of their diversity. It involves what Howard Thurman, the black spiritual leader and philosopher, describes as listening for "the sound of the genuine" in the other. It awakens compassion. It makes possible dialogue, forgiveness, and cooperation. The nation's many social problems in the twenty-first century involving sexism, sexual abuse, racial discrimination, interreligious hatred, oppression of minorities, and economic inequality, as well as the contempt and hatred that pollute the nation's politics, are rooted in a failure to respect the inherent dignity of the other.

In concluding, it is important to ask: from the perspective of the twenty-first century, what fundamental ideals and values are missing in our federal and state constitutions? The science of ecology has made clear that human beings are an interdependent part of the greater community of life on Earth and that the degradation of the planet's environment by human activity threatens to undermine the right to life, liberty, and the pursuit of happiness for present and future generations. The Preamble to the Constitution does recognize that the American people have a basic responsibility to "secure the Blessings of Liberty to ourselves and our Posterity." In this regard, it needs to be made explicit in the nation's legal systems that future as well as present generations have a right to a clean and healthy environment. Were there to be a constitutional amendment on the environment, it should include a declaration affirming the interdependence of humanity and nature and the ethical imperative to respect and care for the greater community of life in all its diversity.[12]

The moral and spiritual transformation necessary for the renewal of our democracy will have to come from the bottom up, beginning with families, educational institutions, religious organizations, local communities, and voluntary civic associations. Only pressure from the people will force the national political parties to find ways to work together intelligently and responsibly for the public welfare. A transformation at the local level in how people interact, deliberate, and build community is what is needed. It is the direct experience of a better way of life that will change people's thinking, attitudes, and behavior. Such change can help to promote a national dialogue about the spiritual and moral values essential to the flourishing of a free society in an age of economic globalization and the internet. Hopefully it might lead to what Michael Sandel calls "a new politics of the common good" that generates healing and reconciliation, and a compelling vision of America's national purpose.[13]

John Dewey argued that the most effective way to promote social reconstruction is to start with a transformation of the schools, and one promising development is the growing support for PreK-12 school reform movements that promote education of the whole child. These initiatives include social and emotional learning, character education, education in compassion, training in mindfulness, and citizenship education. In addition, guided by new scientific research demonstrating the close correlation between the well-being of young people and their spiritual and moral development, a National Council on Spirituality in Education has been formed with strong support from educators.[14] Many schools are already committed to promoting the spiritual, moral, and aesthetic dimensions of development as well as social, emotional, and academic learning. Some have a religious affiliation and some are secular. Renewing American democracy will require taking the spirit of holistic education and spiritual democracy into all the nation's schools.

How American history is taught is an especially critical issue if the American people are to recover a sense of shared national identity. The most promising approach is to highlight what is truly enlightened and innovative in the revolutionary founding of the nation and its history and to celebrate America's extraordinary diversity and the contributions of all groups. The times also demand an honest account of the injustices and suffering that are tragically very much a part of the story. If there is to be progressive change, hope is essential. The nation's founding ideals and the struggle to realize those ideals by women and men of courage and good will from all races, ethnic groups, and religions should be viewed as one major source of hope that can inspire oncoming generations.

In his inaugural address as president, John F. Kennedy invoked the spirit of the civic republicanism of the founders when he stated: "Ask not what your country can do for you, ask what you can do for your country." One way to awaken a new sense of national identity, solidarity, and commitment to the common good among the American people is to require of all citizens, women and men, one or two years of national service after high school or college. The requirement could be fulfilled by serving in the military, teaching in public schools, or through any number of other socially beneficial domestic or international projects.

In conclusion, if America is to come together to address the great social, economic, and environmental challenges we face in the twenty-first century, it will require deepening our understanding of how to live meaningfully, responsibly, and joyfully with freedom. In this regard, the upcoming 250th anniversary of the American Revolution presents a unique opportunity to rediscover the common sense in the founders' republicanism and to commit ourselves to a fresh vision of the democratic faith infused with reverence for the mystery of being, a passion for what is right and just, and a new respect for Earth, our shared home in the universe.

AMERICAN LAND, AMERICAN DEMOCRACY

Eric Freyfogle

Soon after Illinois entered the union in 1818, Englishman John Woods paid an extended visit to a pioneer region in the southeastern part of the state near the Wabash River, a region largely settled by immigrants from England and centered on, appropriately, the town of Albion. Woods spent two years on this "English prairie," as he termed it. His regular reports back home, published in book form in 1822, were widely read. Among the surprises Woods described were the ways new Americans were taking charge of their landscapes to satisfy their frontier wants, collectively reshaping land-use norms as they did so. Under the English common law of property, landowners could complain about wandering livestock that damaged their crops and could similarly ward off public hunters and foragers. Not so in the new Albion, Woods explained. There, landowners could exclude live-stock only if they erected sturdy fences to keep them out; otherwise the livestock were free to enter. The same rule applied to hunters and foragers, who could wander the land freely so long as they stayed out of the rare, en-closed spaces. A new freedom was in the air, a new sense that nature's riches existed for all. Private property was honored, but settlers exerted a shared role in setting land uses and redrawing the lines between public and private. And they did so, in the case of land use, by favoring the public side. "The time for sporting," Woods explained in a vivid dispatch,

> lasts from the 1st of January to the last day of December, as every person has a right of sporting, on all unenclosed land, for all sorts of wild animals and game, without any license of qualification as to property. . . . Many of the Americans will hardly credit you, if you inform them, that there is any country in the world where one order of men are allowed to kill and eat game, to the exclusion of all others. But when you tell them that the occupiers of land are frequently among this number, they lose all patience, and declare, they would not submit to be so imposed on.

These land-use practices in frontier Illinois mirrored developments occurring in other states and territories. In a lawsuit resolved just as Woods reached Illinois, a South Carolina appellate court expressed surprise that a landowner in that state would even suggest he had the legal right to exclude hunters from unfenced land:

> Until the bringing of this action, the right to hunt on unenclosed and uncultivated lands has never been disputed, and it is well known that it has been universally exercised from the first settlement of the country up to the present time; and the time has been, when, in all probability, obedient as our ancestors were to the laws of the country, a civil war would have been the consequence of an attempt, even by the legislature, to enforce a restraint on this privilege. It was the source from whence a great portion of them derived their food and raiment. . . . The forest was regarded as a common, in which they entered at pleasure, and exercised the privilege; and it will not be denied that animals, *ferae naturae*, are common property, and belong to the first taker. If, therefore, usage can make law, none was ever better established.

These reforms to trespass law were among the many changes Americans felt free to make to English common law to take account of their wants and sensibilities and the continent's topography and vast resources. Immigrant Americans, as is often noted, yearned to become property owners. Yet they carried in their baggage grievances about the ways big landowners in their home countries used their powers to exploit and dominate. In England, for instance, the public could fish only on waters subject to the ebb and flow of the tides; not so in the freer land of America, where all "navigable in fact" waterways were open to a wide range of public uses, even when river bottoms and banks were held privately. In the arid parts of the continent, the first arriving settlers claimed legal rights in scarce water flows by the simple act of diverting the water and putting it to use. As they did so, they pushed aside the English law of riparian rights, which reserved water exclusively to owners of riparian lands. English law on the ability of landowners to drain lands took a new shape, as did the common law rule under which subsurface gold and silver deposits belonged to the sovereign, not to the landowner where found.

Foreign visitors like John Woods also commented often on another way that American lands bred new ways of thinking and living. From the beginning, settlers coming from Europe were awed by the continent's vastness and natural bounty. They spread out quickly, resisting communal efforts to maintain compact communities. As they went about cutting down forests and exhausting soils they embraced resource-use practices that visitors deemed wasteful. By the end of the eighteenth century, older settlements in eastern Massachusetts and elsewhere did develop more land-conserving farming practices. But land-grabbing and westward expansion would admit no enduring constraint, particularly when so many national voices celebrated the moving frontier as a positive American asset; as a key source and protection of individual liberty and democratic political culture. So it was that, as the generations unfolded and migrants crossed the Mississippi into semi-arid grasslands, they felt free to plow and plant following humid-land farming methods that were ill-suited to the plains and its recurring droughts and winds. When migrating farmers reached lands more arid still, they pushed the government to construct reservoirs and irrigation works, which over time degraded water quality and radically disrupted riparian ecosystems. In much the same way, settlers along major rivers, wanting to plow, plant, and build in the fertile floodplains, pressed governments to fund and build levees, confining rivers to narrow channels, distorting silt flows, and compelling communities downstream to erect even higher levees. With the coming of the internal combustion engine, cities stretched across countrysides while ever-growing tractors and combines transformed farming and farm landscapes almost beyond recognition.

Underlying any civilization, ancient or modern, is the land itself, the complex mix of soils, rocks, waters, plants, and animals that undergirds all terrestrial life. A civilization can flourish and endure only if it tends its lands and waters with reasonable care, limiting what is done to nature, where, and how. Failure to do so, particularly misuses of soils, has brought down more civilizations than any other cause. Before a civilization finally collapses it is beset with public health declines, political conflict, and weakened defenses. Bad land use, that is, ties directly not just to malnutrition and wars but also to internal conflict, exploitation, and despotism. In the case of democracies, bad land use and its consequences can sap the collegiality and good will essential to their operation. As for good land use, it is a considerable challenge, particularly when managed over entire landscapes. It requires ecologically informed, well-reasoned, collective decisionmaking. It is frustrated by the many cultural and economic forces of fragmentation.

Land and democracy have long intertwined in American history. The availability of vast lands to the west, as often pointed out, bred feelings of liberty and self-worth that supported popular demands to broaden suffrage and level social distinctions. It offered a kind of safety valve that reduced social pressures in built-up and congested areas, diminishing risks of mob action and, at least for a time, sapping the powers of the wealthy to exploit workers and dominate the poor, both economically and politically. Available land and frontier liberties promoted democracy and, in the view of many, were essential to it.

Today's links between land and democracy are rather different, even as there remains merit to the claim that widespread land ownership encourages people to sink roots and become better citizens. The kind of liberty as license that the frontier fostered has come back to haunt us, not just by empowering bad land- and water-use practices but also by weakening the kind of government required to bring changes to our ways and means of dwelling on land.

News outlets these days offer a regular drumbeat of reports on ecological decline, many stemming from our ongoing efforts to manipulate and press against the continent's physical fabric. A handful of such dispatches can help frame where we stand.

- By May of 2018, the Rio Grande River was already running dry for the year, its meager runoff from snow-melt lost to the parched riverbed and irrigation pumps. By the beginning of April, federal wildlife officials were capturing silver minnows, an endangered species native to the Rio Grande, and relocating them upstream to spots where the river still flowed. Irrigators, meanwhile, continued to divert scarce river water to produce low-valued crops.
- On September 14, 2018, the much-anticipated Hurricane Florence struck the Carolina coastline. Its torrential rains combined with strong storm surges—reversing the flows of coastal rivers—produced massive flooding as far as 150 miles inland, making a mockery of historic floodplain maps.
- In October 2018, the World Wildlife Fund for Nature released a sobering report on declining wildlife populations. It concluded, based on numerous scientific studies worldwide, that populations of terrestrial

vertebrate species over the previous forty years had declined by an average of 60 percent. The following month, a detailed article in *New York Times Magazine* drew similar attention to massive ongoing declines in insect populations. On May 6 came a U.N.-sponsored report on worldwide losses of animal and plant species at rates unprecedented in human history and accelerating.

- In November 2018, the California Air Resources Board announced with frustration that sprawling housing patterns were undercutting state efforts to reduce greenhouse gas emissions due to the lengthening of daily commutes.

- On February 26, 2019, voters in Toledo, Ohio, by a wide margin approved a measure granting legal rights to Lake Erie by way of lamenting and combatting the environmental calamities afflicting the lake, particularly its expanding algal outbursts caused by fertilizer and animal-manure runoff.

- In March 2019, heavy rainfall in the Missouri River basin brought weeks of massive flooding to much of Nebraska, Iowa, and Missouri. High waters breached levees and devastated farms, roads, and towns. On April 3, the governors of the three states asked the Army Corps of Engineers not just for short-term help to fix levees but for longer-term, innovative solutions. "We can't do the same old thing we've been doing," one of the governors asserted.

- As the Missouri's waters surged, noted science writer Elizabeth Kolbert reported on the continuing, inexorable loss of land in Louisiana. A century of flood-control efforts had kept silt-laden floodwaters from carrying to the state's coastal lands the mud vitally needed to offset the land's inevitable compaction. Since the 1930s the state has lost more than 2,000 square miles of land, with another football field's worth disappearing every ninety minutes. An advisory group appointed after the ravages of Hurricane Katrina in 2005 recommended resettlement of only the highest parts of the city. Politically, Kolbert explained, the proposal was a non-starter, inconsistent with individual liberties and the still-potent urge to keep nature under heel.

So long as the continent's resources appeared unlimited, Americans mostly looked upon conservation and planned land use as unneeded and unwanted, at least outside cities. The guiding urge was to expand liberties and unleash human enterprise. Individual choice and market forces, not bureaucrats, would dictate where and how people made homes and drew incomes. Nature in this shared view appeared as a warehouse of resources—of land parcels, water flows, minerals, and forests—its interconnected elements broken apart, valued, harvested, and exploited largely based on short-term human wants.

Looking back, many liberty-guided Americans made poor choices as they charged ahead, manipulating nature with too little regard for its ways and means. Until the New Deal era, those who did mostly had to shoulder the harsh consequences, the crops lost to drought and flooding, the livestock killed by frigid winters, the homes and businesses swept away by fires, mudslides, and coastal storms. But liberal America was becoming more compassionate. Families and businesses ill-treated by nature increasingly appeared as victims, not as foolish actors. Spotty private relief gave way, starting in the 1930s, to massive federal outlays, spending that, in retrospect, enabled recipients to continue their costly practices. Federal efforts to save Dust Bowl farmers from their follies—from plowing semi-arid lands that should have been left in grass, to overreliance on wheat monocultures—encouraged struggling farm families to stick it out rather than leave. Propped up with federal money, they could await the return of the rains and continue the practices that had brought them down. Had the federal government remained hard-hearted toward drought-ruined farmers—had it similarly refused to build levees, dams, and irrigation networks; to tame rivers for navigation; to expand coastal flood and crop insurance programs—our landscapes would function better ecologically and display richer biological diversity.

To draw together these various land-use reports from present and past is to amass a rather powerful case for reconsidering the ways we live on and with the interlaced soils, rocks, waters, plants, and animals around us. They expose the stark need for Americans to do what their colonial and antebellum predecessors did, to take charge of their landscapes, to craft ways of living that foster the common welfare, and to revise laws and cultural norms to help make it all happen. Sometimes a problem stems from a particular, ill-chosen land use: from "ponds" full of coal ash, for instance, that a power company situates next to, and that leak pollutants into, a National Scenic River (to cite an example not far from John Woods's

Illinois prairie). There, a site-specific remedy might work. But today's major ills by and large are ones that call for remedies that unfold at larger spatial scales, for land-use shifts over multiple square miles, even hundreds and thousands of square miles, transecting township, county, state, and even national borders. A reformed American democracy somehow will need to rise to the overall challenge. The work tasks will be many.

- Most obvious here, to begin a quick list, are the challenges brought on by a changing climate. As sea levels rise, as ocean salinity invades groundwater and kills protective coastal vegetation, widespread shifts are needed in coastal land use. The sensible route, plainly, is to evacuate most coastal areas and allow nature to do what it will. Only the highest-valued coastal areas should receive the costly (and ecologically problematic) protections of rigid barriers—meaning, typically, cities located on stable (nonsinking) land that enjoy water supplies immune to encroaching salinity. Similar evacuations and relocations are in order along riparian flood plains, with levees breached and natural, life-enhancing flood regimes revived. Merely to mention such prospects, before even pulling out maps, is to glimpse the magnitude of the challenge: the long-range planning and decisionmaking required at large spatial scales along with the vast reforms to American democracy and culture required for this all to happen.
- Wildfires in the West similarly highlight the benefits of better-planned settlement patterns. Fires are often blamed on longstanding firefighting efforts that have disrupted natural fire regimes. Yet scattered human land-use patterns are also at work, blocking fires from running their natural courses. Worsening things are insect infestations, tree diseases, and climate shifts. Prescribed burns could help, as we look ahead. But fires burn more freely, and prescribed burns are more feasible when occupied zones are relatively few and compact.
- As for wildlife declines, proposals to combat them tend to entail identifying and rehabilitating wildlife corridors, particularly along river corridors. Yet wildlife habitats everywhere are increasingly fragmented and degraded, often by the same land-use changes that enhance fire risks. Industrial farm practices have taken terrific tolls on wildlife, as have levees and other river structures.

- The California Air Resources Board report on urban sprawl and long-distance commutes highlights only one of the nagging costs of urban sprawl. Many of these costs were anticipated a century ago by early regional planners such as Benton MacKaye, who warned of the "metropolitan invasion" of the countryside and urged Americans to take charge of their fates and institutions. Many Western European nations—and others such as South Korea—have found ways to contain urban growth. A revived, empowered American democracy could do the same.

- Too often overlooked are the many ecological ills caused by modern farming, so productive (too productive) yet so destructive of lands as biologically rich, functioning ecosystems. Farm problems go well beyond wide-spreading fertilizers and pesticides, harmful as they are. Monocultures of annual crops (corn, beans, most wheat) require tillage that releases soil carbon. Eroding soil, still a problem, clogs rivers and reservoirs while killing freshwater mussels. Far different farming and ranching methods—far more ecologically healthy methods—are available to try out and refine when farm policy is redirected to encourage if not mandate them.

- Special attention is warranted for the particular ills of irrigated agriculture, which according to the USDA accounts for 80 percent of all water consumption in the United States (90 percent in many Western states): the rivers drained and polluted with farm runoff; the estuaries degraded by low water flows and farm chemicals; the falling groundwater tables; and the costly, energy-consumptive efforts used to meet the water needs of urban areas. Since World War I America's central farm challenge has come from overproduction and the resulting need to deal with farm surpluses. A well-functioning democracy, attentive to the common good, would severely curtail irrigation of most major crops—corn, beans, cotton, rice, alfalfa, pasture grasses. (Vegetables and orchards use about one-eighth of all irrigation water, far less than corn alone.)

We need to see our plight more clearly. Today's water-supply ills have little to do with physical water shortages; we have as much or more water than we need. They are caused instead by a collective incapacity to make sensible water-use (and land-use) decisions. Underlying that deficiency, as already noted, is the foundational matter of American culture and the many reasons, often at a gut level, why Americans resist planning and governing that cramps personal liberty. If the United States is going to deal successfully with a changing climate, if it is to shift to patterns of land and water use that are good for people, wildlife, and future generations, it is going to have to embrace different cultural understandings and values, and then, based on them, to create democratic institutions to take on the re-settlement of the country.

Americans by and large grasp and appreciate the fact that what one landowner does can have spill-over effects that hurt neighbors. Whether happily or begrudgingly, they mostly endorse laws that restrict harm-causing land uses. What we see less well are the countless ways that land uses trigger ecological ripple effects that spread widely and, to most eyes, invisibly. Overlooked too are the harms caused by land uses that are innocent enough taken alone but become problematic when too many people engage in them. Who notices the ways residential housing fragments critical wildlife habitats? Who notices how ordinary drainage practices for subdivisions and farms collectively alter the timing and quantities of water flows, eroding streams and rivers while worsening flooding and droughts?

To these points we can add the reality that many environmental goals are simply out of reach unless landowners work together. No well-meaning riparian landowner alone, for instance, can clean up a river and restore a natural flow. Real wildlife recovery requires coordinated habitat improvements over broad areas. What is called for, plainly, are democratic means to reconsider land and resource uses at larger spatial scales. This means getting people generally to see land use as a matter of public business, even on private land. It means overcoming also the long-held view that land use is strictly a matter for local government. The land planning called for today requires action by multiple levels of government working at various scales.

Land planning of this type will not come easy. Earlier attempts at it mostly stumbled, for reasons worth study. A form of federal land planning began in the 1890s when federal administrations took steps to conserve federal lands, particularly forests, and to buy back key lands that private owners had abused. A step closer to national land planning came during the New Deal, when the Roosevelt administration and Congress directed the Department of Agriculture to help bankrupted farmers in the Dust Bowl region, Appalachia, and elsewhere and to propose land policies to diminish further land abuses. The most thoughtful of the federal land planners could see that the underlying culprit was modern culture rather than economics. An extraordinary government report issued in 1937, *The Future of the Great Plains*, ripped into the bad practices one by one, while calling out the "attitudes of mind" that had brought them about ("man conquers nature," "natural resources are inexhaustible," "what is good for the individual is good for everybody," "an owner may do with his property as he likes"). The few New Deal programs that really sought to control bad land uses—other than by paying farmers, year by year—were soon nixed by agribusiness political power and by the economic upturn of World War II. The mindset that brought on bad land uses also resisted attempts to remedy them. Still, the challenge was announced, and the root causes laid bare.

Federal land planning first gained significant national support in the early 1970s with key senators (Henry Jackson, Edmund Muskie) and President Richard Nixon in the lead. The bills introduced in Congress were modest enough, mostly designed to push states to do more. Driving the planning impulse this time was urban sprawl and associated infrastructure costs rather than degraded farmlands. Nixon's Watergate troubles diverted attention from the effort, and the Chamber of Commerce resisted fiercely. A variety of economic woes in 1973 and 1974 saw the end of it.

What careful observers could see was that legal reform at the federal level was unlikely unless and until fundamental shifts took place in modern culture.[1] As historian Donald Worster explained in his penetrating study, the ecological catastrophe of the Dust Bowl "was the inevitable outcome of a culture that deliberately, self-consciously, set itself that task of dominating and exploiting the land for all it was worth." For Worster, the various flaws identified in *The Future of the Great Plains* were best captured by the word "capitalism," a word hard to define but illuminated by the words associated with it: "private property, business, laissez-faire, profit motive, the pursuit of self-interest, free enterprise, an open marketplace, the bourgeoisie." Americans simply didn't see that landscapes, given their ecological and social interconnections, are best understood as types of commons and are subject to easy misuse. What brought tragedy to a commons at root was neither the lack of individual private property

rights (as conservatives would claim) nor the lack of a collective management system (as commons scholars urged). The root cause lay deeper, in
the inability of users of a commons to see that they were better off if they
worked in tandem, setting limits on their exploitation. The shortcoming
was a cultural one, not an institutional or legal one.

Many of today's challenges, social as well as ecological, are rooted in the
land-use practices of private landowners. It has always been thus. Misuses
of public lands, now much mitigated, have been less common and, when
occurring, are due to government agencies too weak and ill-funded to resist private pressures. Merely to raise a concern about private land use,
however, is immediately to collide with private property, so dear to Americans and yet so poorly understood as a dynamic, evolving, morally complex institution. Americans care about environmental ills and the social
ills mixed with them. But they care too about private property and about
individual rights. Not wanting to infringe upon the latter they look for
ways to address environmental ills that respect them, usually coming up
empty-handed.

American democracy can make real progress on land-use ills only if
it gains control over private property as an institution, taking the lead
from early Americans in their willingness to tinker with the elements of
ownership. This means, as a first step, taking property seriously, studying it as an institution, reflecting on it morally, and considering the many
ways the law can define what owners might possess and what ownership
entails. America's blindness on the issue—its failure to see private property as a coercive, morally complex, potentially beneficial form of state-
backed power—is saddening and costly. An awakening is overdue also on
the misleading dichotomy between public lands and private lands; in reality, all lands reflect varied mixes of the public and the private. To think
about early America and its wandering livestock and hunters is to catch
a brief glimpse of how private property has had widely varied meanings
even within the United States, to say nothing of its many manifestations
in other cultures. Property is a dynamic, highly flexible institution. Property as we know it is long out of date.

The reform of private property is best begun by giving thought to the
ways a well-structured private property system can bring benefits.[2] It begins,
too, with an understanding of the institution's moral complexity. When a

wandering hunter or hiker is arrested for trespass and put in prison, it is state power that is interfering with her individual liberty—a morally problematic act that demands justification. It is hardly enough to say that the hunter or hiker is violating private property rights, because it is the rights themselves that are at issue. Take the modern farmland owner who demands one-half of the total farm produce from a farm while doing no work. How can this be fair? What about the owner of urban land who demands a king's ransom to sell a vacant land parcel when, as political economist Henry George pointed out more than a century ago, the high value of the land has come about, not because of anything the owner did, but because of the collective activities of the surrounding community? When a community creates value, why does it not get to claim at least a sizeable part of it?

Private property, we need to see, is not at all an individual right like those mentioned in the Bill of Rights. One does not own property simply by dwelling in the United States. The Constitution offers limited protection for property, but it protects only rights that arise under some other law. Mythology aside, private property is not first and foremost an individual right. It is better grasped as a tool that a majoritarian lawmaking community recreates and refines over time to promote the common good. Property norms, to be sure, require careful revision to avoid disrupting the institution and undercutting its benefits. But many changes to property law would not diminish its benefits appreciably, and even major legal changes are possible when landowners receive lengthy notice. Overdue legal change could come, too, if lawmakers took more seriously the public's own property rights in rivers, wildlife, and beaches.

Perhaps no specific issue exposes the stark cultural challenge ahead on this private property issue better than does the current resistance to the government's exercise of eminent domain. Governments have wielded this power for centuries for a variety of public purposes, exercising the power, as they exercise all powers, sometimes for good reasons and with good results, other times more questionably. James Madison, drafting the Bill of Rights, added on his own initiative a provision in the Fifth Amendment requiring the federal government to pay just compensation for any lands it took for a "public use." The historical record gives no evidence that he proposed to curtail this governmental power by referring to "public use" (other than by requiring compensation), and no one debating the proposed Bill of Rights seemed to take the provision that way. As the leading historical account concludes, the term was no more restrictive than "public purpose" or "common good." Looking ahead, a revived American democracy will need to make regular, extensive use of eminent domain if it is going to bring about significant shifts in land and water uses.

For generations, as noted, American thought linked the plight of democracy with land, particularly open land on the frontier. Open land no doubt served as a safety valve in various ways, just as it fostered the kind of freedom and weakened the communal structures that John Woods witnessed on the English prairie. But this role for open land—stimulating an aggressive, exploitive, libertarian land-use ethic—came at great cost. The land itself, understood as an ecologically complex, biologically rich community, paid the price and still does. The appetite of settlers for private lands helped fuel an understanding of private property as somehow an inherent right, one that existed apart from and before property laws secured it. In culture, private property became a kind of shield to keep government away, a power to resist communal demands. That libertarian culture, still alive, itself became a root cause of environmental ills, a reason why Americans even now are so slow to see and condemn bad land uses all around them and to understand private land use as legitimate public business.

The particular property-law changes that took place in the English prairie, in South Carolina, and elsewhere in the early nineteenth century slowly gave way. As for the legal power of landowners to exclude, American law now largely tracks the old common law of England, even as England itself, paradoxically, has followed the lead of Scotland and Scandinavia and opened up many rural private lands to responsible public use. (We could do the same; according to a January 2019 study, the landholdings of America's one hundred largest landowners has risen to 42 million acres, up 50 percent since 2007.) The spirit of law reform that Woods saw in action, though, continued for generations, most evidently (in the mid- to late nineteenth century) with the tailoring of land-use rules to allow the more intensive, disruptive land uses of industrialization and urbanization. Those legal changes in turn fostered ills that triggered countervailing demands for greater limits on noisy, polluting activities.

America today needs to put its pioneer era behind it, more fully than it has, and take a harder look at the settlement patterns brought on by the culture of exploitation—of "capitalism," as Donald Worster termed it. A more land- and community-respecting culture, one less driven by a zeal for individual liberty, would likely have produced on the continent far different settlement patterns.

Strong democracy is essential to accommodate climate change sensibly and to deal with other lingering ills. Strong democracy here means something far different from the neutral night-watchman image of generations back, and is different too from a government designed simply to help everyone, regardless of race, ethnicity, or gender, get ahead individually. Rather, it means government also committed to, perhaps first-and-foremost committed to, protecting and enhancing the ecological foundations of all of our lives and fostering the functional health and biological diversity of our natural homes. This kind of strong democracy cannot arise, history suggests, without significant cultural change, which is to say today's reform agenda goes well beyond the political.

We might help foster this kind of democracy by encouraging people to reconnect to nature, perhaps by gardening or nature study, perhaps by taking interest in the sources and quality of their food. Yet such measures, useful as they are, fall far short. They don't help people take charge of their landscapes as a whole as did the frontier settlers on the English prairie. They don't get people to see land use at the landscape scale as legitimate public business suitable for collective action. They don't get people to take charge of private property as an institution and to reshape its norms to accommodate resource exhaustion, biological declines, and disruptions of basic ecosystem processes. Mostly they don't offer up to people visions of what our landscapes, riparian corridors, coasts, and settlement patterns could look like one day if we succeeded in resettling the continent, this time as if we meant to stay. This kind of work calls for leaders with vision, leaders who can capture the public's imagination with vivid talk about life as it could be.

RACE AND DEMOCRACY: THE KENNEDYS, OBAMA, TRUMP, AND US

Michael Eric Dyson

"Politics is the art of the possible, the attainable—the art of the next best," Otto von Bismarck famously said. The politics of race, then, is the art of the impossible, the elusive—the art of achieving what was never meant to be. In our nation, the politics of race is shaped by hard truths: that politics, and the state, exist to defend white interests and identities; that witness is an important means to express black grievance and resistance, and to shape public policy; that dormant and resurgent white bigotry, even at the highest level of government, must be identified and opposed; and that a new politics must be formed to fulfill true democracy.

Black folk make it in America despite being denied everything many whites take for granted: justice, the benefit of the social and moral doubt, and ample incentives to believe the nation is great. But the republic that whites are willing to die for has had a hand in killing the ancestors and friends of their black compatriots. The men who fashioned democracy portrayed African people in America as traitors to the cause of building a nation. They questioned their humanity and their intelligence, so that even after they got freedom, black people would be found without merit in the claim to citizenship.

Both formal political culture and informal cultural politics reflected the will of the nation to negate the existence of black folk. Enslaving black people exploited their labor while denying their bodies legitimate rights. Black bodies had no "inalienable rights"; they existed at the pleasure and permission of a white society. Laws and covenants, compacts and contracts, folkways and mores, institutions and civic culture existed for the benefit of white folk—to concretely realize their moral and social aspirations and to serve as ready reference of their norms and ideals. There was robust argument among white folk about how and when these norms and ideals should apply. But they agreed that the circumference of their newly forged civilization should exclude blacks, natives, and a rolling cast of "others." Nativist thinking and xenophobic instincts were baked into the framework of society. These notions were also central to the Constitution, which declared the enslaved would be counted as three-fifths of the number of white inhabitants of a state. These ideas also cropped up in the Declaration of Independence, which saw Africans as "domestic insurrectionists" and Indians as "merciless savages."

To be sure, black folk found room to breathe within the smothering confines of white society. They crafted an existence outside of the slavish demand for total surrender. But their lives were controlled to a large degree by white supremacy. Schools, churches, social clubs, businesses, and courts were run by and for white folk. The point of politics was to defend white interests.

Politicians did not have to name white interests, because they were considered American interests. The founders and the original citizens made whiteness the default position of American identity and humanity. American citizens were allowed to be white without having to say so. They could rely on its benefits without having to name them—one of which was the celebration that attended the notion of the self-made man. But the "self" in that equation, viewed as the epitome of American idealism, was an identity shaped by the larger white world. It was an identity that gave white folk a false sense of achievement by connecting to an ancestry whose claims to glory rested on a lie of hard work—work that was instead outsourced to enslaved black folk.

White politicians took office to maintain the status quo well into the twentieth century. Nativist and xenophobic figures were only portrayed as out of step once civil rights leaders and other black activists challenged their politics and the society that would elect them. Racial progress forced an adjustment in the means of propagating the idea that America is a white society. Dixiecrats like George Wallace maintained the earlier political consensus of white superiority. Later politicians were conflicted: they were lodged between the unspoken endorsement of white supremacy and the effort to do away with old-style politics. But was it a genuine effort? Often white politicians fought the appearance of old-style racism while leaving in place the benefits and privileges of whiteness. Even northern Democrats largely accepted the status quo as the given.

The strategy of some white politicians was to accept existing racial politics to get elected and then use their position to remedy the most troubling aspects of the racial order. It was a risky bargain, and one that often left black folk in the lurch. Lyndon Baines Johnson pulled it off to perfection with incredible results when he managed to pass the holy trinity of civil rights legislation: the 1964 Civil Rights Act, the 1965 Voting Rights Act, and the 1968 Fair Housing Act. If LBJ is the gold standard, then John F. Kennedy was far less glorious in his fatal hesitancies about civil rights as president. His brother Bobby, who was his older sibling's attorney general, is sandwiched between the two, lauded for the scope of his aspiration near the end of his life, and yet lacking the broad tableau on which to completely inscribe, and fulfill, his promise.

President Kennedy was a northern white liberal who subscribed to the idea of equality in the abstract without endorsing a revolutionary overhaul of racial politics. He saw the conflict between Bismarck's art of the possible and the demand for radical change by the black freedom struggle. These forces were in dispute: politics as usual, even liberal politics, clashed with a movement that argued for social change. But there was at least a dual strategy to black protest: some leaders met with a president to argue for change, while other black figures, either because they chose not to go or, more likely, because they were locked out, made a virtue of their exclusion. Those who were barred from such meetings sought to enhance their political authority by claiming deeper discernment and superior representation of black interests. Black leaders who got in the door of the White House sought to leverage their access for social change—even as they were wounded for going by fellow black leaders. Thus, Malcolm X, who neither sought out nor was invited to such closed-door meetings, called Martin Luther King Jr., who was invited, an Uncle Tom and dubbed King's signature protest in the nation's capital the "farce on Washington."

President Kennedy was hardly exuberant in his pursuit of a civil rights agenda. He got a big boost in black communities because of a symbolic gesture—as a presidential candidate, the Massachusetts senator placed a telephone call to Georgia's governor, Ernest Vandiver, to get King out of jail in October 1960, right before the election that put Kennedy in the Oval Office. While the gesture endeared him to black folk, Kennedy was careful not to alienate his white supporters. He had infamously courted white southern voters by meeting with their leaders to reassure them he would not be a vigilant advocate of civil rights. Kennedy pledged to Vandiver that as president he would never use federal authority to coerce school desegregation in Georgia. In office, President Kennedy was ingenious at manipulating the appearance of liberal dedication to civil rights while all along stalling the progress through legal feints and legislative hints that never came full throttle. He put conservative bigots on the federal court, recoiled at the sight of the interracially married entertainer Sammy Davis Jr. when he appeared in the White House with his wife, Mai Britt, and attempted to string along King and other black leaders as much as possible. His equivocations and hesitancies amounted to precious little for black folk. President Kennedy gained a greater reputation for civil rights support in death than he had earned in life.

Bobby, if not quite his brother's opposite, was at least his sometime foil: he knew less about civil rights than Jack, yet he hungered more to make a difference. It is not that he wasn't problematic racially too—his appeal in 1968 to white paranoia about the black invasion of suburbia is well documented—but his political pragmatism didn't obscure his desire to understand black folk and improve race relations. On May 24, 1963, in a famous meeting in New York City between Kennedy and James Baldwin and several of the writer's compatriots—including Harry Belafonte, Lena Horne, and Lorraine Hansberry—it all came to a head: the history of white politics, the function of white politicians, the tension between white politicians trying to tread water and those seeking to make change, and prominent figures who funnel the rage of the black masses. When Bobby confronted Baldwin and his confreres in an effort to bring them under heel and within a moderate sphere of racial understanding, he presumed the legitimacy of politics in a way that may have worked for King, but surely not for Baldwin, ever the skeptic of white power. King was committed to working within the parameters of political legitimacy. Baldwin and some of his mates felt differently; they doubted the will of the state to reconcile itself to black destiny, because they realized black folk were viewed, fundamentally, as an enemy of the state.

Baldwin could more easily acknowledge his doubts because he wasn't in the same position as King, Roy Wilkins, Whitney Young, and other black leaders. Their raison d'être was to uphold the state as the bulwark against black suffering. In King's view, the state is not questioned as to its function and intent; it is criticized in terms of its delivery and performance.

But Baldwin questioned the intent of the state because it had collapsed into—become identical with—whiteness. King understood white supremacy as a distortion of democracy, as an interruption of the delivery of social goods; thus, his "I Have a Dream" speech suggested that the American Dream was sufficient to accommodate the aspirations of black folk. The adjustment had to be made in society's laws, customs, habits, traditions, and conventions. Baldwin believed the state was doing exactly what it was set up to do: to undermine blackness and to eviscerate the black race as the measure of its fidelity to American principles. Thus, black animus was a condition of the state's very existence. Recognition of black people's humanity was an aberration, a failure of the system, a weakness.

When Bobby butted heads with Baldwin's group over patriotism, he was proclaiming his vision of the state as a bulwark of protection of its citizens, who, in exchange, repay the state with their loyalty. Their mutual adherence rests on the belief that the best interests of the citizen are realized through the state, and that the state's true existence is measured by the loyalty of its citizens. That is why, at the beginning of America, the American Revolution sparked a transition of its members from subjects of the empire to citizens of the state. The authority was wrested from a monarchy and bestowed on a nation that embraced the kingship of every man. That understanding ended in the black body. The state attempted to deny black agency. Jerome Smith, a highly decorated young veteran of the war in the streets and fields to make America more racially just, attended the Baldwin meeting. When he protested that he had no traditional interest in defending his country, Bobby took that as a sign of utter disrespect. What he failed to see is that Smith and other black folk had already endured the gravest form of disrespect possible: the denial of active citizenship and the rich realization of American identity with a full complement of rights. Although he thought of himself as empathetic to black folk, Kennedy was acting from the basis of projection: he cast onto Smith and the other blacks the notion that what he was, they could be. That is why Bobby easily asserted that his immigrant family was the perfect example of how black folk could be absorbed by the state. What Kennedy didn't acknowledge is that black folk were rejected as full citizens of American society. Thus, there was no parallel track that black and white folk could travel. Baldwin knew that tinkering with public policy was of little use if the value of black life had not been established. That's why he and his fellow blacks spent so much time insisting on being heard and, most important, seen.

The dual meaning of witness becomes clear: Baldwin as witness, and Baldwin's being witnessed, being seen, and thus, as their representative, of black people as witnesses, of black people's being seen. Baldwin as witness brought the full panoply of his gifts to bear in speaking on behalf of black folk. Baldwin's witnessing constituted a serious counternarrative to the state's lapsed function and duty. Since Baldwin is an individual, and not an institution, what he could offer, at best, is notice of the interior landscape of black psychic resistance to white supremacy. His voice was a weapon of witness.

Optics are critical in discussing politics and race. Who is seen and witnessed is as important as who gets the spoils. If knowledge is at least partly rooted in sight, then Baldwin's witness held special value and power. When Baldwin and his friends spoke, it may have been dismissed as merely emotional, but it was so much more: it was the data of the internal dimensions of racial experience; it was blackness seen through the prism of pain and trauma; it was knowledge rooted in black priorities—what an experience means, how it registers, and what effect it has on the black body. That is why Smith's witness was so compelling: it was the knowledge his body brought, the knowledge rooted in the hardship he endured, the knowledge that the white world wanted to avoid, that it couldn't afford to know, because if it knew what Smith knew, felt what he felt, it would upend their view of the world. It was more than a problem of knowledge; it was an ethical question, too, a problem of how they could morally accommodate the knowledge his suffering brought, and what it implied about the immoral character of white society.

Kennedy's desire to talk policy without hearing the group's pain seemed like a dodge. Policy is undoubtedly important in transforming black society, but knowledge derived from experience is crucial in shaping policy and driving law. For instance, the experience of lynching drove protests and was motivation to change laws in the South. The existential and the ethical, the philosophical and the political, legislation and lived experience are united. Bobby's preference for policy made sense in his world. But in order to understand why the policy had to be implemented, why it had to exist in the first place, why the existing laws weren't enough to right the wrongs, he had to first understand the lives, experiences and perspectives of the black folk he intended to serve.

A different kind of challenge loomed when a black president was elected: How, and to what degree, would experience and witness play into policy? And what experiences did Obama have? Were they ones that many black folk could identify with? That is why during his first run for the presidency there was a great deal of anxiety over whether Obama was black enough. What was the quality and nature of his experience as a black man, how would it shape his understanding of his role and job, and how would it add, or subtract, from his duties? Would his blackness constitute an existential weight, a knowledge of suffering, and also one of possibility, and thus color his views of democracy and shape his approach to making laws? How would it positively and negatively impact his view of himself as president, and would it somehow lessen his efficacy as a black man who was president?

For the first time, a black face was on the machinery that had worked hard to undermine black agency. But a black face in a high place does not guarantee a new order. Obama offered the state legitimacy more than he offered black folk inclusion. One black face could not possibly overcome the historic legacy of black erasure or solve the perception of unreliable blackness. One black body could not negate the past or reverse the vicious legacy of white supremacy. Obama was a walking legitimation crisis, throwing into conniptions the very state he represented because it meant, by implication or extension, that the blacks it had historically demeaned and excluded were now part of official American identity, were that much closer to being perceived as full citizens. And so, an equally powerful wind blew back, insisting that Obama could never be truly American, truly a citizen, truly the symbol of the nation as its putative father, because he was, in essence, illegitimate, a bastard president, a political orphan with no lines of kinship to authentic American identity. No matter, or amount, of policy can solve that.

Obama's blackness, no matter how curtailed, made him, even as president, an enemy of the state. The white refusal to concede Obama's legitimacy is the articulation of the deeply rooted refusal to see blackness as American. Donald Trump's birtherism was the extended unfolding of such an idea. For those who take solace in the belief that Trump is a marginal player in whiteness, they are sadly mistaken. He is, indeed, the extension of the logic of American ideas about blackness found at the nation's roots and beginnings. Baldwin and friends understood the roots of whiteness as the determinant of our politics before King could acknowledge it. It is true that Malcolm X and the black nationalists were capable of seeing this, but their handicap was two-fold: first, they didn't get involved in electoral politics to make the claim from within the boundaries of political argumentation where it might have been most effective. And second, they bathed in a politics of racial resentment that matched whiteness in spirit. That is why Malcolm could meet with white supremacists from the Nazi Party, like George Lincoln Rockwell, in 1961 to map out their mutual strategies for racial separation. For all of its ferocity of black self-love, there was about Malcolm's position a galling naïveté about how such things operated in the real world of politics. The black nationalists' belief that they and white supremacists wanted the same thing is fatally ignorant.

Recently, as bigotry resurfaces, such as in Charlottesville, Virginia, the lie is put to the belief that "this is not American, this is not us," when, indeed, it truly is. We do not want to acknowledge how true it is, because of how it makes us look complicit in prejudice we thought we had gotten over. Donald Trump is far more representative of the nation than many whites would like to admit.

But there is a development with Trump that is unique: he is treating the nation—which, by default, is white and Christian (though technically it is neither)—as white folk have treated black folk throughout our history. Trump is treating the entire nation as black. More particularly, he is treating the entire nation as "the nigger." One of the reasons for the special outrage of many white Americans toward him is that he has forgotten the rules; that sort of treatment is for blacks, the others, not whites. That need not be a conscious belief for it to be true. The reason his views on immigration can be abided is because those immigrants are "them." However, when it comes to insulting folk, spoiling his office in narcissistic displays, acting vengefully—this is the heart of whiteness, and the force of whiteness against blackness and other colors. It has always been a rather juvenile affair: drinking at a white water fountain was not simply a marker of rigid, though unscientific, anthropology; it was also the symbolic height of adolescent bravura and competition—mine is better than yours. Except such displays are rigged from the start to favor petulant whiteness. It is unbearable for white Americans who don't support Donald Trump to tolerate him because he is treating "them" like "they" treated "us." In short, he's confused his pronouns. If they could abide the language and grasp the comparison, many whites would cry out with James Baldwin: "I am not your nigger."

After a great deal of resistance, combat, and protest, some white folk have come around to seeing race, especially this brand of whiteness, as a fiction, something Baldwin said more than fifty years ago. Many whites now see its truth because they believe that what Trump is doing is deeply and profoundly flawed, lunatic. His obsessions and perverse preoccupations are the stuff of a whiteness that never had to be accountable. Trump's total lack of knowledge, and the enshrinement of ignorance as the basis of power and authority, is the personification of white supremacy and white arrogance.

Obama and Trump are thus wedged between two poles of unbelievability: that Obama, the ultimate "traitor" to American identity, could be elected, and that Trump could cavalierly give away the family secrets by exposing the twisted logic of whiteness for the world to see. It is unthinkable to many whites that such a man could be president, that such a figure with his array of flaws could take command. After all, a subtler, or more sophisticated, whiteness often occupies the presidency. But the truth is Trump harkens back to original and founding whiteness.

Even before he took office Donald Trump was plagued by chronic ignorance of black life, an ignorance spiked by a mean-spirited incuriosity about even the fundamental facts of black existence, a pose amplified in the Oval Office as he addressed Frederick Douglass as if he were alive and starring as the second baseman for the Baltimore Orioles. During his 2016 presidential campaign Trump tweeted out a grossly inaccurate image from a nonexistent "Crime Statistics Bureau," which suggested that the bulk of white folk are killed by black folk. We are reminded, with the trial of Dylann Roof, that white bigots have long parroted this belief as the reason for their racist revenge. That same inaccurate tweet portrayed police killings of black folk as far fewer than those of blacks killing white folk. In truth, whites die overwhelmingly at the hands of other whites. The supposedly unique scourge of so-called black-on-black crime cannot withstand the deluge of fact and statistics: the majority of people kill where they live.

The fact that white-on-white homicide has no resonance in the culture reflects the ideological and political purposes of a narrative of black intraracial savagery, a narrative that Trump and too many right-wingers are all too willing to embrace.

Trump also argued on the campaign trail that "African American communities are absolutely in the worst shape they've ever been in before. Ever, ever, ever." President Barack Obama drolly declared, "I mean, he missed that whole civics lesson about slavery or Jim Crow."

Trump's ignorance about race, his critical lack of nuance and learning about it, is disheartening enough, but it prevails among liberals and the white left too in their 2016 post-election calls to forego identity politics. If there is a dirty secret in American life, it is this: the real unifying force in our national cultural and political life, beyond skirmishes over ideology and party, is white identity masked as universal, neutral, and therefore quintessentially American. The greatest purveyor of identity politics today, and for the bulk of our country's history, has been white citizens. This means that among the oldest forms of "fake news" in the nation's long trek to democratic opportunity has been the belief that whiteness is identical to, and exhausts, the idea of what it means to be American.

Senator Bernie Sanders, despite his dramatically different politics and ideology, is, in many ways, the mirror image of Donald Trump: a brash, older white male with sympathies for the white working class and limited knowledge, at least early on, of black folk. From the start of his 2016 presidential campaign, Sanders was prickly about race, uncomfortable with an outspoken, demanding blackness, and resistant to letting go of his preference for class over race—or really, of subsuming race under class. Though he made efforts to correct his poor racial sight, Sanders remained at heart a man of the people, especially if those people were white working-class folk. After the election, Sanders sounded an increasingly familiar theme among liberals that they should "go beyond identity politics." Sanders warned that "to think of diversity purely in racial and gender terms is not sufficient," and that we need candidates "to be fighters for the working class and stand up to the corporate powers who have so much power over our economic lives." In a speech in California, Sanders said that it is "very easy for many Americans to say, I hate racism, I hate homophobia, I hate sexism," but that "it is a little bit harder for people in the middle or upper middle class to say, maybe we do have to deal with the greed of Wall Street."

This is a nifty bit of historical revisionism. For the longest time there was little consideration for diversity, even among liberal elites, much less the white middle and working classes. Diversity was calculated in terms of region, sometimes religion or vocation, as long as they were all white. Race and gender, and sexuality too, were late to the game. It seems more than a little reactionary to blame the loss of the election on a brand of identity politics that even liberals were slow to embrace, and which not all of them are completely sold on. Moreover, Sanders, like so many liberals, spurns the very diversity that gave the ideals of democracy legs. It is not that attention to diversity and identity somehow undercuts our nation's embrace of democratic ideals; it strengthens them. The black struggle for freedom has ensured that other groups could follow along in the wake of our demand for equality.

When the 1964 Civil Rights Bill was in doubt in Congress, crafty and bigoted white representatives thought they could sink it by attaching the issue of gender, hoping to appeal to the sexism of those who might otherwise be cajoled to offer their support. Instead the bill passed and paved the way for both black rights and, with Title VII, those of women. What's good for black folk is good for the nation. It is more than a little curious that, in the name of a mythical universalism that is stripped of race, gender, or sexuality, advocates across the political spectrum now advance a notion of populist anti-identity politics that rests, ironically, on their vigorous defense of white identity politics in their lauding of the white working class. It is not that the white working class is unworthy of serious attention and broad support. It is that their fortunes are cast over against the masses of folk of color, many of whom are also working class or poor, but whose interests hardly factor into considerations of class-consciousness, class rebellion, or class solidarity.

To accept the framework being advanced by Trump and Sanders, we must be resolutely ahistorical. The interests of the white working class have often been used by white political elites to stave off challenges to inequality and discrimination by black folk and other minority groups. First, in the early twentieth century, the rights of black folk were denied because they would undermine white working-class stability. Then, in the various worker unions in the middle part of the twentieth century, black agency and mobility were curtailed by protecting the race-based interests of the white working and middle-class folk. In the late sixties, Richard Nixon even supported a variety of affirmative action policies because he deemed it useful to break unions by accusing them of racial exclusion. In the eighties, Ronald Reagan appealed to disaffected white Democrats who resented being forced to share a small measure of the enormous gains they had accumulated through bigotry and official discrimination. And now we hear again the hue and cry that the neglected white working class is the linchpin to the 2016 election and the future of American progressive politics. The more things change, the more they stay the same.

The truth is that American politics has hardly neglected the interests of the white working and middle classes. The progress experienced under the banner of the movement for racial, gender, and sexual justice has forced white folk to share just a little of their bounty with blacks, Latinx, women, and queer folk. To be sure, these groups are hardly homogenous or univocal. Yet concern for their own interests leads whites to think of their own well-being at the expense of other groups' interests. Instead, there is talk of restoring America to a nostalgic vision of white dominance under Donald Trump, or, in progressive circles, to a mythological, coherent, homogenized group that lacks the plagues of identity politics. But identity has always been at the heart of American culture. We must confront a truth that we have assiduously avoided: the most protected, cherished, and nurtured identity of all has been white identity.

That whiteness is the nation's preferred identity becomes painfully obvious when white bigots scamper out of their closets at the first sign of support by our government. It is difficult to believe that the ugly bigotry unleashed in 2017 in the streets of Charlottesville, Virginia—when white supremacists and Neo-Nazis rallied in a "Unite the Right" march to protest the removal of statues of Confederate generals from city parks, resulting in the death of valiant anti–white supremacist protester Heather D. Heyer—had nothing to do with the election of Donald Trump, one of the whitest presidents, with one of the whitest administrations, in the history of this nation. White separatist David Duke declared that the alt-right unity fiasco "fulfills the promises of Donald Trump." Trump infamously offered false equivalencies between white bigots and their protesters by suggesting that there were "some very fine people on both sides."

The ungainly assembly of white supremacists in Charlottesville rides herd on political memory with a willfully ahistorical version of the past. Their resentment of the removal of public symbols of the Confederate past is fueled by revisionist history on steroids. These whites fancy themselves the victims of the so-called politically correct assault on American democracy that propelled Trump to victory. Trump and white nationalists are flip sides of the same bigoted coin. Their currency in our present political climate reveals how each feeds on the same demented lies about race and justice that corrupt true democracy and erode real liberty. Together, Trump and white nationalists constitute the repulsive resurgence of a virulent *bigotocracy*, a loosely organized confederation of white racists who seek to institutionalize their ideology as national habit, social custom, cultural convention, and, when possible, legal precedent. Trump and the white bigotocracy have little patience for real history. If there's one word that calls whiteness to account, if there's a single phrase that conjures all the heartbreak that bigotry created and that blacks have endured, that word, that phrase, is slavery. White bigots think black folk have pimped that term for far too long, lived too long on the memory of something that happened so long ago and can't possibly have anything to do with what's going on today.

Of course, the bigotocracy ignores how the destiny of the black folk they despise is tied to the history and destiny of white America. It overlooks fundamental facts about slavery in this country: that blacks were stolen from their African homeland to toil for no wages in American dirt and turn it to cotton and gold. When black folk and others point that out, it grieves white bigots. They are especially offended when it is argued that slavery changed clothes during Reconstruction, then got dressed up as freedom, only to keep menacing black folk, as it did during Jim Crow. The bigotocracy is angry that slavery is seen as this nation's original sin. They cling for life to a faded Southern aristocracy whose benefits—of alleged white superiority, and moral and intellectual supremacy—trickled down to ordinary whites. If they couldn't drink from the cup of economic advantage, at least they could sip what was left of such a hateful ideology in the belief that at least they weren't black. The renowned scholar W.E.B. Du Bois called this alleged sense of superiority the "psychological wage" of whiteness. President Lyndon Baines Johnson once argued, "If you can convince the lowest white man he's better than the best colored man, he won't notice you're picking his pocket. Hell, give him somebody to look down on, and he'll empty his pockets for you."

It is disheartening for black folk to see such a vile and despicable replay of history before our very eyes. To know that in 2019 we are still beset by the most reprehensible symbols of our fractured past means that our present is shred and torn by hate as well. It is depressing to explain to our children that what we confronted as children may yet be the legacy they bequeath to their children as well. It is more disheartening still to realize that the government of our land, at least in the present administration, has shown little empathy for victims of white bigotry, and indeed has helped to spread the paralyzing virus of black hatred, as much by turning a deaf ear and blind eye as by actively encouraging our fretful gaggle of hate mongers. Nothing could more clearly declare the moral bankruptcy of our country.

There is little hope that the Trump administration will give a quarter in the fight for the nation's democratic legacy as it deepens the stakes of white supremacy through memory warfare and a nostalgia that masks political failure and historical distortion.

What James Baldwin and his friends exposed in that room continues to resonate with us today. The "other" is the fuel that drives ideas of American society, that feeds American identity. If we are committed to discerning, then defeating, the contemporary logic of racism, we must separate it from its ties to democracy itself. In order to be true patriots, we must become disloyal to chronically prejudiced views of American society that persist in our rather ignoble Trumpian moment. We earn the politicians we deserve, inherit the systems we admire and find useful, no matter our protests to the contrary. What Baldwin and his cohort understood is that we must be full of redemptive rage, and, simultaneously, fire every argument and emotion we can at the hate that threatens to sink our society. That is the only way to rescue our democracy.

LIBERTY AND JUSTICE FOR ALL: LATINA ACTIVIST EFFORTS TO STRENGTHEN DEMOCRACY IN 2018

Maria Hinojosa

I remember clearly the first time I saw video of Ana Maria Archila and Maria Gallagher stopping U.S. Senator Jeff Flake in the Senate elevator during the Supreme Court nomination hearings of Judge Brett Kavanaugh in 2018. I knew the contours of the breaking news: two emotionally distraught women cornered the senator to demand he stop supporting Kavanaugh's nomination after Professor Christine Blasey Ford accused him of attempting to rape her several years prior when they both were high school students in Bethesda, Maryland. Immediately, I wanted to know who'd acted so boldly to be heard.

"What you are doing is allowing someone who actually violated a woman to sit on the Supreme Court!" accused one of the women. I thought, wait a second. That's a Latina immigrant. Listen to her accent. Then I recognized her: Ana Maria Archila, an immigration activist I had met before. There she was, making news. A Latina with an accent taking on a powerful white male senator from Arizona. The encounter played again and again on our televisions, our computers, our phones. A shift in political possibility because two women spoke out at a crucial moment while CNN cameras were rolling.

Archila herself stressed to *Washington Post* reporter Elise Viebeck that her advocacy experience was not the only reason they were heard that day. "The people who have been coming to Washington, DC, [to protest the Kavanaugh nomination] are not people who have been activists for twenty years," Archila said. "Maria [Gallagher] was there for the first time. She told her story for the first time. She spoke with an elected official for the first time."

Senator Jeff Flake (R-AZ) and Senator Christopher Coons (D-TN) soon brokered a deal to postpone the committee vote for one week to allow the Federal Bureau of Investigation to perform an investigation of the sexual assault allegations. While one week is not much time, the brakes had been hit, and many people credited the "#ElevatorLadies." The brakes, however, did not hold. Despite credible testimony from Professor Ford, Judge Kavanaugh was confirmed and now sits on the United States Supreme Court.

If political change is about battles and wars, protestors lost the battle of Judge Kavanaugh's confirmation. I would argue, however, that Latina protestors speaking out in that elevator gave courage to other activists and changemakers fighting the longer war, and they did so alongside other Latina activists who spoke out and organized, or, in the case of Alexandria Ocasio-Cortez, ran as a candidate for the U.S. House of Representatives. Their actions, collectively, breathed life into the dreams of our founding documents, creating space for people of color to embrace and exercise our civic duties as Americans.

In this chapter, we will look closely at the actions of activist Ana Maria Archila, Congresswoman Alexandria Ocasio-Cortez, as well as the Latina activist who led the way, Dolores Huerta. I argue that these women, with their bold and strategic actions, are strengthening our endangered U.S. democracy.

2018 was a year of trauma—lived and remembered—for too many Americans and those who sought refuge in this country. I've covered U.S. immigration policy and its consequences for thirty years. I know that inhumane policies did not begin with the Trump administration. According to data from the Department of Homeland Security, removals were highest during the Obama administration, with 3,094,208 from 2009 to 2016, while the most deportations—if we also include returns—were committed during the Clinton administration, with 12,290,905. Returns are when migrants are detained and immediately returned to their country of origin. Removals are when they are separated from family and communities established in the United States and sent back to their countries of origin, countries that are no longer their homes, places that are often deadly for those who came here for asylum. If those who are returned or removed are dangers to our society, these actions can be justified. But lawyers and activists called out ICE in 2018 over their priorities. Mary Bauer, deputy legal director for the Southern Poverty Law Center, told the *Washington Post*: "It used to be that there was a sense that they were looking for people who had committed serious crimes." The *Washington Post* quoted a 2018 ICE report that noted that ICE apprehended more than 158,000 people in 2018. Many of those apprehended were convicted criminals. But the largest number of criminal convictions were for driving under the influence (DUIs) at approximately 54,000. The next top reasons were "dangerous drugs," other traffic offenses, and immigration violations. "People [are getting deported] in large numbers because of minor traffic violations," said Bauer, declaring that it is "appalling and morally unconscionable that this is the place we find ourselves." While a DUI is not a minor traffic violation, I'd argue that one poor decision that did not result in another's death should not result in expulsion from this country, that the convicted can pay their debt to the community without being cast out of the community.

If deportations weren't at an all-time high, immigrant detentions were. According to ICE statistics acquired by CNN, ICE detained an average of more than 42,000 immigrants per day throughout the 2018 fiscal year. The peak recorded amount before 2018 was 38,000, in 2001. Leaving aside the morality of mass detention, recent reporting, including that from NPR's *Latino USA*, which I host and executive produce, informs us that mistreatment and sexual assault run rampant in detention centers and that the detained have no idea how long they'll be imprisoned. Hopelessness abounds in places where due process is denied.

The Trump administration's immigration policy in 2018 hurt in other ways. Many immigrants who fled violence in their home countries suddenly found their temporary protected status (TPS) terminated. In January, the Trump administration rescinded TPS for nearly 200,000 Salvadorans. In April, the administration announced that in twelve months, 9,000 Nepalese would lose their TPS status. In May, the administration announced that in eighteen months, TPS status would be rescinded for Hondurans. So much security families had been able to create in the United States was wholly undermined by Trump administration policy reversals.

These policies alone filled families with grief. But the April announcement by then–Attorney General Jeff Sessions that he'd told U.S. Attorney offices along the border to enforce a "zero tolerance" policy for people crossing the border undocumented has rattled this country to the core. Suddenly "zero tolerance" meant family separation at the border. When investigative independent news outlet ProPublica shared a smuggled-out audio tape of a six-year-old child desperately calling for officers to call her aunt, that she had the number memorized, and no one would do it; or when Senator Jeff Merkley was denied entry into a detention facility; or when more leaders joined the public outcry against this barbarism as President Trump referred to immigrants as "animals"—suddenly the nation could see clearly what I and other journalists had been reporting on for many years, how the United States government consistently violated the due process and human rights of immigrants at the border and in this nation. The Trump administration is engaging in the same inhumane actions but is doing so despite court orders to cease family separation and to hasten family reunification. In March 2019, we're reading reports that U.S. Customs and Border Protection is *still* separating families.

What makes things even more grotesque now is the Trump administration's persistent criminalization of migrants in both rhetoric and fact. We have a propaganda arm in this administration that every single day, twenty-four-seven, creates a narrative of immigrant threat. Before, I used to want to hear the conversation about immigration during a U.S. president's State of the Union address. Before, we were almost invisible. We were never mentioned. Now, the State of the Union is all about immigrants and immigration. In President Trump's 2019 address he lauded U.S. Immigration and Customs Enforcement (ICE) agents, spotlighted parents whose children were killed violently by undocumented migrants, accused the Mexican government of rounding up migrants to flood our border, and declared a "see-through steel barrier" would be the solution. This new hypervisibility has rendered us invisible because we're talked about as vicious threats. In his day-to-day rhetoric, President Trump presents himself as the man who will save us from the "animals" and will stop America from becoming a "migrant camp."

Frankly, I have a hard time waking up every morning hearing that my community and my family and strangers just like me are being talked about in ways that are foreign and hateful.

In 2018, I embodied everything you're supposed to be afraid of in Trump's America: I'm a journalist, therefore I'm an enemy of the people. I'm an immigrant, therefore I'm invading this country. I'm Mexican, therefore I have some kind of sinister reason to be here. I'm a woman, therefore I am less trustworthy, somehow, or somehow perceived to be problematic. According to Trump, you should fear me and anyone like me. Trump cultivated this fear through speech and action. He is very good at understanding discomfort with demographic change. The problem is, people have allowed messaging around fear to replace what they're actually living with in their own lives. Scapegoating is not new, of course. But in 2018, we contended with a U.S. president who repeatedly messaged "be afraid of these people who don't look like you, who don't speak like you." We're hearing this repeated on Fox News and other outlets. Believers of this rhetoric are not opening their eyes and saying, wow, look at my community. Look at the people who actually live in my community. Am I really afraid of them? Who are these kids that my grandson or daughter is playing with? I believe if they did, it would lessen their fears of their own displacement.

If the problem is fear, I say the solution is speech and action. Latina leaders in 2018 showed us this was the way when many realized they had absolutely nothing to lose and believed they could use their voices for change.

Alexandria Ocasio-Cortez

Women like me aren't supposed to run for office. I wasn't born to a wealthy or powerful family. Mother from Puerto Rico. Dad from the South Bronx. I was born into a place where zip code determines your destiny.
—2018 Alexandria Ocasio-Cortez for Congress ad copy

In July 2018, Bronx-born Alexandria Ocasio-Cortez defeated ten-term Democratic incumbent Joe Crowley in New York's 14th Congressional District with 57 percent of the primary vote. She would go on, at age twenty-nine, to become the youngest woman ever elected to the U.S. Congress. Her strategic actions secured a victory that has led to a sea change in policy discussion and power dynamics in Washington. As *Washington Post* media columnist Margaret Sullivan wrote in January 2019: "[Ocasio-Cortez] has only been on the job for less than two weeks and already has generated more national press coverage than some members of Congress get in their whole careers." In Washington, attention is power, and she has used this intense spotlight to make her "Green New Deal" policy framework a living possibility and not a fringe dream.

I interviewed Ocasio-Cortez twice in 2018, once for my politics podcast *In the Thick* and once for *Latino USA*, a weekly syndicated news magazine that airs on NPR. In both interviews, I queried her about messaging and campaign decisions. She has been both hailed and criticized for her messaging, which is seen as either heroically progressive or socialism at its worst. Critics may despise the content of her speech, but they will praise the efficacy of her campaign message delivery, a potent combination of traditional "shoe-leather" organizing, such as door-knocking, and social media outreach.

In our *In The Thick* interview that took place on July 24, 2018, Ocasio-Cortez shared compelling insights that illuminated her experience as an insurgent candidate. "Fighting a Democratic machine means people are scared to take pictures with you," she said. "It means that when you're walking in a parade, no one wants to be in front of you or next to you." She spoke to the gender divide, noting that the county machines were almost all-male. How, when she realized that the system wasn't going to embrace her, she decided to build her own. "I said, hmm, let me see whose needs aren't being met. Oh, almost everybody's? I'll go organize there."

Organizing means knocking on doors, and a famous picture is that of Ocasio-Cortez's worn-down shoes at the end of the campaign. Winning means galvanizing voters, and she credited much of her success to a "bottom up" approach: winning over young people, who in turn motivated their elders to vote for the candidate. Young people were the first to start organizing on her behalf. "We really touched community organizers who were younger, who were really animated about a lot of issues impacting our generation: student loans, gentrification, income inequality. They started talking to their parents." When I asked her how the young people found out about her, she replied: "Digital. It's where the influence is." Back then, if someone direct messaged her a question via Facebook, she could answer. "Digital was really important because it gave people a direct connection," said Ocasio-Cortez.

Ocasio-Cortez's campaign win is a grassroots organizing story, though one complicated by the fear felt by undocumented immigrants, mixed-status families, and naturalized citizens living in a country with an administration that is targeting them for detention and deportation. For our *Latino USA* episode on October 26, Ocasio-Cortez invited us to see her campaign office and take a walk through the Queens neighborhood between East Elmhurst and Corona. She noted how Latino it was, specifically Colombian, Mexican, and Ecuadorian. "This community is actually one of the most difficult to organize, electorally," said the candidate. "The presence of ICE has created so much fear, it's much more difficult to knock on doors in Corona, because if a stranger is knocking on your door, you do not answer here." She credited the decision to have a listening tour community stop that was open to the neighborhood but closed to the press as a risk worth taking. "I always put my community first," said Ocasio-Cortez. "I got a lot of blowback that week. But you know what the community was telling me that week? Thank you. They thanked me for creating a space for them, because in every other context in politics right now you need to pay $10,000 a plate to get that kind of intimacy with your public official."

Proof of electoral success rests in the numbers. In our *In the Thick* interview, Ocasio-Cortez declared that her campaign expanded the electorate by 68 percent over the previous off-year midterm primary. As she knows, to be successful she needs allies and continued grassroots support. Autopilot is not an option. "Movements cannot be on one person's shoulders," Ocasio-Cortez said in our *In the Thick* interview. "That's the mistake we made with Obama . . . he needed continued grassroots movement and support." If we're to use Ocasio-Cortez's own words as a guide, legislative success will depend upon continued execution of movement-building work. Ocasio-Cortez is showing herself capable of this as she tweets out fundraising appeals for colleagues, especially other freshmen congresspeople, and redirects some of the voluminous attention she receives to them and their policy proposals. She continues to push the possibilities of social media outreach. Ocasio-Cortez will cook up rice and beans or assemble IKEA furniture on Instagram Live on a Sunday night and engage thousands of viewers. You don't often hear members of Congress consistently engaging and referencing their constituents this way. She'll say that these are her constituents. That she's listening to them. Bonding with them. Solidifying her political base.

In my two 2018 interviews with Alexandria Ocasio-Cortez, I seem to have only once caught the candidate off-guard: when I asked her about her father during our *Latino USA* interview. She compared the moment to having someone walk next to you for months and months without that person being acknowledged, then suddenly someone asks, "What does this guy think?" Her father had been deceased for years, but it's clear that he has long been a motivating force in her life. He offered her love, support, and trips to both Puerto Rico and Colonial Williamsburg. She spoke of how when he died, she took jobs in the service industry—e.g., bartending—to support her family. How so much heartbreak and struggle led to this moment.

I can't help but return to the impact her parents and community have had on the congresswoman. She is a middle-class Puerto Rican young woman in New York City. Her parents were highly aware Puerto Ricans, around New York City in the sixties, seventies, and eighties. Puerto Ricans were *the* Latino activists at this time. They ran the show. People forget that the last time—the one and only time—that the crown of the Statue of Liberty was used as a place of protest was when Puerto Rican nationalists placed the flag over her crown in 1977. Ocasio-Cortez takes that Puerto Rican activism and broadens it for her diverse community of constituents in the South Bronx and Queens. In 2019, Alexandria Ocasio-Cortez has taken that radical street activism and actually rooted it in a basic politics-grassroots 101, which is speaking to your neighbors. Organizing your neighbors. Organizing the people in your community. Organizing the people on your block. Then representing those people in the halls of power.

Ana Maria Archila

If there has been a movement that has deployed the power of storytelling to transform the consciousness of a nation, it's the immigrant rights movement.
—Ana Maria Archila, from "The Immigrant
Woman Who Confronted Senator Flake,"
Latino USA, *October 2, 2018*

I interviewed Ana Maria Archila for *Latino USA* after her elevator confrontation. She shared the personal story that had motivated her to speak out, and her professional and volunteer experiences that had pushed her to be at the right place at the right time. As the co-executive director for the Center for Popular Democracy, an umbrella organization in New York City for several social justice organizations, she trains people across the country in "bird-dogging"—a tactic of staking out elected officials in order to engineer a moment for contact. "It's about seeking connection," said Archila. "It's about allowing elected officials to remember who they represent." She had joined several organizations in Washington, DC, that were protesting Judge Brett Kavanaugh's nomination, and had met Maria Gallagher only a few minutes before the two of them were able to corner Senator Jeff Flake in a Senate elevator with the CNN cameras rolling.

On that evening's broadcast, Anderson Cooper declared the encounter "one of those rare instances when a story's emotional center of gravity seemed to shift before our eyes." He then aired an extended cut of the video, in which we again heard Archila's strong and trembling voice:

> What you are doing is allowing someone who actually violated a woman to sit in the Supreme Court . . . you have children in your family . . . think about them. . . . I have two children . . . I cannot imagine that for the next fifty years they will have to have someone in the Supreme Court who has been accused of violating a young girl. What are you doing, sir?

Archila was followed by Maria Gallagher, who cried:

> I was sexually assaulted and nobody believed me . . . look at me when I'm talking to you. You're telling me that my assault doesn't matter!"

Archila often repeated in interviews that the moment was not just about them, that they weren't the only ones telling their stories, that the power was in so many women coming to Washington to tell their stories, to stand in solidarity with Dr. Christine Blasey Ford. As a journalist, I do not attend protests, and I do not advocate for political outcomes. However, I felt compelled to tell, for the first time, my own story of rape.

The Kavanaugh hearings were very challenging for me because it was part of my own reckoning and understanding that I am a survivor. Never before had I spoken publicly about it, but it happened when I was sixteen years old. I think a lot of women in the United States were struggling with traumatic memories. I shared my story for the first time on *In the Thick*. I felt very much like other American women who struggled internally, very quietly, with their own processes. And then there was this reaction, part of what American women do, which is to make it very public, very in your face, take it to the streets, from the suffragettes to the bra-burners in the 1960s. Women in the United States have this way with frontal activism.

When I heard Ana Maria Archila's voice that day, I thought, *Wow, she created this moment with Senator Flake because of the fact that she's actually trained as an activist in the immigrant rights community.* When people talk of intersectionality, that's exactly what it looks like. There's no schism in these two things. In 2006, she and other immigrants, including those without papers, protested against Congressman James Sensenbrenner's anti-immigrant legislation. "Millions of immigrants came out of the shadows, walked out of their jobs, walked out of schools, across the country, everywhere," said Archila in the *Latino USA* interview. She shared how her activism began, in a tiny Port Richmond, Staten Island, storefront. Young people would work twelve-hour days in kitchens or as day laborers, and they'd come to the storefront to take her English classes. She said it was incredibly moving "to be in the presence of people who had dreams, who said, 'I want to learn English and I'm gonna buy myself a motorcycle and I'm gonna do this.'" When she worked with two fifteen year-old boys who'd been mistreated by a boss, who referred to both of them as "Pancho," Archila said at the time: "You and I are going to set this course correct." She was able to help them sue the boss and get back thousands of dollars in stolen wages.

Archila's path led her to the U.S. Capitol and the moment she seized by "bird-dogging" Senator Jeff Flake. Archila struck me with these words: "I didn't even know the voice that was coming out of me. I had never raised my voice in that way. I had never used that tone to talk to anyone." That's trauma. That's what trauma looks like when it's unleashed. And it's very honest. This is the raw power of storytelling. "Young people came out of the shadows to tell these stories. And many of those young people have become young women leaders. They have demonstrated what it looks like to fight both for your country and for your own life and how those two things are one in the same."

Archila and Gallagher spoke up for their lives and for our country. They did not singlehandedly stop the Kavanaugh confirmation. But they shifted the story. They bought time. They let others know, through their example, that our stories matter and could be heard if we told them. For years I'd been waiting for these Latina voices to rise to the top. But they couldn't be doing it without the legacy of those who came before them.

Dolores Huerta

I quit [teaching] because I couldn't stand seeing kids come to class hungry and needing shoes. I thought I could do more by organizing farm workers than by trying to teach their hungry children.
—*Dolores Huerta, from the National Women's History Museum biography*

Alexandria Ocasio-Cortez and Ana Maria Archila stand on the shoulders of generations of Latina activists who stood up for their families, their communities, themselves. In 2018, *Latino USA* aired an interview with the most visible elder activist we have, the eighty-eight-year-old Dolores Huerta, and her daughter, Juana Chavez. Juana interviewed her mother for the piece, and we heard about the special difficulties and epiphanies women activists face at home and in the world.

As a young woman in Stockton, California, Dolores Huerta decided she could do more for her impoverished students, so many of them the children of farm workers, as an organizer than as a teacher. She quit her job, and in 1955 she and visionary organizer and mentor Fred Ross co-founded the Stockton chapter of the Community Services Organization. Later, Huerta started the Agricultural Workers Association (AWA). After Huerta met César Chávez, another CSO officer, they, along with fellow organizer Gilbert Padillo, co-founded the National Farm Workers Association (NFWA). Ultimately they'd merge AWA and NFWA to become the United Farm Workers Organizing Committee (later the United Farm Workers). The United Farm Workers (UFW) staged the Delano Grape Strike in 1965. Because of their efforts, 17 million people boycotted table grapes across the United States. Huerta became famous for her rallying cry of "sí, se puede!" or "yes, we can!"

Huerta's work has been so significant because she fights for workers across the board. She never just fights for Latinos or a single community. Again, solidarity. Intersectionality. I can't overstate how meaningful it was for me to see a Latina raising these issues. I remember seeing César Chávez, and that was great. We were so happy that he was leading the farm workers, but seeing Dolores Huerta felt very real to us. To have a woman right next to him. She may not have had the microphone, but we understood that the woman was always there. Dolores was always there.

But was she there enough for her family? This is the question that haunts every working woman I've known, including myself. We are forever battling the issue of guilt and whether we've done enough for our kids. "I always loved children, I guess that's why I had so many of them," said Dolores Huerta, mother of eleven, in the *Latino USA* interview. "I know there's been lots of criticism . . . if you love children so much . . . you sure didn't do a good job of taking care of them. In my work, I had relatives taking care of them, I had friends, sometimes people I barely met, helping me take care of my children. But, they all survived."

Huerta spoke of the major fights she had with her husband over dishwashing, whether daughters should do that first instead of homework. Huerta spoke of the difference in attitudes when men were recent immigrants, as opposed to her family, who had been in California for several generations. While we didn't have this particular fight in my household, I know the struggle is real when it's time to shift gears and be present at home. Dolores Huerta needed to know she was worthy enough to stand next to Robert F. Kennedy and say *I'm right there with you, Mr. Attorney General. I'm going to educate you.* But at the same time, the ego that pushes us to do this important work can take us away from our families. We're so busy fighting for visibility and power and equality that we can neglect domestic roles that require our nurturance, our time and patience as caregivers.

We cannot save our country and lose our families. We cannot save the U.S. Constitution but lose our partners or our kids. The beautiful thing is that we have a generation of women who are talking publicly about these struggles. As Latinas, we're trying to model new ways of achieving this balance. We do so hoping our kids—like Huerta's, like mine—ultimately will understand why the sacrifices were happening. If that reckoning comes too late, there are mistakes that can't be forgiven. All of us—women and men—need to be present in the sphere of those closest to us: our families and friends and the village that raises us.

Dolores Huerta's words from her *Latino USA* interview with her daughter Juana are always in my head. She said there's "something you can't walk away from, and that's people power." She helped organize the most powerless, invisible group of people in the United States: undocumented farm workers. The most unlikely group of people to ever be able to unify and pose a challenge to power. They did that. People power is real. People organized are a mighty force.

This is not a drill. Our democracy is under threat. I think many of us are just coming to terms with the dangers. What does it mean if the United States is the world's greatest democracy and it's under threat? What do we have to do? I put my faith in action. As journalists, we work to inspire people to believe in and value their own participation in democracy. With strong journalism, Americans are hearing themselves and their stories in voices they understand. I can do this. I have a voice. My voice also means I should vote. I love to imagine that through the work I'm doing, I'm inspiring people to be engaged in that democracy.

As someone who wasn't born in this country, as someone who had to raise my right hand and pledge allegiance to take up arms and defend this country, I think we have to remember our duties, especially civic duty. A great democracy would be everyone feeling fired up and engaged to vote and take on other kinds of activism. I think about certain public policy changes that can create buy-in and equity. Expanded access to voting, including online voting registration. Election Day as a national holiday. Voter protection protocols that ensure the will of voters is respected. A reassessment of the Electoral College.

I consider the recent work of Latina activists and I am hopeful. In some ways, Latina activists are the most invisible activists in this country. They're still struggling for basic visibility in our culture. Yet Alexandria Ocasio-Cortez and Ana Maria Archila stand on the shoulders of Dolores Huerta and create new narratives for what political engagement looks like. In this chapter, I could have focused on so many changemaking Latinas, including Parkland teen activist Emma Gonzalez, Los Angeles teen activist Edna Chavez, and freshman Texas congresswoman Veronica Escobar. I could have focused on great American black women heroes of resistance Harriet Tubman or Ida B. Wells, for the liberation of black women liberates us all. Or the work of Susan B. Anthony and other white suffragettes who laid the groundwork for all we do as women voters in this electoral system. The Latinas I wrote about are not the first to speak out. There is nothing new here. But this new evolving leadership is inspiring a new generation of Americans. These Latina leaders are specifically empowering to Latina immigrants, and they are inspiring women—and men—all across America, no matter their race, age, sexual orientation, religion, or national origin. They are leaders for all of us, and they are changing history. When women of color, especially Latinas, have had enough of a situation, when they have reached the boiling point, look out, because they understand they have nothing to lose and everything to gain.

That's when it gets fascinating.

WHAT BLACK WOMEN TEACH US
ABOUT DEMOCRACY

Andra Gillespie and Nadia E. Brown

I f you google the words "Alabama 2017 Senate election black women," the growing mainstream perception of black women as political saviors of American democracy quickly becomes apparent. The first few headlines speak for themselves: "Why Black Women Voters Showed Up for Doug Jones;" "Long Before Sinking Roy Moore's Candidacy, Black Women in Alabama Were a Force for Change;" "Twitter Thanks #Black-Women for Voting for Democrat Doug Jones in Alabama Senate Election." The last headline nods to social media, incorporating the hashtag that started trending after the election. The takeaway message is that black women's high turnout and 98 percent Democratic voting rate in the 2017 special election played a critical role in Doug Jones's narrow victory.

Does black women's near unanimous Democratic vote choice represent a kind of groupthink? If not, what are the rational reasons that black women are such a cohesive voting bloc?

Even if the very vocal praising of black women in politics by political commentators and Democratic Party leadership were new, for those who study African American women in politics, black women's prominent role was not a surprise. The truth is that black women are the most loyal Democratic voting bloc in the United States—and have been for a long time. The phenomenon started way before Donald Trump became president.[1]

Race and Gender Gaps Among American Voters

To best understand what motivates black women's political participation, it is important to think about them intersectionally—to explore the ways that their preferences and patterns of activity distinguish them from white women and also black men. Political analysts started to notice differences in voting patterns between men and women in 1980. Women were voting for Democrats at higher rates than men, leading to the creation of a formal definition of the term "gender gap": the percentage of women voting Democratic minus the percentage of men voting Democratic.[2] Scholars speculated that the gap detected in 1980 may have been the result of the Republican Party's more conservative policy positions on abortion and equal rights for women. As the pattern persisted, researchers presented a number of different rationales to explain the gap, many of which focused on the ways that gender socialization and household roles may prompt men and women to prioritize issues such as war or education differently. Given the state of partisan issue ownership, they proffered that women prioritized issues related to their roles as mothers and caretakers (e.g., education, health care, etc.), which were and continue to be perceived as issues on which Democrats have an advantage.

In early gender gap studies, scholars ignored the possibility that the gender gap might manifest itself differently across different racial or ethnic groups. Racial blind spots no doubt contributed to this, but Barbara Norrander, in her essay "The History of the Gender Gaps," also points to earlier findings that may have steered some public opinion scholars from even considering the relationship between race and gender gaps.[3] She notes that early research about civil rights and gender did not detect a relationship between gender and support for civil rights.

Moreover, strong support for the Democratic Party within black communities also masks small but important gender differences. The African American vote has broken for the Democratic Party since the New Deal, and almost unanimously so since Lyndon Johnson shepherded the Civil Rights Act of 1964 through the legislative process. Johnson's support for civil rights (and Barry Goldwater's opposition to it) solidified Democrats' perceptual advantage on civil rights, an advantage that has not changed since. As such, many researchers have not seen the need to explore the nuances in black political behavior.

If investigators had dug further, they would have found that the gender gap in the black community predates popular observations that denote 1980 as the start of that phenomenon nationally. Our data analysis shows that with the exception of 1980, the gender gap was wider in the black community from 1972–96. The gender gap narrowed among blacks (and did not keep pace with whites) from 2000–08, but widened in 2012 and 2016. Blacks had a wider gender gap than whites in 2012, while blacks and whites had the same gender gap in 2016.

This data suggests the necessity of a revision of some of the gender gap narratives in previous elections. For instance, the story of the 2004 election is the rise of the "security mom," or the married, suburban white woman who voted Republican in 2004 out of a sense of concern about national security as a result of the 9/11 attacks. To be sure, the gender gap does narrow overall from 2000–04 and among whites because white women were less likely to vote Democratic. However, the black gender gap narrows because black men were more likely to vote Democratic in 2004. It is important to remember that even when overall trends mask racial and gender differences, we should examine the trends further to see if the explanations for certain observed behaviors ring true across different groups.

If we move beyond presidential vote choice to look at congressional vote choice, we continue to find gender gaps across all racial groups. There are years, like 1982 and 1992, when the black gender gap far outpaced the white gender gap; years like 2008, where the black and white gender gaps are identical; and years like 2018, where the black gender gap pales in comparison to the white gender gap.

The most interesting observation is the difference in the Hispanic gender gap relative to the other groups. Exit polls did not consistently capture enough Hispanic respondents to report gender gaps before 1988. Since then, the Hispanic gender gap has been inconsistent. In some years, like 2012, we see a big difference in the Democratic voting behavior of Latinas and Latinos, with Latinas being more likely to vote Democratic. In many years, though, the differences between Latinas and Latinos are negligible. What is surprising is the finding that among those who answered the exit polls in the years 1990, 1992, 2006, and 2008, Latinos were slightly more likely to vote Democratic than Latinas. We acknowledge, though, that some of these observed differences may relate to sampling decisions in exit polls that do not effectively capture the entire Hispanic electorate.

Overall, blacks remain the most loyal Democratic voting constituency. But black women have been the most loyal of the loyal Democratic voters for two generations now—which provides important context to the now common refrain that black women are the backbone of the Democratic coalition.

Gender, Turnout, and Structural Inequalities

But we cannot talk about vote choice without considering voter turnout. Anemic turnout among African Americans means that even if 90 percent of those blacks who do turn out vote Democratic, their votes, in concert with others, may not lead to Democratic victories, especially in places where blacks do not comprise a majority of the electorate.

Hillary Clinton won the popular vote in the 2016 presidential election by nearly 3 million votes. However, she lost the all-crucial Electoral College vote—which actually decides who wins the presidency—by 77,744 votes. These nearly 78,000 votes reflect Donald Trump's margin of victory in the three states (Michigan, Wisconsin, and Pennsylvania) whose electoral votes allowed him to surpass the 270 votes needed to claim the White House.

If we were talking about an election in a small or sparsely populated jurisdiction, finding an additional 78,000 votes might be an impossible task. But in a presidential election—and especially in states that had major cities with large black populations, it is hard to see how the Clinton campaign did not have opportunities to improve voter turnout. For instance, in Wayne County, Michigan, which includes the City of Detroit, only 59 percent of registered voters in the county turned out for the 2016 election. In Philadelphia, only 64 percent of registered voters turned out to vote. And in Milwaukee, only 56 percent of voters cast a ballot in the 2016 election. Had turnout rates in these Democratic cities been higher, the outcome of the 2016 presidential election might have been different.

Here, structural considerations and institutional racism, in combination with gender, presented particular challenges to black voters—amplifying the importance of black women voters. In the wake of the passage of the Voting Rights Act (VRA), self-reported black voter turnout (as a percentage of the voting-age population) continued to lag white voter turnout. Scholars attributed this difference to the cumulative effects of historical discrimination. They anticipated natural lags in turnout in the immediate wake of the VRA passage. Later, they attributed black-white differences in voter turnout to socioeconomic factors like lower income and education levels, which also have their roots in discrimination. Others considered the role of psychological factors, arguing that a sense of empowerment and efficacy could increase voter turnout.

The turnout gap between blacks and whites narrowed considerably in the Obama era. Blacks turned out at a slightly lower but nearly identical rate to whites in 2008; and in 2012, for the first time ever, they reported voting at higher rates than whites. The turnout gap between blacks and white reemerged in 2016, when blacks were nearly 6 percentage points less likely than whites to report having participated in that year's election.

This popular narrative of the relationship between race and voter turnout seems simple: blacks have historically voted less often than whites, directly because of discrimination or voter suppression in some cases and indirectly because discrimination disadvantaged blacks socioeconomically, making it more difficult for them to vote; black turnout increased in 2008 and 2012 because of excitement about Barack Obama's candidacy, and it fell in 2016 because of a combination of Obama not being on the ballot, Hillary Clinton not being an inspiring candidate, and voter suppression tactics, like the implementation of strict voter ID laws.

The discussion of how the manifestation of discrimination affects turnout warrants a deeper examination, though—one that incorporates gender differences into the discussion. Using data from the U.S. Census Bureau's Current Population Survey, we find that gender gaps have long existed in both voter registration and turnout. Black women are more likely to report being registered to vote, and they are more likely to report having voted in elections than black men. Moreover, the gender gap in turnout appears to have increased ever so slightly in more recent elections.

Structural factors help to explain these registration and turnout gaps. Keep in mind that these figures are reported as a percentage of all adults, not just those who are eligible to vote. This means that these figures include people who cannot vote because they are not citizens and people who cannot vote because they have had their voting rights taken away because of felony convictions. Felon disenfranchisement has a disproportionate impact on the black electorate, particularly black men. Political scientist Wendy Smooth, in her essay "Intersectionality in Electoral Politics: A Mess Worth Making" noted, "Using an intersectionality framework, the larger percentages of African-American women voting must be considered in tandem with the loss of voting rights for an ever-increasing number of African-American men through felony disenfranchisement laws."[4]

To address this disparity, it is helpful to calculate voter turnout as a percentage of eligible voters who cast ballots, not just those who are age eighteen and older. Yet, even when we account for eligibility, we still see gender and race gaps. Using data compiled by the Center for American Women and Politics at Rutgers University to look at voter turnout by race and gender in presidential elections going back to 1984, we find that though black women have consistently turned out at higher rates than black men, the voter turnout rates of both groups increased at about the same rate until 2012 and fell at about the same rate in 2016. Most important, though, we see that in the last six presidential election cycles, black women's turnout rates have consistently rivaled (and in the past decade, sometimes surpassed) the turnout rates of whites, particularly white men.

Black Women as Political Candidates

But if we are to gain a deeper understanding of black women's political participation, we must, of course, look beyond just voting. The crowd-sourced "Black Women in Politics" database boasted of a searchable list of 468 black women candidates who ran for office in 2018. The 2018 midterm elections were dubbed a new "year of the woman," in part because of the critical mass of new members of Congress who were women of color. Thirteen of the forty new female members of the House of Representatives in 2019 were women of color. Five of these new members were black women. As of the 116th Congress, the Congressional Black Caucus is nearly evenly split between male and female members, a level of gender parity that cannot be rivaled by the partisan caucuses in either chamber of Congress.

In 1968, Shirley Chisholm (D-NY) became the first black woman to be elected to Congress. The following year, Chisholm would later go on to co-found the Congressional Black Caucus (CBC), and then in 1970, she would become a co-founder of the National Organization for Women (NOW). Chisholm famously stood up to racist and patriarchal politics, lambasting sexists and racists alike while using her voice to challenge structures that marginalized subordinate groups. The first black woman to seek a major party's nomination for president, Chisholm took on the leadership of the Congressional Black Caucus—black men—who believed that the first black person to run for president should be a black man. Likewise, leading white feminists of the time failed to support her candidacy. Chisholm's deeper belief in the transformative power of democracy sustained her during a political career in which friends and colleagues did not support her because she was black woman. The acknowledgment that the playing field was not equal did not deter her. Indeed, Chisholm famously said, "If they don't give you a seat at the table, bring a folding chair."

Chisholm's legacy is the 25 black women currently serving in the 116th U.S. Congress. These women brought their folding chairs and several have had a seat at the table for a sustained period of time because of the groundwork that Chisholm laid. In the fifty-one years since Chisholm was elected, there have been 45 black women elected to serve in the House of Representatives (including three nonvoting delegates) and two to the Senate. The vast majority of women of color to be elected to Congress are black women. The Center for American Women in Politics notes that there have been 73 ethno-racial minority women who have served in the House of Representatives. Given black women's overrepresentation in the House of Representatives compared with that of their ethno-racial minority sisters, would Chisholm celebrate these accomplishments today?

The glass is rather half full. Today, women comprise 23.7 percent of Congress. There are 25 women in the U.S. Senate and 102 in the House of Representatives, the vast majority of whom are Democrats. Indeed, the current Congress is the largest class of women ever elected. Women have made tremendous inroads to elected office since Jeannette Rankin, a white woman, was elected to Congress in 1916. A total of 153 blacks have served in Congress, mostly in the House of Representatives. Since 1965, Congress has become increasingly diverse in nearly every legislative session. And with 52 black voting members of the House of Representatives, the proportion of blacks in the current House is approaching parity with the proportion of blacks in the U.S. population today.

Conversely, the glass is half empty. While nonwhites are 39 percent of the population, 78 percent of members of Congress are non-Hispanic whites, whereas this population is only 61 percent of the U.S. population. Increased racial diversity in Congress, while on the rise, still has not eradicated the structural inequities that plague black women in American politics. Much of what Chisholm advocated for still challenges many black women elected officials as well as black women citizens.

The electoral power of black women has largely been a story of voters, not candidates. The misnomer surrounding the 2017 special election of Doug Jones—and others—is that there has been an 11 percent drop in black women's support of the Democratic Party between 2016 and 2017.

"Power of the Sister Vote," a 2017 poll conducted by the Black Women's Roundtable and *Essence* magazine, found that black women believe more than ever that neither political party supports them. While black women vote at high rates (94 percent voted for Hillary Clinton—a figure that represented 64 percent of all black women eligible to vote, this was a 6 percent drop from black women's historically high turnout in 2012), the 2016 presidential election witnessed a decline of black voter turnout for the first time in twenty years. There is a widening chasm between white and black female voters that mirrors America's unspoken, yet persistent, whitewashing of feminism. Black women consistently vote at high proportions and for the Democratic candidate. Despite these distinctions, the persistent underrepresentation of women of color among officeholders raises important questions regarding the way gender, race, and ethnicity continue to affect candidate's electoral successes.

Still, black women's visibility in electoral politics, especially the numbers of black women in leadership positions, was manifold in 2016 and 2018. Take for example, Donna Brazile and Marcia Fudge's highly publicized roles in the Democratic National Committee, or the election of Senator Kamala Harris (the second black woman elected to the Senate), or Ilhan Omar's election to Congress, the first Somali-American female to hold this distinction. Seven black women currently serve as mayors of America's 100 largest cities. Of the 2,131 women state legislators, 312 are black. These electoral gains happened at a point in time when black women's median wages were $36,735 per year compared to the median wages of $60,388 annually for white men.[5] They are also occurring while levels of inequality and discussions of racial and gendered prejudices are paramount. Not only do black women still often face significant challenges to securing political representation and advocates who will champion their issues, but simultaneously President Donald Trump is waging a public battle against four newly elected progressive junior congresswomen—two of whom are black (Ilhan Omar [D-MI] and Ayanna Pressley [D-MA]).

Despite these challenges, black women officeholders have been able to leverage their identities to effectively represent their communities. Black women are inclusive legislators who champion policy preferences that affect the most marginalized in society. In the legislature, black women tend to push legislative agendas that differ from their black male and white female colleagues. They draw on their distinct racial and gender identities to promote policy innovations aimed at bettering the lives of all African Americans. And they frame their advocacy in both racialized and gendered terms. Nadia Brown and Sarah Gershon found in their 2016 study "Exploratory Study of Minority Congresswomen's Websites; Biographies" that black congresswomen are known to discuss issues such as domestic violence, children, and the economically marginalized in ways that acknowledge the differential experiences of and policy impacts on women of color.[6] And Alvin Tillery demonstrates in his recent essay "How the Congressional Black Caucus Used Twitter in the 113th Congress" that the most consistent indicator of black congressional discussion of racial issues on Twitter is gender.[7] Indeed, it is black congresswomen who are two-and-a-half times more likely to engage with Black Lives Matter activism and issues on Twitter than their male counterparts. These findings, among others, demonstrate that electing black women leads to substantive policy changes, dynamic symbolic engagement, and inclusive advocacy for disenfranchised and underserved communities: to the extent that more black women have been elected, disenfranchised populations are ensured greater voice in the body politic.[8]

The roots of black women's distinctiveness run deep and wide. The manifestation of structural inequalities, and racial and gender discrimination, all have implications for how many black women turn out and for whom they vote. It also has implications for whether black women seek elected positions of leadership and how they govern once they are in those positions. These experiences provide black women with a different set of motivations for their political decision-making. In part because of their perceived resilience to the structural inequalities that beset black communities as a whole, black women play a unique role in American politics. Successful black women candidates stand on the shoulders of countless, nameless black women who demonstrate their power from grassroots activism to the voting booth. And they often achieve large progressive political outcomes with few resources. But it is incorrect to believe that black women's efforts to challenge the existing political status quo happens with ease or is done out of a benevolence for the American polity. To be sure, black women are magical—but they would not have to perform political magic if the political terrain were equal for all Americans.

ENGINES OF DEMOCRACY: RACIAL JUSTICE AND CULTURAL POWER

Rashad Robinson

W hen we talk about democracy, we often talk about its importance in terms of its outcomes. The conventional thinking goes: once we have a true democracy, democracy will produce progress. But the more pressing question is: *What produces true democracy?*

We need to put just as much thought and effort into that question if the next decade's fight over democracy is going to be strategic and successful. One answer is to understand racial justice as a strategy for securing, powering, and producing democracy, rather than merely as an eventual outcome of it. Racial justice movements have tremendous capacity to both disrupt unjust norms and establish norms that favor justice and equity, which means they must figure largely into any strategy to protect and expand democracy. That requires investing in both the communities they represent and in the different types of power necessary for them to win—from the power to influence policy and political candidates, to the power to influence cultural norms and corporate practices.

The Role of Cultural Power in Politics

I assumed the helm of Color Of Change in May 2011. It was at an important moment in the life of the left—a painful moment of missed opportunity that would come to haunt us, one that dramatizes an indispensable insight about the fight for democracy: the role of cultural power.

At the time, the organized backlash against the diverse and hopeful President Obama coalition had just entered a new phase of power following the 2010 midterm success of the Tea Party. The left (unsuccessfully, in the end) was trying to figure out how to prevent the Koch-backed political insurgency of the Tea Party from derailing progress on a range of issues

related to health care, social equity, economic security, and the environment. Activists across the country were putting inequality center stage as
a winning issue for 2012, culminating in the Occupy Wall Street moment and the popular banner of the "99%." Both helped us win back
some degree of moral high ground and cultural momentum going into
the election.

Yet, at the very same time, "birtherism" and other fantastical attacks
against President Obama were proving successful in undermining his very
legitimacy in the minds of millions of Americans, as well as signature
achievements like Obamacare and the denuclearization of Iran. Birtherism was just one of many political ploys, mainstreamed through popular
culture, that would exploit racial attitudes in order to build right-wing political power. It was one of the leading ideas in an overall onslaught of
false symbols, false scandals, false threats, and false narratives. This right-
wing strategy undermined public confidence in the idea of diversity in
our democracy as a force for good, and empowered attacks on anyone who
challenged or competed with white, male power. It's an engine still running
on all cylinders today.

While the Tea Party and Occupy had popularized their ideas about
the economy and channeled public support at different success rates, Color
Of Change saw a new threat: the mainstreaming of deeply anti-democratic
ideas at an ever-larger scale, rising across several powerful and popular
cultural channels. All of these anti-democratic ideas were rooted in race—
from revisiting the role of religion in politics, to questioning who gets
federal funding, to who counts in the census and votes in elections, and
even who is loyal to the country. We believed these forces were powerful
enough to turn a defensive backlash against President Obama into a highly
offensive assault on progress, democracy, and freedom.

In the racist "birther" charade led by Donald Trump, we saw the danger of someone who was both steadily rising in his cultural profile and
also willing to stir up a blatantly racist frenzy for personal gain and political base-building, while also validating that approach as an effective
strategy. Trump wasn't only on conservative talk radio or Fox News. He
was on NBC—prime time. Every week, NBC enjoyed their profits while
The Apprentice positioned Donald Trump as a serious, competent, and ju-
dicious businessman—someone to trust and take seriously. While Obama

had been a unifier across race—in his political organizing, policy agenda, and media presence—racializing Obama to his core made the Obama legacy a liability for the right to exploit rather than an asset for the left to rely on.

Trump's political screen test worked: it demonstrated that the networks had no rules or limits when it came to giving credence to race baiting. They allowed their networks to be used as vehicles for race-based attacks on Obama, despite all the progress on racial equity they claimed to have made. It also tested well in the electoral context, popularizing racism as a powerful organizing platform for driving dangerous changes in political power in local and state races during the 2012 elections, the 2014 midterms, and in 2016.

But you can't see the impact of culture on politics if you're only looking at the impact of politics on politics. Color Of Change launched a campaign to hold NBC accountable and end the legitimacy they were giving to both birtherism and Trump. Yet, it was extremely difficult to get other progressive organizations to engage in our campaign—to see outside the world of pure politics and take on *The Apprentice* as a dangerous political vehicle. Consequently, we could not hold NBC accountable and interrupt the political rise of Donald Trump before it began, nor disrupt the dangerous political discourse he was popularizing as an insurgent and entertaining form of "truth telling."

There was a line between those who did and didn't think what Trump was doing really mattered. Partly because culture didn't matter in how many institutional leaders and political influencers thought about politics. But also because the politics of racism didn't matter to them, either. They thought the country was past the point of explicit racists being able to gain ground and become powerful politically.

Racial justice organizations knew better. We were painfully aware of how race, politics, and democracy have always been intertwined. But too many people on the left thought racist attacks on political leaders of color couldn't really hurt us, and would dissolve into irrelevancy once we took control of the things that really mattered in politics, the important stuff: the policy fights, the news cycle of the day, the politicians who were (it was assumed) going to win. In the end, we heard the same exact thing repeatedly: *Donald Trump? He's just a TV star; what damage could he possibly do?*

Investing in Cultural Power

The obvious lessons for the left are not to sideline issues of race while, at every turn, the right wing is building a race-based case for rolling back democracy, and also to remember that, historically, the fight for racial justice has always led the way to progress that benefits everyone.

Racial justice is a powerful American narrative. It inspires people to grow, motivates people to participate in broad coalitions, and helps people to find value, peace, and power in one another. It also mobilizes people to change systems and change history like few other passions can. Racial justice has powered corporate accountability, workplace change, criminal justice reform, and the expansion of democracy and social programs that strengthen all communities.

The less obvious lesson for the left has to do with the power of culture to shape democracy, and the power of media to shape culture. Conservatives love to promote the boogeyman of Hollywood as a proxy for the dangerous and corrupting cultural dominance of the left. But it is actually painful to consider how little of the media landscape the left truly "owns" and influences, compared to the right wing and the neoliberal center. We have not invested in it or believed in it.

As a result, we cannot win a game we are not really playing. We cannot compare the occasional shout-out to a progressive cause on a popular TV show to the nonstop racial stereotypes, moralizing attacks on poor people, mythologies about work and the economy, dismissiveness toward activism, and endless stream of anti-progressive ideas spewed across the entire television landscape every single day. Nor can we possibly compare the political influence of new progressive voices on television news with the outsized political impact of entire right-wing news platforms, like Fox News and talk radio, which have mainstreamed extremist ideas over two decades and also mainstreamed the propagation of conspiracy theories (from birtherism to Benghazi).

The latter established their place in people's lives as a cultural phenomenon, much more than a political one, largely because they were tied into deeper social networks and tapped into the internal logic and base-building potential of faith institutions, business networks, lifestyle social clubs, and fan bases organized around popular culture (e.g., heavily police-influenced, crime-focused television dramas, which promote highly inaccurate ideas about crime, race, politics, and democratic freedoms). Meanwhile, the prospect of supporting independent media that could tie into the communities of the Obama coalition was never taken seriously by most political consultants, strategists, and operatives on the left, and nor was the need to make interventions in the rules and norms of popular culture (outside of the LGBTQ context).

We failed our stated vision for gaining political power when we failed to invest in engaging popular cultural channels and in helping to scale up culturally rooted media outlets with the ability to educate, agitate, motivate, and ultimately expand the progressive coalition (e.g., small town press, online subcultures, Black-owned radio stations, and religious media networks).

NBC, whether through *The Apprentice* or *Saturday Night Live*, truly failed the public by enabling the rise of Trump politics—as did many of the broadcast media industry's corporate executives who joked throughout 2016 that Trump was dangerous for society but great for profits. But the left shares part of the blame because we did not invest in the infrastructure to hold those media outlets accountable—to change the rules and norms of the broadcast media industry so that its platforms could not be so easily played by the right wing, nor find so much profit in aiding them. Those who advocated for these strategies could not gain the momentum they needed when the moment called for it, and when the opportunity to strike was hot.

Creating just and effective guardrails for *media* in politics is no less important than doing so for *money* in politics. Media accountability is critical for democracy: whether the medium is television, tech platforms, publication, or others. Not censorship. Not purity. Rather, mechanisms that ensure fairness, equity, and outcomes based on the public interest, rather than partisan interests or corporate interests. And racial justice is highly relevant here, as always, because holding both new and old media platforms accountable to the movement for racial justice is a much stronger proposition than holding them accountable to the more abstract principles of democracy. Efforts to bring Silicon Valley to the table, and hobble ALEC from propagating voter suppression, both escalated when the narrative of racial justice was leading the charge.

To that end, we must never merely accept the business model of corporate media as corporations themselves define it, but rather fight to hold them accountable to powerful, people-powered movements that demand more of them and can set firm expectations with consequences. Holding corporations accountable when it comes to racial justice invariably holds them in check when it comes to standards of truth and equity in the service of the public interest, which help prevent the most dangerous political narratives from taking hold of the mainstream. On the other hand, when we let profit alone drive the corporate media's values and practices, we find them enabling the demonizing of people of color, intentionally or not, which is the linchpin of any successful assault on American democracy. In this way, democracy may best be served by a movement that, on the face of it, may not be about democracy at all.

This accountability strategy must run parallel with an equally critical strategy of investing in the cultural and media channels that capture the public imagination on our own terms—channels we own that, through larger cultural channels, put us in direct engagement with people we are organizing and aiming to make more powerful in politics.

Winning with Cultural Power

Building and leveraging cultural power is a precondition for driving major system change, including democratic freedom. One example is the strategy to end the matrix of norms and policies that have led to the criminal justice system's devastating economic, emotional, and physical impact on Black, Brown, and poor communities, and on democracy itself.

The movement for transforming our criminal justice system broke through and ushered in the current period of progress by using the power of a racial justice narrative to create a range of leverage points beyond policy alone. We applied the racial justice strategy to corporate accountability (making the bail industry toxic and less able to do business and defend the status quo of financial exploitation and mass incarceration driven by unnecessary money bail); electoral accountability (replacing status quo defenders and enablers with true reformers in prosecutor races across the country); and to cultural leverage (turning the public consensus against the status quo by creating undeniable and un-ignorable validation of both the reality of injustice and our vision for change—from amplifying cell phone videos of everyday people on the street to engaging major cultural influencers). In fact, the corporate accountability and electoral accountability strategies, let alone progress on the policy front, would not have been possible without a cultural strategy exciting participation among people not initially interested in "political issues" at all. It was the combination of investing in cultural power, and then translating that power into both corporate accountability and electoral momentum. A ballot initiative to restore voting rights in Florida, for example, was mostly the outcome of a racial justice movement, not a democracy reform movement.

More to the point: It was critical to advance the understanding of the criminal justice system as a corrupt, racist system that represented an unchecked assault on all of our freedoms—including our freedom to vote and participate in democracy. The criminal justice system first had to be widely understood as a fundamentally disempowering mechanism of control and sabotage targeting Black communities and other vulnerable communities—an extension of the brutal, senseless, immoral, and destructive history of racial oppression that has held the entire country back. It was the larger fight for freedom, a cultural turn toward racial justice as a standard for well-being in society at large, which brought about the conditions in which democratic reforms could also take hold. The fight against voter suppression took on a new level of passion, and found a new level of momentum, because of the larger racial justice framework that racial justice movements had elevated to a new level.

We must remember that Nixon's war on drugs was first and foremost a war to undermine and neutralize his political threats. His team realized that by demeaning Black people in the eyes of other Americans (a cultural strategy), they could then destroy the organization of Black communities and therefore the Black political base (a political strategy). This was going to be easier and also far more rewarding for Republicans in the long term, they concluded, than simply attacking Black voting rights unto themselves (a policy strategy).

The national movement to elect progressive prosecutors, and reject status quo prosecutors, is an outcome of using this cultural strategy in reverse: using cultural channels to build a much wider investment in the fate of Black people and other people of color in the wake of police murders and other injustices, and then translating that momentum into winning elections in which racial justice can be the defining issue both in terms of motivating participation and choosing among candidates. A cultural rejection of the criminal justice status quo, combined with motivating

local instances of injustice—Sandra Bland in Houston, Laquan Mc-
Donald in Chicago, Tamir Rice in Cleveland, Eric Garner in New York,
and so many more—both stoked demand for a new kind of leadership *and*
cleared the way for it. It renewed trust in the leadership of organized communities of people of color who have been suffering from the criminal
justice system status quo. It also renewed trust in the political figures those
communities supported and could hold accountable.

Each progressive prosecutor who emerged became more than just another politician. They became symbols and vehicles—manifestations of
a movement—that would finally expose and overturn the status quo
(e.g., failing to hold police accountable, depriving people's freedom
through exploitative money bail) and elevate the visionary ideas that once
seemed impossible to mainstream (e.g., massive decarceration, alternative
sentencing, community investment). But the engine that gives them power
is the immense, well-organized cultural force of the larger racial justice
movement, reinforced as a powerful norm through multiple media channels and also on-the-ground experiences in cultural spaces.

Conservatives have long used racism to build cultural power and win
elections, and now we have used racial justice to do the same. Whether
the campaigns are for prosecutors, or candidates for governor like Stacey
Abrams and Andrew Gillum, racial justice is giving greater moral weight
to political campaigns, and ultimately greater weight to the need for true
democracy in America.

Corporate Accountability Is Culture

Racial justice must be understood as a powerful intervention in moving
our democracy forward, both directly (as in the case described above) and
indirectly (as in the case of corporate accountability). Racial justice is a
critical path toward achieving the level of corporate accountability that
can lead to major democratic reform and justice.

Unchecked capitalism has allowed corporations to run our democracy.
If we do not build movements powerful enough to challenge the written
and unwritten rules of corporations—shaping the parameters in which
they operate—then we will never have the power to win structural change
on any issue, including democracy itself.

We must first weaken the cultural loyalty that corporations have established with so many Americans, while at the same time turning people's attitudes toward demanding corporate accountability. Not merely embracing and propagating anti-corporate attitudes. But more importantly, embedding in millions of people's minds and hearts the motivation to see corporations play their part in creating an equitable world, and a deep desire and affinity for participating in movements capable of making them do it.

How can this be achieved in a strategic, effective way? Corporations play a clear role in attacking democracy. But corporations also play a major role in sustaining and worsening the forces of racial inequity, a role that presents among the starkest and truest pictures of the dangers of corporate power. Media corporations—whether news, entertainment, or social media—saturate our culture with stereotypes and racist misinformation, now widely understood to play a role in escalating division, hate, and violence.

Corporations hurt our communities in a thousand ways—from widening the racial wealth gap to widening the racial health and achievement gap—and yet they are incentivized toward offering up fake solutions for injustice that we allow them to pass off as real. They are celebrated for sending bottled water to victims of poisoned public water in Flint, Michigan, but they face no consequences for dodging the taxes needed to fix the water system or for causing any of the pollution that led to its harmful effects. Corporations pay pennies in donations to civil rights organizations: the silence of those organizations is easily bought with no real concessions or social fixes exchanged. So it's an easy trade for corporations to avoid doing anything real to rectify their racially exploitative or harmful practices.

Corporations are also incentivized to expand exploitation rather than remedy it. The past and present of work in America has been dependent on Black servitude, from domestic work to the factories and the fields. Today, we see corporations trying to write the exploitation of our labor—and all workers' labor—into the law in permanent ink. And we know that undermining workers is another means to undermining democracy. As work changes, corporations are trying to change the rules of work, which means we must create a level of cultural power strong enough to prevent them from doing it.

Again, one of our strongest yet most unrealized levers is racial justice: powering movements to fight the rampant rise of unpaid prison labor, the exploitation of fast-food workers, college basketball players, and more. It's a leading edge for making corporate accountability an American cultural norm, and thereby decreasing corporate power in our democracy. But this can happen only if we invest in the ability of communities of color to lead and win those fights.

The threats to democracy we face must often be fought first as cultural fights, which means they must be fought as fights that may not—on the face of it—seem to have anything to do with democracy at all. Yet those are the fights in which the power to save and improve democracy is forged. We have seen cultural momentum on the right make heroes out of villains, make lies accepted as truth, and swing an election. Waiting to invest in these movements, especially racial justice movement, until we improve democracy will only lead us to lose even more of our democracy than we have lost already.

CIVIC AND ENVIRONMENTAL EDUCATION: PROTECTING THE PLANET AND OUR DEMOCRACY

Judy Braus[1]

O ne of my most pivotal educational experiences did not happen in a classroom. As a teenager in Cincinnati I helped organize a cleanup of the Little Miami River, a tributary of the Ohio River that flows through gorges, forests, and farmlands in the southeast part of the state. The cleanup was a big deal for a bunch of high school students. We organized hundreds of volunteers to pick up discarded tires, drowned shopping carts, and other trash. The National Guard hauled out the big stuff, like rusted cars, tractors, and refrigerators. By all accounts, it was a great success.

Planning that event and watching it lead to the protection of the river had a life-long effect on me: I realized that one person, even a teenager, can do something to make a difference in their community. I've never forgotten that feeling.

In the decades since, the world's problems have become far more complex and urgent than I could have imagined as a teenager. Yet instead of linking education with those real-world challenges, our education system has turned away from the kind of education that motivates students to protect the world they're inheriting. It's as if we're leaving our children a burning house, but only teaching them how and when the house was built, rather than how to put out the fire.

And our house is definitely on fire. Humans are causing the most devastating extinction event since the asteroid impact that wiped out the dinosaurs. Sea levels are rising, while sea life is disappearing; plummeting insect populations could lead to an "insect apocalypse"; and global temperatures continue to climb. Scientists give humanity less than a dozen years to reduce CO_2 emissions to avoid a two-degree warming and the onset of "climate chaos."

And perhaps not surprisingly, the decline of environmental health around the world is intertwined with the decline of democracy. According to Freedom World's 2018 "Freedom in the World" report, countries around the world collectively are experiencing the thirteenth consecutive year of decline in global freedom.[2] In the United States, more than 100 million eligible voters—including more than half of eligible adults between the ages of eighteen and twenty-nine—stayed home in the 2016 presidential election.

Moreover, the number of people engaged in civic life overall, and the quality of that engagement, has dropped dramatically in the last two decades, a number based on a notion of "civic life" that includes much more than voting. It's about volunteering for nonprofit organizations and other community activities, helping your neighbors, deliberating with others on complex issues, advocating for policies, running for office, serving on juries, being involved in community organizations, serving in the military, and all the activities that make our communities and our democracy stronger."[3]

At such a pivotal time for both democracy and the environment, education is critical because both democratic and environmental engagement depend on what people know, care about, and do. We are dual citizens of political and ecological communities, so failure in either realm spills into the other. Environmental and civic education are sister approaches that help people understand the natural, political, and social systems they inhabit. Securing a prosperous future for humanity requires that people have ready access to clean and plentiful water, a stable climate, and a rich array of biodiversity. This, in turn, requires the active support of people at all levels of society who make informed decisions for land management, health policy, public education, infrastructure planning, the economy, and beyond. Such engagement requires a fundamental understanding of the impacts of those decisions on the natural systems that sustain humanity.

With more than 58 million students attending U.S. public schools, we have an unprecedented opportunity to create a system that lays the groundwork on many dimensions for a more sustainable future. Creating a more inclusive, just society is essential to strengthening democracy, protecting natural systems, and ensuring that all have access to high-quality education. For democracy to work, everyone needs the power to create change, just as I saw in Ohio. Together, civic education and environmental education are key to sustaining a strong democracy and a healthy planet. Instead of ensuring that our students get the best civic and environmental education possible, however, we are doing the opposite. Support and funding for both is minuscule compared to the need. And quality education is not equally available to all students.

Education Gone Awry

John Dewey believed that education should equip students to become full-fledged citizens, able to make informed, intelligent choices that support the public good. Since democracy requires knowledgeable and wise citizens, he reasoned that education has a moral purpose and should foster a passion to improve society.

In our current era of constant testing, however, many schools have lost sight of their larger responsibilities to develop citizens ready for the responsibilities of living in a democratic society. Instead, schools have become hyperfocused on college preparation and career readiness. Of course, it's important for students to be ready for college and career, and to measure students' progress and teacher performance. The problem is that the obsession for testing has pushed subjects like environment, civics, and the arts to the margins. They are underfunded and largely ignored in many school systems.

For example, although all U.S. states require some kind of civic education, the quality varies widely, with most programs focusing on facts rather than experiences. A study by Kei Kawashima-Ginsberg, the director of the Center for Information & Research on Civic Learning and Engagement (CIRCLE) at Tufts University, found that fewer than half of fourth-, eighth-, and twelfth-grade students experience simulation-based educational experiences—such as a mock trial, mock election, or model legislature—in civics. In her words, "You can't learn to be a citizen," she writes, "by memorizing dates and taking multiple-choice tests."

The result is an astonishing level of civic ignorance. Only a quarter of Americans can name the three branches of federal government, and nearly a third cannot name a single one of the three; fewer than half can name the chief justice of the Supreme Court, and more than six in ten say they are pessimistic that Americans who hold different political views can come together to solve the country's problems. A survey by the Woodrow Wilson

National Fellowship Foundation found that "just one in three Americans would pass the U.S. citizenship test," which is intended to be a baseline level of knowledge for new citizens.[4]

Worse, the quality of U.S. civic education varies according to zip code. If you look across the country, students who are in wealthier districts get a much better civic education than students in low-income and underserved communities.[5]

Is that also the case for environmental education? No one knows for sure, but we do know students in low-income schools have less access to green spaces, and that green spaces are essential for teaching kids about the natural environment.[6] Systemic racism in America has led to a variety of gaps across society: a wealth gap, an educational achievement gap, and even a nature-access gap.

No student, regardless of race or income, receives as much environmental or civic education as they need. Experts say that students should receive ongoing environmental education throughout all grades to develop and support civic and environmental literacy skills that persist over a lifetime. But the amount of environmental education that students receive varies by state and district, and many schools touch on the environment less than an hour on average per week. Kevin Coyle, vice president of education at the National Wildlife Federation, estimates that environmental education is taught sporadically in about 50 percent of U.S. schools, while another 30 percent don't teach about the environment at all. There is so much more we could do to integrate environmental education into formal education and advance environmental literacy.

Although the increasing emphasis on science, technology, engineering, and mathematics in education, coupled with the Next Generation Science Standards, has helped, many schools still don't make time for community-based projects that facilitate deeper learning and the development of lifelong skills that are essential in confronting today's challenges. For example, we know that when kids tackle community projects that they care about, which is core to both environmental education and civic education, there are enormous benefits for students—from promoting critical thinking skills and collaboration to better decisionmaking and public speaking. According to Heather Buskirk from the Knowles Teacher Initiative, "project-based learning's biggest hurdle is that not enough students have access to it. For every classroom that works in this way, there are 99 others that still resemble what public education looked like in the 1950s. It is something close to a moral imperative that our schools embrace new ways of educating students so they all get the opportunity to learn and be inspired."[7]

Part of the problem is that there simply isn't enough funding to support large-scale inclusion of civic or environmental education in schools today. As a result of long neglect, the foundation of civic education that was built after World War II has crumbled. The current crisis of faith in democracy is one consequence of the failure of government to invest in forming students who are prepared to participate in civic life.

The same is true in environmental education, which largely receives its funding from foundations, government agencies, and corporations. A study funded by the Environmental Grantmakers Association found that environmental education represents a very small portion of overall environmental and educational philanthropic giving.[8] Part of the problem, however, is that teachers and administrators do not have the time to fundraise, even for important initiatives such as designing new facilities with gardens and solar systems.

At the federal level, funding for environmental education is sparse. The National Environmental Education Act, passed in 1990, is one of the few federal programs that supports environmental education. This critical funding has remained at about $8 million annually for more than two decades, but the need is much larger. The gap between the need and federal funding reflects a failure to invest in the future of our young people and to prepare them to be stewards of the planet.

Discomfort with Complex and
Controversial Topics

The conduct of the public business in a democracy and the sustainable management of the environment are related. It is difficult to imagine democracy flourishing in a damaged environment and *vice versa*. Both, however, arouse strong opinions, and citizens must acquire the ability to talk across differences to find common ground. In the words of Louise Dubé, a leader in educational technology and the Executive Director of iCivics: "We're teaching kids to talk to somebody (they) disagree with, how to find evidence, how to have a conversation, how to listen attentively . . . but that's the kind of public discourse that we've lost."[9] The challenge to educators is to equip students with the knowledge and aptitude for civil discourse necessary to our democracy and to protecting the environment.

In this regard, one of the toughest political issues is climate change, which crosses social, economic, and political boundaries. According to an NPR and Ipsos poll, more than 86 percent of teachers feel that students should learn about climate change, but only 42 percent teach it. Many school boards and parents try to limit what is taught, often for political reasons. In their recent climate-change policy statement, the National Science Teachers Association (NSTA) stated that "teachers are facing pressure to not only eliminate or de-emphasize climate change science, but also to introduce non-scientific ideas in science classrooms." NSTA recommends that teachers "recognize the cumulative weight of scientific evidence that indicates Earth's climate is changing, largely due to human-induced increases in the concentration of heat-absorbing gases." They also recommend that teachers emphasize that "no scientific controversy exists regarding the basic facts of climate change and that any controversies are based on social, economic, or political arguments and are not science."[10]

We are definitely doing a huge disservice to our kids—and the planet—if we continue to ignore climate change and other controversial issues, both inside and outside the classroom. Climate change is the most serious threat to the planet that we've experienced as a global society. It is our responsibility to prepare students for the future they will lead.

How Environmental and Civic Education Can Help

When considering how to best prepare people for a world that is changing faster than ever, we need to remember that our education system was created to prepare students for the responsibility of living in a democracy, for solving problems, and for building a better future.

Environmental education can help; it empowers people to address today's problems and prevent those of tomorrow. Environmental education focuses on helping people gain, enhance, and clarify the knowledge, skills, motivations, values, and commitment to create healthier communities and a livable planet. The goal of education from this perspective is "an environmentally literate person . . . who, individually and with others, makes informed decisions concerning the environment; is willing to act on these decisions to improve the well-being of other individuals, societies, and the global environment; and participates in civic life."[11]

The core of environmental education is to equip students to see the world as a unified system with definable rules. Understanding those rules as systems dynamics requires crossing conventional disciplinary boundaries to address societal issues as well as understanding the places in which we live. Ecosystem health and people's health are related. Human health, for example, is impossible to sustain in a polluted and destitute environment. That reality operates at various scales and across divisions of race, income, and religion. In other words, we are all in this together, or as Benjamin Franklin once said in other circumstances, "We must indeed all hang together or most assuredly we shall all hang separately."

The rise of social media can facilitate or complicate that sense of solidarity. Ours is a new world, and no school ought to ignore its responsibility to prepare students for navigating the digital reality. Students have to constantly consider their online identity, privacy, and safety, as well as deal with deliberate misinformation, deep fakes, bots, and radical ideology. Developing the critical thinking skills needed to evaluate information sources, question motives and accuracy, check facts, listen to a variety of opinions, and engage in civil debate has always necessitated learning and honing new skills, but now requires an even higher level of discernment.

Environmental education fosters critical thinking and learning across disciplines, just as a good civic education does. As students are evaluated and tested in independent subjects, like science and math, teachers have less incentive and time to help students make connections between disciplines. But because solving today's complex problems requires people with a variety of talents and perspectives to work across disciplines, interdisciplinary learning is at the core of both civic and environmental education. We need input from science, civics, history, and engineering, and we need to bridge different learning experiences to create solutions.

Research shows the positive impact of interdisciplinary approaches for overall student achievement and civic engagement. A 2017 study from

Stanford University indicates that environmental education not only increases knowledge gained across subject areas—including science, mathematics, and language arts—but also

- improves social and emotional skills, such as confidence, leadership, autonomy, and teamwork;
- fosters environmental behavior;
- improves academic skills, such as critical thinking, analytical skills, and problem solving;
- increases motivation, enthusiasm, and interest for learning and civic engagement, including instilling a sense of personal responsibility and motivation to address community and environmental issues; and
- helps young people apply their classroom learning experiences to real-world settings and address complex environmental and social issues.[12]

In these ways and others, environmental education enhances students' overall educational experience. Civic education has many of the same cross-disciplinary, democracy-strengthening benefits. Yet, Florida is one of the only states to require introductory civic education in elementary school, which is why experts say the state has seen an upswing in students' civics proficiency.

Civic education should start in the earliest grades and be integrated across the curriculum. The science necessary to understand water pollution, for example, should be connected to the history of the policies that have caused water pollution in places like Flint, Michigan, and other poor communities. Together, science and history become more relevant and motivating to students, and the same is true across the standard discipline-centric curriculum.

This is also true of civic education. Connected across otherwise isolated disciplines, it provides many benefits, such as agility in thinking, skill in communication, commitment to civic causes, willingness to participate in community affairs, increased life satisfaction, and, last but not least, a lower dropout rate.

With such clear evidence that environmental and civic education advance student performance and civic engagement, it's time to bring them in from the margins.

Reimagining Education

Education either functions as an instrument which is used to facilitate integration of the younger generation into the logic of the present system and bring about conformity or it becomes the practice of freedom, the means by which men and women deal critically and creatively with reality and discover how to participate in the transformation of the world.

—*Paulo Freire*

Young people today are already living with the consequences of climate change, but instead of feeling disempowered, many are stepping up. All over the world, they have been marching for action against climate change, with signs that say, "Sea levels are rising, but so is the next generation." Just last year, a group of young people in Florida filed a lawsuit against the state, declaring that decisionmakers are not doing enough to protect the planet for future generations. Nine states currently face similar lawsuits. This is environmental education and civic engagement in action!

And it's not just climate change that young people are taking on. When Maddie Vorva was eleven years old, she and one of her fellow Girl Scouts decided to save orangutans. They learned that rainforests, where orangutans live, are being cleared to grow palm oil plantations in Indonesia and Malaysia, and were horrified to learn that palm oil from those very plantations was used to make Girl Scout cookies. So they boycotted the annual cookie sale and launched a campaign to get the Girl Scouts to stop using unsustainable palm oil. It took eight years, and help from other organizations, but the girls successfully convinced Kellogg, which sells the cookies, to use responsibly grown palm oil.

Lesha Baldwin is working to protect Proctor Creek in her watershed, near Atlanta, Georgia. She conducted water tests with elderly members of the community to help them learn more about the water quality around them. She also traveled to Washington, DC, to speak with members of Congress about environmental issues pertaining to food insecurity and the number of fast food restaurants located near low-income communities and how this impacts the health of black families.

Swedish student Greta Thunberg, age sixteen, has led a movement to force policymakers to address climate change. She is inspiring young people to strike and speak out about the potential catastrophe that might

result from inaction. More than 270 cities around the globe have responded and are taking part in the "strike for climate" movement.

Students have shown that they have an incredible capacity to engage
to make the world better. We need a world full of Maddies, Leshas, and
Gretas, but that will only happen when we have a system that gives every
student access to great education and experiences that will last a lifetime.

Here are four goals that can help get us there:

1) Prioritize Environmental Education and Civic Engagement

Organizations, educators, administrators, and parents need to demand
funding and support for civic education and environmental education. High-quality civic education and environmental education should
be required in every school across the country, which means a focus on
the approaches known to advance deeper learning and positive student
outcomes.

The good news is that more than thirty-five states have adopted
environmental literacy plans that highlight how formal and informal
education can together help advance environmental literacy at the local and state levels. More plans are in development, but the majority of
states don't have the resources and support needed for full implementation. Only Maryland, however, requires environmental literacy and
service learning.

Another promising step is that many of us in the field of environmental education are collaborating with our colleagues in civic education to
scale up our collective work—from leadership training to policy changes—
to advance civic engagement that tackles environmental challenges.

And many districts are making policy changes. In Portland, Oregon,
a resolution passed that directs the school system's superintendent to work
with students, teachers, and members of the community to come up with
a plan to ensure all Portland public schools include climate change and
climate justice in their curriculum. And in Massachusetts, an ambitious
new act was passed in late 2018 to promote and enhance civic engagement and ensure that every student is ready for civic life.

The bottom line is that we need more and better environmental and
civic education. And by doing so, we will be strengthening democracy and
sustaining the protection of our natural resources.

2) Address Equity and Inclusion

We cannot protect our democracy or the environment unless everyone has equal access to high-quality education. That means, among other things, effective teaching, which in turn presumes high-quality teacher education and schools with enough resources and sound infrastructure.

Equity and inclusion are central to education at all levels, including policy, curriculum, and professional development. "Learning in an engaging and participatory environment," Dana Bennis, chief learning officer at the Institute for Democratic Education in American (IDEA), writes, "is not just for the privileged few. Because equality and justice are at its core, democratic education must be available to all young people and their families." A sustainable and democratic future, in other words, will require that everyone has a voice that is heard.

3) Increase Professional Development Opportunities, with a Focus on Student Voice and Choice

One of the most important things we can do is to ensure that students' experiences, knowledge, and perspectives inform and shape the curriculum. The good news is that many organizations, including Generation Citizen, Earth Force, CIRCLE at Tufts, the MIKVA challenge, and many others, are promoting learning that is student led and action oriented. Not only do students identify the problems they want to work on, but they also research possible solutions, engage with the community, look at options and trade-offs, take part in discussions and deliberation, and present their findings to those in power to create change. They also reflect on what they learned and talk more about what it means to be an engaged citizen. Through this process, students learn about policy, about creating changes in their community, how to work with other team members, and how to engage with civic leaders to tackle tough issues.

Educators cannot do this critical work without effective professional development, ongoing support, and access to high-quality resources. It is key that educators know how to facilitate discussions across social, political, and cultural differences, and how to facilitate experiential, student-led, project-based learning. We also know that to achieve deeper learning in civic engagement, we need more civics courses for students; more opportunities for simulations, role-playing, and deliberative discussions; and more opportunities to work on real issues in their community.

4) Building Bridges, Not Silos

Although environmental and civic education share many approaches and outcomes, both fields often operate in silos. By collaborating more, both fields could potentially have much more impact—especially in helping people and communities understand their roles and responsibilities in sustaining our democracy and protecting our environment. Environmental education can be a model for civic engagement. I believe that climate change is one of the civic engagement issues of our time. Greta Thunberg has shown the world what it means to be an agent of change. And there are thousands of examples of young people taking informed action to address other environmental and social challenges—from local to global.

In addition to more closely linking environmental and civic education, we also need to look beyond schools as stand-alone entities and instead envision them more as learning hubs for the community. One of the most exciting trends in the country is the breaking down of sectors and silos. Some of the most successful programs showcase schools as a hub for linking nonprofit organizations, universities, corporations, religious organizations, and citizen groups to create healthier communities. Young people are working in communities to create change—and they're partnering with zoos, museums, religious groups, businesses, governments, and more. They're learning what it means to work across boundaries and understand that building more-resilient communities is part of our work as citizens of a democracy. If we do education right, our students will thrive, our communities will thrive, and our democracy will thrive.

Conclusion

Education is the foundation of democracy. The founders of the United States spoke freely and convincingly about the critical relationship between education and democracy, emphasizing the importance of education for preserving freedom, equality, and well-being. John Adams, our second president, went so far as to say, "Laws for liberal education of youth . . . are so extremely wise and useful, that, to a humane and generous mind, no expense for this purpose would be thought extravagant."

Environmental education and civic education use student-centered, experience-based approaches that help young people understand their power to be agents of change. Both focus on developing the skills, values, and motivation to be an active member of the democracy.

In 1971, the full length of the Little Miami River was designated a National Wild and Scenic River. Being a part of the river's transformation was an experience that transformed my life. Education should be transformational. It should be experiential. And this kind of excellent, meaningful education should be equally available to all students. Education forms the foundation of democracy, and it's time we demand that our educational system embrace its larger mission as though our country's future depends on it—because it does.

THE SUPREME COURT'S LEGITIMACY CRISIS AND CONSTITUTIONAL DEMOCRACY'S FUTURE

Dawn Johnsen

President Donald Trump has routinely violated longstanding norms that govern and undergird the United States' constitutional democracy. His disregard for rule-of-law and other foundational norms—in some instances in violation of the law—has inflicted damage and exposed vulnerabilities throughout government and in the vital supporting institutions of civil society. Special Counsel Robert Mueller documented one high-profile set of violations. His investigation into Russian interference in the 2016 U.S. election revealed the difficulty of constraining a president willing to flout norms and the law, particularly with prosecution of a sitting president off the table, a divided Congress disinclined to act, and an excessively deferential Supreme Court.[1]

In our democratic system, change ultimately depends upon the outcomes of elections. The Twenty-Second Amendment guarantees that, notwithstanding any authoritarian tendencies, Trump will leave office no later than January 2025. We cannot yet know whether, as constitutional scholar Jack Balkin predicts, Trump's presidency represents an end-of-era "disjunctive" presidency (using political scientist Stephen Skowronek's taxonomy) and the final collapse of Reagan-era conservatism. Balkin holds out promise that "when we get through it—about five to ten years from now—the present will seem like a distant, unhappy nightmare, or an illness from which one has recovered."[2] Others warn against taking such solace, pointing to signs that Trump instead will prove to be a "reconstructive" president who transforms the terms of debate and expectations for future presidents.[3] Time and future elections will tell.

In one vital respect, however, recovery will require more than winning the next election or two. Long after Trump leaves office, those he appoints to the Supreme Court and lower federal courts will continue to serve. The post-Trump courts may be profoundly out of step with the nation for decades to come.

The treasure of an independent federal judiciary is a cornerstone of our constitutional democracy. Federal judges appointed for life following Senate confirmation uphold the rule of law during political storms and in the face of partisan and populist threats. At one essential level, the federal judiciary and the rule of law seem so secure that the American people take for granted that the courts will adjudicate, as is said, without fear or favor. This contrasts with stressed and failing judicial systems in some other nations, where tenure-insecure and poorly resourced judges risk retaliation for rulings against powerful interests and are susceptible to political pressures and even bribery.

These very attributes of judicial independence, however, contribute to the lasting harm of President Trump's transformative appointments. Moreover, Trump has continued a decades-long Republican strategy of aggressively—at times, clearly wrongfully—prioritizing judicial appointments in order to achieve radical ideological ends. Given the numbers and ages of those who serve, Democratic (big "D") electoral victories cannot soon restore balance and eliminate the threat that the federal courts, particularly the Supreme Court, will reverse some of the last decades' progress and stymie future democratic (little "d") change.

Trump's appointments of Neil Gorsuch and Brett Kavanaugh secured a solid right-leaning majority on the Supreme Court. Kavanaugh's confirmation hearing attracted broad public attention for the differences between himself and his predecessor, Justice-in-the-Middle Anthony Kennedy, on key issues, and for sexual misconduct allegations met by Kavanaugh's shockingly partisan, intemperate behavior.

Even more consequential, if less dramatic, was Justice Gorsuch's wrongful appointment in derogation of constitutional norms. Had Senate Republicans not, in effect, stolen that seat from President Barack Obama and all those who elected him, Merrick Garland's appointment would have created a Supreme Court with a majority appointed by Democratic presidents *for the first time since 1969*, thereby altering the court's direction on many, varied issues. A historical anomaly further diminished stabilizing democratic influences on the judiciary: the current Republican-appointed majority includes four justices appointed by presidents initially elected despite having lost the popular vote, thanks to the role of the Electoral College.

Many vital, even life-altering issues require judges to exercise discretion, with judgment influenced by judicial philosophy and legal views. At stake are voting rights, reproductive rights, racial justice, economic justice, access to health care and education, the environment, and the climate. A judiciary that fails to protect rights damages not only individuals, but also the prospects for an inclusive, well-functioning democracy. So, too, judicial rulings that wrongly invalidate the actions of democratically accountable officials. Particularly insidious to democracy are judicial rulings that support partisan entrenchment—that is, keeping Republicans in power beyond their public support, as in the Roberts Court's refusal to guard against gerrymandering and uphold Voting Rights Act provisions designed to protect minority voters and the integrity of elections. On these issues and more, the federal judiciary is likely to advance the Trump agenda—or, more to the point, the agenda of the ideological right—for many years to come.

A Crisis of Legitimacy

A defining feature of the current federal judiciary is the outsized, imbalanced role of partisanship in the confirmation and appointment of judges: partisan polarization in ideology and partisan asymmetry in priorities and methods.[4] Beginning with President Reagan, the Republican Party leadership has prioritized judicial appointments to achieve radical legal transformation, while generally moving to the ideological right. Among their ends: to weaken government regulation and especially congressional power, to support business interests, to entrench Republican political dominance, and to advance electorally advantageous social objectives on issues such as abortion and affirmative action. With Trump's appointments, Republicans have solidified a judiciary poised to thwart democratic and progressive values and at odds with norms of judicial independence.

This politicization of the federal courts and the public's perception of politicization undermine the judiciary's very legitimacy—a problem likely to worsen with future rulings. The old adage is true: the courts rely for their authority on public perception and support, because they lack independent means of enforcing their decisions.

Supreme Court Justice Elena Kagan has cautioned that it is "a dangerous time for the Court" because "people increasingly look at us and say 'this is just an extension of the political process.'" Shortly before his death in 2019 at age ninety-nine, retired Justice John Paul Stevens similarly expressed concern that the public increasingly sees justices as no different than politicians. He warned that the Supreme Court "seems to be more ideological than it's been since the 1930s." Stevens, himself a Republican, took the extraordinary step of publicly opposing Kavanaugh's confirmation. President Gerald Ford appointed Stevens shortly before the party prioritized ideology in appointment. Stevens explained that his movement toward the relative left reflected not a change in his views, but Republican appointments that had moved the Supreme Court to the right over his thirty-five years of service.

To legal scholars Daniel Epps and Ganesh Sitaraman, the court's legitimacy problem is so dire that "The Court must radically change—or die."[5] They and others have proposed changes in the court's structure, but each brings difficulties that make adoption unlikely. The best-known proposal would expand the number of justices, which clearly is within Congress's authority. In the nation's first century, the number of justices fluctuated between five and ten, before Congress settled on nine. "Court-packing" has been widely viewed as unacceptably counter to norms of judicial independence ever since President Franklin D. Roosevelt's 1937 proposal of fifteen justices, but future pressures might cause public perception to shift. "Court-packing" also presents the prospect of unstable counter-expansions, although discrete arguments would support an expansion to redress the 2016 Republican theft of the seat that was President Obama's to fill. Legal scholars Paul Carrington and Roger Cramton, among others, have proposed a more moderate and sustainable structural change: replacing life tenure with an extended term of service, such as eighteen-year terms staggered to equalize appointments among presidents. Although strong on the merits, any version of term limits with a chance of adoption likely would require an unattainable constitutional amendment.[6]

For now, the path forward remains murky and intractable and is unlikely to be cleared by any structural change. A clear priority for reform efforts is to improve public understanding and engagement, informed by constitutional history, regarding what precisely is at stake and the proper place of courts within the United States' constitutional order. That understanding reveals an arduous path to recovery.

How We Got Here

A remarkable fact bears repeating: for an unbroken string of the last fifty years, a majority of justices serving on the Supreme Court were appointed by Republican presidents. Republican dominance since 1969 has moved the court's center substantially to the ideological right on issues that fundamentally affect the nation. Issues of racial and economic justice were early targets: remedies for the nation's horrific history of slavery, Jim Crow segregation, and continuing discrimination, as well as issues of criminal justice and poverty marked by persistent, severe racial disparities. On some core concerns, however, a right-wing voting block solidified only with Justice Kavanaugh's 2018 appointment.

If this Republican dominance of the judiciary represented the democratically expressed will of the people, the Court would not be facing a legitimacy crisis. Presidents and senators consider judicial philosophy and ideology in selecting judges, creating opportunities for the American people to influence judicial interpretation and constitutional meaning through elections.

In fact, Democrats have been winning elections. In stark contrast with Republican domination of the courts, election results during this fifty-year period have been quite balanced. Democratic presidents were elected in five—and won the popular vote in seven—of the last twelve terms. And Democrats controlled the Senate during more than half of that time.[7]

One factor behind this electoral mismatch is chance. In an irony of history, Jimmy Carter remains the only U.S. president to serve a full term with no Supreme Court vacancy to fill, while Richard Nixon appointed four justices before resigning in disgrace. This allowed Republican presidents an astounding string of ten consecutive appointments, from 1969 to 1992.

Additional influences are anti-democratic features of the constitutional structure: the role of the Electoral College in presidential elections and uniform state representation in the Senate notwithstanding huge variations in state population. The presidential elections of 2000 and 2016 resulted in the remarkable fact that four of the five current Republican-appointed justices were appointed by presidents initially elected despite having lost the popular vote (John Roberts and Samuel Alito by George W. Bush and Gorsuch and Kavanaugh by Donald Trump). (The fifth, Clarence Thomas, barely won Senate confirmation after a grueling hearing that included Anita Hill's testimony regarding sexual misconduct.) Moreover, Gorsuch and Kavanaugh both were confirmed by senators who represented less than a majority of the country's population, made possible by the fact that the Constitution gives each state two senators, even though California's population is seventy times that of Wyoming.

This disjunction between democratic outcomes and the makeup of the Roberts Court counsels special regard for the core interpretive principle of *stare decisis*; that is, the justices should give great weight to the court's precedent that upholds constitutional rights and implements constitutional principles upon which the American public has come to rely. Some hold out hope that Chief Justice Roberts will forestall radical legal shifts and join the moderates, as he twice did in cases that put the Court under intense public scrutiny (involving the Affordable Care Act and the National Census). However, the story behind the making of the current court suggests that absent such unusual pressures, we likely will see aggressive, regressive rulings from justices who were appointed in highly partisan, sometimes legally dubious, circumstances.

Trump's disdain for constitutional norms has been an extraordinary—one hopes unique—aberration, but his actions with regard to the federal judiciary are better understood in terms of continuity with this long-established Republican strategy to transform the Court. Contrary to his self-proclaimed status as a disruptive outsider, with regard to the courts Trump has strictly and faithfully toed his party's decades-old line.

The Republican strategy has seeds in Nixon's 1968 campaign, which targeted an "activist" Warren Court, complete with "Impeach Earl Warren" bumper stickers (ironically targeting the Republican-appointed Warren). Nixon's four appointments proved enormously consequential to the court's ideological direction in the short and long run. For example, shortly before his 1971 nomination, Lewis Powell penned a now-infamous memorandum to the U.S. Chamber of Commerce recommending how to expand corporate influence including "vast opportunity for the Chamber" by focusing on the courts: "the judiciary may be the most important instrument for social, economic and political change."

President Reagan and his attorney general, Edwin Meese, further prioritized the president's ability to shape law through judicial appointments to further ideological and political ends. The Federalist Society (founded in 1982) and other ostensibly nonpartisan organizations increasingly have assisted. The Republican Party emphasized wedge issues—abortion, crime, guns, race—in order to court working-class Democrats to vote Republican against their economic interests. And they held out judicial appointments in presidential and Senate elections as the way to advance these issues. The Republican Party's opportunistic shift on abortion provides a prime example. At the time of the court's 1973 decision in *Roe v. Wade*, Republicans were more pro-choice than were Democrats. Republican strategists determined that a party switch in positions to oppose legal abortion would attract Catholic and other religiously conservative Democrats. The Court decided *Roe* by a solid seven–two margin, with five Republican-appointed justices in the majority, but that margin shrank with appointments by Presidents Reagan and George H.W. Bush, both elected on party platforms that called for overruling *Roe* through judicial appointments.

Presidents and senators of course consider nominees' legal views and judicial philosophies. But the comprehensiveness of Reagan's constitutional vision and strategy was unprecedented, as well as substantively wrong for the nation and violative of norms in its call to overturn doctrine across issues. A series of Department of Justice reports, ostensibly public but not widely known until a decade later, detailed how they sought to remake constitutional law, with lists of landmark cases targeted for overruling. The reports endorsed (but did not consistently apply) an overarching theory of "originalism," with frequent citations of the works of the right's intellectual leader, then-lower-court judge Robert Bork. The introduction to one report explained: "There are few factors that are more critical to determining the course of the Nation, and yet more often overlooked, than the values and philosophies of the men and women who populate . . . the federal judiciary."[8] The Reagan/Meese blueprints were as dismissive of precedent and stare decisis as was their guru, Bork, who told one audience: "I don't think that in the field of constitutional law precedent is all that important. . . . If . . . a prior court has misread the Constitution, I think it's your duty to go back and correct it. . . . I think the importance is what the framers were driving at . . . ."[9]

It is worth noting that if the Senate had confirmed Reagan's nomination of Bork to the Supreme Court in 1987, a reliable right-wing block would have been solidified more than thirty years before Kavanaugh's confirmation. The Democratically controlled Senate rejected Bork after a hearing that thoroughly aired his extreme views, with negative votes from six Republicans just prior to the extreme partisan polarization to come. In a pivotal moment in constitutional history, Reagan appointed to that seat the more moderate Anthony Kennedy, who would become the deciding vote in support of some rights that Bork had decried. For example, Bork surely would have provided the fifth vote to overrule *Roe*; instead, Justice Kennedy's deciding vote in 1992 in *Planned Parenthood v. Casey* preserved a weakened form of protection. Kennedy's 2018 retirement created the opening to which Trump appointed Kavanaugh, unsettling numerous issues.

President Trump's very election was facilitated by the partisan imbalance in attention to the courts. In a campaign decision that helped secure his election, Trump took the unprecedented step of releasing a list of right-wing potential Supreme Court nominees, prepared with the guidance of the Federalist Society—to whom President Trump has continued to defer. Trump and his surrogates regularly invoked the president's authority to appoint judges, to the end of reassuring otherwise shaky supporters who disagreed with Trump's positions, for example, on the economy and trade, and in the face of revelations of his moral and legal failings, including his sexual misconduct and business practices. Trump implored those who might be wavering in their support to keep in mind just two words: "Supreme Court." For many, the magnitude of his impact on the judiciary became apparent only two years after his election, with his nomination of Kavanaugh.

Scholars debate to what extent certain Republican actions with regard to the judiciary should be considered "unconstitutional," notwithstanding that any violation would be judicially unenforceable due to doctrines that limit judicial review (such as standing requirements for plaintiffs and the court's avoidance of "political questions"). Even when not unconstitutional, actions may violate constitutional norms and conventions. The Republican Party clearly has been engaged in what commentators describe as "asymmetrical constitutional hardball"[10] by which they have moved "off-the-wall" constitutional arguments "on the wall" and even into doctrine adopted by the Court.[11]

Whether of laws or norms, Republican violations undermine the court's legitimacy. Absent the following three instances of Republican "hardball," four of the five justices who make up the current far-right majority might not even be serving on the Court.

Bush Versus Gore

In a breathtakingly partisan ruling that experts excoriated as wrong on multiple grounds, the Court intervened effectively to resolve the 2000 presidential election in favor of Republican George W. Bush. Five Republican-appointed justices selected Bush as the victor, over the vigorous dissent of the other four justices. After improperly substituting its resolution for the process the Constitution provided, the Court went on to declare its ruling was of no precedential value, a ticket good for one ride only. Among the countless effects, many immeasurable, of the court's action, in his second term Bush appointed two justices who otherwise might have been selected by Al Gore—who incidentally had won the national popular vote.

Merrick Garland Versus Neil Gorsuch

Within hours of Justice Antonin Scalia's unexpected death in February 2016, Republican Senate Majority Leader Mitch McConnell announced plans to block the confirmation of *anyone* President Obama nominated, with the fabricated claim that a nominee should not be confirmed in an election year. The Senate refused even a hearing for Obama's nominee, Merrick Garland, the eminent Chief Judge of the U.S. Court of Appeals for the District of Columbia, for reasons entirely related to the Republican commitment to playing extreme constitutional hardball to control the Court. The Senate's refusal to consider Garland—an unimpeachable, consensus-style nominee—at a minimum violated historical precedent and constitutional norms. Many argue it violated the Constitution, albeit without the possibility of judicial remedy. The partisan theft of the seat thwarted democratic influences the Constitution provides and prevented what should have been a Democratic-appointed majority on the Court for the first time in half a century. McConnell confirmed the unprincipled nature of his action with a hypocritical statement in 2019 that, should a vacancy occur on the Court the following election year, he would push through a Trump nominee.

Justice Brett Kavanaugh

Kavanaugh's path to appointment was strewn with controversies characterized by extreme partisanship. Just a month before the November 2018 Senate elections, every Senate Republican voted to confirm Kavanaugh by a bare-majority vote of 50–48, in a process that disregarded established norms. The Judiciary Committee rushed hearings without taking the time to secure most of his record and also inadequately investigated credible claims of sexual assault. Kavanaugh's closing testimony was widely condemned as disqualifying for its erratic, combative, hyperpolitical tone unbecoming a justice, including wild allusions to a possible conspiracy behind Dr. Ford's allegations for the purpose of avenging Trump's defeat of Hillary Clinton.

Three additional norm violations darken the cloud of illegitimacy over Trump's judicial appointments and contribute to the threat to democracy. First, unprecedented expenditures of tens of millions of dollars in dark money advanced the confirmations of Gorsuch and Kavanaugh, with Republicans importing the worst aspects of our failed campaign finance system to infect our judiciary in new ways. Second, far more than his Republican predecessors, Trump has ceded his responsibility to make judicial appointments to right-wing ideologues; his appointments also are astonishingly lacking in racial, ethnic, gender, and experiential diversity. The final general cloud is the fact of Russian interference in the 2016 election to aid Trump's election.

Fifty years of Republican dominance on the Supreme Court has been potent. It is powerful to imagine the implications for our nation if that unlikely run had ended with the confirmation of Merrick Garland or an appointment by a President Al Gore or a President Hillary Clinton. Instead, the Supreme Court faces many more years of Republican dominance.

What's at Stake

The current out-of-step federal judiciary threatens a multitude of issues important to the lives of individuals and the health of constitutional democracy.[12] The right's specific objectives have remained remarkably consistent over the decades. The Reagan/Meese agenda of the 1980s targeted Supreme Court precedent that protected individual rights and that broadly interpreted Congress's power to regulate commerce and enforce the Reconstruction Amendments. Ever since, the right has beat the drum for "judicial restraint" against so-called liberal activist judges, but its hypocrisy is evident from calls for "judicial engagement" and rulings expanding protection for favored "rights," for example, to unregulated guns and property. Cross-cutting themes also have endured: advancing corporate and moneyed interests, obstructing democratic change through partisan entrenchment, diminishing protections for historically disadvantaged groups, and restricting the government's regulatory authority to protect rights and the public interest.

In modern times, Americans have seen the Court protect individual rights and promote social progress by breathing practical, real-world life into the Constitution's often abstract, undefined provisions. Landmark decisions reflect and reinforce great social and political movements to redefine who is part of "We the People." *Brown v. Board of Education* started the end of Jim Crow racial segregation; *Griswold v. Connecticut* and *Roe v. Wade* protected women's reproductive autonomy and equality; and *Lawrence v. Texas* and *Obergefell v. Hodges* protected the equality and dignity of same-sex couples. Over time, many of those previously stigmatized and excluded have been included more fully in America's Great Experiment. The Court also has directly protected the democratic process with doctrines such as "one person, one vote."

In addition to interpreting the Constitution to protect rights directly, over most (though not all) of U.S. history, the Court has respected Congress's broad authority to enact legislation to advance constitutional interests and the public interest. Landmark federal laws have created the nation as we know it, including the Social Security Act, Medicare, Medicaid, laws establishing minimum wages and worker and consumer protections, the Civil Rights Act of 1964, the Voting Rights Act of 1965, the Clean Water Act, the Clean Air Act, the Family and Medical Leave Act, and the Affordable Care Act.

In the contexts of both individual rights and congressional power, the Court typically has rejected a narrow search for original intent or meaning as the guiding principle, an approach that certainly would have precluded, for example, *Brown, Griswold, Roe, Lawrence,* and *Obergefell*.[13] In its decision in *McCulloch v. Maryland*, the Court upheld Congress's authority to establish the Bank of the United States and set the stage for "fair and just interpretation" of the Constitution and for judicial deference to Congress's choice of means for implementing it. Far from a cramped originalist approach, the Court emphasized that "we must never forget that it is a *constitution* we are expounding:" "the basic charter of our society, setting out in spare but meaningful terms the principles of government" and "intended to endure for ages to come, and consequently, to be adapted to the various crises of human affairs." In 2003, Justice Kennedy's majority opinion in *Lawrence* similarly rejected originalism in interpreting the meaning of liberty for gays and lesbians: "As the Constitution endures, persons in every generation can invoke its principles in their own search for greater freedom."

Throughout history, however, the Court has not been consistent on matters of rights and federal power. A brief review of episodes from the court's dark, discredited past helps in understanding potential risks ahead. During efforts to abolish slavery, reactionary judicial decisions wracked the country. The Court also impeded progress and protected moneyed interests at other key moments of social and economic change: during Reconstruction, the record economic inequality of the Gilded Age, and the Great Depression. The Court wrongly "interpreted" congressional power and rights of property and liberty to invalidate many efforts by Congress and state legislatures to enact protections and address economic and social crises, among them the Missouri Compromise on slavery, the Civil Rights Act of 1883, a national income tax, prohibitions on child labor, minimum wage and maximum hour requirements, and numerous worker and consumer protections.

The court's infamous "*Lochner* Era" (named for the court's *Lochner* decision, but encompassing many decisions from the late nineteenth century through the late 1930s) is especially instructive. A regressive, dangerously out of step court invalidated numerous federal and state laws aimed at improving a desperately failing economy, unprecedented economic inequality, and life- and health-threatening working conditions. Although Congress did not adopt Roosevelt's 1937 court-packing proposal, the Court changed direction that very year, perhaps influenced by the threat of the proposal. Roosevelt achieved his ambitions with appointments over his record twelve-plus years in office (a length now constitutionally prohibited). This set the stage for Democratic majorities on the Court for almost all of the thirty-year period from 1939 to 1969 and landmark progressive decisions such as *Brown* and *Griswold*.

A consensus both on and off the Court condemns the *Lochner* Era as a cautionary tale and national tragedy, and the Court since has upheld broad governmental authority to address major economic and social challenges. Cracks in that consensus began off the Court in the 1980s in plans formulated in the Reagan administration, the writings of Robert Bork and others, and the Federalist Society and other right-wing organizations. On the Court, cracks emerged in decisions of the Rehnquist Court in the 1990s. Trump's additions to the Roberts Court threaten rapid erosion.

The Federalist Society's Leonard Leo, who serves now as President Trump's judicial nominations advisor, harkens back to *Lochner* with promises of legal "transformation" and "revival" the likes of which "I don't think has really happened since probably before the New Deal." A *Washington Post* investigation uncovered that Leo helped nonprofits raise more than $250 million for right-wing judges and causes in contributions referred to as "dark money" because no law requires the disclosure of sources. In raising funds, Leo exhorts that "judicial confirmations these days are more like political campaigns."[14]

Some immediate responses to Justice Kavanaugh's replacement of Kennedy foreshadow that "transformation." Most prominent, emboldened abortion opponents have secured new restrictions in red states in the hopes that the newly constituted Court will eviscerate what remains of the Constitution's protections. In some states only one or two clinics that perform abortions have survived, and the procedure's costs have skyrocketed, frustrating access. Drawing an important line in the sand, in 2016 Justice Kennedy cast a necessary fifth vote in *Hellerstedt v. Whole Women's Health* to invalidate some particularly onerous abortion restrictions, bogusly framed as beneficial to women, that would have shut down most of Texas's abortion providers. With Justice Kavanaugh, the Court is widely expected to gut what remains of *Roe* and overrule *Whole Women's Health*.

The assaults on some constitutional rights have been more circuitous. For example, without Justice Kennedy's moderating influence, the Roberts Court is likely to expand religious exemptions from generally applicable laws, including civil rights protections for women and the LGBTQ+ community, and to halt the recognition of further protections. The Court almost surely will continue its erosion of the Establishment Clause's protections against government endorsement of religion. Kennedy also had prevented the Court from a broad invalidation of voluntary race-conscious remedies to desegregate schools, which now are at great risk. Kennedy also was the swing vote holding out a role for the Court in protecting against political gerrymandering; in 2019 Kavanaugh joined the bare five-justice majority to open the door to relentless partisan entrenchment through sophisticated computer-drawn electoral maps, which justice Elena Kagan denounced as a "tragically wrong" "abdication" that undermines democracy.

The "transformation" also targets vital governmental powers. The Court is likely to narrow Congress's authority to enact laws to promote the public interest as democratically determined. Among the existing and future federal laws and regulations at risk are those that address, for example, staggering economic inequality, worker and consumer protection, access to health care and education, environmental protection, and the existential threat of climate change. One specific example: a new federal tax on wealth should be viewed as within Congress's authority but could be deemed unconstitutional under the terribly flawed reasoning of the *Lochner* Era.[15]

Additional clues to potential judicial constraints on federal power rest in creative doctrine devised by the Rehnquist and Roberts Courts: a congruence-and-proportionality test to limit Congress's authority under Section Five of the Fourteenth Amendment, an equal state sovereignty principle to invalidate provisions of the Voting Rights Act, a distinction between economic and noneconomic activity to invalidate the Gun Free Schools Zone Act and portions of the Violence Against Women Act, and a distinction between economic activity and inactivity to find that portions of the Affordable Care Act exceeded Congress's commerce power. The Roberts Court likely will continue to disguise the radical nature of its changes with complex, reasonable-sounding doctrine that undermines the effectiveness of democratic response.

When justices obfuscate the import of their analysis, we must look for guidance from dissenting justices and legal commentators. For example, Ian Millhiser titled an article "Justice Alito just wrote the most terrifying sentence to appear in a Supreme Court opinion in years," which drew attention to Alito's startling interest in resurrecting the court's *Lochner* Era nondelegation doctrine, which would drastically limit Congress's authority to delegate regulatory authority to executive agencies. Justice Alito declined to join Justice Gorsuch's alarming dissent for three justices, which advocated just that, but Alito wrote: "If a majority of this court were willing to reconsider the approach we have taken for the past 84 years, I would support that effort." Justice Kavanaugh now might provide that majority for the radical position that, as the headline to Nicholas Bagley's analysis suggests, "Most of Government Is Unconstitutional."[16]

Another notable characteristic of the Roberts Court's decisions is the astounding, rising success rate of the Chamber of Commerce and business interests. A study by the Constitutional Accountability Center reveals that "since Justice Samuel Alito joined Chief Justice John Roberts on the bench in 2006, the Chamber has won over 70% of its cases [which is] in contrast to the Chamber's 56% success rate before the late Rehnquist Court (1994 to 2005) and its 43% success rate before the late Burger Court (1981 to 1986)."[17] Among these decisions, *Citizens United* overruled longstanding precedent to strike down federal statutory limits on corporate campaign expenditures as contravening the First Amendment. The Court similarly invalidated other congressional efforts to regulate money in politics. Big money in politics presents very direct threats, but democracy also degrades when the Court strengthens the interests of the wealthy and corporations across a range of contexts, from First Amendment obstacles to organized labor (prompting Justice Elena Kagan to warn against a "weaponized First Amendment") to diminished access to courts by employees and consumers seeking to vindicate wrongs inflicted by businesses.

Conclusion

The alarming path that lies ahead for the federal judiciary and our democracy has been charted intentionally and persistently over many decades. Preeminent Supreme Court analyst Linda Greenhouse warned of the partisan asymmetry: "What we're seeing now . . . are the fruits of decades of laser-like focus on the courts by one party, and a kind of laissez-faire attitude by the other—an asymmetry of intentionality, you might say, that's brought us to where we are today."[18] Correcting that asymmetry and reclaiming our constitutional democracy demands equivalent unremitting commitment and political action. The future of the world's longest-surviving democracy is at stake.

Part III

POLICY CHALLENGES

CAN DEMOCRACY SURVIVE THE INTERNET?

David Hickton

In 2010, the heads of U.S. Steel and the United Steelworkers of America came to me as U.S. Attorney for the Western District of Pennsylvania and announced that Chinese hackers had penetrated their networks. China had been accumulating market share for years, at a pace that suggested they weren't just taking advantage of global trade rules and their own advancing domestic technology. Manifestly, they were stealing trade secrets over the internet, with grave consequences not only for the steel industry but for American companies generally.

American manufacturers had in fact been making similar complaints to the U.S. government for more than a decade. Critical to the Chinese assault on our manufacturing base was intellectual property theft, which was crimping the ability of American companies to protect hard-won copyrights and patents and thus taking away much of their incentive to research and innovate. China's aggressive cyber-theft efforts contributed to the loss of 50 percent of American manufacturing jobs in the decade after it entered the World Trade Organization in 2001. Negotiations and litigation couldn't solve the problem, and neither could an executive order issued by President Barack Obama declaring U.S. intellectual property to be a strategic asset. Factories closed, and workers pushed out of their jobs and stripped of their futures were treated as casualties and transaction costs of the new information era.

These developments had many underlying causes, starting with the growing power of China and the emergence of new, flourishing markets in the Pacific Rim. The tectonic shift in global power had some parallels with the rise of the United States itself as an economic powerhouse in the late nineteenth century. The difference was, the Chinese weren't *competing* with American technology; they were *stealing* from us, taking advantage of our own digital highway to conduct a borderless theft they could not have accomplished in the pre-digital age. It was invasion by keystroke, illegal and highly damaging, and something had to be done.

What we did in the Justice Department was build the capacity to take on complex cyber-crime cases. After an exhaustive investigation, in which we used the most sophisticated digital forensic tools available, we indicted five members of a Chinese military hacking unit for economic espionage. Our investigation showed that in addition to U.S. Steel and the USW, the Chinese had hacked Alcoa, Westinghouse, and other companies to hunt for trade secrets that could give them a competitive edge. They came away with a large haul of proprietary product information, business strategy plans, bidding information and proposals—and, in the case of Westinghouse, plans for nuclear power plants. They also gained access to confidential legal communications about cases filed against China with the World Trade Organization.

Our indictment was the first of its kind, a bold statement that the United States would pursue cyber-criminals whether they were operating individually or in the employ of a foreign government. We were also determined to establish international norms and laws to the digital realm. The internet had become the Wild West, a place where theft, espionage, and attacks on infrastructure flourished largely beyond the reach of any authority. As long as individuals and countries benefited from participation in our markets but ignored our laws, they were making a mockery of efforts by the United States and its Western allies to establish common legal principles for international cooperation. Our political and economic institutions were at risk.

Five years after our prosecution, the challenges have only deepened. It is now evident that we made a grave error in watching the explosive growth of the internet without thinking through the implications. Policymakers have been asleep at the wheel.

Not only are we contending with a virtually lawless international cyber-environment; we are also seeing how the ubiquity of digital communications and social media is fueling a rise of authoritarianism, the concentration of economic power in technology and e-commerce companies, and a decline in institutional journalism. These alarming trends threaten our ideals of freedom and democracy in ways never previously contemplated.

Take the rise of Donald Trump as Exhibit A. It would have been inconceivable, before the digital age, for a real estate developer turned reality TV host to rise to the pinnacle of American politics with a bigoted and deceitful campaign challenging his predecessor's legitimacy, twinned with an assault on our institutions, our minority populations, our international alliances, the norms of political discourse, and, ultimately, our system of government. Trump understood early on that the internet allowed him both to bypass and to manipulate traditional media outlets, in a way that resonated strongly with voters who were sick of the status quo and willing to back someone promising to overturn it. His daily tweet storms, which have not abated in office, are designed to keep his base energized, his detractors outraged, his political opponents unfocused, and the facts perpetually obscured by a torrent of grievance, hostility, self-aggrandizement, and blatant falsehood.

Trump is hardly the only leader to have achieved power on the back of the digital revolution. China under President Xi Jinping has established an unprecedented surveillance state, working hand-in-glove with its tech industry to police ethnic minorities and political opponents while also launching cyber-attacks on political and economic targets overseas. An increasingly confrontational Russia has regained global influence via aggressive disinformation campaigns aimed at social media users in Western countries. North Korea and Iran are honing their skills in cross-border cyber-attacks of their own, putting critical infrastructure at risk. Resurgent far-right movements in Europe have mobilized online, aided by the ease with which hate and conspiracy can spread on social platforms. This was key in the Brexit vote, and we see it too in the horrifying resurgence of white nationalist terrorism here in the United States.

The global rise in authoritarianism has coincided with a concentration of power within tech and e-commerce companies reminiscent of the monopoly power of the robber barons of the late 1800s and early 1900s. The giants of Silicon Valley have almost unchecked economic power and unlimited access to our personal information as they vacuum up data on our movements, buying habits, and intimate communications. This vast access constitutes a surveillance infrastructure unprecedented in human history, accruing power in these firms to rival that of nation states.

We have entered a new epoch, which scholars Erik Brynjolfsson and Andrew McAfee have termed "the second machine age."[1] Just as in the Industrial Revolution, humans are developing new ways of working in concert with machines and significantly reducing the need for physical labor in manufacturing. Now, though, machines have also entered the realm of cognitive labor, making decisions about everything from diagnosing diseases to marketing groceries. The algorithms behind these decisions frequently operate in opaque fashion, and without accountability. No one has measured the disruption they might bring to our culture, our economy, and our way of life. What will people do if machines take over the labor market? Where will they work, if they work at all? Across a broad spectrum of issues, we have more questions than answers. Can America sustain its global leadership and advance its national interests in a world shrunk and changed by the internet? Have nations become obsolete? How do we establish e-commerce rules and governance when a few small players control our communications and know all of our private information? Without a robust and economically viable journalism industry to put a reliable spotlight on abuse, injustice, and oppression, how can we know what the players are doing?

The new era forces us to confront a variety of interrelated issues with implications for the future of democracy: privacy, the power of the tech industry, the spread of extremism, the rise of authoritarianism, new kinds of warfare, and the Balkanization of the web. We must begin crafting policy responses before it is too late.

American jurisprudence says we should have a "reasonable expectation of privacy," but it is far from clear we still can. Is privacy dead, or transformed beyond recognition? What do we do about the corporations that have built their empires atop a mountain of personal data? Facebook now has more users—over 2.3 billion—than there are Christians. On Google's YouTube, users stream one billion hours of video each day. These companies present many of the same governance challenges as other large corporations—lobbying, monopoly power, regulatory capture, tax avoidance—but their stranglehold on our attention and their incomprehensibly vast trove of personal information make them a new kind of threat. Engagement with these companies is key to addressing the phenomena that have placed our politics in peril.

Put simply, people behave differently when they know they are being watched. Expressing controversial ideas, a vital part of the democratic process, entails greater risk. The fear of being perceived as "other"—for reasons of ethnicity, religion, sexuality, or lifestyle—can push them into concealing or denying who they are. It can also inspire harassment, shaming, and verbal and physical attacks. The tech titans have established their surveillance operations through Byzantine service agreements that give most users little understanding of privacy trade-offs. That is by design. With their knowledge of our browsing habits, communications, and physical location, Facebook and Google can develop ever more sophisticated techniques to draw us to their services and manipulate our behavior for the benefit of their advertisers. We know, for example, that cellular providers have sold location data to unscrupulous operators. Bounty hunters, jilted lovers, and many others can exploit the knowledge that someone is seeing a mental health counselor, say, or a divorce lawyer.

It is a lesson of history that unaccountable bureaucracies collecting personal data without scrutiny will inevitably abuse their power—which explains why European countries with recent histories of just such abuses have taken the lead on this issue. Here in the United States, we are also familiar with worries about how much the government knows about us; the debate about security versus privacy has been with us a long time. But we need to understand that the right to privacy applies at least as much to our relationship with Google, Twitter, and Facebook as it does to our relationship with the government.

The privacy question enjoys unusual bipartisan support in Congress, suggesting that legislation is not too far off. Europe's General Data Protection Regulation offers some guideposts on what such legislation should include: data portability to enable easily switching between competing services, along with consumer protections requiring companies to seek consent before collecting data and erase it upon request. We must also ask whether tech companies have become too large, just as our leaders did with Standard Oil in its heyday. We should consider forcing Facebook to divest Instagram and WhatsApp, and Google to cut loose YouTube and Gmail. That would promote greater competition and make it easier for new businesses to enter the tech arena and differentiate themselves on user privacy.

We must also examine the way these companies have seized control of our public discourse, a dynamic Jameel Jaffer of the Knight First Amendment Institute has described as a "privatization of the public square."[2] It is impossible to communicate as a politician, journalist, or public figure without acquiescing to terms of service from Facebook and

Twitter, and there is no way to appeal their censorship decisions in a legal proceeding. At present, these platforms cannot even be compelled to reverse decisions on banning users or removing content. It is not a stretch to imagine Facebook labeling vitriolic criticism of Mark Zuckerberg as a violation of its guidelines, nor Apple removing content from its App Store that enables scrutiny of its supply chain.

Facebook, Google, and Twitter have so far evaded questions about their responsibility to promote healthy discourse and prevent harassment by claiming that they are not publishers, just neutral parties providing communication infrastructure. But this is disingenuous at best. The content users see is determined by what will best drive advertising revenue. This has created online silos of likeminded people consuming information that speaks to their pre-existing biases. Even worse, the algorithms privilege provocative content, regardless of factual accuracy, because it is more likely to go viral and prompt "engagement" in the form of shares, replies, and comments.

Like it or not, social media has become part of our twenty-first-century infrastructure, and we can't wish it away. What we can do, though, is treat it as we do many other utilities and subject it to robust public charter. This may seem like a radical step, but there are numerous precedents. The British Broadcasting Corporation, for example, is required under its charter to promote education and learning, sustain citizenship and civil society, and stimulate creativity and cultural excellence. In the United States, PBS and NPR are governed by the 1967 Public Broadcasting Act, which found value in media established "for instructional, educational, and cultural purposes" and which set out to "address national concerns and solve local problems."

Imposing similar imperatives on the largest social media platforms could substantially improve our public discourse and provide some measure of democratic control. Tech magnates like Tim Cook and Mark Zuckerberg have themselves called for some level of regulation as they struggle to manage complex issues like free speech and user privacy without guidance from policymakers.

These companies don't need to be nationalized, but they do need a much tighter leash. The U.S. Supreme Court swung and missed on this when, in the 2010 *Citizens United* case, it afforded unlimited political power to corporations based on a finding that they are "persons" with First

Amendment rights, ignoring the fact that they are chartered by the states and therefore have public interest responsibilities. A renewed debate in the light of our struggles with speech on the internet could reset perceptions and help reestablish rules of corporate public and social responsibility.

Coincident with the rise of the tech titans has been the collapse of professional journalism. More than half the jobs in the newspaper industry disappeared between 2001 and 2016; more journalists lost their jobs during this stretch, in fact, than coal miners. The demise of classified advertising played a major role in the initial decline, but the major culprits these days are Facebook and Google, which together account for more than 60 percent of U.S. digital advertising.

In short, the economics of internet publishing are a disaster for journalism. Newspapers are laying off their investigative teams and local government reporters, making it ever easier for corrupt companies and politicians to evade scrutiny. Harder to measure, but no less damaging, is the social cohesion lost when a community lacks a comprehensive chronicle of local events.

Where real news has suffered, fake news has filled the gap. In the months preceding the 2016 election, the top twenty stories from fake news sites out-performed those from legitimate outlets in Facebook engagement.[3] Fraudulent publishers like the *Denver Guardian* and *Ending the Fed* mastered the art of virality, racking up pageviews to rival the *New York Times* and CNN. Some of these publishers are simple con artists, penning outrageous content in search of display-ad revenue. But a significant portion, we now know, were operated by the Russian government, which aimed to provoke conflict, assail trust in our institutions, and suppress voter turnout. They succeeded beyond anyone's wildest dreams.

"Everyone is entitled to his own opinion, but not his own facts," Daniel Patrick Moynihan famously said. The fake news boom offers a worrying challenge to the senator's claim, with conservatives and liberals increasingly existing in alternate realities. Conspiracies are circulated to millions, whether it's the farcical "Pizzagate" scandal, or Alex Jones accusing the bereaved parents of the Sandy Hook school shooting victims of inventing their grief to deny gun owners their Second Amendment rights. In the pre-digital age, when fools claimed that the moon landing was staged, they were ridiculed or ignored. Now lunacy has a place in the social media mainstream.

The alternate realities incubated on social media threaten to make our country a very hard place to govern. If we cannot agree on basic facts, we cannot hope to define problems, much less resolve them. The Rand Corporation researchers Jennifer Kavanagh and Michael Rich refer to this phenomenon as "truth decay," and in their 2018 book, they argue that the most damaging consequences include "the erosion of civil discourse, political paralysis, alienation and disengagement of individuals from political and civic institutions, and uncertainty over national policy."[4]

One essential response to truth decay is the resuscitation of professional journalism. As Louis Brandeis might say were he here to survey the landscape, the best defense against fake news is real news. One way to start would be to allow media outlets to negotiate collectively with social media platforms for better terms. Carriage fees, like those television providers pay to networks, would allow news outlets to recoup lost revenue. Social platforms operating under public charters could be compelled to pay them fair rates. The platforms must also do a better job of highlighting legitimate news. The fact that a *Denver Guardian* story can appear visually indistinct from a *New York Times* article on Facebook or Twitter is an obvious and easily remedied design failing.

What do we do, then, about orchestrated disinformation campaigns like the one Russia launched during the 2016 presidential election? Back then, social platforms were caught off-guard; so convinced were they of the virtue in their corporate mission that they failed to consider how their tools might be abused. To their credit, they have since made significant investments in stemming the tide of fake content, but much remains to be done. Mark Zuckerberg has expressed confidence that improvements in artificial intelligence will automate away much of the Herculean task of moderating what appears on his site, but this claim deserves skepticism. The question of what constitutes truth in the political context will always be contested, and it is hard to imagine large numbers of human moderators ever becoming unnecessary.

Social media platforms also have to acknowledge and address the problem that their business models favor inflammatory content of the sort peddled by fake news publishers. As prominent digital media critics such as Tim Wu and Jaron Lanier have noted, content that spreads on social platforms tends to be based on "startle" emotions: humor, for one, but also outrage, disbelief, and disgust for out-groups, of exactly the type outrageous fake news articles generate. Nuance seldom goes viral.[5]

It is not just fake news publishers who benefit from this culture of outrage; a new class of extremists have as well. The Islamic State has recruited fighters and established global affiliates through digital propaganda. White nationalism has made a terrifying resurgence in the United States, with new adherents falling under its sway via rabbit holes of anti-Semitic conspiracy videos on YouTube and incendiary forums like 8chan. We should require YouTube and other platforms to recommend deradicalization content for serial consumers of hate speech, and we should prevent links to extremist forums from being posted.

Authoritarian-minded politicians have also benefited from the perverse incentives of social media's attention economy. They have taken advantage of popular anxieties over issues like immigration and global trade to demonize their enemies and weaponize social platforms, which are already primed, as the historian Timothy Snyder has written, to serve up posts "according the individual's psychological preferences and vulnerabilities." No wonder, then, that the politics of resentment is sharply in ascendance. The platforms, Snyder argues, "offer content known to align with the user's emotions, and then mix in extreme versions of the views or practices of another group." The new populists have free rein to repeat false claims about their opponents, knowing that their supporters will do the work of propagating these claims over social media long before mainstream journalists have an opportunity to fact-check or contextualize. As Snyder writes, "We hear what we want to hear . . . and then we fear what we want to fear."[6]

Once in office, authoritarians have even more dangerous digital tools at their disposal. The surveillance methods pioneered in Silicon Valley can be put to work to spy on citizens in ways that trample on our constitutional rights and stifle our fundamental freedoms. While there is the potential for democratically minded leaders to work with tech firms to safeguard constitutional rights, authoritarian leaders have collaborated with industry to achieve the opposite effect. In China, for example, citizens can be arrested just for searching a controversial topic like "Tiananmen Square," while Uighur Muslims and other minorities are tracked and logged in databases via facial recognition technology. The Chinese tech sector functions essentially as an arm of the state, creating an environment that makes *1984* look like Pleasantville.

It is therefore essential, as we contemplate any new privacy legislation, to regulate the government's own digital practices. We should anonymize data wherever possible, allow citizens to access data collected on them, and store personal data no longer than absolutely necessary. We must walk back the excesses of the post-9/11 Patriot Act that sanctioned warrantless surveillance. Our operating principle must be to imagine the worst abuses of power possible under current law and to safeguard against them.

It is also important to identify the positives of the internet age—the ways in which digital tools have enabled global connections and democratic participation.

To be sure, America's institutions feel unstable in ways we have not experienced since the upheaval of 1968, but part of this tumult is the result of progress. Social friction inevitably occurs when marginalized groups assert their rights, and the internet has given them a forum to do so in profound and unprecedented ways. Take the Black Lives Matter movement, which has grown in part because of the power of smartphones to record and distribute episodes of police violence against African Americans. It's not that excessive force by police officers is new or unknown to those who have been at the blunt end of an unbalanced criminal justice system for more than two centuries, but when video evidence is at hand, it becomes impossible to look away. The Rodney King beating in Los Angeles in 1991 was an early example of the power of video footage to stir public outrage—and, ultimately, to enact reforms. Now you don't need an expensive video camera to shoot the footage, and you don't need to lobby a local television affiliate to air it. Whipping out a smart phone is all it takes for the world to learn about Eric Garner in Staten Island or Philando Castile in Minnesota.

Without the internet, news stories about Harvey Weinstein and other prominent entertainment figures accused of abusing women might never have lit the fuse of the #MeToo movement. The #MeToo hashtag was tweeted by the actress Alyssa Milano in October 2017, and within twenty-four hours it had been repeated 4.7 million times, transforming the national conversation.[7] Without the internet, survivors of the February 2018 mass shooting at Marjory Stoneman Douglas High School in Parkland, Florida, would not have been able to pull off the remarkable and unprecedented feat of becoming better known than the shooter and launching an impassioned national campaign attacking America's epidemic of gun violence.[8]

Grassroots organizers have also been empowered at the ballot box, thanks to their ability to mobilize and raise money online. While the influence of big money in politics remains a significant threat to democracy, the likes of Barack Obama, Bernie Sanders, and Conor Lamb—who ran a successful insurgent campaign for Congress in Pennsylvania in 2018—have shown that it is possible to build successful campaigns with digital tools and small-dollar contributions. As we consider the future of the internet, we must preserve its power to fuel activists and give voice to the voiceless.

We also should not forget the internet's extraordinary power to disseminate knowledge and ideas of all kinds, or its ability to foster personal and business relationships across the globe. The worlds of work, education, and research are transforming before our eyes, and many of those changes have been positive. The rosy, liberal, cosmopolitan future that Thomas Friedman envisaged in his 2005 book, *The World Is Flat*, is still a part of the story.[9] The internet has broken down barriers of time and distance and offers people the chance to gain access to new cultures, ideas, and friendships. The world's economies are more connected as a result, an important buffer against interstate conflict.

What we need to avoid is a Balkanization of the digital realm, in which authoritarian states wall off domestic audiences from the rest of the internet and restrict the flow of incoming information, to the detriment of entrepreneurs as well as individuals. One startling example of such backtracking arose during the Arab Spring, when autocratic Middle Eastern governments turned the online organizing tools of the uprisings into instruments of oppression. Where at first governments in Tunisia, Egypt, and elsewhere were caught off guard by the protests, they soon became adept at cutting off online services, using social media posts to identify and round up organizers, and spreading disinformation to discredit them.[10]

Clearly a continuation of our laissez-faire approach to digital regulation is not tenable. What we need instead are multilateral agreements on the flow of online information and commerce, similar to those that have established norms for warfare and global trade. "The lack of consensus or cooperation," investor Fred Hu and Council on Foreign Relations fellow A. Michael Spence have argued, "could lead to the emergence of national digital borders, which would not only inhibit flows of data and information, but also disrupt trade, supply chains, and cross-border investment."[11]

Certainly there are limits to this kind of cooperation. It is naive to think we will change China's mind on domestic censorship, and other governments will come to their own conclusions about surveillance and free speech. But the global nature of the internet is worth preserving. We can start by passing reforms at home that can act as a model to the rest of the world. We should also start a global conversation about rules that could, for example, protect the ability of citizens to communicate across borders, limit the data that corporations and governments can collect on foreign citizens, and protect companies from state-sponsored hacking. President Obama made a start on this in the aftermath of my office's indictment of the Chinese hackers, securing an agreement from Xi Jinping to refrain from cyber-theft of intellectual property. That agreement, though, was non-binding. We need to establish an international tribunal to impose penalties on countries that violate agreed-upon norms. The greater our openness in digital communication and commerce, the more stable our international relations will be.

This cooperation must also extend to security, as one of the most terrifying aspects of the digital age is its application to new forms of warfare. We have already seen Russian attempts to hack our electoral infrastructure and flood us with disinformation. The Russians have also launched brazen hacking attacks on our electrical grid, and we are not the only targets. In 2015, Putin's forces cut the power of more than 200,000 Ukrainians. They also appear to have been responsible for a 2017 cyber-attack that shut down a Saudi Arabian petrochemical plant.

We need to make clear that attacks on infrastructure will be met with international sanctions, and may even trigger our NATO mutual-defense obligations. We cannot tolerate the prospect of assaults on our hospitals, transportation networks, or financial system. One possibility is to fold these security-related concerns into the Geneva Conventions; they could also come as part of a new accord. In any case, we have established the broad international norm that civilians are not legitimate targets in a conflict, and we must extend that principle to cyberspace.

The Trump administration has been skeptical of international cooperation and opposed to new government regulations, but American isolationism is neither desirable nor possible in the internet age. We cannot allow a monopolistic industry to continue expanding unchecked and threaten the stability of the global political system, nor a new class of digital weapons to threaten our economy and security. Our democratic institutions have already suffered, but there is still time to enact domestic reforms and secure international agreements that will limit the damage and establish a better way forward. We have to decide what our politics will look like in the internet age. Our democratic freedom is in the breach.

THE NEW NEW DEAL: HOW TO REREGULATE CAPITALISM

Robert Kuttner

Outside the Federal Trade Commission in Washington, DC, are twin pieces of Roosevelt-era statuary that capture in metaphor the New Deal project of harnessing raw capitalism in the broad public interest. The magnificent limestone statues are titled "Man Controlling Trade," and each shows a rider struggling to rein in a wild horse. One suspects that if such a statue were commissioned today, it would show the horse dragging the man up Constitution Avenue.

In the 1930s and 1940s, Americans benefited from a regulated brand of capitalism. Not only did the economy grow at record rates; it also grew more equal. Bankers were kept in their proper role of providing capital to the real economy, not feathering their own nests. The right to organize unions was protected. Antitrust laws were vigorously enforced. Housing was affordable; likewise higher education. Children on average could expect to do better than their parents. In the postwar era, government began extending needed regulation to new realms of the economy and society, such as the environment and consumer protections.

Not all was well, of course. It took until the 1960s for the government to even begin guaranteeing African Americans rights that had been promised a century earlier by Lincoln. Women were second-class citizens, lawfully shunted to inferior support jobs and earning less than sixty cents for every male earner's dollar. That status also began to be remedied in the 1960s—though the work is far from over. Still, looked at as a strategy for governing capitalism in the broad public interest, the postwar system was a good start.

The question we need to ask now, in an age of rampant inequality built on concentrated corporate power, is whether that grand bargain was a temporary anomaly, and what it will take to restore and then build on it. Spoiler alert: The answer has to be a much stronger democracy. Otherwise, the sheer power of the capitalist system will run roughshod over efforts to harness it in the public interest, no matter how good the regulations are on paper.

Since the 1970s, the gains of the postwar era have largely been reversed. In every major realm where salutary forms of regulation made the economy more efficient and more equitable, we have seen both major parties collude in deregulation, beginning with the presidency of Jimmy Carter. The result is an economy that is less fair and less reliable. Instead of the pendulum swinging back to more regulation on behalf of a fairer system, the resulting political backlash against diminished prospects for ordinary people has been substantially captured by the far right.

A democratically regulated economy remains possible—and urgently necessary. And the task of the progressive movement is to build a democracy strong enough that leaders find it impolitic to try to dismantle public-interest regulation. Regulated capitalism needs to be combined with direct public provision of goods and services in some realms where public is more efficient than private, and where even regulated private provision is too easily corrupted.

Why Markets Require Regulation

History has proven three realities about market capitalism and democracy. First, regulated markets are more efficient, more equitable, less prone to corruption, and more legitimate than unregulated markets. Second, the state needs strong democratic institutions to regulate markets effectively and efficiently; otherwise, capitalism overwhelms the capacity of the democratic state to regulate broadly in the public interest. And third, when elites weaken democracy and capture the state, they not only rig the rules to reward themselves; they also undermine the legitimacy of democracy itself, and the far right gains. Reversing this downward spiral of disaffection and distrust is necessary in order to reclaim a decent economy and to restore and strengthen democracy itself. The details will be different from the New Deal era, but the principles and politics are enduring.

Why are laissez-faire markets inefficient as well as inequitable? Despite the claims made on behalf of the standard economic model and its more extreme neo-liberal variant, markets do not in fact price things accurately. The market has treated the environment, for example, as a free sink. The true costs to the economy and to the planet are not captured in the market price of each transaction. Economists call that form of market failure an externality. The standard model treats externalities as a special case, but in fact goods and services that markets price inaccurately account for something like half the economy—everything from education, to health care, to workers' wages, to research and development, to the costs of pollution.

Financial markets are an extreme case of the unreliability of laissez-faire. They are prone to fads of boom and bust. Bankers and investment bankers are in the habit of inventing securities whose true risks are opaque to the purchaser. Because they create the security and then promote it, bankers are in a conflict of interest relative to the retail buyer. Financial players use a variety of tricks to disguise the true degree of debt within a particular category of security, or in the entire system. This is also a form of systematic market mispricing. When buyers suddenly dump securities and the crash comes, as it did in 1929 and again in 2008, the damage to the real economy overwhelms whatever purported efficiencies resulted from "innovative" new forms of financial product and market price-setting. In 2008, the loss to the real economy was in excess of $15 trillion.

In the idealized market model, the interplay of supply and demand determines an appropriate "market-clearing" price, which translates consumer preferences into signals of what producers should offer for sale. But that premise assumes a rough equivalence of information between buyer and seller, no monopoly pricing power, and no externalities. The more the true political economy is tilted in favor of powerful corporations and banks, the more power these elites have to rig the economy's rules in their own favor, pushing the actual economy ever further away from the textbook marketplace, which was not all that efficient in the first place. What we need are not freer markets, but the opposite: reregulation.

The Regulation of Capital

Following the Great Depression, the Roosevelt administration regulated financial markets very tightly to eliminate the conflicts of interest that had pumped up the stock bubble of the 1920s and led to the Great Depression. Public capital was needed to break the deflationary spiral, because businesses and homeowners were making distress sales in a falling market and fueling further debt deflation. The New Deal regulatory structure was the right model, and now it needs to be reclaimed and adapted to the twenty-first-century economy, because we have repeated the catastrophe of 1929. Here's how it worked then:

The **Glass–Steagall Act of 1933** separated commercial banking from investment banking so commercial banks could not package sketchy loans as securities and peddle them to unsuspecting customers. In exchange, the commercial banks were eligible for deposit insurance to reassure their customers. Investment banks were able to take more risks, but had no government backup in the event of failure.

Under the **Securities Act of 1933** and the **Securities Exchange Act of 1934**, stockbrokers, underwriters of securities, and stock exchanges were for the first time required to disclose all financial information considered "material" to a potential investor. The **Investment Company Acts of 1940** consolidated these reforms, while the **Public Utilities Holding Company Act** cracked down on pyramiding. New independent regulatory agencies were created and existing ones strengthened in several sectors of the economy.

When this edifice was complete, the financial system had been turned into something not far from a public utility. Incomes of commercial bank executives were comfortable, but not lavish. The legacy of the 1930s and 1940s was a financial system free of panics, crashes, or scandals, virtually for the first time in the history of the American republic. A well-behaved financial system helped to underwrite the postwar boom and lasted until the inflation of the 1970s and the 1980s and the right's return to power.

Regulating Housing Finance

The mortgage finance system also required drastic overhaul. Until the 1930s, a mortgage was typically a short-term note, often of just five years. The homeowner paid only interest until the note came due. In normal times, the note was rolled over at prevailing interest rates. But during financial panics when banks were short of funds, homeowners lost everything because they could not get a new mortgage.

In the Great Depression, housing values collapsed and thousands of banks failed. Even a bank that had money would not make a mortgage loan on a house that was worth less than the loan amount, and many people could not afford to meet their payments because they were out of work. In the spring of 1933, half of the mortgages in America were in default, and banks were failing by the thousands.

In response, the Roosevelt administration invented deposit insurance and remade the entire mortgage system, starting with the Home Owners Loan Corporation, which eventually refinanced about one mortgage in five. The 1934 National Housing Act created long-term, self-amortizing mortgages with low down payments, and a new agency, the Federal Housing Administration, to insure them. Over time, a changing mix of interest and principal would not just carry a loan, but also pay it off. A secondary mortgage market, the Federal National Mortgage Association, was created in 1938 to purchase mortgages from banks and thrift institutions so their funds could be replenished and they could make more loans. Under the GI Bill of Rights in 1946, down-payment requirements were lowered even further.

The whole system worked like a Swiss watch. Standards were high but not punitive. The homeownership rate rose from 40 percent to around 62 percent by 1960. Defaults and bank failures were vanishingly rare.

In the 1970s, inflation began to stress the system. The thirty-year fixed rates that banks had offered effectively accrued negative interest as inflation increased. Bank losses led to calls for deregulation so the banks could pursue other profit opportunities. As corporate political power increased and free-market conservatives took over government, Wall Street's capacity to "innovate" overwhelmed regulators' capacity or appetite for protecting the public interest. The non-regulation and deliberate deregulation that followed, were cheered on by neo-liberals in government and by their allies in the financial industry.

The consequence was a proliferation of new forms of financial instruments, whose risks were opaque to both consumers and regulators. As allies of the financial industry took over government, regulators regarded these new instruments with studied incuriosity. Wall Street simply had its way with the economy. As in the 1920s, the result was a pyramiding of hidden, speculative debt unbacked by actual capital, and it all finally came crashing down in the collapse of 2008. The Federal Reserve and the Treasury responded by pumping several trillion dollars into the financial system to bail out banks that were insolvent, but not to clean them out.

The Regulation and Deregulation of Labor

Under the New Deal, the government for the first time championed labor's right to organize unions. It also inaugurated wage and hour laws, setting a minimum wage and requiring overtime pay for hours beyond the standard forty-hour work week. Worker economic security was increased via an unemployment compensation system. Social Security also enhanced the standing and power of workers by providing government-organized pensions as well as a federal disability program.

During World War II, the role of unions as legitimate social partners was further enhanced. In exchange for a no-strike pledge, the government vigorously enforced the National Labor Relations Act, to the point where any war production contractor was compelled to have a union if workers wanted one. By the war's end, more than a third of all American workers were unionized, and labor organizing was accepted as the new normal in major companies across all industries. The trend continued for a while after the war, as unions were able to bargain for an equal share of rising national output, and wage settlements in unionized workplaces set the pattern for the pay of all workers, unionized or not.

It did not take long, however, for corporate capital to assert its temporarily suppressed power. The Taft–Hartley Act of 1947, passed by the new Republican Congress over President Harry S. Truman's veto (with the support of scores of Southern Democrats, who feared unions as agents of integration), cut union power back again. States were given the option to pass anti-union "right-to-work" laws, and sympathy boycotts were outlawed.

By the time Ronald Reagan became president in 1981 and as one of his first moves broke a strike of air traffic controllers, government had ceased being an ally of the right to unionize, and companies had declared open warfare against unions. One famous study demonstrated that about one worker in twenty who sought to organize or join a union was fired. Penalties against employers who pursued flagrantly illegal union-busting tactics were mild slaps on the wrist, just the cost of doing business. The percentage of unionized workers in the private sector dropped from more than one in three to about one in twenty.

There were other, more insidious measures that weakened worker power in the 1980s and 1990s. Increasingly conservative courts denied the federal Arbitration Act to allow employers to deny workers the right to go to court to challenge employers who curtailed their rights or failed to enforce anti-discrimination laws. Instead, workers had to take their case to an arbitrator selected by management (and so the arbitrator usually sided with management).

Trade agreements expanded the rights of corporations to move operations around the globe in search of cheaper labor or weaker regulations, but were silent on the question of worker rights. Products made under conditions that would be illegal in the United States could be freely brought into the country—thus importing the degraded labor and social conditions along with the product. Domestic workers who sought to protect their rights could be threatened with outsourcing. Millions of jobs were lost, and millions more people suffered worsening pay.

Companies also made creative use of bankruptcy laws to loot worker pensions. They would point to an inflated stock market to claim that pensions were over-funded and to find ways to take out money. Then, when the market fell, they claimed they needed to cut benefits. The traditional pension system was largely converted to a far less reliable 401(k)-style system, under which a worker could outlive the plan and be left with nothing for old age.

The protections of minimum wage, meanwhile, lagged badly behind inflation, and corporations got more clever at redefining regular payroll jobs as contingent jobs, and workers as independent contractors. Unlike payroll workers, contractors don't receive most benefits, their employers no longer pay half their payroll taxes, they lose their right to unemployment compensation, and they may lose the ability to organize or join a union.

As courts have become more right-wing, Supreme Court decisions have added to the assault on unions and worker rights. In the 2018 case *Janus v. AFSCME*, the Supreme Court overturned forty years of precedent and ruled that public-sector unions with contracts covering a given workplace cannot collect dues from workers who don't want to pay dues, even though they are covered by the contract and derive benefits from it.

The expansion of the so-called gig economy, and the technology that enables it, serves to further weaken worker power relative to employers and facilitate new abuses. Uber and Lyft drivers are treated as independent contractors, even though the employer controls all the conditions of work except for the worker's schedule. Under the 1938 Fair Labor Standards, if the employer dictates the conditions, the worker must be treated as an employee. But administrative and court rulings have allowed on-demand driving services, warehouse companies, trucking services such as FedEx, and employers in countless other sectors to evade that standard.

Weakened Consumer Protections

Beginning in the late 1960s and early 1970s, America benefited from a mobilization of consumer and environmental activism resulting in the **Clean Air Act** and **Clean Water Act**; the **Fair Credit Reporting Act** and the **Truth in Lending Act**; the **Occupational Safety and Health Act**; and measures to ensure fairer treatment of mortgage applicants, such as the **Home Mortgage Disclosure Act** and the **Community Reinvestment Act**.

Even in the full flush of these reforms, though, an anti-regulation undertow was already in motion, influenced by the renewed popularity of free-market economic theory and the resurrection of corporate power. Some industries that had been thought to be natural monopolies or oligopolies in need of regulation, such as airlines, electricity, telephones, and long-distance trucking, were now regarded as free-market competitors after all. The regulation of these industries had already been corrupted by industry influence, so regulation in practice did not work as well as it did in theory. Thus, in the Carter era some liberals joined conservatives in calling for deregulation. These included Carter's economic adviser, Fred Kahn, as well as Senator Ted Kennedy and his then counsel and future Supreme Court justice, Stephen Breyer. Even Ralph Nader was in favor of eliminating some regulation that he felt had been corrupted.

Deregulation swept through one sector after another. Beginning in 1978, airlines, trucking, electric power, and, later, telephones were deregulated. Even the hospital industry was substantially deregulated and many nonprofits converted to for-profits. The result was far from what enthusiasts had intended: these sectors were soon rife with mergers, concentration, and monopoly pricing power. Airlines went through a spate of bankruptcies, leading to price gouging and a deterioration in travel conditions as well as some bargains. Electric power went from a regulated monopoly to a deregulated monopoly, with no savings for the consumer. Hospital charges soared. Telephone service was soon in the thrall of two unregulated giants, AT&T and Verizon.

Regulatory capture intensified. The conflicts of interest were not as extreme under Democratic presidents as under Republican ones, but anti-regulators maintained a fortress at the Office of Management's Office of Information and Regulatory Affairs (OIRA), which regularly vetoed regulations required by statute on the dubious grounds that they did not pass cost-benefit tests. In the Obama administration, OIRA under the leadership of Cass Sunstein blocked or weakened several rules at the Environmental Protection Agency in this way.

Can Regulation Be Made to Work?

The time for a counter-revolution has come. A mixed economy is efficient and equitable only when markets are heavily regulated—and when democratic institutions protect regulators from capture by the industries they are overseeing.

Financial Regulation

Globalization has enabled a swollen banking sector to outrun national regulation and to use global trade deals to weaken the rules that govern finance. Yet the United States, as the world's deepest financial market, still retains vast power to set the rules, since most of the world's capitalists do business with its banks.

The next administration will need to restore a tightly regulated financial system. This means drastically simplifying finance so that there is far less securitization of credit. The whole system of slicing and dicing mortgages and repackaging them as securities should be simplified. There should be no subprime loans. We need to restore the Glass–Steagall wall so commercial banking is once again separate from investment banking. Reserve requirements need to be raised so as to reduce excessive leverage in the system. The largest banks should be subject to extra reserve requirements and, in some cases, broken up. Usury ceilings on interest rates, which had been standard until the 1980s, need to be restored. Credit-rating agencies, which escaped scrutiny under the Dodd–Frank Act, need to be tightly regulated.

Savings and loan associations were once almost entirely nonprofits. They did not pay their executives exorbitant salaries and had no incentive to speculate. We should either prohibit for-profit thrift institutions or expand public banking and the credit union sector so consumers and homebuyers have more not-for-profit options. We also need a lot more social housing.

The Dodd–Frank Act was a good start, but some of its provisions have been weakened administratively, while others have not even been implemented. More than a decade after the crash of 2008, we still have not come to grips with root causes. We do not have final regulations on executive compensation, credit default swaps, reform of credit-rating agencies, or rules on commodity speculation by banks. The next administration needs to put teeth into all these initiatives.

We also need a much tougher set of policies on banks deemed too big to fail. Because these behemoths believe the government will always bail them out, they are able to take grave risks and still get cheaper capital in money markets than do smaller, more community-minded banks. In 2018, America's six largest banks made $120 billion, accounting for more than half the profits of the entire banking sector. It's time to change reserve requirements to create a disincentive for banks to grow beyond a certain size. No bank should control more than 5 percent of the nation's banking assets.

Under Donald Trump's presidency, banking regulation and deregulation have been going in the wrong direction. Trump has crippled the Consumer Financial Protection Bureau, the most important innovation of the Obama years. At the time of this writing, plans are underway to dismantle or weaken some of the key protections of the Dodd–Frank Act by lowering capital requirements, allowing more proprietary trading and derivatives dealing, and watering down the terms of stress-testing and so-called living will requirements that require a bank to make contingency plans for what it would do in the event of failure. All these provisions need to be strengthened, not weakened. In addition, we need public banks to offer services that commercial banks fail to provide at a reasonable cost and inject some measure of what Franklin Roosevelt termed "yardstick competition."

Private Equity and Hedge Funds

Private equity firms and hedge funds make up one of the most abusive parts of the post-1980s financial system. Many have wriggled through what started out as a very small loophole in the 1940 Investment Company Act, which exempted family financial management firms from disclosures and regulations required of publicly traded companies. This loophole has been widened so far that so-called private equity companies can now evade regulation on the premise that they are not selling shares to the general public. What these companies are doing, however, is taking over businesses with mostly borrowed money (a maneuver known as a leveraged buyout), piling the debt onto the balance sheet of the target company, stripping assets, selling off real estate, laying off workers, cutting pension plans, and paying the private equity managers exorbitant dividends and management fees. Even if the operating company goes broke, the private equity owners typically make back their own small investment many times over. Today, some eleven million American workers are employed by companies ultimately owned by private equity, and may not be aware of the true source of the relentless pressure to cut their wages.

Despite the name, private equity firms seldom contribute equity. They are nothing like true venture capitalists, who put their own capital at risk. Mainly, they burden target companies with debt and act as parasites on the real economy. They cause countless bankruptcies. The real economy performed better when there was no such industry. Public policy should drive private equity out of business by closing the disclosure loophole and using tax policy to penalize companies that acquire other companies by loading them up with debt. Excessive extraction of dividends at the expense of the operating company should be prohibited as a conflict of interest.

Economic Concentration and Platform Monopolies

One of the great abuses of our era is the near collapse of antitrust enforcement and the extreme industry concentration. One result of the merger and acquisition mania of the past several decades has been price-gouging and reduced consumer choice. The proof is in the astronomical incomes of corporate executives and the monopoly profits of their industries. For the most part, these have not been challenged by the Federal Trade Commission or the Antitrust Division of the Justice Department.

Some of the abuse has been achieved through the extension of patents, trademarks, and copyrights, the result of decades of industry lobbying. The pharmaceutical industry represents a toxic brew of failed direct regulation by the Food and Drug Administration, failed antitrust enforcement, excessive patent protection, as well as trade policies that seek to extend drug company abuses internationally. We not only see astronomical price-gouging on new drugs, but also industry manipulation of the pricing of drugs long in the public domain, such as insulin.

Across the economy, concentration has reached such an extreme that just two companies control more than half of the market share in sectors as diverse as car rentals, drugstores, airline reservation systems, aircraft manufacturing, hardware stores, optical companies, and smartphones. Hospital ownership is ever more highly concentrated, too. In the tech sector, Amazon, Apple, Facebook, Google, and Microsoft managed to buy out 436 independent companies in the decade after the crash without a single regulatory challenge. One of the first orders of business of the next administration has to be reversing these trends. What, after all, is market capitalism without meaningful competition? This is not just about economic fairness. It's about the bedrock legitimacy of the system.

Today, the giant platform monopolies—Google, Facebook, and Amazon—are parasitic on the rest of the economy, as attested by their exorbitant profits. But other abuses are new and require new doctrines and enforcement techniques. For example, Amazon provides a platform for companies that wish to sell products to the public, but it also competes with those companies by offering similar products. That should be an antitrust violation, because Amazon can use its privileged access to user data to gain an unfair advantage. Senator Elizabeth Warren has proposed a principle similar to the doctrine of "common carriage." Amazon should either provide market services to all comers, or sell its own products, but not both.

Platform monopolies generally should be subject to much tougher constraints on the purchase of potential competitors, and should also have strict limits on the use of consumer data. Facebook and Google need to share their advertising proceeds with bona fide media organizations and other content originators who attract users to their sites but recoup few of the financial benefits.

Warren's proposed regulation would designate platform companies with $25 billion or more in revenue as "platform utilities." They would have to divest themselves of subsidiaries that sell products or engage in ancillary businesses, such as advertising or data collection. Some mergers would be reversed, such as Amazon's purchase of Whole Foods, Facebook's acquisition of WhatsApp and Instagram, and Google's buyout of Waze and Nest. The common ill here is too much concentrated market power.

Reregulating Labor

We need to reregulate labor markets if we want better jobs. Congress can clarify that arbitration clauses were never intended to destroy other rights. The Wagner Act needs to be updated so that when a majority of workers sign union cards, the union is certified and there is no protracted delay during which management can harass or fire pro-union workers. The minimum wage needs to be raised to at least $15 an hour nationally.

Millions of jobs that ought to be payroll jobs have been improperly reclassified as contingent jobs, but prosecution for misclassification, a form of payroll fraud, is extremely rare. There has also been an increase in outright wage theft. These practices tend to be more flagrant under Republican administrations. Even under Democratic ones, though, the resources of the Labor Department and the National Labor Relations Board are no match for the proliferation of abuses, and regulators are able to prosecute only the most flagrant cases.

We need a whole schema of regulation for part-time, temp, and contract workers. Gig workers and franchise employees should enjoy the same rights as other payroll workers. Pension rights need to be restored. Under the Obama administration, the Labor Department and NLRB issued guidelines suggesting that the parent company of a franchise chain like Burger King has the same legal responsibilities as an employer. This has not been enforced under Trump, and Trump's Labor Department has suggested that gig workers do not, in fact, have the rights of payroll employees. All this needs comprehensive revision.

Resorting good jobs with good wages is not just a matter of better regulation. A comprehensive infrastructure and energy transition could generate many millions of good jobs, an argument made explicitly by congressional advocates of the Green New Deal.

Strong Democracy and Strong Regulation

In the absence of a strong countervailing democratic movement, regulated industries find ways to capture their regulators. This is not a technical problem that requires better forms of regulation. It is a deeply political one. In an economy that remains fundamentally capitalist, powerful industries keep finding allies in the two major political parties to help them game the rules. Though Trump has taken the corruption of regulation to a grotesque extreme, it is important to remember that deregulation began under Jimmy Carter. Deregulation of finance really took off under Bill Clinton, and many of Clinton's former top financial officials profited directly when they parlayed their government positions into lucrative jobs on Wall Street. The debasement of the Food and Drug Administration has spanned several administrations, Democrat and Republican. The scandal of the Federal Aviation Administration delegating safety certifications to airplane manufacturers began long before Trump. The collapse of antitrust began under Reagan, but continued under successive administrations of both parties.

Public interest regulation was more robust from the 1930s to the 1960s because democracy was more robust. The labor movement, the consumer movement, and the civil rights movement all served to exercise countervailing power. The electorates of those decades also elected Congresses that regularly conducted investigative and oversight hearings. Lawmakers kept corrupt industries under pressure and put regulators under a spotlight. The inference is clear: the movement to restore public interest regulation necessarily requires a complementary movement to strengthen democracy.

FIRST UNDERSTAND WHY THEY'RE WINNING: HOW TO SAVE DEMOCRACY FROM THE ANTI-IMMIGRANT FAR RIGHT

Sasha Polakow-Suransky

I Feel Your Pain, but Reject Your Remedy

Two years after her calamitous defeat in the 2016 presidential election, Hillary Clinton was asked why the mainstream center-left politics that she and many once-successful European politicians embraced now appeared to be failing. She immediately seized on the issue of immigration. "I think Europe needs to get a handle on migration because that is what lit the flame," she told *The Guardian*. "I think it is fair to say Europe has done its part, and must send a very clear message—'we are not going to be able to continue to provide refuge and support'—because if we don't deal with the migration issue it will continue to roil the body politic."[1]

Clinton's diagnosis was mostly correct; immigration has indeed transformed the worldwide political landscape since 2015. Americans might not have faced a refugee crisis on a scale to match the European experience of millions fleeing the Syrian civil war, but they were certainly familiar with the anxieties associated with a large influx of immigrants across their long land border with Mexico. Indeed, Donald Trump had exploited those anxieties to propel himself to victory.

Clinton's policy remedy, however, was wrong. It was based on the erroneous assumption that migration is the principal driver of voter discontent and accounts, on its own, for the success of politicians like Trump or Marine Le Pen, when in reality the key problem has been the failure of establishment parties, including Clinton's Democrats, to adequately defend the economic interests of their traditional constituents.

Understanding that failure is vital for anyone seeking to make sense of the fraught immigration debate on both sides of the Atlantic. Despite the United States' very different history, self-conception, and demographic makeup, Trump's deliberate stoking of white resentment for electoral gain has made the political climate in America remarkably similar to that of many European countries where unapologetic white nationalism has become a central feature of right-wing politics. Trump, like many European populists, has paired nativism with economic populism to appeal to angry white Americans whose jobs and factories have gone and whose futures look uncertain.

That does not mean that to win back those angry white voters the Democrats have to play Trump's game and throw immigrants—or, for that matter, gays or blacks—under the bus. Building an electoral coalition is not a zero-sum game. A party can address economic insecurity *and* champion minority rights. The problem for many on the left is that they too often dismiss supporters of a candidate like Trump as incorrigible racists without seeing that many of them are alienated ex-Democrats. That is a recipe for disaster. As the British writer Nick Cohen has observed, "When the liberals despise the working class the opportunities for backlash politics are boundless."[2]

Clinton's comments were music to the ears of far-right politicians on both sides of the Atlantic whose greatest victory has been to move the goalposts and push the terms of acceptable debate firmly onto their turf.

Indeed, Trump's popularity among working-class whites in 2016 showed that when there is no clear economic agenda articulated by the left, inflammatory rhetoric and cultural appeals can quickly fill the void. Once the old battle lines disappear, realignment becomes very easy. Much the same has happened in Europe, particularly in the wake of the Syrian refugee crisis. Populist parties that were already ascendant began winning many more seats in European elections after 2015.[3] Whether or not the arrival of large numbers of desperate foreigners "lit the flame," the blaze was consciously and meticulously stoked by the likes of Le Pen in France, Geert Wilders in the Netherlands, and upstart populist parties like the AfD in Germany, the League in Italy, and Vox in Spain.

In France, the January 2015 attack by Islamist extremists on the satirical journal *Charlie Hebdo* only encouraged Le Pen's National Front to amp up its hostile rhetoric toward immigrants and Muslim citizens. For Le Pen, the refugee crisis was the greatest political gift imaginable, and she expertly conflated the *Charlie Hebdo* assailants—and other Muslim terrorists—with the hundreds of thousands of innocent Syrians fleeing

ISIS terrorism and the Assad regime, in much the same way that Trump conflated Mexican and Central American migrants with murderous drug kingpins. In the mind of a significant portion of the French public, Muslim killers and Muslim refugees became one and the same.

Just as Trump's anti-immigrant rhetoric resonated with working-class whites in the upper Midwest, some of Le Pen's most enthusiastic supporters were former Communist Party voters in France's post-industrial north. "It was socialist-communist for eighty years," Le Pen said of the Pas-de-Calais region in 2016, a few months after local elections there. "I won 45 percent," she told me. She performed even better in the presidential election two years later, appealing to traditionally left-wing voters who resented the capitalist class but no longer saw the left as representing their class interests. In Calais, as in Canton, Ohio, voters were angry about their factories closing and their jobs going abroad. They were fearful of Islam and the growing number of immigrants they saw in their towns (or heard about on TV). And they bristled at the triumphalism of a globalist class that appeared to be succeeding while they fell further behind.

It doesn't have to be that way, as Elizabeth Warren and Bernie Sanders, both left-wing champions of the working class, have discovered on the 2020 presidential campaign trail. Sanders was applauded on Fox News, the house channel of the Trump administration, when he called for universal health care, while Warren earned nods and a few cheers in the heart of Trump country when she talked about the opioid crisis in Kermit, West Virginia (80 percent pro-Trump in 2016).[4]

The irony is that nativist politicians like Trump are not particularly concerned with bread-and-butter issues, and their economic policies aren't terribly helpful to workers and the poor. The challenge for the left is to offer policies that address these voters' economic grievances without making moral concessions that lead to scapegoating of immigrants, reactionary illiberal policies, and outbreaks of politically motivated violence.

Indeed, as the Dutch political scientist Cas Mudde has pointed out, the impulse to cave in to the right's immigration agenda is not empirically sound, because the working class is not exclusively white, and most of them do not vote for the far right anyway. "Centre-left parties have been trying to 'act tough' on immigration for decades," he argues, "and have often supported policies to limit immigration, but it has not prevented their decline."[5]

Where the far-right has succeeded is in combining xenophobic immigration policies with a populist economic agenda and so pulling in votes from both right and left. Because there is no recent historical antecedent to Trump in the United States, we must look elsewhere for political lessons in how—and how not—to defeat him.

The Defenders of the White Race

On the night of November 13, 2015, Islamists shot up a series of Parisian bars and restaurants, detonated a bomb at a crowded soccer stadium, and attacked the Bataclan concert hall, firing indiscriminately into the crowd and killing ninety people. President François Hollande declared the attacks "a horror" and imposed France's first nationwide state of emergency since the Algerian war. Coming just a few months after the *Charlie Hebdo* killings, this bloodletting was met with shock and rage. A new intellectual undercurrent had already begun to paint Muslims as a fundamental threat to the nation, and the arguments now became more strident.

The United States had its own Bataclan moment in June 2016, when a Muslim American sprayed an Orlando nightclub that catered to the LGBTQ+ crowd with gunfire, killing forty-nine people. It came six months after an attack on a county health department holiday party in San Bernardino, California, in which a U.S. citizen of Pakistani descent and his Pakistani wife killed fourteen people. Like them, the Orlando shooter, Omar Mateen, appeared to have been radicalized by Islamist propaganda on the internet, without forging ties to a broader organization. Still, Trump did not hesitate to use the news to his advantage. "This is a very dark moment in America's history," he told a campaign rally, depicting Mateen as a "radical Islamic terrorist" who wanted to kill Americans without mentioning that Mateen was an American himself.[6] Trump also picked up on a favorite tactic of European far-right politicians—by presenting himself as the only true defender of gays against Muslims who hate them.

On both sides of the Atlantic, the far right has exploited such violent episodes—and ignored others perpetrated by non-Muslims—to transform the debate over immigration into something larger: a culture war against a civilizational enemy seen as fundamentally incompatible with Western democratic values. Party leaders have presented themselves as the last bulwark protecting a besieged Judeo-Christian civilization from the barbarians at the gates.

By stoking fear about immigrants and minorities, they have—sometimes deliberately and sometimes inadvertently—encouraged other extremists to act. Some of this violence has been perpetrated by jihadists and some by white nationalist extremists taking up the civilizational fight for themselves.

The two groups are in many ways two sides of the same coin. They might see each other as sworn enemies, but they share a worldview premised on an irreconcilable clash of civilizations. Both share a nostalgic obsession with a purist form of identity: for one, a medieval Islamic state; for the other, a white nation unpolluted by immigrant blood. "The two sides feed off each other," argues the British writer Kenan Malik, "creating ever more exaggerated fears. . . . It helps create a siege mentality, stoking up anger and resentment, and making communities, both Muslim and non-Muslim . . . more open to extremism."[7]

In the United States, white supremacist violence has become noticeably *more* prevalent than its Islamist mirror, in part because white supremacy, in Trump's America, has received some measure of mainstream acceptance.[8] The nadir, for many, came when Trump described the neo-Nazis who descended on Charlottesville, Virginia, and killed an anti-racist protester in August 2017 as "very fine people." And the trail of violence has grown only bloodier since. In 2018, a gunman massacred eleven Jews at a Pittsburgh synagogue, and a year later another attacked a synagogue in Poway, California, near San Diego, killing a woman and injuring several others.

The violence has also gone beyond American shores. The world's most devastating white nationalist attack took place in Christchurch, New Zealand, in March 2019, when an avowed anti-immigrant crusader (himself an immigrant from Australia) gunned down fifty-one worshippers at two mosques. Like those who chanted "Jews will not replace us" in Charlottesville, he drew explicitly on the French writer Renaud Camus's notion of a "great replacement"—the nativist myth that there is no hope of whites and Muslims living together.[9] Like his fellow killers in the United States, he was also an avid user of 8chan and other dark corners of the internet that receive far less law enforcement scrutiny than jihadist chat rooms and message boards.

It's a strange irony: nobody questions the public-safety imperative of tracking potential ISIS sympathizers, but rooting out violent white supremacists is viewed as a possible infringement of free speech—both by government agencies and by tech companies with the power to police their own online spaces. "The political will to establish such surveillance with the resources and tools needed to make it work is unlikely," Oxford University's Bharat Ganesh has argued, "given that politicians and CEOs continue to prioritize the free speech rights of white supremacists over the security of their potential victims."[10]

The double standard stems at least in part from cultural identification, because the core ideology of white supremacism has a natural constituency in Western democratic nations in a way that radical Islamism does not. But it is also motivated by fear of that same "great replacement" that has spurred the growth of the National Front in France. White Christian America became a minority for the first time during the Obama presidency, as Robert P. Jones of the Public Religion Research Institute has noted, falling from 54 percent of the population in 2008 to 45 percent in 2015. "The passing of a coherent cultural world—where working class jobs made ends meet and white conservative Christian values held sway—has produced this powerful politics of white Christian resentment," Jones has written.[11]

One reason white supremacists pose an exceptionally grave threat is that they present themselves as natives valiantly defending the homeland. Because they look and sound like many of their co-citizens, they garner sympathy in ways that Islamists never could. Trump himself has been unafraid to mobilize white nationalists and earn their enthusiastic support, only to disavow them or become evasive when they commit acts of terrorism.[12] Many other Americans are similarly receptive to their views but ambivalent about the political violence they've unleashed. It is clear that white nationalists are no longer a fringe group. They are influential, and they are growing.

When the Right Goes Extreme, Centrist Voters Go Green

Just because politicians have made immigration a hot-button issue doesn't mean it has to be. Managing asylum and refugee status requests is largely a legal and logistical problem. The U.S. government could, if it so desired, create a well-regulated asylum system like Canada's and provide a path to legal status for undocumented immigrants without separating children from their parents or detaining people in unsanitary, overcrowded facilities. European countries could choose to establish consular screening in transit countries like Turkey, issuing visas to those deemed legitimate refugees and letting them fly to Germany or Sweden rather than risking their lives at sea or living in inhumane and potentially deadly conditions in detention camps in war-torn countries.[13] The problem is, politicians know that fomenting fear wins votes.

That said, it is important to draw a bright line between rabid nationalists who see immigration as a civilizational threat and those conservatives, in the United States and Europe, who advocate restricting asylum and immigration numbers without resorting to culture war rhetoric. The latter group—like many Republicans before Trump decimated that wing of the party—are interested in slowing the pace and controlling numbers because they believe that it is the wiser path to integration. And they are an important part of the debate, as became clear in Germany after Chancellor Angela Merkel first welcomed large numbers of Syrian refugees in 2015.

A minority within Merkel's CDU party challenged her position and did not buy the business community's view that a fresh infusion of labor was what an aging German workforce needed. "You don't solve that by uncontrolled asylum migration," the former parliamentarian Philip Lengsfeld said. The concern, for Lengsfeld and other restrictionists, was that integrating large immigrant populations could take decades, not just years, and that it would be better to focus on narrowly humanitarian cases, not on anyone and everyone seeking a better life.

The pressure on Merkel only intensified after the CDU lost sixty-five seats in the 2017 national election and struggled to form a coalition. Merkel came under particular pressure from the CDU's Bavarian sister party, the CSU, whose leader, Horst Seehofer, became interior minister in her coalition government and declared, in direct contradiction to Merkel, that "Islam does not belong to Germany."[14] Seehofer was an unapologetic friend of Hungary's anti-immigrant leader, Viktor Orban, and his ascendancy appeared to signal a sharp rightward lurch on immigration. But the voters had other ideas. Seehofer's colleague Markus Soder ran on an anti-immigration platform in the 2018 Bavarian state election, and the CSU—which had dominated state politics for decades—lost its absolute majority.

The lesson was clear. Mimicking the far-right does not necessarily win votes. Rather, it empowers nativists. The far-right Alternative for Germany (AfD) took 10 percent of the vote, precisely the same amount the CSU lost. A considerable number of centrist voters, meanwhile, flocked to the Green Party, which won nearly 18 percent—double its previous showing.

As the World Grows Hotter

The Greens' strong showing in the context of a fraught immigration debate was no coincidence, because climate change is rapidly becoming an immigration issue, too. For now, many migrants are motivated either by economic opportunity or by the pressing need to flee violence. Soon, though, the primary factor driving people to flee to another country will likely be sudden and devastating climate emergencies. They will flee to eat, drink, and find shelter.

Already the political effects are proving unpredictable, as attested by a "Trump supporters for Ocasio-Cortez" sign hung outside the congressional office of the rising superstar of the American left, Alexandria Ocasio-Cortez of New York. The man who made it told Ocasio-Cortez she was one of the few politicians from either side of the aisle willing to take decisive action on climate change, which for him was the most important issue of the age. "If you don't understand this man's sign or don't approach it with a desire to," Ocasio-Cortez said, "then you do not understand this political moment."[15]

In some countries exposed to extreme seasonal weather, climate migration is already underway. In Bangladesh, thousands of people leave the countryside during monsoons to seek a living in the cities. As water levels rise and once-in-a-century storms become annual events, even parts of low-lying nations like Bangladesh that are currently considered safe may no longer be habitable. The World Bank has found that as many as 143 million people could be forced to migrate internally within their home countries by 2050.[16]

Those forced from their homes in search of basic sustenance will not stop at borders. If an arid and populous nation like Egypt or Pakistan faces

devastating droughts, or if coastal countries like Bangladesh and Nigeria—
or, closer to home, Honduras—are faced with catastrophic floods, the mass
movement of people is likely to dwarf the numbers that Europe has
struggled to absorb since 2015, or, for that matter, the Central American
caravans that have been arriving at the Rio Grande.

Many will seek a future in the closest wealthy Western democracy.
Some of those countries, like Australia, Italy, and the United States, already have draconian policies toward refugees and asylum seekers formulated against a backdrop of bitter political divisions. And the upheavals
will only grow worse.

Pulling Up the Ladder

The conservative writer and Manhattan Institute president Reihan Salam
has a different set of reasons to envision a dark future if current immigration trends in the United States continue—one that could have unwel-
come and unexpected consequences for the Democratic Party. Salam
predicts a clash pitting current Latino immigrants and poor African
Americans against a new wave of low-skilled Latino immigrants competing for their jobs in ten to twenty years.[17]

This is not a shocking idea if you look at Australia, where some of the
staunchest opponents of immigration are themselves recent immigrants
who want to pull up the ladder and maintain their gains without new competition. Likewise, in the United Kingdom, immigrants and their descendants voted in significant numbers for Brexit despite a campaign that
featured constant fearmongering about an immigrant invasion, including an ad showing a long line of brown-skinned migrants and the tagline
"We must break free of the EU and take back control." Leave campaign-
ers made a direct appeal to immigrant restaurant workers from South Asia
by promising them preferential treatment over EU citizens from Eastern
Europe.[18]

Democrats in the United States tend to take the Latino vote for granted,
but many Latinos are hostile toward further immigration and would prefer to pull up the ladder, too. Even John Judis, whose widely read 2002
book, *The Emerging Democratic Majority*, predicted a bright future for the
Democrats as the United States became less white and more brown, has
started to worry about this. Latinos, he now says, may be following a

political trajectory more like that of the Irish than that of African Americans, and their vote may be far from automatic.[19]

Salam echoes this line of thinking, and also draws a particularly grim portrait of the political future if the pampered, privately educated children of the Democratic Party elite fail to make common cause with the children of their nannies and cleaners. The class divide, after all, is stark and growing. "What if working-class Latinos aren't especially interested in serving as junior partners in a coalition led by their self-proclaimed white allies?" Salam asks. "What if they instead support new forms of anti-establishment politics, rooted in grievances and vulnerabilities that place them at odds with liberal white elites?"[20]

These tensions could bubble over into a much broader cultural and political realignment if a future populist—perhaps one who has brown skin and speaks fluent Spanish—mobilizes a stagnating underclass of second-generation Latinos and, in Trumpian fashion, stokes their resentment of the white elites for whom they toil, or working-class blacks with whom they compete for jobs. Indeed, a future Latino candidate—more populist than any on the scene today—could conceivably emerge and run on a harsh anti-immigration platform while holding up his or her own Latino identity as a defense against charges of racism and xenophobia.

These are scenarios that most Democrats—content with the party's current broad church identity—have not contemplated. The demise of stable centrist majorities and long-dominant parties in Europe should give them pause.

The Disappearing Left

In March 2017, the Dutch Labor Party was decimated, plummeting from thirty-eight seats to just nine in the 150-seat House of Representatives. Meanwhile, the GreenLeft party, headed at the time by the boyish and charismatic Jesse Klaver, increased its share from four seats to fourteen, with nearly 10 percent of the national vote. Klaver, just thirty years old at the time, called for a "realistic, humane and just asylum policy" that would provide "protection to people fleeing war, violence and persecution." His advice to the mainstream left: "Don't try to fake the populace. Stand for your principles. Be straight. Be pro-refugee. Be pro-European."[21] It was precisely the message the country's Labor Party had failed to heed.

Indeed, the Labor Party had all but abandoned its mission as a voice of the working class and was seen as largely identical to the center-right VVD, with which it had governed in coalition for five years. Increasingly, the party's base was turning to the far right.

The same wave hit the French center-left a few months later. After five lackluster years under President François Hollande and a series of terrorist attacks that shocked the nation, French voters reduced Hollande's Socialist Party to a mere 6 percent in the first round of voting for a new president—a distant fifth place. To add insult to injury, the Socialists went on to lose 249 of their 279 seats in the Assemblée Nationale, a devastating defeat that left the outgoing governing party with virtually no legislative presence and led to such a loss in party funding that it was forced to sell its iconic headquarters in central Paris. Le Pen's National Front took 29 percent of the vote from those identifying as blue collar, according to exit polls; the Socialists pulled in just 8 percent of them.[22]

The French Socialists—like their center-left counterparts in the Netherlands, Germany, and the United States—had ceased to be seen as authentic representatives of the class for which they claimed to speak. These parties once drew on divisions between bosses and workers, or landed aristocrats and the urban bourgeoisie. But all of that had now been disrupted, and old electoral certainties no longer held.

Immigration is typical of the issues that no longer sit easily within a left–right class framework. As the British political scientist Matthew Goodwin has described, university-educated suburbanites and blue-collar workers tend to hold vastly divergent views on border security and asylum policy, even as center-left parties are still trying, in vain, to appeal to both constituencies. Meanwhile, new actors have stepped in to fill the vacuum—taking bites from either side of the political spectrum.[23]

Goodwin's description holds true even in Denmark, a country Bernie Sanders is fond of citing as a model for many of his own Democratic Socialist policies and where the center-left Social Democrats still enjoy enough support to win power—but at a price. The far-right Danish People's Party, like many of its European cousins, has perfected Le Pen's strategy of courting ex–left wing voters. As early as 2001, the DPP leveraged the immigration issue to siphon away voters from the Social Democrats' traditional base, positioning itself early on a key issue that has come to define Danish politics.

Danes pay high taxes and in return get excellent education and health care for free—as Sanders is keen to point out. But the generosity of the welfare state has also become a wedge issue for far-right populists. The fear the populists stoke is that as more people come to the country and claim benefits, Danish citizens will find their bread being buttered more thinly. The DPP has long stressed the need for quality health benefits and care for the elderly—but for "us," not "them." This vision of a nativist nanny state has helped make the DPP kingmakers in Denmark's closely divided political landscape and, more important, political trendsetters.

Many of their policies that were once seen as fringe—outsourcing the detention of asylum seekers and paying poor North African countries to detain potential refugees before they reach European shores—became key planks of the center-left Danish Social Democrats' platform in the 2019 campaign. Yes, the Social Democrats returned to power—and indeed the DPP suffered its worst showing in twenty years—but few analysts stopped to ponder the cost of the victory. The DPP may have a much diminished presence in the Danish parliament, but it has won the war of ideas and can watch from the sidelines as a Social Democratic prime minister pursues many of its policies.

The Spanish Exception

Spain's politics, meanwhile, have been shaken up in a different way, with immigration still a major issue—but one that the right has failed to weaponize. The signal moment came in September 2018, when eleven migrants were picked up in the Mediterranean, and the ship was refused entry to Italy. "Go wherever you want, but not to Italy," the freshly elected Italian far-right deputy prime minister Matteo Salvini declared. Spain's Socialist prime minister responded very differently. "It is our duty to help avoid a humanitarian catastrophe and offer a safe port to these people, to comply with our human rights obligations," Pedro Sánchez said.

"The decision to admit the *Aquarius*," the Spanish researcher and activist Gonzalo Fanjul commented, "was both a moral and symbolic triumph for Spain, showing that the country is not afraid to row against the populist tide."[24] Indeed, Spain has remained largely immune to the explosion of populism that has affected other EU countries, despite experiencing similar economic crises and mass immigration from Africa.

There have been various explanations for the Spanish exception: memory of Francisco Franco's fascist dictatorship; Spaniards' recent history of mass emigration; or the fact that nationalist sentiment had for a long time been directed at Basque and Catalan separatists, not at immigrants.

That said, Spain does have its own far-right populists, the Vox Party, which took 11 percent of the vote in Andalusia's regional elections in December 2018 and joined the region's governing coalition. Even if it hasn't yet broken through in the way that France's National Front has, Vox still won 10 percent of the vote nationally; in post-Franco Spain, no far-right movement had previously managed more that 1 percent. And the principal victim of its success has not been the old-guard left, but rather the old-guard center-right.

The leader of the conservative Partido Popular, Pablo Casado, had hoped to capitalize on anti-separatist sentiment and anti-immigration anger and put his party back in power; instead, he led the PP to its worst electoral defeat in history. Casado reacted to Vox's success by calling for tighter border controls and cultural assimilation standards for new arrivals. It proved disastrous in the national elections of 2019 because the PP imploded, losing half its seats.

Conclusion

The United States, unlike most of Europe, has long defined itself as a nation of immigrants but it has not been immune to periodic bouts of nativism—from the anti-Irish and anti-Semitic movements of the nineteenth and early twentieth centuries to the Chinese Exclusion Act and the World War II–era internment of Japanese Americans.

The current moment in U.S. politics qualifies as another such episode, as children are separated from their parents at the border and armed militias masquerading as law enforcement officers engage in vigilante "arrests" of migrants. Trump has manipulated the country's latent tendencies toward nativism at a time when the country's longstanding white Christian majority feels both demographically and politically threatened.

His actions also reflect broader global trends. Nativist parties in Europe may not win much governmental power through elections, but they have leveraged their popularity to force draconian immigration policies on center-right and center-left politicians, who live in constant fear of losing ground to them. It is an extremely effective form of political blackmail.

By introducing once unthinkable policy ideas into the mainstream, far-right parties have created a new normal in which refugee boats are turned back, migrants are detained offshore, and families are separated. The European far right has, at different times and in different places, shut down or even outlawed mosques, banned the construction of minarets, forbidden Muslims from wearing burqas, ended the sale of halal meat, and confiscated the valuables of arriving refugees. These and other dog whistles have normalized extremist white nationalists and empowered them to go on the offensive.

In such a political climate, defenders of liberal democracy on both the left and the right need to convince economically vulnerable voters that the threat they face comes not from immigration but from something else. Future waves of climate-induced migration could make the current clashes over immigration seem tame.

No one in the United States has yet found the winning formula, but the model offered by the Dutch, the German Greens, and the Spanish Socialists—an unapologetic defense of immigration, coupled with a combative economic agenda—points a way forward. The solution lies not in appeasing or mimicking the far right, but in pressing an economically populist message that places the blame for declining living standards where it belongs, on politicians who have abandoned the working-class voters they once claimed to speak for. Nativism is a siren song, but it can and must be resisted.

NO TIME LEFT: HOW THE SYSTEM IS FAILING TO ADDRESS OUR ULTIMATE CRISIS

Bill McKibben

As of 2020, the temperature increase resulting from climate change is closing in on two degrees Fahrenheit. The volume of meaningful legislation passed by the U.S. Congress and signed by the president, meanwhile, is closing in on zero.

There may be no clearer indictment of our dysfunctional democracy.

If, as seems almost certain, climate change is the greatest crisis our species has yet faced, it may be worth looking at the unhappy story in a little detail.

Congress has never done more to highlight the dangers of climate change than it did on a June afternoon in 1988, more than thirty years ago, when James Hansen testified before a committee chaired by Colorado Senator Tim Wirth. Wirth had deliberately scheduled the hearing in the middle of a savage heatwave—and a drought so deep that shipping was halted along much of the Mississippi. The temperature in Washington that afternoon topped 101 degrees, and some contend that the air conditioning was turned way down in the committee room.

Hansen was sweating, that's for sure—partly because of the heat, and partly because he was about to bring the greatest crisis the world has ever faced into clear public view. He presented a series of elegant charts to show that the Earth was warmer than at any time in the history of instrumental measurements. "There is only a 1 percent chance of an accidental warming of this magnitude," he said. "The greenhouse effect has been detected, and it is changing our climate now." In those days, you had to wait for the morning papers to see how a story was going to play, and when the *New York Times* came off the press, the verdict was clear. "Global Warming Has Begun," the story at the top of the front page said.

People believed him—why wouldn't you? *Time* magazine made a beleaguered Earth its "man of the year." George H.W. Bush, running for president, memorably declared his intent to fight what was then called the greenhouse effect with the "White House effect."

And that was about as far as we got. Two years later, Bush undercut the initial Rio conference on the environment by telling reporters en route that "the American way of life is not up for negotiation." Almost a decade after *that* I watched as the developed world seemed to come together in Kyoto around a modest plan to rein in emissions, only for the chief lobbyist for the fossil fuel industry to turn to me and say: "I can't wait to get back to Washington, where we've got this under control." I thought he was whistling in the dark, but it turned out he was right. The United States never came close to ratifying the Kyoto accords, and the second president Bush reneged almost immediately on a campaign promise to treat carbon dioxide as a pollutant. A decade after *that,* U.S. diplomats helped preside over the failed Copenhagen climate conference, and a U.S. Congress with sixty Democratic Senators failed to pass cap-and-trade legislation.

Six years after *that,* President Barack Obama did manage to sign the Paris climate accords, but the pact was less than overwhelming. It was not a legal document, only a series of voluntary pledges by different countries. The rest of the world had long since recognized there was no way that two-thirds of the U.S. Senate would ever sign a climate treaty. Three years after *that,* President Donald Trump withdrew the United States from the Paris accords anyway; the country that had poured the most carbon into the atmosphere was now also the only country unwilling to even pretend it was joining the international effort to solve the problem. Indeed, the president held that climate change was a hoax "manufactured by the Chinese," a statement dumb enough that if you heard someone muttering it on a public bus you'd change seats. Did his party—for much of the twentieth century the party of conservation—complain? It did not. In fact, the man it chose to head the energy committee was an Oklahoma savant named James Inhofe, who chose to illustrate his party's approach to the climate problem by carrying a snowball into the chambers of the world's most august deliberative body. To show that it was cold outside.

While this parade of failure ran back and forth down Pennsylvania Avenue, what else was happening?

For one thing, the problem that we once called the greenhouse effect was growing steadily into the crisis we now call climate chaos. The planet's twenty hottest years on record have all come since that first Senate hearing. The last five years have been the five hottest in human history. As that heat has spread, all the dire effects scientists warned us about have come true, more quickly and on a larger scale than they predicted (scientists being by instinct conservative). So: half the summer sea ice in the Arctic is now gone, and with it a nice white mirror that used to bounce a great deal of incoming solar radiation back out to space. In the Antarctic, we're passing the point of no return with one giant glacier system after another. In the oceans, some combination of rising temperature and acidity from the carbon absorbed from the air has killed vast swaths of coral reef. The Great Barrier Reef is still the largest living structure on Earth, but it's only half as living as it was a few years ago. On land, we've watched record heat lead to record evaporation and hence record drought. Once that water vapor is up in the air, it comes down in torrents, leading to record rainfall.

Were all this happening only to poor people in distant places, we might expect American political leaders to ignore it. But it's not. Certainly, other places are paying a higher price, the iron law of climate change being that the less you caused, the more you suffer. But America has been hit pretty squarely too. New York's financial district, our square mile of greatest wealth, took a direct hit from Superstorm Sandy as the tides rolled in on an elevated ocean. (*Business Week*'s verdict: "It's Global Warming, Stupid.") California, our wealthiest, most populous, most politically powerful state, has been visited with one climate plague after another: years of drought so deep that the Sierra Nevada lifted inches skyward because of the disappearing weight of water; intermittent periods of rainfall so prodigious that they threatened to topple giant dams; and wildfires so freakishly intense that people died by the score as they sat trapped in their cars. Texas, where the hydrocarbon industry wields its greatest influence, saw the greatest rainstorm in American history as Hurricane Harvey dumped four and a half feet of water on Houston in late 2017. Weeks later, Puerto Rico was raked by a monstrous storm of its own, Hurricane Irma, whose damage equaled a year of the island's GDP. Miami Beach, the ultimate American playground, now floods even on sunny days just because the tide has risen so fast and so far.

In other words, while DC has fiddled, America has burned.

Is it for a lack of alternatives? It is not. Over the same thirty years, engineers have engineered, succeeding in their work almost as profoundly as politicians have failed in theirs. The price of solar panels has steadily fallen, year after year. The same with wind turbines. Renewable energy is now the cheapest way to produce electrons, both in this country and worldwide. Electric cars are no longer toys; they accounted for most of the growth in Chinese car sales last year. Electric buses are not a novelty; in China, 385,000 of them now ply the streets.

While we face a crisis of remarkable scale—one, it should be noted, that comes with a time limit—we certainly have the tools to begin to solve the problem. And yet Washington has not acted in significant ways to speed up the necessary transition, ignoring the large majority of voters who tell pollsters they want action. If this is a stress test of our democracy, our democracy is failing.

Why?

None of the reasons are shocking or new. They are merely better illustrated by the climate change crisis than by any other issue.

The first is the role of money and corporate power in our politics. Since the fossil fuel industry is the richest in the history of the planet, it stands to reason that it would wield great influence. Journalists at the Pulitzer Prize–winning website *Inside Climate News*, at the *Los Angeles Times*, and at the Columbia Journalism School began laying the ugly story bare some years ago by showing that the fossil fuel industry had known everything about climate change that James Hansen did back in the 1980s. Exxon, which at the time was the biggest company on planet Earth, had squadrons of fine scientists, and since carbon was its product they were set loose to investigate its effects. They provided executives with a clear view of how much and how fast it was going to warm, and they were believed. Indeed, Exxon began adjusting the specs on its drilling rigs to compensate for the coming rise in sea level. Just imagine if those executives had shared their findings with the rest of the world—if, say, they had bought space in the newspapers in the wake of Hansen's congressional testimony to say their scientists had found much the same thing. Nobody would have accused them of alarmism, and we could have gotten down to work with modest steps (a small but rising tax on carbon, say) that would have given us a head start and dramatically shifted our trajectory.

That, of course, is not what happened. Instead, Exxon hired new squadrons of experts, this time from the public relations arena, including a number of veterans of the fights over tobacco and DDT. They and other oil, coal, and utility companies set up front groups, harnessed the political power of the fossil fuel and manufacturing industries, enlisted coalitions like the Chamber of Commerce, and rallied them all behind the project of convincing Americans that there was ample doubt about climate science. Remember, this was precisely the period when scientists were removing that doubt. And remember, too, that these companies knew the truth. Still, the PR offensive proved powerful enough to prevent our participation in the Kyoto accords, powerful enough to scare the Senate off taking so much as a vote, powerful enough to allow Dick Cheney and the rest of the Bush administration to put an end to any attempts to regulate carbon.

Environmentalists fought back, and had some success in pushing the big oil companies away from their denialist positions into softer forms of evasion and "greenwashing." Al Gore's *An Inconvenient Truth* made it harder for consumer-facing enterprises to continue engaging in outright falsehoods. Over time, though, this hasn't mattered all that much, because the hydrocarbon giants have been replaced as dynamos of inaction by a slightly different set of moneyed actors, the network of right-wing billionaires built primarily by the Koch brothers, who are (not coincidentally) among the country's largest oil and gas barons, running a network of pipelines and controlling a vast swath of Canada's tar sands. They and their organizations have worked tirelessly to prevent action on climate issues at both the federal and state levels. The Kochs are by far the biggest funders in American politics, and they have—as Jane Mayer recounts in her classic investigation, *Dark Money*—in essence bought one of our political parties and intimidated the other.

I used to think about money in politics as a distant abstraction, the way you think about a disease you have not yet contracted. That changed with my first personal interaction with DC politics, over the boondoggle, climate-busting Keystone XL pipeline. We had mustered millions of Americans to oppose the project, yet we barely survived one narrow congressional vote after another. The oil industry was so sure of prevailing that during one Senate roll call it put out a victory press release, only to fall a single vote short. After each of these near-death experiences, our friends at Oil Change International would issue a scorecard showing how much money the various congressional representatives had taken from the fossil fuel industry, and in each case the correlation between the money and the members' votes was virtually perfect. The money was a much better predictor of voting outcomes than party, geography, or ideology.

The reluctance to lead on climate change issues crosses all lines; the idea that it's entirely the fault of Republicans is an oversimplification. It's not just the oil companies that fear change; the unionized workers who labor in those industries are just as invested in the status quo. On the Keystone XL question, Democrats told us again and again what a terrible choice we were forcing on them. The building trades unions were so closely allied with the companies building the pipelines they were in effect company unions. They pressured the AFL-CIO to back them, and the AFL-CIO put pressure on the Democratic Party, to the detriment of environmentalists, who were championing retraining projects for the affected workers. It was in many ways a retread of an earlier climate fight in which the auto workers union, powerfully represented in Congress by the stalwart Michigan liberal John Dingell, worked with GM, Ford, and Chrysler to stymie calls for better auto mileage.

Another way of saying this is that money in politics plays a real and pervasive role, and "money" comes in many forms, including the electioneering prowess of labor. Politics is not like other forms of financial investment. In politics, it is the industries that have already made their money that exert the greatest power, because they have cash flow, essentially captive employees, and longstanding political connections. Coal companies are a good example of this. In the financial community, by contrast, what matters is not who has made money in the past, but who is likely to make it in the future. And that makes Wall Street much more adept at imagining where we are headed than Washington. The stickiness of the status quo can be an asset, of course; on many issues, a politically enforced gradualism may serve societies better than the whiplash that comes from following the fast-twitch impulses of the financial markets. But the climate change challenge is not one of those issues, because it is a timed test, perhaps our first. If we don't solve it within the timeframe imposed by physics, and on the scale required by physics, we will not solve it. A solution to climate change that lies forty years in the future is, by definition, not a solution. Winning slowly is just another name for losing.

* * *

The power of the status quo is not the only thing that has limited our re-action. The failure of the media to help people make sense of climate change has been epic. It was particularly poor luck that the rise of the cli-mate issue coincided with the rise of an ideologically driven media and the death of a postwar journalistic model that, for its many flaws, usually got people to reach consensus on reality. Think of the war in Vietnam: it took six or seven years, but eventually the television networks were able to show Americans how badly the war had gone off the rails.

The rise of Fox News, and ideologically driven journalism in general, has complicated this process, perhaps fatally. If disinformation is perva-sive, it warps everyone's response. If an entire TV network insists that sci-ence doesn't work the way scientists say it does, the chance of reaching a consensus is greatly reduced. And that, of course, has been the goal of the fossil fuel industry from the start. Just as amazing as Fox News (which, after all, is news for change-resistant elderly people) has been Rupert Murdoch's other key property, the *Wall Street Journal*, the predominant source of news for rich people. Between 2012 and 2016, even as the scien-tific case for climate change became overwhelming, the *Journal* published 303 op-eds, columns, and editorials on the subject, 287 of which were judged by the climate information watchdog DeSmog to consist of "mis-leading and debunked denial talking points, conspiracy theories, and po-litical attacks." Put another way, roughly 95 percent of what Murdoch's paper put out conflicted with the conclusions of 97 percent of climate scientists. Democracy may not be able to work if it is flooded with lies. Indeed, the other country that has shown complete political paralysis on the climate question, Australia, is also hamstrung by Murdoch's media.

It's a commonplace of political scientists that our system was designed for inaction, but it bears repeating when we are faced with a problem that . . . calls for immediate action.

Think of the Green New Deal, the embryonic legislation designed to address climate change on the scale at which the problem now exists. Given how long we've gone without action—how fully we've succumbed to what the writer Alex Steffen has called the "predatory delay" of vested interest groups—we now need to change much faster than is comfortable. Instead of reducing carbon emissions by a percentage point or two a year, we now need to see drops of five, six, seven percent annually, and take extraordinary measures, as laid out in the Green New Deal, to reach 100 percent clean power generation by 2030. Now imagine a president committed to this task. It's not impossible, since at this writing many of the leading Democrats running in 2020 have endorsed it. Now imagine what political analysts have described as the best possible outcome for Democrats in Congress—fifty-three seats in the Senate, perhaps, along with continued control of the House. Now imagine (I realize this is a lot of imagining) the Senate debate on the Green New Deal, the most massive program of its kind since the Great Society and perhaps since the original New Deal in the 1930s. All the usual forces, on both sides of the aisle, would be concentrated in opposition, making fifty votes a struggle and a filibuster-proof sixty votes flat-out impossible. So you would also have to get rid of the filibuster rule, itself a hurdle of great difficulty. Even if you somehow engineered that, you'd then have to shepherd the legislation through a court system that, for the relevant time frame, will be bulging with Trump-era appointees, especially on the Supreme Court.

It seems far more likely that, under mounting public pressure, Congress and the oil industry will craft a modest carbon tax, of a sort that would have done a lot more good if it had been introduced three decades ago. If one were cynical, one might even imagine the fossil fuel industry counting on such an endgame. Indeed, the oil companies have begun floating ideas for minimal carbon taxes, all of them attached to provisions that would remove any liability for the damage they have already done.

If we want to learn to grapple more successfully with climate change, other, more functional democracies around the world can offer us clues. Take Germany, which played a significant role in bringing down the price of solar panels. Beginning in the 1990s, Germany signaled it was willing to pay a high price for solar panels, and over time China learned how to make them more cheaply. Why was Germany willing to pay that high price? Because environmental consciousness was a powerful political force, and because the country had a strong parliamentary system that repeatedly gave the Green Party leverage over the formation of governments. The Greens' price came to be called the *Energiewende*, an innovative (and not inexpensive) feed-in tariff system that made it possible for Germans to convert in large numbers to renewable energy, even in a nation not renowned for its sunshine. Anyone who has taken a train across

Germany will have seen the results on one rooftop after another. And, conversely, anyone who has invested in the big German utilities will know how those massive enterprises were bankrupted by the surge in solar energy. America's utility companies certainly know this, which is why they have exerted political influence in state after state to make sure no such thing could happen here.

In our country, of course, things work differently. People inclined to back the Green Party because of their commitment to environmental protection know that their vote runs the risk of backfiring; it's what helped George W. Bush prevail over Al Gore, or Donald Trump over Hillary Clinton. There are fixes to our system short of wholesale conversion to parliamentary democracy that might square this circle at least a little: ranked choice voting, for example. But I confess I am not convinced that these changes will come fast enough to help us deal with the crisis of global warming, which—at the risk of repeating myself—is a test with a time limit.

Given that time limit, I think the best chance—not a great chance, but the best chance—lies in continued organizing outside and alongside the electoral process. Only by building a groundswell of public opinion massive enough to overwhelm the formidable redoubts of money and influence and disinformation do we have a chance. Progress is a matter above all of changing the zeitgeist, of so dramatically shifting perceptions of what is normal and obvious and necessary that the system has no choice but to bend sharply in that direction.

Environmentalists can hark back to the first Earth Day in 1970, when—against all odds—20 million Americans, roughly one tenth of the population, took to the streets and changed the terms of debate in profound and unmistakable ways. A conservative Republican administration headed by Richard Nixon, who had not an environmental bone in his body, was forced to enact virtually all the legislation that, to this day, undergirds our efforts to safeguard the planet.

Ten percent of our current population would be 35 million people. We can hope, and we can organize.

POWERING DEMOCRACY THROUGH CLEAN ENERGY

Denise G. Fairchild

An energy transition can only occur if there is a decisive shift in power towards workers, communities and the public—energy democracy. A transfer of resources, capital and infrastructure from private hands to a democratically controlled public sector will need to occur in order to ensure that a truly sustainable energy system is developed in the decades ahead . . .
— *Trade Unions for Energy Democracy*
2012 International Trade Union Roundtable[1]

A global energy war is underway. It is being waged on numerous fronts with distinct battle lines. On its face it's fossil fuel versus clean energy. But much deeper issues are at stake: man versus nature, global north versus global south, globalization versus local sovereignty; the powerful moneyed class versus low-income, indigenous, and communities of color—the haves versus the have nots. The war is over an economy that is extractive, not regenerative; one that exploits rather than restores and enhances our natural and human capacities. The battle lines have been clearly drawn between the mammoth fossil fuel industry and a converging movement of interests for a clean-energy future that operates at the intersection of environment, economy, and equity.

The stakes are high for everyone. This is about the health of the planet and whether humans will survive as a species. How—and if—we and the larger ecosystem co-exist will be determined by which of the warring factions emerges victorious. These David and Goliath battles over our energy future are taking many forms and springing up across urban and rural America. But, at their core, they are a fight for democracy, an *energy* democracy that puts decision-making, natural resource management, and access to clean technologies into public and community hands.

Energy: A Battleground for Democracy

Goliath in this story is the fossil fuel industry, and it exemplifies everything that is wrong with our system. Its economic weight, and the undue influence it wields over our political leaders and institutions, has given rise to an uneven and unfair distribution of the benefits and burdens of fossil fuel extraction that fail all reasonable tests of democratic ideals. Not only has the industry created stark economic, political, and social inequalities, but it has also actively colluded in the fight against a cleaner, healthier, and more egalitarian energy future.

We're talking about an empire as much as an economic sector, one that spans the exploration, extraction, refining, transportation, distribution, and retailing of oil and gas and other fuel sources. In 2019, the ten energy and utility firms in the Fortune 500 approached $500 billion in market value, benefitting from natural monopolies created by the exclusive rights they enjoy to our energy infrastructure.[2] The fossil fuel firms own and operate a centralized energy grid consisting of a complex, capital-intensive network of refineries, transmitters, transformers, and distribution lines. They have capitalized on the dependence of our industrial economy on this infrastructure. Close to 250 investor-owned utilities that deliver electricity to 220 million Americans are regulated monopolies, permitted to power our homes and businesses on a noncompetitive basis and at great profit.

Monopolies are not in themselves bad if their economic benefits are broadly distributed. But that is emphatically not the case across the fossil fuel industry, where they are crippling competition and economic freedom, both founding principles of the U.S. Constitution. In 2018, the median energy/utility CEO pay package (compensation plus stock options) was $9.6 million, with some CEOs awarded over $30 million; that is, between 150 and 500 times the 2017 median U.S. family income of $60,000.[3] Such income gaps clearly signal structural inequalities, and they are amplified by the reality that one in three residents struggles to keep their lights on.[4] U.S. taxpayers are also subsidizing the industry to the tune of $10.2 billion a year in direct tax breaks and subsidies, without considering hidden costs.[5]

This grim picture only worsens when we account for its environmental and social costs. The havoc wreaked by oil spills from tankers, pipelines, and on- and offshore rigs is relentless. Resourcewatch has documented 137 oil spills in the United States in 2018 alone—more than one every three days—resulting in uncontrolled oil releases, blowouts, and fire breaks.[6] Pipelines rupture or catch fire three hundred times a year on average, affecting areas from the Kalamazoo River in Michigan[7] to Allentown, Pennsylvania,[8] and suburban Mayflower, Arkansas.[9] The resulting damage to our aquatic ecosystem, birds, marine mammals, fish, wildlife habitats, and breeding grounds compromise our biodiversity and the future of our water and food supply. There are also significant economic dislocations for local communities that rely heavily on natural capital—water, air, forests—for their economy and a range of ecosystem services.

And it is not just oil. Fracking for natural gas, coal mining, and fossil fuel processing are equally devastating to our environment. The scarred mountain towns of Appalachia are one obvious example. So are the many neighborhoods shadowed by power plants and refineries across the country, neighborhoods in many cases notorious as cancer alleys or superfund sites, whose economies have been sapped of vitality and whose public health is severely compromised. There are the even more alarming effects that scientists have attributed to fossil fuel extraction and combustion: storms of unprecedented frequency and ferocity, floods, tornadoes, hurricanes, earthquakes, heatwaves, wildfires, and crop failures.

Invariably, it is low-income people and people of color who take the brunt of this devastation. Their communities are the ones most likely to house power plants and refineries and to see unusually high rates of asthma, cancer, and premature death—a problem compounded by poor access to health care. They are the ones who tend to live in areas vulnerable to floods and other natural disasters, on top of which they lack the financial resources to bounce back after disaster strikes, or to pay the rising price of food and other necessities under conditions of scarcity. The highest rates of injury and mortality in Hurricane Katrina were suffered by low-income African American women, and that finding is typical.[10]

The mandate for cleaner energy technologies is clear, and so is the hostility and resistance we see from the energy industry. In a fully democratic system, the clean energy mandate would win, because a majority supports it.[11] Instead, we have the Koch brothers, and Harold Ham of Continental Resources, and North Dakota Bakken drilling, and all the old-guard Big Oil companies—the Chevrons and the Exxons—along with the

American Petroleum Institute and its affiliated industry-controlled think tanks and research groups, who collectively wield an outsized influence on our democracy with their lavish campaign spending and lobbying muscle. It wasn't popular pressure that caused the United States to pull out of the Paris climate accord, because seven out of ten Americans wanted to stay in. And it's not voters who have pressed the Trump administration to roll back fossil fuel regulations or open up new offshore oil and gas leases despite the glaring environmental and social costs.

Even the minority of the electorate that does support these measures is subject to manipulation. The industry spent $1 billion in 2018 on re-branding to suggest it was more committed to alternative energy than was in fact the case. While Facebook ads and Instagram touted the industry's bona fides as fearless warriors in the fight against climate change, the same industry was busy spending $31 million in Washington state to kill a carbon tax ballot initiative and spending millions more on ballot measures in four other states.[12]

The Energy Revolution

The fossil fuel industry may be rich and powerful, but it is experiencing an existential crisis from the mounting pressures of an aging energy grid, new market actors with new energy technologies, and growing consumer demands to reduce its impact on the environment, on our health, and on our climate. For the first time in a hundred years, we have an opportunity to re-imagine, re-engineer, and re-build our energy sector. How we do that, however, is the contested issue.

The easy part, relatively speaking, is to switch from dirty to clean, renewable energy. A lot of this is already underway, spurred by the policies of local and state governments in the face of resistance from Washington: greener buildings; sustainable urban design; cleaner, more fuel-efficient cars and appliances; a transition to solar, wind, and other clean-energy technologies. These fixes are certainly part of the solution, but they are also analogous to putting a Band-Aid on a cancer, because they fail to address the deeper underlying issues: profits, property, power, privilege, and the titans that control them. There is no guarantee that a clean-energy revolution will put energy decisions, production, and money into the hands of consumers, or that it will break the monopolies and decentralize the energy grid. Without these things, the energy revolution could end up looking a lot like the digital revolution, hailed as the Great Equalizer in addressing gaping economic inequality but in fact only reproducing and magnifying it.

The big oil and utility companies have too much to lose to move over quietly, to shift their capital investments from a centralized to a decentralized energy grid that they do not own and control. In fact, the fossil fuel industry is moving rapidly to capitalize on the inevitable transformation to renewable energy, precisely to ward off this prospect. They are pushing to harvest the sun, wind, biomass, and other renewables and build scaled-up new energy systems that use the pre-existing central grid. The business model is not changing, only the sources it draws on to operate.

A more radical vision for alternative energy must be transformative, comprehensive, and egalitarian in scope. It must be about system change, about the struggle for decentralization, for community health, for community resilience, for community empowerment. It is a struggle for social justice and an opportunity to build community. It is a struggle for a transformed democracy rooted not just in new technologies, but also in new values: environment and property rights, new cooperative economic models, a new social compact in which the cost and burdens of electrification do not fall on the poorest, and new governing institutions.

This is the vision of energy democracy.

Energy Democracy: An Emergent Movement

The forces of David are descending upon the industrial Goliath, and they are converging around the idea of energy democracy. It is an emergent movement that has captured the imagination of community groups and has become an organizing principle for their work. The decentralization and democratization of the power sector are at the heart of it—to make energy the core of the Lincolnian idea of power to the people, for the people, and by the people. This implies a profound shift in how we think about not only our energy infrastructure, but also our economy and our democracy.

Like all good movements, the energy democracy movement has no clear beginning or singular leader. It was born out of a long legacy of struggle for land rights, civil rights, human rights, political and economic justice, and the rights of nature. It is a movement precisely because of its broad-based appeal to a higher moral authority that lives in the hearts and minds of people outraged by the callous disregard and exploitation of our natural and human resources. The power of this moral outrage is that it is found in all walks of life. It never dies and is inevitably passed forward to future generations until justice is served.

It was the climate crisis that began threading these strands around the central concept of energy democracy. Hurricane Katrina and the extreme weather disasters that followed brought the connections between fossil fuels, the environment, the economy, and equity into sharp relief. Katrina not only galvanized interest in rebuilding Louisiana's poorest communities, the ones hit hardest by the hurricane, but also threw a spotlight on the root causes of the environmental, economic, and social dislocations that the storm caused. People didn't just demand a more resilient energy infrastructure; they also understood the need to confront the related challenges of pollution, poverty, and the planet.

Fifteen years on, energy democracy has become a recognizable movement and field of practice bringing national and local organizations together to work at the nexus of energy, economy, and equity. My organization, Emerald Cities Collaborative, builds coalitions of unions, community organizations, activists, businesses, and policy gurus, with a view to "greening our cities, building our communities and strengthening our democracy." Statewide energy democracy alliances can be found in Louisiana, North Carolina, New York, and California, as well as other localities on the front lines of the environmental havoc being wreaked by climate change and our broken system. They have organized campaigns around the key questions of a new energy future: Who pays for it? Who owns it? Who governs it? Who benefits? Who has access? How do we deliver it?

The growing energy democracy networks share research that helps inform their values and principles[13] and offer models for what has been termed a "just transition."[14] Thought leaders and activists meet regularly to learn and share best practices. And other organizations are putting energy democracy policies and plans into action. One Voice in Jackson, Mississippi, for example, has established the Electric Cooperative Leadership Institute to educate residents about their rights as members and owners of rural electric co-ops. The Asian Pacific Environmental Network is training Laotian refugees in Richmond, California, and Chinese immigrant families in Oakland, California, about the connection between Chevron's smokestacks and their family's high incidence of respiratory illness. The Community Power Network, a national nonprofit organization based in Washington, DC, is helping people across the country start their own solar co-ops.

Energy democracy unifies what can appear to be amorphous networks through an intersectional framework that traces a panoply of issues—equity, the environment, the economy—back to the ills of our extractive system, which for too long has revolved around mass production, mass consumption, and the mass accumulation of wealth. The energy democracy agenda, by contrast, starts with democratic values, principles, and practices and from there establishes three key pillars: civic engagement (democratizing governance), an energy commons (democratizing the environment), and energy cooperatives (democratizing the economy).

The Equity Imperative: Civic Engagement

To some in the larger environmental or climate movement, the term "equity" means providing communities with access to renewable technologies and making certain they are not overburdened by the fallout from energy-related decisions. And that is all good. But it has to mean more than that. If decisions are to be equitable, then those directly impacted have to be the ones making them. When we talk about civic engagement in energy democracy, what we mean is engaging citizens directly in policy decisions that affect their future.

When it happens, we see the difference: democracy comes alive, and decisions are more effective because they are informed by lived experience. When low-income, racial, ethnic, and immigrant communities are given a voice, they bring a very different sensibility to energy challenges and come up with solutions that traditional environmentalists might not think of.

Such engagement has multiple knock-on effects. Citizens learn how politics and policy decisions affect their lives. They learn about the legislative process. They understand how to craft policies that work for *them*. They develop public-speaking abilities. They attend community meetings and evidence the power of collective action. They are politicized and motivated to vote.

Collectively, they also upend the conventional wisdom of Western democracy that says only the privileged and elite have the capacity for self-rule. Energy can be highly technical, if not impenetrable, but the energy democracy movement prides itself on making it understandable and relevant to everyday citizens. And to good effect. They are showing up at public service commission meetings, running for utility boards, lining up policy wins, and developing clean-energy projects.

The Environmental Imperative: The Commons
The energy democracy movement sees natural resources as a public good. If we do not move toward sharing those resources, democracy will not survive. It requires a significant mental shift to reframe natural resources not as commodities to be exploited and monetized, but as elements of an ecosystem that can serve human needs as long as we respect, preserve, and replenish what we take. Making that shift, though, is now essential to our survival.

One place that labor unions in our network have started is to campaign to give municipalities control over their energy sources. This guarantees a large number of good-paying jobs and also increases public oversight and accountability. It is only a start, though, and we need to go much further. Giving cities control over their electricity, gas, and water supplies does little to address vital questions of resource depletion and resource sharing. This is where the Commons comes in, an idea derived from the cultural legacy of First Nations, the African diaspora, and other indigenous and traditional cultures. The Commons denotes a respect and stewardship of nature, as well as a culture of cooperation and interdependence.

That may sound utopian, but there is ample evidence that resource sharing and cooperation are in fact deeply ingrained human traits, if not also biologically encoded ones.[15] The Roman republic recognized natural resources as belonging to no one. The Commons was also embraced in the Magna Carta and the thirteenth-century Charter of the Forest. Even in our own time, we have a large body of "public trust law" that has given us such fundamental concepts as habeas corpus and due process.

The Commons saw its heyday during America's Progressive Era and later under the New Deal. This was when municipal utilities and rural cooperatives were conceived—as both moral necessities and economic or civic entities (although their democratic underpinnings have been lost over time). A similar spirit imbued the establishment of Yellowstone, the Grand Canyon, and other major national parks. And we have contemporary examples, too: the internet (back in the days of net neutrality), Wikipedia, and other open source data systems.

Protecting and expanding the Commons is now vital. The threats to land rights, water rights, public spaces, infrastructure, knowledge, and culture are manifold and constantly multiplying. Mineral extraction rights on federally protected lands are being put up for sale. Federal protection of rivers and waterways is being challenged in court as an infringement of private property rights and due process.

Furthering the idea of the Commons requires effective citizen engagement, or else we risk losing it altogether. As David Bollier writes in his book *Think Like a Commoner*: "There are no commons without communing." And that won't be easy. Private property rights, after all, are firmly embedded in the U.S. Constitution. We need to organize both locally and globally, exercise vigilance over the public lands we still have, and work painstakingly to build the idea that we all share a common fate, which makes cooperation a stronger democratic value than individual freedom.

The Economic Imperative: Cooperative Economics

The dominance of the fossil fuel industry and its monopolistic practices represents the worst fears of our founding fathers. This is precisely "the aristocracy of our monied corporations" that Thomas Jefferson wanted to crush at birth.[16] Taking up the struggle against monopolies is not just about economic, social, racial, and environmental justice. It is also about protecting democracy. The growth of renewables and a decentralized energy infrastructure—rooftop solar, community grids, energy storage, demand response—opens the door not only to decarbonizing our environment, but also to new business models and a new, alternative economy that will make control of energy systems more democratic.

Energy cooperatives exemplify these values, as Lynn Benander, Diego Angarita Horowitz, and Isaac Baker have argued in describing their work at Co-op Power, a regional renewable energy collective in New England and New York.[17] Their vision is not just to distribute energy to their members, as the rural electric co-ops of the 1920s and 1930s did, but also to include members in decision-making and reinvest profits in the community. They are, in other words, advocates not of *representative* democracy but of *direct* democracy. They put decisions about the sourcing, production, distribution, and management of energy into the hands of those who consume it. The idea is still in its infancy, but it is growing.

Conclusion

We can stage a new American revolution with the same premise as the first: freedom from domination and control of a self-serving ruling class. Yes, we must democratize our political institutions, but we must also democratize our economy. The task might seem overwhelming given the size and power of our current multinational energy economy. But the seeds of change are everywhere, and that is heartening. The cells of energy democracy are global. We also have allies in other sectors of the economy—just think of the slow food movement, which is breaking up the central food distribution system, shortening the supply chain, spurring small-farm economies, improving health and nutrition, and reconnecting rural and urban communities.

The question is not whether we can transform our democracy, only how. Freedom should not extend to the exploitation of people and the environment. We need to rethink our relationship to capital, the environment, and each other.

This is the moment. As opinion polls show, we the people want a greener, healthier, more sustainable, more affordable, more inclusive, and more just society. This is our time to leverage the transformations in the energy sector to achieve just that.

THE LONG CRISIS: AMERICAN FOREIGN POLICY BEFORE AND AFTER TRUMP

Jessica Tuchman Mathews

The post–Cold War era has seen five profound transformations in the short span of thirty years, each nearly revolutionary in scope. Globalization, the global war on terror, the dawn of the digital age, China's growth explosion, and the emergence of populism and weakening of democracy worldwide have together dramatically altered the United States' external environment and had far-reaching domestic impacts. Yet in the face of this tsunami of change, U.S. foreign policy scarcely deviated from the ideas and practices that both political parties championed from the end of World War II—until the Trump administration took office.

While the Trump presidency has sowed worldwide confusion about U.S. aims, weakened core American alliances, aligned itself tacitly or explicitly with authoritarians and dictators, undermined the international rule of law, and eroded the worth of America's word, most of this damage can be repaired, though not quickly and not without cost. The hardest things to change will be shortcomings that predate Trump's years in power. Assuming that his administration ends by 2021, and does so without a major crisis, it may prove in retrospect to have been a needed transition from a time of worn-out thinking that was increasingly out of step with profoundly new conditions. By indiscriminately trampling on the good and the bad, the Trump period will have inadvertently underlined the longstanding elements of U.S. policy that remain at the core of its national interests and made available, if not a clean slate, at least an opportunity to undertake long overdue fresh thinking.

Where We've Been

Globalization preceded the end of the Cold War, but the sudden seeming triumph of democracy and capitalism in 1989–90 gave an enormous boost to its entwined threads of political and economic change. The first postwar decade saw an explosion of multilateral activity in every sphere of economics and geopolitics. The European Union—a greatly reinforced version of the old European Community, with closer economic, political, and security ties—was founded in 1993, followed nine years later by the adoption of its common currency. The General Agreement on Tariffs and Trade (GATT), a loose set of rules, was replaced by the more ambitious World Trade Organization (WTO), which had a far broader scope and membership. Trade grew at twice the rate of GDP during the 1990s, and foreign direct investment was substantially faster than trade. By 1994, there were seventeen United Nations peacekeeping missions—more in a single year than in all of the preceding half-century. The following year, the parties to the Nuclear Non-proliferation Treaty agreed to transform what had been a temporary agreement into a permanent one. The founding statute of the International Criminal Court was adopted in 1998.

These and similar steps were major commitments to multinational problem-solving and involved significant concessions of national sovereignty. The notable outlier to the trend was the United States. In the first few hopeful years of this era, the Senate ratified three treaties: the International Covenant on Civil and Political Rights (which had been awaiting action since 1966), the Framework Convention on Climate Change (an easy vote since it contained only a broad goal and no emission limits), and the Chemical Weapons Convention, banning the production, stockpiling, and use of such weapons. Congress also approved two trade agreements in the early 1990s: NAFTA and the Uruguay Round, which led to the formation of the WTO. Since then, however, there has been nothing. The U.S. Senate has been unable to approve a single multilateral treaty, even those explicitly modeled on U.S. legislation.

No matter how determined the Senate has been to ignore their impact, globalization and digital technology have made national borders ever more porous to the movement of information, arms, pollution, criminal activity, money, popular culture, foreign investment, and even people, meaning that ever fewer challenges can be met without substantial international cooperation. National security within set boundaries is harder to achieve and to maintain. Citizens' expectations can be framed by conditions half a world away. Multinational corporations and financial institutions are increasingly mobile and less committed to the fortunes of their home countries. Fair taxation and effective regulation are harder to achieve on a national basis. Moreover, the demand for multinational problem solving keeps rising. Cybersecurity, social media regulation, climate change, and global epidemics are among the issues that, left untended, carry the risk of catastrophe.

Digital technology has long been considered an element of globalization, but it has grown so huge, its impacts so pervasive, and its threats so diverse that it now must be considered separately. Trade in digital technology grew forty-five-fold in the decade from 2005 to 2014. Cybersecurity has become an overriding concern of governments, businesses, and individuals, with consequences that span domestic politics, crime, and national security. Social media has transformed society, from early childhood to adulthood. Without major new regulations, machine learning and big-data analytics threaten to erase individual privacy. Cheap cyber technologies, easily accessible to weak, and even failing, states shift the global balance of power. Weapons systems have to be reimagined, and new offensive and defensive doctrine must be developed to respond to attacks that do not involve killing but that can nonetheless inflict massive damage. The loss of jobs in manufacturing has already been significant, but the progression of artificial intelligence and the advent of quantum computing hold potentially earthshaking implications for the future of employment.

What makes these challenges so terrifying and so different from anything that has been tackled heretofore is that the cyber world overlaps the public (governmental) and private (commercial and individual) domains. Foreign policy experts talk of an "all of government" response to the most challenging threats, but cyber issues require an "all of country" response and eventually an "all of all countries" response to be effective. In the United States, government and the private sector are unused to working together, and the task is massively complicated by the need to keep military and intelligence capabilities highly classified. Designing and enforcing such "all of country" new regimes is consequently hard to imagine domestically and seems almost unattainable globally.

For the United States, the second and third decades of this post–Cold War era have been dominated by the aftermath of the terrorist attacks of September 11, 2001, and the unending conflict that has followed. The 9/11 attacks tore away the illusion of safety provided by the massive oceans on its borders that had shaped Americans' thinking about their security since the nation's founding. The attacks launched the war in Afghanistan and led to the debacle in Iraq—the two most expensive wars in our history. Afghanistan, also the longest war in our history, is costing American taxpayers $45 billion annually with almost nothing to show for it. Every approach the United States has tried in these and similar conflicts, alone or in concert with others—regime change, nation building, counterterrorism, counterinsurgency, red lines, responsibility to protect—has failed to achieve its objectives.

China, meanwhile, has been exploding. Its economy grew at double-digit rates in the twenty years from 1990 to 2010, a staggering fifteen-fold increase, and doubled again between 2010 and 2017. (These are the official Chinese figures and are almost certainly exaggerated.) In the early post–Cold War years, China still thought of itself as poor and weak, a victim of past colonialism. It continued to hew to Deng Xiaoping's famous dictum to "hide your strength, bide your time." As the economy surged, however, Beijing began to feel its way to a quite different international persona. Its theorists argued that China would accomplish a historically unprecedented "peaceful rise." Washington responded by urging Beijing to define its national interest as a "responsible stakeholder" of a U.S.-led international order. Xi Jinping, who became president in 2012, had other ideas. After many years of regular transfers of power from one Chinese leader to the next, Xi effectively made himself ruler for life, rolled back many of Deng's economic reforms, and put the Communist Party back at the center of power. China's increasingly assertive global economic and political ambitions, including hegemony in the Western Pacific, are part of the result.

Finally, the post–Cold War era has seen a weakening of democracy and a rise in populism around the globe. The last twenty years of the Cold War saw the so-called Third Wave of democracy, a doubling of the number of democracies around the world. In the following decade, the wave ebbed and then rolled back as governments of every type became more authoritarian or less democratic. This was evident in China, and in semi-authoritarian, partially democratic countries like Hungary, Turkey, Egypt, and Brazil, among many others. Even in the consolidated democracies of Western Europe and the United States, resentment of immigration, rejection of elites, distrust of government, and a belief in the mythical wisdom of "the people" have weakened norms and institutions central to democracy. According to the annual assessment produced by the respected nonprofit Freedom House, 2017 was the thirteenth consecutive year in which global freedom declined.

Taken together, these five transformations have changed global and regional power balances and created a strategic environment that is fundamentally different from that of 1990. Yet the thinking behind U.S. foreign policy has adapted hardly at all. Tired foreign policy debates still revolve around the century-old tension between interests and values. Realists argue for a tough but narrow interest-based policy, focused on the small number of major powers. Neoconservatives, at the opposite pole, take an interventionist view of America as a global policeman, driven by what they incorrectly see as "universal values" of freedom, democracy, and capitalism. Liberal internationalists emphasize multinational institutions and agreements as the principal instruments for advancing U.S. interests. Primacy among the three camps has largely depended on who occupies the White House at any given moment. Their circular policy debates have grown stale and have become poor guides for policymaking.

In one respect, however, U.S. foreign policy has changed dramatically, and that is in its growing dependence on military power. Without the constraints of the Cold War and the ever-present threat of conflict with the Soviet Union, Washington has grown more reliant on its military and less able in its diplomacy. America has been engaged in conflict for all but a few months of the past quarter-century, including three of the five major wars it has fought since 1945. The brief Gulf War to reverse Saddam Hussein's 1990 invasion of Kuwait was a clear-cut success, but the George W. Bush administration's war of choice in Iraq thirteen years later was a catastrophic mistake. And the immense cost of Afghanistan will far outweigh any gain to U.S. interests, or to the Afghans who have borne its brunt in blood. Yet, Washington has been willing to spend whatever has seemed necessary to prevail in these wars—regardless of ballooning federal deficits. It has spent more on reconstruction in Afghanistan, in real dollars, than it did on the Marshall Plan. At the same time, it has denigrated the alternative tools of diplomacy—negotiation, international cooperation, foreign aid, the creation and nurturing of institutions, and the making of international law—as slow and often ineffective. Because of its essential need for compromise, neocons have even portrayed diplomacy as harmful to U.S. interests. The only non-military tool embraced in this period has been the use of sanctions, and these have often been unilateral and minimally effective. Far too often the United States has treated sanctions as an end in themselves, unconnected to active diplomacy, rather than as a means to a negotiated outcome. Six decades of sanctions on Castro's Cuba testify to the futility of this approach.

Both Democratic and Republican administrations have chronically underfunded the non-military elements of policy. On average, the funding of defense has been sixteen times greater than that of the State Department and other foreign operations. In recent years, as dependence on the military has grown, the gap has become grotesque. The Trump budgets for fiscal years 2019 and 2020 proposed *increases* for the defense budget larger than the entire State/foreign operations budget—while at the same time proposing massive cuts in the latter.

The disparity in funding translates into huge differences in operational capacity and human capital. It means that foreign service officers have only a fraction of the opportunities available to the military for advanced training in language, culture, and history of key countries and regions, in the study of strategic thought, and in the development of planning and management skills. At the time of this writing, ambassadorships in Brazil, Egypt, Iraq, Jordan, Mexico, Saudi Arabia, Turkey, and the United Arab Emirates, among others, remain unfilled, a shocking state of neglect two years into an administration, and one that would never be tolerated in positions of comparable weight in the military. Because the Pentagon generally has money and resources while other agencies do not, the military is often tasked with humanitarian and governance duties for which it is not well suited and is nearly always the most expensive option.

The effects of chronic underfunding at the State Department are compounded by a patronage system in which campaign donors and others owed political debts are paid off with appointments to critical ambassadorships and important positions within the hierarchy in Washington. Such a spoils system would be unthinkable in the military (and in many other countries) and should be equally so in the foreign service. Yet, the practice has penetrated ever further down the State Department hierarchy. There is of course a link between the lack of funds and the lack of respect for diplomacy as a profession, exemplified by the use of patronage appointments. Efforts to recruit, train, and develop top talent fall short if the posts at the top of the career ladder are unavailable. Morale can't survive long if professionals watch the most coveted overseas assignments go to individuals who don't speak the language or know the players, or the history, or the issues, or the culture in a country or region critical to American interests. The best will leave; those with no other options will stay. Congress then responds to poor performance with further budget cuts, even though it was underfunding that contributed to the problem in the first place.

All these problems were enormously exacerbated by Trump's first secretary of state, Rex Tillerson. Tillerson ruled the State Department as he had from what was known as the "God Pod" at ExxonMobil: through a tiny group of advisors cut off from the rest of the organization. Partway through his "redesign" of the department, five of the six top-ranked people, more than 40 percent of the next grade, and a quarter of the third rank all left. The intake of new officers was cut by more than half. At the time of Tillerson's departure, a staggering third of the top 152 positions requiring Senate confirmation had no nominee. In a doomed effort to build a relationship with the president, Tillerson obliterated what morale remained by accepting Trump's proposed draconian cuts to an already deficient budget.

Looking Ahead

Before the United States can develop and apply a coherent strategic vision to the world as it now is, it will need to address problems at home. Domestic dysfunction directly impacts our ability to formulate and execute foreign policy.

A degree of accord on national aims requires some level of public trust in government, otherwise resentment, conspiracy theories, and kneejerk policymaking will rule. For the United States to exercise leadership abroad, most Americans must feel that domestic needs are at least being addressed, if not fully met. Progress on addressing inequality and reversing the stunning loss of intergenerational mobility over the last several decades is a necessity. As Raj Chetty and his colleagues have shown, only 50 percent of Americans born in 1980 could expect to earn more than their parents, whereas 90 percent of those born in the 1940s did so.[1] The "American dream," at least for now, is more a memory than a reality. The public also needs to have some baseline understanding of the issues, which means that politicians must forego some partisan point-scoring for more honest communication. There can be no meaningful debate on trade policy, to take an example, if a significant portion of the public has been led to believe that tariffs or other trade barriers can magically restore manufacturing jobs lost forever to technological change.

Most of all, it is vital to find a way to melt the hyperpartisan polarization that so distorts current policymaking. Other governments will be less willing to make meaningful commitments to Washington—participating in military coalitions, supporting diplomatic initiatives, sharing intelligence, hosting bases, joining U.S.-led sanctions—if they fear that the U.S. position is shallowly rooted and likely to switch with the next election.

Morale and performance in the Foreign Service and the State Department's civilian workforces can certainly revive after Trump, under a secretary of state who values their expertise and in an administration that reinstates a disciplined interagency process. There will be no quick way to recapture the experience and deep knowledge lost in the exodus of the first two years of the Trump administration; only considerable time can remedy what has been lost. But the use of patronage appointments can and must be cut back. The State Department can become less hierarchical, less tangled in endless layers of internal review and approval. Most difficult of all, it may also have to shift its focus from bilateral relationships with individual countries to a regional organizational structure, comparable to the Defense Department's integrated combatant commands.

None of these steps will make much difference, however, unless Congress, working with a reform-minded State Department leadership, finally addresses the funding question. More than a decade ago, Defense Secretary Robert Gates took what was then seen as the extraordinary step of calling for "a dramatic increase in spending on the civilian instruments of national security—diplomacy, strategic communications, foreign assistance, civic action and economic construction and development." Future conflicts, he argued, "will be fundamentally political in nature and require the application of all elements of national power."[2] Since then, military leaders—those in the best position to know what is being short-changed—have made the same point over and over again. Before he became secretary of defense, General James Mattis put it bluntly in Congressional testimony: "If you don't fully fund the State Department, then I need to buy more ammunition." A few years later, more than one hundred retired military leaders urged Congress to recognize that "elevating and strengthening diplomacy and development alongside defense are critical to keeping America safe." The military, they wrote, "needs strong civilian partners." So far, all of this has fallen on deaf ears, and the gap between military and non-military funding has widened.

The Key Challenges

Sharing Sovereignty

We live in a world where an increasing number of challenges—cyber regulation; arms control and proliferation; financial stability and trade; climate, health, and the environment; crime; money laundering; and the rule of law—can be dealt with only through multilateral diplomacy. The United States cannot continue to shun new agreements and pull out of those it has previously joined without losing much of its capacity for global leadership and much of its influence over the rules and norms of the international order. A strong military alone cannot change that reality.

Among the agreements the United States has rejected since the end of the Cold War are the Law of the Sea Treaty; the Comprehensive Test Ban Treaty; the Antipersonnel Landmine Ban; and the International Criminal Court. Most of the rest of the world approved them. It has also refused to ratify treaties protecting genetic resources, restricting trade in conventional arms, controlling trade in tobacco, banning persistent organic pollutants and cluster bombs, and protecting persons with disabilities. In the first two years of the Trump presidency, it rejected the Transpacific Partnership (TPP) trade agreement, withdrew from (and then renegotiated) NAFTA, the Paris accord on climate, the INF treaty on intermediate range missiles, the UN Human Rights Council, UNESCO, the Extractive Industries Transparency Initiative (to control corruption in oil and mining), and the Iran nuclear deal. Few Americans appreciate how the United States looks from abroad in the light of this uncompromising record.

Trump and Secretary of State Mike Pompeo do not hide their low opinion of nearly all international agreements and institutions. In a major speech in Brussels, Belgium, home of the European Union, Pompeo opined in December 2018 that the international order has "failed us, and it failed you." Europeans who think the United States is not acting in the free world's interest by taking this view are "just plain wrong." In swift succession he criticized the UN, the EU, the Organization of American States, the African Union, the World Bank, the IMF, and the World Trade Organization (WTO). NATO, he noted, was "indispensable," but the president he serves has repeatedly suggested otherwise.

Today's economic realities—global markets, lengthy international supply chains, trade, and foreign investment—make traditional Republican isolationism impossible. The wholesale rejection of international agreements is just another iteration of the same impulse. The longer the GOP clings to an outdated notion of national sovereignty, the more American leadership will be weakened and with it the promotion of American interests around the world.

Meeting the Cyber Threat

When digital technology first emerged, it seemed to pose a huge challenge to closed societies. How could a regime like the Soviet Union, which required a permission slip to make a Xerox copy, deal with technology that opened the world on a single click? The consensus view was that Russia, China, and other authoritarian states would either have to relinquish their tight control of information or fall hopelessly behind. The vitality, scope, and power of the new technologies seemed to confirm the superiority of open democratic societies.

A quarter of a century later, nearly the opposite has proven to be true. China, Russia, North Korea, and others have been able to construct firewalls that allow them to exploit cyber technology while at the same time tightly controlling their citizens' access to information. Open societies, on the other hand, have turned out to be unexpectedly vulnerable to attacks by criminals and hostile governments. Their social media platforms have become such efficient high-speed delivery systems for incendiary messages, conspiracy theories, and false information that their media-drenched citizenry has become a destructive force from within. Cyber technology has proven so effective at sowing division within democratic societies, in fact, that it is not clear how these societies will be able to protect themselves without sacrificing the values they most cherish.

After the hate-driven March 15, 2019, mosque shootings in New Zealand, the *Washington Post*'s technology reporter noted: "The New Zealand massacre was live-streamed on Facebook, announced on 8chan, reposted on YouTube, commented about on Reddit, and mirrored around the world before the tech companies could even react." Controlled, authoritarian societies avoid the problem.

Foreigners have, of course, intruded into other countries' domestic politics for decades. The United States has itself been a frequent perpetrator.[3] What is new is the speed of such attacks, their massive scale, and the specificity of their targets. Together, these features are transformative. To date, the governments of open societies have been unable to regulate the commercial tech behemoths effectively, though Europe is well ahead of the United States. The situation will get worse: the pace at which governments are able to develop and apply sound regulations, especially in a new arena, is far slower than the pace of technological change.

Nowhere is the need to adapt to the cyber technology revolution more urgent than in the world of intelligence, weapons systems, and national security operations. Digitized militaries will soon be relying on swarms of very low cost, unmanned weapons guided by sensors in every spectrum and targeted and controlled with networked satellites and AI. Unfortunately, the U.S. weapons-acquisition process is terribly slow and is still largely wedded to high-capability, high-cost, manned systems. These are so expensive to buy and to operate—the F-35 joint strike fighter, for example, costs $90 million per plane—that only a few can be purchased. Everyone along the long procurement chains—planners and designers, factory workers, military officers, defense contractors, and politicians who depend on the jobs these industries provide and the campaign contributions they make—has a vested interest in protecting what they are already doing. Authoritarian states like China, by contrast, can overcome the political drag and force a rapid transformation by dictate.

America needs a military that takes full advantage of new technology. Equally, it needs domestic legislation and regulation to force social media companies to recognize that they are not passive platforms for any and all content, but publishers who must bear the same level of responsibility as traditional media. Serving the national interest by controlling the disruption their technology creates may require a change in their core business plans. We need rules to protect privacy and to impose limits on the ownership and monetization of individuals' data, an issue that will become more pressing with the development of machine learning, AI, and quantum computing. As hard as these policies will be to achieve at the national level, they are necessary precursors to the much more difficult task of conceptualizing and negotiating comparable rules internationally.

Confronting Great Power Adversaries

The United States now faces an external environment that has morphed from the afterglow of victory in the Cold War, and the seeming triumph of democracy and capitalism, to a confrontation with two determined great-power adversaries. For most Americans, the transition has been rapid enough to cause cognitive whiplash.

Economically, Russia is anything but a great power. Its GDP is 2.5 percent of the global total—one-tenth that of the United States and just one-twentieth that of the United States and the European Union combined. Its military budget is also about one-tenth that of America's. Yet Russia thinks of itself as a great power, and with massive nuclear forces, diplomatic agility, and deep enmity toward the United States, it is a formidable adversary. Its use of so-called hybrid warfare—a combination of military force and subversion, espionage, assassination, propaganda, cyber-based crime, and political deception—has been deployed in various forms over the past decade in Georgia, Ukraine, the Baltics, Europe, and the United States. After decades with almost no position in the Middle East, Russia has parlayed relations with Iran, Syria, and others into a broad-based footing there. Its aims are to halt and reverse the eastward expansion of NATO and the EU, to undermine the confidence and domestic strengths of the United States and European democracies, to weaken their ability to influence events abroad, and to destroy their credibility as advocates of democratic governance and political freedom.

China, under Xi Jinping, has shed its past caution and embraced the role of great power. It has flexed its economic strength through its Belt and Road Initiative and Asian Infrastructure Investment Bank to dominate its immediate region—fourteen land and three maritime neighbors—and beyond into Eurasia. It has stolen intellectual property on a colossal scale through human spying and internet-based theft and pursued foreign technology through targeted investment abroad. It has relentlessly forced foreign companies that want access to its huge domestic market to transfer their most valuable technology as the price of entry. It has asserted ownership of a good part of the Western Pacific by turning tiny rocks and reefs into artificial islands and building military facilities on them, by laying claim to airspace, and, where it can, by buying off small countries that object. Its "Made in China 2025" initiative is an ambitious agenda for technological dominance. Domestically, its new "social credit" system aims to use ubiquitous surveillance and big-data analytics to control every Chinese person's thoughts, speech, and behavior. It has been increasing defense spending at double-digit rates for many years and is prioritizing new cyber- and space-based weapons systems.

Washington has developed no clear strategy to deal with these profoundly new conditions, and the Trump administration has made things vastly worse by scrambling friends and adversaries and pursuing chaotic, unpredictable policies with no discernable strategic aims. Thanks to President Donald Trump's still inexplicable relationship with President Vladimir Putin, the United States has failed to develop sufficiently rigorous policies for responding to foreign cyberattacks, even though its heavily digitized economy makes it particularly vulnerable to such assaults. It urgently needs large-scale investment to secure critical infrastructure, including election systems, both for defensive reasons and to ensure that its offensive cyber capabilities can actually be used and therefore function as an effective deterrent. Foreign cyberattackers must know that there will be a significant price to pay for their actions.

Beyond the cyber realm, Washington's near-term strategy toward Russia should be modest. It must keep NATO rock solid, support the EU's political cohesion, and maintain close ties to its European allies. It should strive to prevent further subversion of Ukraine but work with Russia on shared interests in controlling nuclear terrorism and proliferation. Preserving the New START agreement beyond its 2021 expiration date is a top priority, for the treaty is the last remaining piece of half a century of superpower efforts on nuclear arms control.

China is a much more demanding challenge. History tells us that an established power and a rising one in the same space usually end up at war. To avoid that outcome, Washington and Beijing need to update their thinking about each other and develop sufficient trust in their mutual expectations to craft a vision of a peaceful shared future in Asia. Washington will have to decide whether it is going to view a powerful China as irredeemably threatening or develop an alternative concept it can live with. It must figure out how to make the most of its many regional allies and friends—especially Japan, Australia, India, and South Korea—without suggesting to China that it is pursuing a Cold War–style strategy of containment. It also has to move beyond the Trump administration's focus on the nearly meaningless bilateral balance of trade, prioritizing instead the critical issues of intellectual property rights, appropriate use of cyberspace, and multilateral trade rules.

Rethinking Military Spending

At 3 to 4 percent of GDP, U.S. defense spending may seem quite reasonable. The politically meaningful measure of affordability, however, is not share of the economy but share of the federal budget. The bite is huge: approaching 60 percent of all federal discretionary spending. Everything else the government does is crammed into the shrinking remainder. The trend is unsustainable.

A different way to appreciate the enormity of this figure is to compare the United States' defense spending to that of other countries. The United States spends more than the next eight largest spenders *combined*, and four of these countries are its treaty allies. Are we actually threatened to this degree? Do real-world military and foreign policy outcomes measure up to this level of investment? Does our global leadership role require this level of spending? Should that leadership role be rethought? These questions don't have generally agreed-upon answers, because they are not being asked.

There is little doubt the Pentagon's massive back-office bureaucracy is bloated and poorly performing in many respects. On the combat side, as many retired military leaders have pointed out, excessive spending does not buy usable capability. The enormous Pentagon budget—now over $700 billion per year—is treated by congressmen and senators as a jobs program for their constituents. Congress keeps funding weapons systems the military doesn't want, and bankrolls bases and facilities the military would rather close. Tellingly, Donald Trump chose to hold one of the first events of his re-election campaign at an Ohio tank factory, even though the army already has thousands more tanks than it can use in any conceivable future combat and has been trying for years to convince Congress to turn off the faucet. But the factory has a few high-paying jobs in a political swing state whose manufacturing sector has suffered huge losses, and so the useless production continues.

President Dwight Eisenhower was right to warn against a "military-industrial-congressional complex" in the first draft of his famous 1961 farewell speech. (Advisors later urged him to drop the third word.) It is doubtful, though, that even he could have foreseen the degree to which military spending would come to be so equated with patriotism that the exercise of hard-nosed rigor in budgeting would be lost. The political momentum that is now driving that spending upward, unguided by clear goals in a drastically changed world, threatens to become unstoppable. It will require uncommon leaders in the White House, the Pentagon, and on Capitol Hill to turn things around. It will be painful, but it must be done.

Implications for Democracy

Democracy, as we have seen, is under threat at home and abroad. Russia is a determined adversary, intent on exploiting every weakness America makes available, and China is no longer willing to be a "rule-taker" in a U.S.-led world. At home, the advantages of America's uniquely favorable geography—with two vast oceans on its borders and two friends for immediate neighbors—have been largely erased by globalization and by missile and digital technology. The enormous attraction of the American model—its fidelity to free speech, the rule of law, the opportunity for all to succeed, and its great economic success—has been greatly diminished. At the same time, Washington's willingness to invest in the global common good, to support democracy and uphold human rights in the belief that these things ultimately serve its self-interest as well as the interests of others, has been tarnished, or worse, by the Trump administration's preference for autocrats over democratic governments and its blatant, greedy "America First" policies. Even if the Trump administration proves to be a brief aberration in the arc of American history, it will be impossible to follow any long-sighted foreign policy without steadier domestic support than can be forthcoming from a society as politically fractured as ours is now.

Strengths remain. The most important is the unique structural advantage of having treaty-based allies around the globe and many other close friends and alliances—around fifty countries in all. Compare this to China's tally: Pakistan and North Korea. The panoply of international regimes and institutions in which the United States is a lead player—the World Trade Organization, the Geneva Conventions, the Nuclear Nonproliferation Treaty, the Bank for International Settlements, and dozens of others—serve U.S. interests more reliably than those of any other country. The continuing strength of these entities is not a given, however. The United States cannot afford to turn a cold shoulder to some of them—a practice Richard Haass has aptly termed à la carte multilateralism—without undermining those it wants to rely on. Given the breadth and gravity of the global issues now demanding a multilateral response, it would be folly to allow these institutions to weaken while also ignoring the need for new ones.

For decades, the United States had the wealth and power to avoid making hard choices in its international relations. It could throw money at problems without having to choose among conflicting foreign policy goals or make painful tradeoffs with its domestic needs. Its military strength was more suited to the twentieth century's conventional interstate conflicts than to today's array of intrastate threats, generally from weak and failing states, and cyber and other non-military challenges. We no longer have the luxury of those advantages. We have become strategically flabby: complacent about keeping pace with changing conditions. We are near a tipping point on military spending, allotting too large a portion of the federal budget, tolerating too much waste, and ignoring a rapidly expanding federal deficit when we should be acquiring a more agile, less wasteful, twenty-first-century military that makes full use of new cyber and space technologies. Most important, we must redress the imbalance in our international posture. Overreliance on the use of military force combined with an undervalued, underfunded, and underperforming diplomatic arm cannot deliver what the country needs.

All of these challenges can be met, but it means abandoning almost everything the Trump administration has stood for. Even harder, it means making a fresh start on much of what preceded it.

Part IV

WHO ACTS, AND HOW?

THE CASE FOR STRONG GOVERNMENT

William S. Becker

One important lesson that American voters have learned over the past 250 years is that a representative democracy is not self-maintaining in a capitalist economy. Government and democracy require course corrections from time to time. This is one of those times.

Three issues must be addressed by this correction. First, what is the best balance between market forces and government interventions to guide the nation's progress? Second, what is the proper balance between the powers of the federal government and the powers of states? Third, what should America's role be in the community of nations?

On the first issue, and contrary to beliefs of free-market evangelists, a free market does not and will not exist in the United States, if it can exist anywhere at all. Our laws and the tax code are filled with rules and incentives that deliberately manipulate the economy, ostensibly for the public good. For example, the federal and state governments have long skewed energy markets by subsidizing fossil fuels responsible for global warming.

Our fettered market economy in the United States has produced an extraordinary quality of life for most Americans, but it has also produced the developed world's largest wealth gap, most of the world's greenhouse gas pollution, and a military-industrial complex that leads the world in selling the tools of war to other countries.[1]

In regard to the second issue, the state/federal power balance has been debated since America was founded. States have a variety of important powers, including several assigned by the Constitution. But their powers stop at their borders while many of the nation's pressing problems do not. For example, states command many of the tools we need to confront climate change, from utility regulation to building codes and transportation planning. But it is up to each state how to use those tools. Between 2009 and 2016, most states achieved net reductions in carbon dioxide emissions, but emissions from Texas rose so much that they canceled out the progress that all other states made.[2]

Similarly, and in regard to issue number three, many problems, present and future, can be tackled only with international collaboration. Nationalism—the policy that considers our nation to be apart from and more important than all others—is a fantasy in a world as interconnected as it is today. Diseases that occur in one country can produce pandemics by stowing away on international flights. One nation's economic hiccup ripples around the world, and any nation's pollution becomes every nation's problem. Refusing to work fully and openly with other nations can be tantamount to criminal negligence.

Each of these three issues begs the question of how active and strong America's national government should be right now. Should it be the minimalist government that many on the far right want, or the proactive government advocated by progressives? We have seen the allocation of power shift dramatically over time as circumstances required, as they did when the federal government intervened in industry to produce the weaponry for World War II. Beyond the assignment of responsibilities in the Constitution, what should the role of the federal government be today?

Purposeful Dysfunction

It's clear that the current government is not what we need. Partisanship—party over country—has rendered government dysfunctional. Important domestic problems are festering for lack of federal action. Democracy itself is threatened by voter-suppression and unlimited donations of money to political campaigns, unaddressed by Congress and validated by the U.S. Supreme Court.

The wealth gap, which began developing in earnest in the 1980s, is the largest among developed countries. It is larger than Russia's or Iran's. In New York City, the gap is the same as in Swaziland; Miami's gap is like Zimbabwe's; and Los Angeles's is comparable to Sri Lanka's, according to urban studies theorist Richard Florida. The solution is not to redistribute wealth; it's to fairly distribute opportunity and revive the American contract that everyone can get ahead if they work hard. The government has done nothing effectively to narrow the wealth or income gaps even though they were important factors in the 2016 election.

The most consequential case of federal ineptitude, however, is the government's failure to deal with global climate change, a real and present danger to the "American way of life," not to mention life on the planet in general. There has been no starker contrast in the role of the federal government than the shift from President Obama to President Trump. During its final two years in office, the Obama administration helped broker the first-ever accord in which all nations committed to carbon-reduction goals; negotiated bilateral climate-action agreements with China and India; developed a detailed national climate plan; and created an outline for America's deep decarbonization by mid-century. President Trump has trashed all of it.

The federal tax code grants tens of billions of dollars in subsidies to fossil fuel industries every year, encouraging them to produce more of the stuff that causes global warming. International scientists say there should be a 65 percent reduction in global oil use and a 43 percent cut in gas use by 2050 to keep the planet from warming more than 2 degrees Celsius above preindustrial levels, yet American companies are doubling down on oil and gas production. The watchdog organization Global Energy Monitor (GEM) reports that U.S. companies plan to invest $1.3 trillion on infrastructure to export liquefied natural gas.[3] In North America, where more than half of oil and gas pipelines are located, expansion plans total more than $1 trillion.

GEM warns of a "pipeline bubble" that will burst and cause a market collapse similar to what coal companies experienced. "Today, investors in the booming expansion of oil and gas infrastructure appear headed for a similar shock," GEM says, "as boom-fueled optimism runs into climate realities and fiscal limits."

It seems that our problem in the United States is not too much federal government, but too little.

Rise of Neoliberalism

The seeds of this situation were planted more than a half-century ago by a group of conservative thought leaders who worried that President Franklin Roosevelt's aggressive New Deal was prelude to an overbearing federal government or even communism in America. They believed that free markets and the private sector—not government spending, regulation, and public ownership—were the way to preserve freedom.

Their point of view was called "neoliberalism." It grew into a movement that involved some of the nation's richest citizens, including billionaire brothers Charles and the late David Koch, who invested part of their
oil fortune in conservative think tanks such as the Cato Institute, Americans for Prosperity, and the Heritage Foundation. Along with kindred
organizations such as the American Enterprise Institute, the Hudson
Institute, and the Hoover Institute, they spread the neoliberal ideology.
In recent history, these organizations have been major influences on the
priorities of Ronald Reagan and Donald Trump.

By 2014, researchers at Princeton and Northwestern University confirmed what had become obvious: "economic elites and organized groups
representing business interests have substantial independent impacts on
U.S. government policy, while average citizens and mass-based interest
groups have little or no independent influence."[4]

"When a majority of citizens disagrees with economic elites and/or
with organized interests, they generally lose," the researchers concluded.
"Moreover, because of the strong status quo bias built into the U.S. political system, even when fairly large majorities of Americans favor policy
change, they generally do not get it. . . . America's claims to being a
democratic society are seriously threatened."

In other words, America's representative democracy is not representative today. The United States is effectively ruled by an unelected plutocratic oligarchy. Government serves these economic elites more faithfully
than it serves the American people. One indication is the persistent gap
between what the majority of Americans want and what Congress and the
president of the United States deliver. The majority of Americans wants
Congress to invest more in infrastructure, education, veterans' benefits,
Medicare, environmental protection, health care, and scientific research.
It isn't happening. More than 70 percent of voters want Congress to do
something about gun violence. Congress refuses to act. Six in ten Americans believe the economy is rigged for the rich, a belief substantiated by
the persistence of wealth inequality.

Most Americans also want the federal government to address the
climate crisis. Research in 2019 showed that 60 percent to 70 percent of
respondents believe that U.S. climate policy is on the wrong track. Actually, it's worse than that: climate action has been completely derailed in

Congress for decades. In the executive branch, two Democratic presidents, Bill Clinton and Barack Obama, created policies and programs to reduce the pollution responsible for climate change, but their initiatives died under the Republican presidents who succeeded them.

The Climate Bubble

Since assuming the presidency in 2017, Donald Trump has asserted considerable power, but in the wrong direction. He has repealed or rolled back as many as possible of Obama's accomplishments including virtually every federal program, policy, regulation, and source of information on global warming. His hostile and erratic work leadership has caused an exodus of the government scientists who know most about environmental stewardship. He has called legitimate science "the same old climate change bullshit." He plans to pull America out of the historic Paris climate accord.

Trump's goal is to make America the world's dominant oil and gas producer. He has ordered federal agencies to repeal regulations that get in the way of oil and gas production. His administration has opened more public lands to exploration and production. In April 2019, U.S. oil production exceeded 12 million barrels, a record. The words "climate change" have disappeared from websites and budgets. Global warming is the crisis whose name cannot be spoken in the Trump administration, even though this is the time that affirmative government action is needed most.

The trillions of dollars that oil companies, investors, and politicians are gambling on fossil fuel production are bad bets. The odds are far better that climate change will become so destructive and costly that all nations will be compelled to dramatically limit the production and consumption of carbon fuels, stranding trillions of dollars in assets.

On our present course, it is inevitable that the carbon bubble will burst. But to keep politicians on its side, the energy and natural resource sector has contributed nearly $346 million to political campaigns since the 2016 election cycle with nearly 80 percent of it going to Republicans.[5] A British think tank reports that since nations signed the Paris agreement in 2015, the world's largest oil and gas companies have spent more than $1 billion on lobbying and public relations to block government regulations that would mitigate the impacts of climate change.

The impacts of Trump's energy policies have been negative for jobs and national security. In 2017 and 2018, employment in the solar industry fell after years as the economy's most dynamic jobs engine. In 2018, U.S. carbon dioxide emissions rose for the first time in four years. The booming economy can't be blamed since nations proved long ago that economic growth can be decoupled from carbon emissions.

Over the last three years, weather disasters linked to climate change cost $415 billion in North America, two-thirds of the world's total. Taxpayers are paying ten times more for disaster relief than in the typical year three decades ago. The best investment we can make is in mitigating and adapting to climate change. Economists figure that every dollar we invest to mitigate climate change will return five dollars in savings on disaster recovery, but Congress has shown no interest.

The psycho-economic impacts of inaction reportedly extend even to the retirement savings of millennials—Americans born between 1981 and 1996. Two-thirds of millennials have saved nothing. Some can't afford to put money aside, but others think there's no sense saving for a catastrophic future.[6]

Sub-Nationals to the Rescue?

If there was a silver lining to Trump's plan to leave the Paris accord, it was that thousands of states, cities, universities, and nonprofits that stepped up to help keep America's Paris commitment. More than 3,500 corporate executives, college presidents, mayors, and governors reassured the world community that the United States "is still in" the pact. Some 125 cities, 9 states, 900 businesses, and 183 colleges and universities joined the commitment. They were said to represent 120 million Americans and more than $6 trillion in the economy.

But are sub-nationals capable of taking the federal government's place on big issues like climate change? States are handicapped by the same red-blue split that gridlocks Congress. Moreover, the cities and counties that stepped forward are only a fraction of the more than 20,000 municipalities in the United States; the 3,500 corporate executives merely scratch the surface of an estimated 250,000 CEOs.

Perhaps the greatest drawback of state-by-state action is the lack of a coordinating national climate-action plan. As the Texas emissions example shows, the United States needs a national road map to reach net-zero carbon emissions somewhere between 2030 and 2050. As a team of scientists and economists told the United Nations in August 2018, "In the modern global economy, (nations) are the only actors that have the legitimacy and capacity to fund and organize large-scale transitions."[7]

This is not to say that sub-nationals cannot make a significant difference. They already have and they will do much more. Largely because of commitments by individual states, the electricity generated with renewable fuels and technologies has grown in all but one of the last twelve years. Coal plant closures doubled in 2018, allowing cleaner and less expensive natural gas, solar, and wind power to take over the job of providing the nation's electricity.

Between 2001 and 2016, renewable energy's contribution to America's energy mix grew from 7.7 percent to nearly 15 percent. And while much remains to be done on the path to a clean energy economy in the United States, one of every five Americans lives today in a community committed to getting 100 percent of its energy from clean and renewable energy resources within a few decades. But we cannot get where we need to go, or get there fast enough, without an active federal government.

Decision Time

Speed is as important as substantive policy now because the world is approaching the point at which climate change becomes catastrophic and irreversible. Weather disasters already are displacing 24 million people around the world each year. Climate refugees from the driest parts of Central America already are among the refugees hoping to get through the U.S. southern border. Millions more climate victims, unable to grow food, will try in the future. The Intergovernmental Panel on Climate Change (IPCC), which has worked since 1988 to monitor and synthesize climate science from around the world, says that by the time Americans elect their next president and Congress, the world will have only a decade to make "rapid, far-reaching and unprecedented changes in all aspects of society."

Australian researchers commissioned by the UN say it's plausible that without an international mobilization comparable to what the United States did in World War II, climate change could end civilization as we know it by mid-century.[8] Continued complacency would result in state failures and resource conflicts, along with nonlinear events beyond any in human experience, all in a world well-stocked with nuclear weapons.

In short, with their firm grip on public policy and politicians, the carbon cartel and its allies in government are putting Americans, the economy, national security, and the world at very grave risk. President Trump and Congress have been warned repeatedly by the military and intelligence communities that climate change poses "immediate risks" to national security, but Trump rejects this counsel. As a result, a recent assessment by the Army War College concludes that the Defense Department remains "precariously underprepared" for the national security implications of global warming.[9]

The Democracy Gap

Democracy also is confronted with an existential crisis in the United States. In an effort to maintain their control over federal and state governments, conservatives are denying many citizens of their right to vote. The first bill the House of Representatives passed in the 116th Congress proposed to address voter access, election integrity, election security, and political spending. Republican Majority Leader Mitch McConnell blocked the bill in the Senate, claiming, "There are no serious barriers to voting anymore anywhere in America." It was a transparent lie to protect the advantage Republicans (and in a few cases Democrats) have created in many states by gerrymandering election districts and employing methods to deny people their right to vote.

Voting in at least ten states is rigged by partisan gerrymandering. Since the last presidential election in 2016, states across the country have implemented voter restrictions. The Brennan Center for Justice reports that five states rushed through new voting restrictions before their legislatures adjourned in 2019. Legislators in twenty-nine states introduced or carried over nearly ninety bills restricting voter access.

These restrictions especially inhibit the voting of minorities and low-income citizens who typically vote Democratic. These are the same citizens who are least able to cope with and who will be most hurt by global climate change.

The First Hundred Days

The most important mission for American voters is to elect people who will put democracy and the federal government back on track.

Let's assume optimistically that voters elect a president and members of Congress in 2020 who understand the balances that must be found between markets and government, state and federal rule, and America's relationships with other nations. What steps should the next president take and what tools should he or she use?

Many immediate priorities are obvious. In the first hundred days, he or she must begin repairing the damage Trump has done to federal science, environmental protections, public trust, race relations, and climate action. Much of this can be done by updating and reinstating the executive orders and regulations implemented by President Obama.

The president should select a cabinet of exceptionally qualified people to replace Trump's team of billionaire cronies and former lobbyists. Federal budgets must be realigned with the country's most important issues; EPA must be brought back to full strength; and the Obama climate action plan should be reinstated after including the best new ideas the presidential candidates issued during the 2020 campaign.

Along with his or her first budget submission, the president should send Congress a well-vetted comprehensive plan for achieving economy-wide net-zero carbon emissions no later than 2050 and net negative emissions by 2075. And as the American peace activist Jessica Mathews writes, the State Department must be restored to help rebuild America's standing in the world, starting with a recommitment to the Paris climate deal.

The president needs to restore the morale of federal employees. Soon after taking office, the president should visit each department to explain his or her goals to career civil servants and to hear theirs. There must be a culture of collaboration between careerists and political appointees. The government does not function well without it.

The First Year

Modern times require modern perspectives and tools. Here are few of them.

Master risk management. The government must become more adept at assessing and mitigating risks. In regard to climate change, the Center for Climate and Security, a nonpartisan group that studies strategic risks, warns "the U.S. is moving backward (in risk exposure) despite the regular warnings coming from the defense, intelligence and science agencies of our government, and the broader national security community."

Federal scientists have an important role here, especially those with broad ranges of knowledge. We used to anticipate the future by studying the past, but the past is no longer prologue. Global warming impacts are nonlinear, ubiquitous, and messy; they cut across political and ecological boundaries. Many impacts have no historical analogs, and some are beyond quantification. For starters, the president could convene a group of risk managers from the insurance industry, the military, and intelligence agencies to recommend an effective risk-management process.

Create an "entrepreneurial state." The world's shift to zero-carbon energy is creating enormous opportunities for new industries and jobs. The global renewable energy market alone is expected to reach more than $1.5 trillion by 2025. But with climate denial, the exit from the Paris deal, and his emphasis on fossil fuels, President Trump is ceding those opportunities to other countries such as China.

The next president should ignore the usual argument that the federal government should not "pick winners" by helping some technologies and not others. Federal research and development does what private industry does not want to do: It expands our technological options by providing risk capital and basic research. Author Mariana Mazzucato argues that the federal government should be an all-in "entrepreneurial state" that shares profits from the successful technologies it helps create. "The dominant political narrative (of leaving the economy to market forces alone) is endangering funding for future innovation and economic growth," Mazzucato writes. The government should be creating markets, not just fixing them.

Use the power of the purse. The federal government is the world's largest consumer of goods and services, spending about $450 billion annually, enough to move markets. The government is the nation's largest energy user with 350,000 buildings and 650,000 fleet vehicles. Its purchases can help beneficial goods and technologies achieve more rapid economies of scale. The result would be lower prices for the rest of the country and a more rapid diffusion of new technologies through the economy.

For starters, the president should reissue President Obama's executive orders for agencies to cut their petroleum and water consumption by 2 percent annually; to buy, lease, and design new federal buildings for zero-net-energy consumption; to cut greenhouse gas pollution 40 percent; and to obtain 25 percent of their energy from renewable resources by 2025, all while saving taxpayers $18 billion in energy costs. Trump repealed these directives and told agencies simply to meet minimal statutory requirements for resource use.

Reregulate. President Trump's war on regulations calls into question whether he has kept faith with his constitutional obligation to "take care that the laws be faithfully executed." Several of our landmark environmental laws contain clear statements by Congress that the government is duty-bound to protect natural resources and the climate for present and future generations. Trump has done the opposite.

Contrary to Trump's claim that regulations stifle enterprise and kill jobs, third-party studies consistently show that well-designed environmental rules deliver benefits that far exceed their costs. In 2018, even the Trump administration acknowledged that annual benefits from regulations between 2006 and 2016 amounted to as much as $695 billion compared to costs as high as $88 billion. The benefits are significantly higher when indirect impacts are counted.

Count what counts. The new administration should adopt national Genuine Progress Indicators (GPI) to supplement GDP in measuring the American people's well-being. GPI already is used by some U.S. states, several nations, and international organizations to measure not only economic activity, but also health, education, income equality, leisure, and so on.

Government decisions should be informed by full-cost life-cycle accounting. Life-cycle costing counts a decision's impacts from "cradle to grave." Full-cost accounting evaluates not only the direct and obvious impacts of a policy or a resource but also its indirect and hidden effects on the economy, environment, and society over time.[10]

An example is how Congress could price carbon. Several proposals would add a fee to coal, oil, and natural gas based on their carbon content.

A full-cost life-cycle approach would tax each fuel's carbon *footprint*—the carbon dioxide it emits as it is produced, refined, and transported, as well as combusted.

Another important metric is the "social cost of carbon" (SCC), a dollar amount that represents the long-term climate damage done by a ton of carbon in a given year. An interagency team during the Obama administration calculated that the SCC should be about $50 per ton of carbon dioxide in 2020. Other analysts set it at $200 or higher to reflect that carbon pollution slows economic growth. To make President Trump's pro-carbon policies look less damaging, his administration manipulated the calculation to set the SCC at only a dollar or two. The Obama SCC should be restored and updated every five years to reflect current data on the physical, ecological, and economic consequences of carbon emissions.

Consider full-spectrum impacts. Full-spectrum analysis (FSA)—also called systems or holistic thinking—recognizes that we live in a world of complex systems where every action produces consequences well beyond itself. FSA often reveals opportunities for synergies that reduce costs while improving performance.

Buildings are an example. Some years ago, DOE began promoting a "whole building" approach where contractors and subcontractors worked as teams rather than individually. Buildings were designed as systems so that components would enhance each other. For instance, proper building orientation and efficiency measures reduce the cost and energy consumption of mechanical systems.

Applied to government, FSA can be as simple as bringing employees out of their stovepipes to collaborate as teams on common goals. The U.S. Global Change Research Program, which includes scientists from thirteen federal agencies, is a good example. Congress embodied FSA in several landmark environmental laws including its first—the National Environmental Policy Act (NEPA) of 1970—which requires federal agencies to conduct full-spectrum assessments for all of their actions.

The failure to use FSA is one of the principal reasons for unintended consequences. As David Orr writes, "The great ecological issues of our time have to do with our failure to see things in their entirety. The failure occurs when minds are taught to think in boxes and not taught to transcend those boxes."

Embrace internationalism. The new president will have to make the decision articulated by François Delattre, the former French ambassador to the United Nations. "The United States faces a fundamental choice," he said. "Does it want to become a new 'Middle Kingdom,' an insular Fortress America? Or does it want to continue speaking to the world and helping to shape it?" And as Jessica Mathews points out in her fine chapter, "We live in a world where an increasing number of challenges—cyber regulation; arms control and proliferation; financial stability and trade; climate, health, and the environment; crime; money laundering; and the rule of law—can be dealt with only through multilateral diplomacy."

Reestablish the Office of Technology Assessment (OTA). This one is for Congress. To keep public policies abreast of rapidly evolving technologies, it should revive OTA. It provided expert, nonpartisan analyses of increasingly complex issues, but Congress shut it down in 1995 in a flurry of budget cutting. "A lot is happening in the technology arena," notes technology journalist Donny Jackson. "But policy lags well behind technology advances and that could be dangerous as the applications are used in more critical settings."

Different times call for different allocations of authority between federal government, states, and markets. Our current challenges require a strong national government fully engaged with states and the international community to de-carbonize the economy, re-democratize the country, revive the American promise of equal opportunity, and more. In short, we need to elect leaders committed to helping us create the future and the country we want.

I have singled out the Republicans often in this chapter, not because solutions must come from left of center, but because, as Jacob Hacker and Paul Pierson of Yale University have written, "Over the last two and a half decades, the GOP has mutated from a traditionally conservative party to an insurgent force that threatens the norms and institutions of American democracy."[11]

The war on government has made us forget what made America prosper, they write. To rebuild America, "the strong thumb of government and the nimble fingers of the market [will] each play a vital role." So must a restored and healthy democracy.

THE STATES

Nick Rathod[1]

The powers not delegated to the United States by the Constitution, nor prohibited by it to the States, are reserved to the States respectively, or to the people.

So reads the tenth and final entry in the Bill of Rights, delegating to state legislatures, governors, and state courts wide swaths of power to shape the working conditions, rights, and dreams of the American people.

As we turn the corner on four devastating years of a Donald Trump presidency and look for ways to rebuild our democracy, we should resist the urge to focus solely on moving forward with federal legislation. We should center the work instead on building a strong set of institutions, laws, and policy reforms to advance the cause of democracy in all fifty state legislatures.

Such an approach may seem short-sighted to most activists, who have been conditioned to spend much of their time fretting over the latest tweet out of the White House, landmark ruling from the Supreme Court, or policy making its way through Congress. To address those concerns, I will first spell out explicitly why states are so important, not just for advocates of democracy but also for the very soul of our country. Second, I will explain why the political right has traditionally outpaced the left in deep investment in state-level infrastructure and what the policy implications have been for our democracy. And, finally, given this new frame of reference, I'll suggest where we go from here.

Why Focus on the States?

A states-first strategy likely does not come naturally for most of democracy's advocates. And really, who can blame us? In the past, those seeking broad-based reforms have turned to federal policy to advance some of the greatest policy achievements in American history. Social Security,

Medicare, the Civil Rights Act, and countless other progressive federal initiatives have permanently changed our quality of life for the better. And, indeed, the last three years of a Donald Trump presidency have shown us perhaps more than ever before just how much damage a federal regime can do to decades of American progress.

In spite of this, it is critical to the fate of our democracy that we consider why a states-first strategy is the best investment for the progressive movement over the next decade. First, state policy matters; second, state legislatures are uniquely vulnerable to corporate influence; third, states hold the keys to democracy; fourth, state movements reinforce federal movements; and, finally, state legislators eventually become members of Congress. I will address these in order.

State Policy Matters

We should invest in a states-first progressive focus and infrastructure because state-level policy has a far greater effect on our lives than policy passed at the federal level. On average, state legislatures across the country pass 128,145 bills every year, making them twenty-three times more productive than the United States Congress. From the schools where our children learn and the air we breathe to the roads and buses that we take to work, the issues that affect our daily lives stem from the constant churn of policy decisions made by the state legislators whom most Americans would not even recognize on the street.

Take public education, for example. Education is traditionally a state issue whose outcomes can vary considerably from state to state. It is consistently a dominant part of any state budget. Typically, states will dedicate roughly 25 to 40 percent of their budgets solely to education, a breathtakingly large amount of money, considering the hundreds of billions of dollars states spend collectively each year, and especially when compared to the paltry 3 percent of the federal budget that is allocated toward education.

Not only can the disparity between states be stark (New York and Alaska, for example, spend nearly three times as much money per pupil as Utah), but also state legislators have the power to shape education policy itself, doling out voucher money to private schools that can discriminate against children with disabilities and even mandating what can and cannot be taught in class. Over the course of the last several decades, we have ceded this sort of power in favor of a federal-first strategy that has allowed conservatives to quite literally dictate the history and science we teach the next generation of leaders, workers, learners, and voters.

Labor rights, the backbone of the progressive movement, are also squarely in the jurisdiction of state legislatures. Though conservatives have for decades slowly built a case for federal right-to-work rulings, the bulk of the labor-rights movement has been fought in the states as a result of the 1947 Taft–Hartley Act, which allowed states to enact right-to-work legislation for the first time. As of 2018, twenty-seven states have decided to do so, directly affecting the paychecks of millions of working-class Americans across the country. The Economic Policy Institute estimates that moving to right-to-work policies leads to $1,558 less in annual salary for a typical worker, even if the worker isn't represented by a union.

Even policy domains traditionally set aside for federal jurisdiction have found their way into state politics. In 2017, for example, state legislatures passed 206 laws and 263 resolutions related to immigration, dwarfing those passed by the federal government.

One now infamous example, of course, was Arizona's SB 1070, which encouraged racial profiling by asking law enforcement personnel to check the papers of anyone they suspected to be undocumented. Though most of the law was later overturned by the U.S. Supreme Court, states have increasingly begun pushing the limits of their power on this issue and many other issues, even when the jurisdiction seems clear. This trend will likely only accelerate as policies that were once considered safely in the federal domain are increasingly vulnerable to state-level tomfoolery.

There's no doubt that federal-level policy is important. Without it, we would not have had so many of the signature pieces of legislation that advocates for democracy hold dear. But every president only has a few such opportunities to make fundamental changes to the way we lead our lives. On the state level, those decisions happen every day. To ignore the thousands of decisions that are made every day about people's lives on the state level is to forfeit nearly unlimited power to conservative and corporate interests.

Corporate Influence

We should care about what is happening in the states because corporations are miles ahead of us in leveraging their resources and power to influence state policymaking. Armed with teams of government-relations lobbyists and a treasure trove of PAC money, corporations in nearly every state have discovered that state legislatures—far more than their federal counterparts—are uniquely vulnerable to the corrosive influence of corporate money.

In part, this unique vulnerability is the result of legislators' being underpaid and understaffed. In fact, in state capitals across the country, a running joke among many legislators is that they are often spending twelve-hour days at their "part-time jobs." Because most state legislatures set their members' own pay, legislators who are in tough re-election battles often opt not to give themselves pay raises. They perpetually block themselves from making enough money to dedicate their full attention to the important work of running their home states. In an extreme example, state representatives in New Hampshire have given themselves a salary worth only $200 every two years. When legislators work part-time, full-time lobbyists step up to fill the void and exploit that lack of attention by supplanting democratically elected officials' work with their own.

I mentioned that state legislators are understaffed. During the 2015 legislative session, state legislatures across the country employed 31,678 people, or about 634 staff per state, including both partisan and nonpartisan personnel. By contrast, the U.S. Congress, far from immune to the influence of corporate lobbyists, employs roughly 15,000 staffers at any given time. And while the number of staff for members of Congress has generally trended upward, state legislature staff has tended to decrease since the 1990s.

Though there is little sympathy in public discourse for the personal financial interests of politicians, the lack of adequate pay and staff support in many state legislatures has created an environment ripe for undue corporate influence. Government-affairs legal teams swoop into state capitals and literally write legislation for elected leaders who otherwise would not have the technical expertise to do so.

All of this is to say nothing of the campaign side of state legislative politics, where even a few thousand dollars is enough to turn the tide of a given election when only a few thousand voters might come out to vote. In roughly half of the states, corporations can write checks to candidates straight from their corporate accounts, an explicitly prohibited practice for federal candidates.

A business owner can write a law exempting his or her company from a particular regulation, spend thousands of dollars of corporate money to elect candidates who will pass the law, pummel legislators with government-affairs teams once they take office, and punish legislators who vote against the law by sending thousands of dollars to their opponents in the next election. It happens every day in the states.

Those who seek to strengthen democracy must be much more serious about focusing on the states in the coming decade; otherwise, corporate influence will continue unchecked in the states, a more fraught possibility than anything happening in Congress.

The Keys to Democracy

We need to pay close attention to states because they hold the keys to the machinations of democracy itself. With secretaries of state as their partners, state legislatures determine how long polls are open, what kind (if any) of ID voters need, when elections are held, and even the actual voting machines used to conduct the business of democracy.

Studies have shown time and time again the racist effect of voter ID laws, which disproportionately turn voters of color away from the polls on Election Day. Those seeking to restrict access to the ballot know it. And as we are seeing once again, state legislators often have the almighty power to redraw the very districts in which they and their federal counterparts will seek re-election.

Influence on Federal Policy

Even if we ignore the influence of state policy on our day-to-day lives and on democracy, state statutes are important simply because they so often become federal policy. Recognizing this phenomenon decades earlier, Supreme Court Justice Louis Brandeis famously called states the "laboratories of democracy." The idea is simple: a few brave states go out on a limb to support a controversial policy, local officials work through the kinks and unintended consequences, and if all goes well, more states slowly adopt similar statutes. Eventually, the federal government has seen enough proof that a policy works in enough jurisdictions that it feels comfortable enacting the policy nationwide.

Marriage equality illustrates that process well, as states slowly but surely began expanding the right to marriage to more and more couples.

Without that, the Supreme Court never would have felt comfortable federalizing the right in 2015. Recreational marijuana legalization is no doubt headed down this same path today, as more jurisdictions knock down the prohibition on cannabis and the federal government starts to warm to the possibility that full legalization seems imminent.

Conservatives, to their credit, have used this idea of state movements reinforcing federal movements not just with policy choices but also with pure political choices. In 2004, for example, conservatives orchestrated a brilliant plan to put anti-marriage amendments on as many ballots in the country as they could ahead of the 2004 presidential election. This was not only a policy choice (though certainly some conservatives delighted in being able to deny same-sex couples the right to marry). It was also a political choice meant to bolster their presidential candidate. By galvanizing their base with a hot-button issue like gay marriage, they drove up George W. Bush's numbers in dozens of states and ultimately played a not-so-insignificant role in re-electing him as president of the United States. We are seeing this play out again with extreme anti-choice legislation being signed into law in states like Alabama, Missouri, and others (following nearly four hundred restrictions enacted across the country since 2011). Once again, nefarious state politics and policies are working hand in hand in a way that many fail to recognize until it is too late.

Investing in Tomorrow's Leaders

Finally, even if we set aside all the power of state legislatures in Americans' daily lives (a Herculean task, indeed), those who remain unconvinced about the necessity of state advocacy should at least care about investing in the next generation of our country's leaders.

According to the National Conference of State Legislatures, roughly half of all current members of Congress got their start in a state legislature, where they honed both their policy and political skills and proved themselves worthy of a promotion to Congress. When members of Congress retire, state legislators are the first prospective candidates for the next election cycle and can often clear the field should they decide to enter.

These state legislators are low-hanging fruit for national campaign committees, state parties, and others who recruit candidates. They understand their districts, they have relationships they can leverage for higher office, and they've run at least a few campaigns before. And, if we're being

honest, when we talk about having a "deep bench" in a certain congressional district, operatives and the media normally just mean that the
district has a plethora of experienced legislators. Raising the name recognition of a newcomer who has not already earned the trust of constituents costs more time, energy, and money. It is a smart investment to elect
more legislators in a district that may one day have an open seat. It will
eventually pay dividends in the form of several viable, well-trained candidates for federal office.

The right has known this for years and has invested tens of millions
of dollars with a laser-like focus on building a farm team of conservative
activist leaders, who have gone on to occupy positions of higher state office, all the way to the presidency. On the left, some groups have begun to
understand this in recent years. There is perhaps no one who does this
better than EMILY's List, the preeminent resource for pro-choice Democratic women. Though EMILY's List has begun to dabble in presidential
politics, its strength has been its ability to see the power of electing pro-
choice women to state legislatures across the country and owning that
space in the progressive movement. It runs effective training for women
to help them become legislators and convinces them to run for Congress,
governor, senator, or even one day president. EMILY's List's dual purpose
is convincing: more women need a seat at the table in the states because
of the robust power those legislative chambers hold, and, yes, we'd eventually like these women to run for Congress, too.

Any one of these five reasons is enough for advocates of democracy to
take stock of our tendency to overemphasize federal politics. Taken together, they should galvanize us all to wholly rethink the way we build
power.

How the Right Prevailed in States and the Implications
for American Democracy

In January 1998, then–first lady Hillary Clinton famously complained of a
"vast right-wing conspiracy" plaguing her husband's presidency and effectively blocking many of his key legislative priorities, including her own
proposals for universal health care. Although she was panned by the media
at the time, she was correct. Since the 1970s, the right had been slowly
building a conservative infrastructure to cement conservative power and

ideology at all levels of society for decades to come. But what was less commonly understood in 1998 was the extent to which that right-wing network of propaganda and political infrastructure focused less on federal legislation like Clinton's universal health guarantee and far more on advancing a corporate, anti-worker agenda in the halls of state legislatures.

As with so many terrible things that happened to the country in the second half of the twentieth century, this story starts with Ronald Reagan. A former governor and a beneficiary of the Heritage Foundation's intellectual infrastructure during his time as president, Reagan was constantly thinking of ways to bolster the conservative movement across the country. That led him to a conversation with Thomas Roe. Roe was no stranger to building conservative infrastructure, having served on the board of the Heritage Foundation and played an active role in Republican politics in South Carolina. Roe and Reagan came up with an ingenious idea: Why not create a miniature version of the Heritage Foundation for South Carolina? In fact, why not have a miniature Heritage Foundation for every state in the union?

And so, in 1992, the State Policy Network was born.

Today, the State Policy Network openly boasts of acting as the umbrella for "64 independent state think-tank affiliates and more than 90 associate partners." This corporate-backed network employs more than five hundred staff members across forty-nine states, with a combined network revenue of more than $80 million. It is currently led by Tracie Sharp, who founded Oregon's SPN affiliate, the Cascade Policy Institute.

The idea was simple: every state needed an infrastructure outside the Republican party and the GOP's elected officials to prop up conservative ideology in order to win the war of ideas after a series of bruising defeats for conservatives during the civil rights movement. And although the issues all stemmed from corporate interests (who funded the network), the causes varied widely, depending on the topic du jour in each state.

In New Mexico, for example, the Rio Grande Foundation's flashy front page bemoans "riding the rails to financial disaster!", referring to Albuquerque's proposed rapid transit bus project. The Alaska Policy Forum reminds its visitors of "the hard truth about Medicaid expansion." In Ohio, the Buckeye Institute pushes work requirements for Medicaid recipients. In North Carolina, the Civitas Institute bashes free community college as "costly and ineffective."

On issue after issue, scores of these think tanks have been pounding the airwaves, editorial boards, and capitol hallways with corporate talking points meant to undermine progressive initiatives and bolster conservative ones. And they've been doing it well for decades.

In fact, the State Policy Network is itself a member of a much more well-known organization: the American Legislative Exchange Council (ALEC). Founded in 1973, ALEC grew in prominence throughout the late twentieth century as a clearinghouse through which corporate lobbyists could move their agendas in the states. ALEC told its investors that it would work directly with corporations to develop "model legislation" around particular issues (insurance, environmental deregulation, taxes, etc.) and then work with state legislators and lobbyists to pass the model bill in as many states as possible. To its credit, ALEC saw the severe understaffing and part-time nature of state legislatures not as an impediment to state-by-state government affairs work, but as an opportunity. By taking the work out of legislating, ALEC made it exceptionally easy for Republicans (and initially even some Democrats) to pass bills written directly by major American corporations and their well-paid lobbyists. With state legislatures so vulnerable to corporate influence, passing a model bill in nearly every state legislature in the country often became a much easier lift than passing legislation in an increasingly stubborn Congress.

Eventually, ALEC became involved in a wide variety of conservative causes, even outside traditionally corporation-friendly issues. In 2005, for example, the state of Florida passed a law stating that "a person who is not engaged in an unlawful activity and who is attacked in any other place where he or she has a right to be has no duty to retreat and has the right to stand his or her ground." This was ALEC's moment to shine. Armed with a cultural flashpoint issue like guns, ALEC seized the opportunity to engage its "model legislation" modus operandi and prove its worth to financial backers.

In 2005, Florida had the only Stand Your Ground law on the books. By 2013, the number had expanded to a jaw-dropping thirty-two states, as ALEC helped state after state take Florida's law and pass it with slight modifications.

With the State Policy Network and ALEC both working overtime to push their respective agendas in the states, conservative causes thrived. Estate tax policies were repealed, Stand Your Ground laws were enacted, and right-to-work laws slowly spread across the country. Meanwhile, more-progressive initiatives languished. Focused so intently on persuading Congress to enact sweeping federal reform of working conditions, voting rights, and environmental protection, progressives slowly lost ground to conservatives in the marketplace of ideas and on policy issues near and dear to progressive hearts.

Meanwhile, conservatives had effectively designed a system of regressive law and policy that solidified their power and their control of American democracy.

Corporate interests weren't just grooming ideas and policies in the states, however; they were also grooming politicians. State by state, Republicans were slowly building a bench of top-notch recruits for higher office with help from corporate-backed outside interest groups. With scores of conservatives sharpening their policy chops in the halls of state capitols across the country, Republicans built a small army of candidates ready to pounce the moment they got a chance to force a red wave. And in 2010, they got their chance.

The political career of Scott Walker illustrates this path well. Walker, one such 2010 winner, first ran successfully for the Wisconsin state legislature in 1993 at the age of twenty-five. With the help of corporate-backed ALEC, he sharpened his policy skills in the legislature and took direct aim at progressive causes by tackling welfare reform, undermining mass transit projects, and, of course, denigrating organized labor. By 2002, he had converted those policy wins into a run for Milwaukee county chairman. And by 2011, he was governor of Wisconsin, a state that had been the beating heart of the labor movement just a generation before.

This intentional grooming of young state legislators who were fully on board with ALEC's corporate, anti-worker agenda has become a centerpiece of the right's strategy over the last few decades. The results have played out in the slow erosion of people's rights. During the Obama administration, Democrats in state legislatures fared especially poorly. From the time President Barack Obama came into office until the time he left, Democrats lost a net of 816 state legislative seats and thirteen governorships.

The flourishing of conservative policy and the uptick in the sheer number of Republican state legislators was not simply the fault of bad messaging or misplaced priorities on the part of progressives. To claim otherwise would be unfair to President Obama's legacy and a partial mis-diagnosis of the problem. Because of the outsized influence of gerrymandering and a concerted conservative effort called the Redistricting Majority Project (REDMAP) in the 2010 election cycle, this was also a crisis of democracy.

In his groundbreaking work *Ratf**ked: Why Your Vote Doesn't Count*, David Daley correctly assesses the reach of REDMAP as "the most strategic, large-scale and well-funded campaign ever to redraw the political map coast to coast, with the express goal of locking in Republican control of the U.S. House of Representatives and state legislative chambers for the next decade or more." REDMAP's overarching goal was to concentrate conservative donors' efforts on winning a handful of strategically significant state legislative races across the country in order to eventually use those legislative chambers to rig the maps in favor of Republican members of Congress and state legislators for the next decade. With just $30 million, operatives like Karl Rove locked in the state legislative majorities the right needed to gerrymander dozens of states after the 2010 Census, effectively blocking progressives from gaining working majorities in several states despite later winning a plurality of the vote. It was an entire decade of conservative dominance for the price of a mere $30 million—less than the total spent on one hotly contested special congressional election in Georgia, for example, between Karen Handel and Jon Ossoff.

To see concretely the effect of REDMAP's strategic investments, contrast Wisconsin (a key target of REDMAP) with a neighboring state like Minnesota, which has been largely spared the scourge of partisan gerrymandering for the last few decades because of court intervention in its redistricting process. In roughly even partisan states like Wisconsin and Minnesota, one would expect a healthy swing back and forth between the two major political parties in terms of control of the state legislative chambers. Indeed, throughout the last decade in Minnesota, that has been the case, with partisan control flipping a few times each for the State House and Senate since 2010.

But Wisconsin tells a different story. While Minnesota saw wild fluctuations every year, Wisconsin's partisan makeup barely changed at all after the 2010 election. Indeed, even with more voters going to the ballot box and voting for Democratic governor Tony Evers in 2018, as well as Democratic legislative candidates, Republicans maintained an almost

	Minnesota House	Minnesota Senate	Wisconsin House	Wisconsin Senate
2010	62 D / **72 R**	30 D / **37 R**	38 D / **60 R**	14 D / **19 R**
2012	**73 D** / 61 R	**39 D** / 28 R	39 D / **60 R**	15 D / **18 R**
2014	62 D / **72 R**	**39 D** / 28 R	36 D / **63 R**	14 D / **19 R**
2016	57 D / **77 R**	33 D / **34 R**	35 D / **64 R**	13 D / **20 R**
2018	**75 D** / 59 R	33 D / **34 R**	36 D / **63 R**	14 D / **19 R**

two-to-one margin in the state legislature, a direct result of REDMAP's work a decade ago.

So, where were those on the left, and why did they not see this coming?

The left's own history of success certainly played a part. Indeed, a healthy skepticism of a states-first strategy in the second half of the twentieth century made sense given the obvious context: the right had manipulated states' rights to drive forward a racist agenda, particularly in the South, around democracy, segregation, and many other economic issues. Progressives' major victories came from a federal-first strategy. Indeed, the crown achievement of the civil rights movement, the Civil Rights Act of 1964, was hailed precisely because it stripped states of their power to discriminate against people of color.

But the left's skepticism of state-based policy came with a price. As we have just seen, conservatives spent the decades after the civil rights movement reassessing their strategy and finding new, creative ways to reassert their dominance by clawing back control of policy and the marketplace of ideas. By the time President Obama took over from President Bush, conservatives already had their battle-tested playbook ready to go. Conservative state attorneys general lined up to attack centerpieces of Obama's agenda—undercutting the Affordable Care Act at every turn, suing to stop DACA and DAPA residents from staying in their homes, and undermining environmental federal legislation. Governors started rejecting federal money for high-speed rail and other economic stimuli. State legislatures refused to implement pieces of the Affordable Care Act like Medicaid expansion that would have stabilized the market and extended help to millions of Americans.

On issue after issue, progressives who had gone all-in on federal policy, thinking we could solve our nation's most pressing problems, failed
to anticipate the strong conservative infrastructure the right had built up
for decades in the states. It was so strong that it often overpowered the
federal government, even when Democrats controlled the White House
and both chambers of Congress.

Steps to Take in a Post-Trump Progressive Movement

So, where do we go from here?

First, those of us who care about building and expanding American
democracy must begin to treat states with the respect they deserve. With
our money and energy, we must elevate groups that focus on investing in
the states. State political parties, which do the heavy lifting of assembling
coordinated campaigns and keeping in year-round contact with voters,
must be taken seriously and be given the resources they need to build long-
lasting political infrastructures. Similarly situated state advocacy organizations should align their strategy to better focus and coordinate on
things like voter education, engagement, and registration, and ensure their
work is supported by an organized donor base (or table) in every state.
And, finally, candidates running to flip control of state legislative chambers must be given the airtime, gravitas, and financial support they
deserve for the kind of power we are entrusting to them.

In 2017, Manka Dhingra, who ran in a district that had been held by
a Republican who passed away unexpectedly, flipped an entire legislative
chamber in her close special election in Washington State. It gave Democrats full control of the legislature and governorship, leading to a series
of democratic reforms. Imagine a world in which she received the same
press coverage, grassroots engagement, and flood of small-dollar contributions as Jon Ossoff did when he raised over $30 million in his special
election in Georgia, or as Beto O'Rourke did when he ran for Senate in
Texas. Our entire frame of reference must change as we head into future
cycles, and we must continue to resist the urge to pivot back to presidential and congressional politics.

Some organizations that sprang up after the devastating 2016 election
are beginning to do this work in earnest. In addition to EMILY's List,
groups such as Run for Something are recruiting, training, and supporting

diverse candidates for state and local offices. They recognize the power of building a pipeline of future federal candidates as well as the importance of contesting every state legislative race in the country.

Second, we must give our hearts and souls to the fight against partisan gerrymandering. Gerrymandering can squander our opportunity to deliver critical relief to working-class families across the country—regardless of what we accomplish at the federal level with a Democratic president. While federal legislation can and should move forward to protect voter rights and move toward independent redistricting commissions, we risk repeating our mistakes from the past if we focus solely on such federal activism. Instead, we must go state by state to build fair maps for both Congress and our state legislative chambers, ceding no ground, even in the reddest states. They could turn purple if not blue in genuinely democratic elections.

Thankfully, former attorney general Eric Holder has stepped up to help fill at least part of this gaping void in progressive politics. His group, the National Democratic Redistricting Committee, which President Obama helped kickstart and which has since merged with Obama's Organizing for America grassroots effort, has zeroed in on states where the legislature or another political arm has a significant part in the redistricting process.

In Wisconsin, for example, the State Supreme Court is especially powerful in the redistricting fight. Kentucky, Virginia, and Louisiana were all 2019 NDRC targets because of their state races in the off year. And as of this writing, Minnesota, Ohio, Pennsylvania, New Hampshire, North Carolina, Georgia, Florida, and Texas were all on NDRC's target list as states where the legislature played an important part in redistricting and that would be up for re-election in 2020.

In 2010, a mere $30 million undermined democracy for a decade through REDMAP's underhanded efforts to insulate conservatives from popular backlash. In 2020 and beyond, the fight will no doubt be far more expensive, with the true power of redistricting now exposed.

Third and finally, we must do the difficult intellectual policy work that is necessary to develop and pass model state legislation across every major issue: environmentalism, education, transportation, economic mobility, racial justice, and housing, to name a few. States-first groups like the State Innovation Exchange, or SiX (which in full disclosure I founded and built into a permanent piece of progressive infrastructure), are doing this work by training and supporting policymaking among legislators across the states. If we can pass paid family leave in every state, for example, the fight to extend those benefits to every American through an arduous (if not impossible) federal process becomes unnecessary. Every state that passes a $15 minimum wage lifts tens of thousands more workers out of poverty wages and offers them a path to economic prosperity. States actively focused on our climate crisis can lay the groundwork for a desperately needed national Green New Deal. We can build policy, establish local narratives, grow smart leaders, and advance the cause of democracy if we refocus our efforts, investment, and attention on the states.

This work begins in earnest today. Already, states across the country are beginning to devise their redistricting plans. A new generation of leaders is beginning to run for state legislatures for the first time. The urgent question now is this: with so much on the line for immigrants, working-class families, people of color, LGBTQ Americans, and so many more, will we make the same mistakes again?

DEMOCRACY IN A STRUGGLING SWING STATE

Amy Hanauer

Flawed democracy delivers flawed policy. Just consider Ohio.

Ohio's political maps are so badly gerrymandered that the congressional districts have nicknames. The "Snake on the Lake," for example, clings tightly to the 116-mile Lake Erie shoreline between Cleveland and Toledo to pack two heavily black, Democratic cities into one district. The result is that in 2018, Republicans captured 75 percent of U.S. congressional seats and super-majorities of both state legislative houses with barely 52 and 50 percent of statewide votes, respectively.[1] Elections throughout this century featured similar disparities.

Ohioans voted in 2015 to reform state legislative districts, and activists negotiated in 2018 to fix congressional districts, but these won't take effect until 2022. Meanwhile, right-wing policies are driving Ohio from the middle to the bottom on many national indicators. This defies citizen preferences, community needs, and Ohio history.

Ohio was home to the nation's first big-city black mayor, is the birthplace of the American Federation of Labor, and is the site of the burning river that sparked environmentalists to demand America's Clean Water Act. It has boasted strong unions, creative community organizers, and a willingness to invest. Both European immigrants and African Americans from southern states came to Ohio for good jobs in the twentieth century, and unions fought to make those jobs better. Compared to the nation, wages were higher, and, despite intense racism, racial wage gaps were lower. The state had above-average high school completion, some of the world's best manufacturing infrastructure and workforce, and a dedication to accessible higher education.

But as the new century got underway, Ohio, battered by deindustrialization, changed course. In 2005, state policymakers eliminated the corporate income tax and replaced it with a system that generates far less revenue. They abolished the estate tax, slashed income taxes, and later created a billion-dollar loophole that lets some business owners earn $250,000 tax-free.[2] Combined, these cost Ohio a staggering $6 billion annually. Dozens of other tax exemptions cost another $9 billion.

Supporters claimed the tax cuts would spur job creation, but since 2005 the nation has added jobs about three times faster than Ohio has. Growth is forecast to continue trailing that of the United States.[3]

Ohio jobs are worse than they used to be. By 2018, six of the state's ten most common occupations paid a full-time, year-round worker less than $26,000, in contrast to even recent Ohio history.[4] The state's median wage has fallen from comfortably above to somewhat below the national average.

Because of reduced revenue, Ohio now ranks in the lower half on many state investments and near the bottom in an alarming, growing share. This is hurting all Ohioans: our larger white and black populations, and our small Asian American, Latino, and Native American populations.

Only two states make it harder for poor families to get childcare subsidies. Earnings of $27,500 put a three-person family over the threshold to enroll. The state ranked a miserable thirty-third for preschool enrollment of four-year-olds in 2018.[5] Our K–12 funding formula has been unconstitutional since 1997.[6] On college affordability, Ohio ranks forty-fifth, and our high tuition and low aid force more than four in ten public college students to work more than thirty hours a week.[7]

Health indicators are just as bad.[8] Ohio ranked third worst in opioid overdose deaths during 2017, yet 90 percent of Ohioans who needed drug treatment the previous year couldn't get it.[9] Going into 2019 budget deliberations, legislators provided less state funding to children's services than any other state. More Ohio infants don't survive to their first birthday than in forty-two states[10]—for black babies only one state does worse.[11] Local governments lost more than a billion dollars a year between 2010 and 2017.[12]

Ohio spends a lot on prisons: only thirteen states incarcerate a higher share of people, and only two keep a higher share on probation. Locking up nearly 50,000 people costs Ohio $1.8 billion a year. This system dramatically over-targets black Ohioans, who face more severe consequences at every step, from being stopped through being sentenced.[13]

Labor standards have eroded, environmental standards are lax, and tax-slashing has hacked away at the public sector. Republicans are using their lock on power to attack reproductive rights, encourage more gun use, and prevent cities and towns from regulating fracking or single-use plastic bags.

As climate change produced the wettest year on record, Ohio's legislature backpedaled on addressing it. While other states were expanding renewable energy in 2019, Ohio policymakers were passing a bill to gut clean-energy standards and make consumers pay fees to subsidize uneconomical nuclear and coal plants.[14]

For a moderate state, Ohio has a pretty right-wing approach. But Ohioans have rebelled against policy excess in the past and may do so again. After policymakers refused to prevent wage erosion, voters increased Ohio's minimum wage in 2006, giving hundreds of thousands of workers a raise. In 2011, Republican policymakers eliminated collective bargaining rights for public-sector workers, but a labor-community coalition decisively reversed the measure with a citizens' veto.

Some leaders from both parties are realizing that the tax-cutting, public-sector-slashing, school-sapping approach is accelerating Ohio's decline. So, alongside abortion bans and clean-energy attacks, some more sensible tax and budget policies are also peeking through. Legislators restored the gas tax after a decade of erosion, expanded the Earned Income Tax Credit, and added somewhat to deeply underfunded transit, school, and higher education spending.

The state's progressive organizations are more energetic, with younger, more diverse leaders. A statewide organizing collaborative with a fiery student arm has been patiently building power for more than a decade. In 2019, teachers at a Cleveland-area school unionized and staged one of the nation's first charter-school strikes, winning their first contract and better educational conditions for their largely learning-disabled students. In recent years, Cincinnati activists won wage-theft protections, more preschool funding, and better job quality for early childhood educators. And, as mentioned, voters and democracy advocates are demanding fairer districts.

A state that once took on problems with gusto, positioning people for decent jobs and good lives, has more recently failed to confront our most pressing contemporary challenges. But when political leaders neglect the common good, voters sometimes force a correction. It remains to be seen whether that happens in Ohio, reestablishing the state as a place that can be more equitable, sustainable, and inclusive. If citizens succeed in this course correction, it will also make for a truer democracy, hewing closer to what Ohioans really need.

CAN INDEPENDENT VOTERS SAVE AMERICAN DEMOCRACY? WHY 42 PERCENT OF AMERICAN VOTERS ARE INDEPENDENT AND HOW THEY CAN TRANSFORM OUR POLITICAL SYSTEM

Jacqueline Salit and Thom Reilly

Since a two-party political system became entrenched more than two hundred years ago, there have been periodic attempts to add a major third party, without success. Now, a third force is rising in American politics with no formal name, no party platform, and no common doctrine. Yet, it could transform the nation's politics.

The rise of the independent voter is one of the most powerful phenomena in U.S. politics today. Independents, or nonaligned voters, make up 42 percent of the electorate. For ten years, they have been the "swing" factor or margin in national elections, electing Barack Obama in 2008 (including in the primary against Hillary Clinton), delivering the GOP congressional majority in 2010, electing Donald Trump in 2016, and giving Democrats control of the House in 2018. While they span the ideological spectrum, independents are guided less by ideology than by values—and by the belief that the two parties have failed the American people.[1]

In the 2018 midterms, two years into the Donald Trump presidency, independents backed Democratic congressional candidates by a margin of twelve points, a twenty-four-point swing from the midterms in 2014. Where statewide political reform initiatives were on ballots, independents played a notable role in the voter coalitions that enacted nonpartisan redistricting, same-day and automatic voter registration, and the restoration of voting rights for felons. In Maine, a vote to reject the state legislature's pernicious override of a citizens' initiative for ranked choice voting brought tens of thousands of independents to the polls, which provided the people's veto its decisive victory.

In other words, in 2018, independent voters carried the Democrats to control of the House, put a check on the White House and on one-party rule, and helped install a varied set of structural reforms that strengthened the democratic process. And yet, this voter community is often made invisible or derided for its refusal to define itself in traditional terms of loyalty to a political party.

Nonetheless, the rise of the independent voter means there is a volatile force with the power to disrupt a status quo, to drive structural reform from the bottom up, and to move "process issues" from the margins to the mainstream. At this hinge moment, when concerns about the state of American democracy are high, it is crucial to recognize, respect, and fully integrate this emergent force into the electoral process—as who they are.

Enforced Loyalty to the Parties

The framers did not insert political parties into the design of our democratic republic. To be truly effective, the reframers—i.e., those concerned today with political and social reform—must respond to the country's thirst for an alternative to the hyper-partisan culture that the parties frequently incentivize. In that culture, party loyalty trumps all else. Primary-season challenges to party incumbents are aggressively restrained. "Sore loser" laws prevent candidates from running as independents if they fail to get a party nomination. The legal matrix governing the electoral process is legislated by partisans who benefit from their own design.

Today, the 42 percent of the electorate that calls itself independent is a protest against that matrix. It includes a diverse cross-section of Americans. Fifty-one percent of millennials, 27 percent of African Americans, and 37 percent of Latinx[2] are independents, yet they are often given second-class status and are subject to subtle and not-so-subtle forms of voter suppression. Currently, they are barred or restricted from primary voting in half the states, and in 2016 it is estimated that close to 26 million independents were locked out of presidential primary and caucus voting. Many of these were millennials who registered as nonaligned in closed primary states, only to discover that they were prohibited from casting ballots. Recent surveys show that upward of 90 percent of independents believe they should be permitted to vote in all presidential primaries and caucuses in 2020 without having to forfeit their nonaligned status.

To a large degree, independents are unrestrained by many of the categories of traditional ideology and political correctness that now (mis)shape the political terrain. In systems that allow voter freedom, unexpected patterns occur. The political appeal of being an independent, combined with the decline of the two major parties, has produced some unimaginable results. In 2016, a truculent outsider with a penchant for political incorrectness and his finger on the pulse of aggrieved Americans marginalized by globalization and the elitism of liberal identity politics defeated sixteen challengers to capture the Republican nomination. It is estimated that one million California independents (No Party Preference) voted for Donald Trump for president and either Kamala Harris, an Indian-Jamaican progressive, or Loretta Sanchez, a Mexican American progressive, for U.S. Senate, a counterintuitive mix-and-match, to put it mildly.

A majority of independent voters, having backed Obama in 2008, changed direction in 2016 and broke for Trump. African American voter turnout was down by an estimated 2 million votes from the Obama years, a mix of targeted voter suppression measures and, many believe, Clinton fatigue. Social media was overheated by domestic and, apparently, foreign interests. And, in a sign of our confusing times, the Democratic Party failed to see the crumbling of the Blue Wall in time to fix it.

While many felt that the result of the 2016 presidential campaign was an aberration, its underpinnings were not. Party loyalty and the boundaries of traditional ideology are breaking down at an accelerated pace. A survey conducted by Morning Consult of 19,000 registered voters across the United States provides a dramatic picture of this shift.[3] Twenty-four percent of respondents are considering voting in 2020 for a different political party than the one they voted for in 2016, including 21 percent of Trump voters and 20 percent of Clinton voters. These data amplify an earlier finding by the University of Virginia's Center for Politics that between 11 percent and 15 percent of 2012 Obama voters, or 7 to 10 million people, voted for Trump in 2016.

The Decline of Political Parties

While the number of independents is growing in the United States, the two-party political system is in flux. The Republican and Democratic parties are torn by internal conflicts between competing parts of their bases. The power struggles *within* the parties combined with the power struggles *between* the parties are producing political chaos, corruption, and deep levels of uncertainty.

Public distrust in government and in the parties is not difficult to explain. The late *Harper's Magazine* columnist Walter Karp—a sharp-tongued critic of the machinations of partisan, including bipartisan, government—wrote back in 1973, "Control of elected officials means real political power, and party organizations use that power, first and foremost in order to serve themselves—party organizations are neither malevolent nor benevolent; they are self-interested."[4]

Today that self-interest has calcified into gridlock, a partisan and polarized media, and abuse of power. Former California governor Arnold Schwarzenegger, who successfully pushed for reforms that would transfer power from the parties to the people, recently told us, "It doesn't matter what party you belong to. The party business is an evil business." Asked why, Schwarzenegger replied, "Because they really don't care about people . . . they're not really interested in getting things done. They're more interested in what gets them elected." And why are so many Americans choosing to identify as independents? The parties "don't have the same hold anymore because they have disappointed the voters."

Former Nevada senator Harry Reid, a Democrat who served as Senate majority leader from 2007 to 2015, shared with us his deep concern over the state of party politics. "I have tremendous affection for the two parties," he said. "But our system has become so filled with tribalism, it's hard for me to comprehend. I know there is tremendous dissatisfaction, which is causing many people, many young people, to not be party-affiliated."

This breakdown in party loyalty and the rise of voter mobility have spurred other new developments in national politics. In his first public exploration of an independent presidential run, former Starbucks CEO Howard Schultz felt that the 42 percent of voters who are independent represent a core around which a new majority coalition can be built.

Shortly before his death in 2019, the iconoclastic pollster Patrick Cad-dell identified the large number of independents not as an ideological force but as an illustration of the "great opportunity for otherness." What is "otherness" in this tumultuous moment? For answers to this, we turn to a more in-depth look at independents and the effort to deny their existence or to deny that their existence has any meaning.

The Controversy over the Independent Voter

The democratic ideal of an independent, "free-thinking" citizen making intelligent, informed decisions has held a place of distinction throughout the history of American political thought. But not in U.S. academic scholarship. For the past sixty years, political scientists have largely discounted or attempted to disprove this notion of "independence." Modern U.S. politics has largely been viewed through the lens of a two-party power structure: Democrats and Republicans. Political and other social scientists have been extremely skeptical and dismissive of independent voters, labeling them as leaners, disengaged, disaffected, and/or shadow partisans. It is as if that many academics are unable to conceive of a voter who doesn't choose between one of the major parties.

The root concept of independent voters as a different political species goes back to the work of Angus Campbell and his colleagues, who first published *The American Voter* in 1960. They acknowledge that something considered an "independent" exists, but they introduced a bias about its significance, stating that independents' "interest in the campaign is less, their concern over the outcome is slight, and their choice between competing candidates seems much less to spring from discoverable evaluations of the elements of national politics."

Nevertheless, since the 1960 study, national and regional surveys for the most part document a growing number of independents. The Pew Research Center, the most oft-cited source, consistently finds that the number of political independents continues to grow, while the traditional parties have lost ground. Self-identified independent voters now make up the largest segment of the American electorate, with Gallup showing a peak of 46 percent of registered voters in June of 2019.

There has been a robust debate about the real meaning of this trend. Gallup attributes it to increasing frustration with government and two-party control over politics. Many authors have been skeptical, however, that those voters who claim the independent label deserve it because they have cast ballots for major-party candidates. Yet in the vast majority of elections, the only choices on the ballot are Republicans and Democrats.

Influencing Elections

Regardless of their "true" independence, the question persists whether independents play a significant role in elections. Linda Killian's 2011 work best represents the research into these questions. In *The Swing Vote: The Untapped Power of Independents*, she dives into an exploration of voters who, in her analysis, contributed a significant margin of victory for Barack Obama in key states in 2008, and for Republican congressional candidates in 2010. Killian found that people increasingly see a disconnect between the priorities of elected officials and voters. She cites polls showing that confidence in the parties is at an all-time low. And, shortly before the 2016 election, Killian wrote in *USA Today*, "Desperate for change and sick of a political system that values wealthy campaign donors over average Americans, many voters have turned to Trump."

Killian's presumption is that disenchanted voters are a growing bloc that evaluates candidates on their likelihood to compromise and seek moderate solutions. Independent voters are also more likely to consider the country's manifest economic conditions, while partisan-identified voters use the cues of party and ideology.

A study of 2,000 voters conducted in 2015 by Arizona State University's Morrison Institute found that nearly half of independents had changed their registration from another party and were more likely to identify themselves as moderates. Additionally, one-quarter of independents still considered themselves liberal or conservative, and shared a diverse range of opinions when asked about specific issues. This perspective was best summed up by one focus-group participant: "We're not a party. We're a mindset."

Key to understanding the potential influence of independent voters in any given election are data about whether independent turnout is the same or lower than partisan voters. Here the "unaffiliated voter" designation, referring to the voter's registration status, is most often cited. In this case, independents have a much lower turnout. But that could be the result of legal and institutional barriers. Both political parties maintain their duo-monopoly status because of federal and state election laws ensuring that third parties have little or no chance of challenging the two-party apparatus.

The Independents' Roots

Recent studies show that independents consume media and information from diverse sources, much more than Republicans or Democrats. They can act as bridges within their own social networks between liberals and conservatives. But they are not necessarily moderates. Independent voters span the ideological spectrum from left to right. But, more fundamentally, they are agents of systemic change. And they have a key role to play in any process of strengthening our democracy and social healing. It is difficult to imagine a wholesome and comprehensive approach to political reform that does not include these Americans and their concerns about the party-driven construct of American politics.

Beginning in the early 1990s, the Term Limits movement swept through the country, passing with 51 percent to 77 percent of the vote in almost every state that permitted citizens' initiatives on ballots. The incumbency protection "racket" was being called to account. The anti-incumbent reform fever lifted up the independent presidential bid of Ross Perot in 1992.

Perot's candidacy drew attention to two new trends: the popular demand to reclaim a corrupt partisan government and concerns about the size of the national deficit and debt. Perot ran again in 1996 not as an independent, but as the representative of a newly created National Reform Party. Its platform focused on reforming the two-party system and limiting the power of political elites. Although the Reform Party soon foundered on multiple conflicts—internal and external—it established that a growing sector of the American public believed that a political restructuring was necessary to redistribute power so that corruption and stagnation would not continue to spread.

Throughout the 1990s and the first two decades of the 2000s, a set of Supreme Court decisions circled the wagons against this nonpartisan reform movement. In *Timmons v. Twin Cities Area New Party*, 520 U.S. 351 (1997), the right to employ fusion voting—a system where candidates can run on more than one party line, which allows cross-partisan and multi-party coalitions to form—was rejected by the court. In *California Democratic Party v. Jones*, 530 U.S. 567 (2000), the blanket primary system enacted by the voters in 1996 to give themselves maximal mobility was declared unconstitutional. In *Shelby County v. Holder*, 570 U.S. 529 (2013), the court declared Section 5 of the Voting Rights Act to be unconstitutional. And in *Citizens United v. Federal Elections Commission*, 558 U.S. 310 (2010), political spending was equated to free speech, thereby nullifying or containing many of the post-Watergate controls on campaign contributions.

Arguably, the political/judicial superstructure was invested in containing an anxious electorate and prioritizing the stability of the existing arrangement. As a consequence, some voting rights attorneys now argue that "the recognition of the rights of unaffiliated voters is the new frontier in the civil rights/voting rights struggle."[5]

At the same time, at the state level, district lines were drawn by the parties in power to cement their advantage. Voter ID laws were enacted or strengthened in GOP-controlled states to depress voting by minority communities that historically support Democrats. Voter rolls were purged in large numbers and not just in "red" states. Purging occurred on a large scale in the bluest of blue New York.

The mounting collision between party control and the independent sector propelled a new reform agenda. New York City mayor Michael Bloomberg and the Independence Party attempted to install a nonpartisan voting system in 2003, which would have enfranchised the city's one million independents, nearly 40 percent of whom were black, Latinx, or Asian. That effort was unsuccessful and was conspicuous for the fact that the traditional good government movement and the liberal *New York Times* opposed it. They argued that voters needed partisan "cues" to make choices and that Democratic Party stakeholders would be disrupted.

This was followed by two attempts led by Governor Schwarzenegger in California to establish a nonpartisan Top Two electoral system. It finally passed in 2010, along with a mandate for an independent redistricting commission, galvanizing support from independent voters and their allies in the major parties. These reforms turned away from a singular focus on campaign finance reform and sought to bring in more voters, to disrupt the hegemonic power of the parties, and to open the political process to more choices.

In the fall of 2017, much of this new ground was codified in two major reports. The Harvard Business School issued its prescription for a dysfunctional democracy, titled, "Why Competition in the Politics Industry Is Failing America—A Strategy for Reinvigorating Our Democracy," by Katherine M. Gehl and Michael E. Porter.[6] In a scathing "dressing down" of the two-party system, Gehl and Porter contended that "the political system is a private industry that sets its own rules." They proposed reforms to break up the unhealthy and monopolistic system. In particular, they advocated for a Top Four nonpartisan primary system, the use of ranked choice voting with instant run-off, nonpartisan redistricting, and rewriting the debate access rules for presidential elections. The report also recommended an aggressive strategy for running independent candidates. The Harvard survey garnered significant media attention and spurred the beginnings of a national dialogue on these initiatives.

At the same time, another report was released by the Schwarzenegger Institute for State and Global Policy at USC, the Morrison Institute for Public Policy at ASU, and the frontline nonprofit Independent Voting. Titled "Gamechangers? Independent Voters May Rewrite the Political Playbook," this survey asked whether independents constituted "a movement for greater enfranchisement, an anti-corruption movement or a unique synthesis of the two?"

"Gamechangers" confronted the skepticism of the political science academy toward independent voters, noting the appeal of political independence in the African American and Latinx communities, and positing that independent voters could be an as-yet-untapped force for democratic reform, an antidote to political polarization, and a force for humanistic development.

The Independent Mindset

If we look more deeply into the independent's "mindset," we begin to see the values that drive these voters. In addition to being ardently pro-reform (90 percent think the presidential primaries should be open to all voters, regardless of affiliation or non-affiliation) and ardently disappointed in the two-party system (66 percent say the reason they decided to become independent is that the two-party system has failed the country and puts its own interests ahead of the people), independents increasingly exhibit a politic that might be described as "Humanist Libertarian."

A survey released by the Pew Research Center illuminates these values.[7] It found that 66 percent of independents feel that the economic system in this country "unfairly favors powerful interests," three points higher than the combined number for all voters. A majority of independents (57 percent) say "the U.S. needs to continue to make changes to give blacks equal rights with whites." And 66 percent of independents believe that immigrants strengthen the country, rather than burden it (23 percent). Sixty-two percent oppose "substantially expanding the wall along the U.S. border with Mexico." The theme of fairness resonates with independent voters, as 70 percent favored the right to same-sex marriage.

With respect to attitudes about environmental problems and policy, a January 2019 Hill-HarrisX survey found that 64 percent of independents feel current environmental patterns are "extremely" or "somewhat" troubling.[8]

While independents hold these progressive values, they are much more libertarian than traditional progressives when it comes to the role and scale of government. By a small margin, 48 percent to 43 percent, most say they believe that "government regulation is necessary to protect the public interest," rather than "government regulation of business does more harm than good." By another small margin, 47 percent of independents prefer "smaller government providing fewer services," while 44 percent prefer "bigger government providing more services."

This distinction sets up an interesting contrast with progressives in the Democratic Party, in particular. The new generation of Democratic Party members elected to Congress, for example, consists largely of Big Government advocates. Many Democratic Party leaders are conflicted about whether nonpartisan reforms should be supported to empower independent voters. This conflict pits party loyalty against demands for across-the-board fairness in the democratic process. Whereas Democratic Party activists tend to see the corporate sector as the pinnacle of corruption, it is reasonable to conclude that many independents believe that while Wall Street is guilty of many sins, the political system itself has the most pernicious corruption.

Social Connection and Political Reconstruction

As independent voters grow rapidly in number, their presence in the system is challenging the major parties' hegemony and disrupting the ways in which we have long analyzed and practiced politics. New research by Arizona State University's Morrison Institute for Public Policy found that social networks—especially among independent voters, who are at ease with interacting with both Republicans and Democrats—can provide an expansion of political inputs into their views.[9]

Pew Research has been a leader in examining media usage across various demographics. Its 2016 report, "The Modern News Consumer," showed a heavy reliance on TV news, followed by online, radio, and finally print.[10] Those under age fifty, however, were more reliant on news from online sources than those on TV.

Pew reported a striking difference between how conservatives and liberals get information about government and politics. It found that consistent conservatives clustered around one news source, Fox News Channel (FNC), while consistent liberals consulted an array of news sources.

Pew's report missed an opportunity to examine the habits of independents in comparison to partisans but the ASU study made the comparison. It found evidence that independents may moderate partisan media consumption with social networks in which they share political news from broader sources in discussions with members of both parties. The study showed that while Republicans with Republican friends use the most conservative media, Republicans with independent friends score average on the media-use scale. This suggests that independents can moderate or broaden the views of conservative friends, exerting a moderating, or broadening, influence. This raises an important question that needs further examination: Can independents help ease the nation's political polarization by sharing conflicting news with both Republicans and Democrats?

Independent Demographics

There is increasing evidence that the attraction of the independent identity has been rising significantly among millennials, college students, Latinx, and African Americans. Significant attention has been paid to the evidence of there being an independent, even anti-party, mindset among millennials (roughly those born from 1980 through 1997). Pew found in 2014 that half of millennials described themselves as political independents, a level "at or near the highest levels of political . . . disaffiliation recorded for any generation in the quarter-century that Pew Research Center has been polling on these topics."[11]

Similarly, a North Carolina poll of college students found a strong independent mindset in this population.[12] The poll found that while independents held a broad range of ideological perspectives, their disapproval of partisan politics and their interest in reforming the political process were common themes.

The growth of Latinx in many battleground states has fueled interest in these voters' levels of independent political thinking. Gallup found in 2012 that a majority of U.S. Latinx identified as political independents. And while the African American community has historic ties to the Democratic Party, there is increasing evidence of a rise in independent identification, especially among younger African Americans. According to a 2019 University of Chicago–affiliated survey,[13] 26 percent of eighteen- to thirty-six-year-old African Americans identified as "independent" and another twelve percent as "something else" for a total of 38 percent. In a 2018 Pew Research Center poll, 27 percent of African Americans of all ages identified as independent.

Might these changes in the electorate impact how the parties relate to independents? While meeting with a slew of Democratic presidential contenders, Senator Harry Reid told us, he gave this advice on relating to the 42 percent: "We, as party members, like to wear that Democratic badge wherever we go. But you better start reaching out to independents and treat them as independents."

Conclusion

Independent voters are both a product of and a propellant for the breakdown in ideology-as-we-know-it and the restructuring and strengthening of American democracy. Those who pointed to the need for process reform at the turn of this century were relegated to the fringe. Today, this has been turned on its head. The first bill introduced by House Democrats in 2019 was H.R. 1, dedicated to the proposition that there cannot be restrictions on or barriers to full voter participation. Ironically, the Democratic Party's control of the House was made possible by independent voters but independents and the barriers they face were not mentioned in H.R. 1.

Nevertheless, the evidence tells us that independents—having made a choice to identify themselves as something other than a political partisan—can help ease partisan divisions in the nation's politics and rework the two-party system. We must be willing to recognize, respect, and amplify their role in the political scene.

PHILANTHROPY AND DEMOCRACY

Stephen B. Heintz

It was the World Economic Forum in 2019. Many of the world's wealthiest and most powerful people had gathered in the Swiss town of Davos to take the pulse of the global economy and geopolitics. Among them was Michael Dell, founder and CEO of Dell Technologies.

Michael Dell is one of the four hundred richest individuals in the United States today. While wages for most Americans have remained stagnant, this group has tripled its share of the nation's wealth since the 1980s. Its members now control more wealth than the 150 million Americans in the bottom 60 percent of the wealth distribution combined.[1] Yet when asked about a proposal that would help rectify this injustice—raising the upper tax bracket in the United States to 70 percent—Dell responded, "I feel much more comfortable with our ability as a private foundation to allocate those funds than I do giving them to the government."[2]

Two days later, on a panel about inequality, Dutch historian and journalist Rutger Bregman veered off script: "I hear people talking the language of participation and justice and equality and transparency, but almost no one raises the real issue of tax avoidance—of the rich just not paying their fair share. We can talk for a very long time about all these stupid philanthropy schemes, but come on, we've got to be talking about taxes!"[3] The video of Bregman's remarks went viral.

Skepticism of Philanthropy and the Democracy Crisis

"All these stupid philanthropy schemes." Bregman's remarks came at a moment of increased public scrutiny and skepticism of the role of philanthropy in democracy. In *Winners Take All*, the most vociferous of the critics, Anand Giridharadas, offers scathing condemnation of concerned elites who grumble about an inequitable and unjust status quo, but whose solutions promise only "elite-led, market-friendly, winner-safe social change."[4] The elites of Giridharadas's "MarketWorld" speak the language of inequality, but refuse to question the neo-liberal market logic that generates it. They speak the language of social justice, but refuse to countenance the obvious path toward advancing it—strengthening participatory democracy and governments accountable to the people rather than to the powerful. When elites "put themselves in the vanguard of social change," Giridharadas writes, "it not only fails to make things better, but also serves to keep things as they are."[5]

Things as they are, it is worth remembering, is not how they always were. In the three decades after World War II, a Keynesian "mixed economy" produced rising wages, shrinking income inequality, and near full employment.[6] The civil rights movement expanded the democratic franchise, cashing in promises made and not kept in the Declaration of Independence and the Constitution. Even in 1972, after leaders in both parties had intentionally misled the public about the progress of the Vietnam War, 52 percent of Americans still trusted government.[7] That was the era of the Great Society. Liberalism swept the country from coast to coast. American democracy was not perfect, but it was moving in the direction of justice.

Today, there is no doubt that democracy in the United States—and around the world—is in crisis. We are living in a second Gilded Age. Economic inequality has returned to levels not seen since just before the Great Depression. Wages peaked in inflation-adjusted terms in 1973, the year cellphones were invented.[8] They have been stagnant ever since. A thirty-five-day federal shutdown beginning in December 2018 was the longest in U.S. history—a historic record befitting a historically dysfunctional government. No wonder only 3 percent of Americans now believe that their government will do what is right "just about always."[9]

The crisis of democracy is described in the language of our age—numbers. But at the heart of the crisis is something numbers cannot capture. Democracy is about more than just rules that can be followed or violated, institutions that are broken or intact. Writing after the Civil War, Walt Whitman put it well: "At the core of Democracy, finally, is the Religious element." In the first half of the twentieth century, American philosopher and educational reformer John Dewey, too, considered democracy a "civic faith." Democracy has always been an ethical and spiritual ideal. The crisis of democracy today is first and foremost an ethical and spiritual crisis.

The world of philanthropy is a reflection of economic inequality. There would be no billion-dollar donations without billionaires. Are those who have profited from our current economic system in a position to challenge its fundamental, undemocratic premises? Faced with the injustices of a second Gilded Age, are the legacy foundations of the first able to untether themselves from the conditions that created them? Can institutional philanthropy respond to the crisis of democracy with more than just "market-friendly, winner-safe social change?"

My thesis is that it can. The paradox of institutional philanthropy is that it is in a special position to address the crisis of democracy that, in some respects, it reflects. The tragedy of institutional philanthropy is that it isn't yet doing so in a meaningful way.

Social Capital Philanthropy Versus Risk Capital Philanthropy

Americans donated $410 billion in 2017.[10] With charitable giving measured as a percentage of GDP, it is fair to say that Americans are the most generous people on Earth.[11] The largest source of the $410 billion comes from small-donor contributions—"ordinary Americans," not the Michael Dells of the world, contributing on average 2 percent of their household incomes to charity.[12] Foundation funding is a much smaller slice of the pie. It tends to hover around 15 percent of total giving.

When talking about individual small-donor contributions versus foundation giving, a distinction is often drawn between "charity" and "philanthropy." In its most common formulation, charity aims to provide relief and direct assistance, whereas philanthropy seeks to address root causes. Donating money to a disaster relief fund after a devastating hurricane, for example, qualifies as an act of charity, according to this distinction. Advancing policies to mitigate climate change—which we know contributes to hurricanes of greater frequency and intensity—is the business of philanthropy. The distinction is imperfect: small donors can and do give money to climate change research institutes; large foundations can and do give money to disaster relief funds. Moreover, confusingly, philanthropic dollars are often categorized (as above) under the larger heading of "charitable giving." Meanwhile, small-donor charitable giving is sometimes called "mass philanthropy."

A better way of thinking about the different forms and functions of philanthropy—of slicing up the $410 billion pie—is to take a short trip through history. The voluntary donation of time and money is deeply rooted in American history and in the American mythos. But it has taken different forms and performed different functions at different times. Early philanthropy in the United States was what we might describe as "social capital" philanthropy. It was the philanthropy of associations—of people identifying needs in their communities (a school here, a church there) and forming associations to build, found, and fund their solutions. Benjamin Franklin was the American social capital philanthropist par excellence. He founded a library, a fire brigade, a university, and a militia. He did so not as a billionaire donor, but as a brilliant leader, convener, and gatherer of citizen contributions. Several decades after Franklin's death in 1790, French nobleman Alexis de Tocqueville found a nation swimming with Benjamin Franklins. "In every case," Tocqueville famously observed, "at the head of any new undertaking, where in France you would find the government or in England some territorial magnate, in the United States you are sure to find an association."[13]

Social capital philanthropy, of course, still exists. Much "small-donor" philanthropy falls within this category. It is the philanthropy of people serving on school boards and donating to their local libraries and religious institutions. It is the philanthropy of ordinary Americans expressing the better angels of their nature, as they have for centuries. And it is vital for our democracy, particularly at a moment when, as political scientist Robert Putnam famously argues, social capital has declined.[14]

But as social capital has declined, another kind of philanthropic capital has increased—risk capital. If the vessel of social capital philanthropy is the association, then the vessel of risk capital philanthropy is the foundation. The modern American foundation did not exist at the time of Benjamin Franklin and Alexis de Tocqueville. It is a creature of the twentieth century. With their vast industrial fortunes of the post–Civil War Gilded Age, John D. Rockefeller, Andrew Carnegie, and Russell Sage endowed the first major American foundations; the Ford Foundation soon followed. All of these foundations still exist today—along with more than 80,000 others.

Foundations have established themselves as important actors in American democracy. Sandwiched between the public sector and private

sector—a giant and an exponentially bigger giant—foundation philanthropy does a job that neither of its larger neighbors does well: it brings a
long-term, bird's-eye-view perspective to vital public goods. The public
sector notoriously suffers from the "short-term-ism" of the election cycle;
the private sector is beholden to the market and the profit motive. Freed
from these constraints, foundations are able to deploy society's "risk capital" to support public goods that don't have an immediate payoff, electoral
or monetary, but that are essential.

The question is—which public goods should foundations support?
Society's risk capital is limited and valuable. Where should it go? Education, health, social services, arts and culture, and the environment are
common destinations. These are all important public goods that foundations have historically supported.

But there is something missing from this list. Do you want a clean environment? A fighting chance at defusing the civilizational crisis of climate
change? For that you need a functioning democracy. Do you want an education system that mitigates, rather than exacerbates, inequality? For that
you need democracy. A health care system that works? Democracy.

Foundation Funding for Democracy

The instrumental value of democracy is well known. When politics are
captured by special interests, goods and policies that are important to the
public suffer. A clean environment, an effective and equitable health care
system, workers' rights, and sane gun control laws are just a few examples. The quality of democracy impacts almost everything foundations as-
pire to do—positively, if democracy is functioning well; negatively, if it
isn't. For this reason alone, whatever else foundations support, they should
support democracy reform too.

Yet this "instrumental argument" is not the only reason foundations
should support democracy. The rise of authoritarianism and ethnic nationalism around the world forcefully reminds us that democracy is more
than a means to an end. Why should we care about democracy? Because
democracy is the only political system premised on universal values of
freedom, equality, and human dignity. Because, as Thomas Mann wrote
at an earlier time when democracy was under threat, democracy is "timelessly human."[15] It was timelessly human in 1776 in the United States; it

was timelessly human in 1989 in Eastern Europe; and it is timelessly human today. The history of democracy in the United States has been sinful, but the idea has always been, and will always remain, noble.

Despite the fact that democracy is facing its most serious crisis in decades, however, foundations continue to take democracy for granted. U.S. foundation support for democracy reform—broadly construed to include money-in-politics reform, civic leadership development, civil rights advocacy and litigation, and journalism—hovers around 1.5 percent of total foundation giving.[16] And the funding that *does* go to democracy reform comes from a relatively small group of foundations; fewer than 10 percent of foundations are involved in advancing democracy reforms. Foundations gave $67 billion in 2017; funding for democracy was not so much a slice of that pie as a crumb.

What percentage of foundation funding should go to democracy reform if not 1.5 percent? (3 percent? 5 percent?) And what percentage of foundations should be involved in the democracy space if not 10 percent? (20 percent? 30 percent?) These are the wrong questions. Just as the crisis of democracy—an ethical and spiritual crisis, above all—cannot be captured in numbers, addressing the crisis of democracy is not, in the first instance, a numerical question. The important thing is that foundations stop taking democracy for granted and start thinking about democracy as akin to education and health—something that they ought to be supporting. Democracy reform needs to become a slice of the pie. The crisis of democracy is exactly the sort of thing that foundations exist to address.

Foundation philanthropy, of course, cannot solve the democracy crisis alone. But together with our partners in civil society and with the other actors discussed in this book—states, cities, and grassroots organizations, for example—we have an important role to play in advancing solutions. How? Foundations are prohibited by law from engaging directly in politics. So politics are off limits. But ideas, advocacy, movements, and culture are fair game.

Ideas and Research

Our country's institutional architecture is robust, and it has helped us weather many storms. But moral compromises were built into our founding documents. And to state the obvious, circumstances have changed profoundly from the time they were written. The work of strengthening our democracy, therefore, cannot be one of nostalgia. Rather, we must *re-invent* democracy for the challenges of the twenty-first century.[17] To do so, we will need new conceptual thinking. We will need ideas—the best and boldest of them.

When the first federal census was taken in 1790, the combined population of the thirteen colonies was less than 4 million, and the average lifespan was less than forty years. We are now living twice as long in a country with a population more than eighty times greater. With lives so much longer, does it still make sense to have life terms for Supreme Court justices? With such vast—and growing—disparities between populations of big and small states, does it still make sense to have equal representation of states in the Senate? How can a representative democracy remain genuinely representative when there are so many citizens to represent? Citizens feel that their voices are no longer heard—that influencing public policy has become the prerogative of corporations, special interest groups, and the wealthy. But how does one conduct a chorus of 328 million citizen voices?

Funding ideas and research has been a quintessential function of foundation philanthropy since its earliest days. The colloquial term "think tank" first came about in the 1950s,[18] but policy institutes designed to help shape policy—the political neurons of civil society—go back much further. The most august of these early policy institutes are now household names. The Carnegie Endowment for International Peace was founded in 1910 with a $10 million gift from Andrew Carnegie; the Institute for Governmental Research, later renamed the Brookings Institute, was founded in 1916, partly through a gift from John D. Rockefeller; and the National Bureau of Economic Research was founded in 1920 by the Commonwealth Fund.

The mandate of these early "think tanks" was to provide unbiased research and impartial analysis to inform policy. In more recent decades, a new generation of think tanks has abandoned the aspiration—or pretense, some would say—of nonpartisanship and impartiality. On the right, the Heritage Foundation, the Cato Institute, and the American Enterprise Institute make no attempt to conceal their conservative and neo-liberal stripes. They helped orchestrate the greatest ideological coup d'état of a century—the neo-liberal revolution of the 1980s and 1990s, which elevated capitalism above democracy and which bears much responsibility for the democracy crisis we now face. On the other side of the spectrum, policy institutes such as the Brennan Center, Demos, and the Center for American Progress advocate unabashedly for participatory democracy from a progressive perspective.

Here is one area in which progressive and conservative foundations can and should agree: elevating the tenor of public discourse and encouraging an informed citizenry. We cannot resolve our differences without adhering to the norms of fair and respectful debate. Providing information is not enough at a time when misinformation and disinformation are rampant. Foundations on both sides of the political spectrum can amplify fact-based, independent journalism and advance limits on the manipulation of social media technologies to spread falsehood, division, and hate.

Institutional and Procedural Reform

Making good on one of his core campaign promises, President Barack Obama signed into law the Affordable Care Act in March 2010. Obama could not have achieved this historic legislative victory alone. He was supported by numerous individuals and organizations that had been advocating for health care reform for years—if not decades. One group credited with having been a major contributor to the Affordable Care Act's passage was a progressive coalition known as Health Care for America Now (HCAN). In 2009, to support its advocacy efforts around the Affordable Care Act, the Atlantic Foundation gave HCAN a $27 million grant. It was, at the time, the largest grant ever made in support of policy advocacy.[19]

The Atlantic Foundation's $27 million grant to HCAN—what I am calling "policy advocacy"—falls within a category that the Foundation Center labels "public affairs/society benefit." In 2014, this category captured 12 percent of foundation funding. Precise data on foundation funding elsewhere in the world is hard to come by, but anecdotal evidence suggests that foundation support for policy advocacy is predominantly an American phenomenon. European foundations, certainly, do not engage in policy advocacy nearly as much as their American peers do.

Yet sometimes what's lacking is not good ideas but the political will to implement them. Analysis can surface new ideas for improving our democracy. But once we determine what the best institutional and procedural reforms should be, we need to advocate for them. And we need to do so transparently; the last thing our democracy needs is more dark money.

The democracy reform ballot initiatives in the 2018 midterm elections provide a template for the kind of institutional and procedural reforms that foundations should consider backing. Michigan enacted same-day voter registration and automatic voter registration; Missouri, Colorado, and Utah all passed initiatives that created independent redistricting commissions or took other steps to combat partisan gerrymandering; Baltimore passed a small donor campaign finance law; and, most stunningly, Florida passed Amendment 4, restoring the right to vote to 1.4 million former felons. Amendment 4 passed with nearly 65 percent of voters supporting it.[20]

Movements and Citizen Engagement

The democracy reform ballot initiatives were not the only reason the 2018 elections were historic. Voter turnout was 42 percentage points greater than during the previous midterm—the largest increase in midterm turnout ever recorded.[21] Ideas and research can help put new policy proposals on the agenda and in the public consciousness, and philanthropy can advocate for a reform agenda directly. But we won't get far unless citizens— on the streets and at the ballot box—march and vote democracy reform into reality.

The role of philanthropy during the civil rights movement provides a template for how philanthropy can support social change through movement building and citizen engagement. Foundations are not—and probably should not be—on the vanguard of social movements. Citizens belong there. But we can help support social movements by amplifying, channeling, and legitimizing their energy and aims. That is what the Taconic Foundation and several of its peers did in the 1960s.

The Taconic Foundation was founded in 1958 by Stephen Currier, scion of a banking fortune, and his wife, Audrey, granddaughter of Andrew Mellon. In 1960, Stephen Currier brought together leaders of the preeminent civil rights organizations—the Congress of Racial Equality (CORE), the Student Nonviolent Coordinating Committee (SNCC), the Southern Christian Leadership Conference (SCLC), and the National Association for the Advancement of Colored People (NAACP), among others—to form the United Civil Rights Leadership Council. The goal was to sponsor voter registration drives and voter education in the South—to change politics at the ballot box where legislation alone had failed. Working together with Attorney General Robert Kennedy, and with a group of liberal foundations, including the Rockefeller Brothers Fund, the New World Foundation, and the Norman Foundation, Stephen Currier and the Taconic Foundation led a stunningly successful effort. Volunteers from all over came together to register African American voters and teach them how to pass the literacy tests segregationists had set up.[22]

The Taconic Foundation's engagement in the civil rights movement is an example of institutional philanthropy at its best. It is an example of risk capital philanthropy (foundations) working hand-in-hand with social capital philanthropy (volunteers); of philanthropy working together with government and supporting leaders in the field; and of foundations marshalling not only their grantmaking budgets, but also their reputations and convening power in order to advance democracy.

Today, as a democracy reform movement takes form and gathers strength, we must follow the Taconic Foundation's example. There is clearly a surge of energy around democracy reform, and foundations need to seize the moment. They can do so by elevating new leaders drawn from the rich diversity of our society; by creating new platforms for collaboration; by bringing together actors from civil society and the public and private sectors; and by using all of our resources—not just our grantmaking budgets, but also our convening power and our reputations.

Democratic Culture

The record voter turnout in 2018—over 118 million votes cast—is reason to celebrate. But it is also a good occasion to remind ourselves that, while voting is an essential act in a democracy, being a good citizen requires more than just showing up at the polls. What happens when the immediate threat is neutralized? When a new administration comes into office? When the most egregious voter suppression laws are repealed? The crisis of democracy has clearly roused the nation's democratic spirit. The key is to keep it awake.

Fixing our institutions—and they are sorely in need of fixing—will not fix our democracy. That is because democracy is not purely a set of institutions. Democracy is, first and foremost, a culture—the "habits of the heart," as Tocqueville would say, that define a democratic people. "To say that democracy is only a form of government," John Dewey wrote, "is like saying that home is a more or less geometrical arrangement of bricks and mortar; that the church is a building with pews, pulpit and spire. It is true; they certainly are so much. But it is false; they are so infinitely more."[23]

Philanthropy can strengthen democracy by supporting ideas and research, institutional and procedural reform, and movements and citizen engagement. These are, for the most part, old and proven tools and tactics. They aim to create legislative and institutional change, and they are often successful. But here is a challenge to philanthropy: How can we go beyond fixing institutions? How can we directly support democratic culture? In the face of an ethical and spiritual crisis, how can we repair the ethical ideals that are at the core of democracy—and nourish the spirit that aches for them?

The philanthropy of the Davos crowd is not the answer. And when the public hears comments such as Michael Dell's, they can be forgiven for believing that philanthropy is part of the problem. People do not want a giant cancellation fee for a broken social contract. They want a new social contract.

Philanthropy can and must help to write one.

KEEPING THE REPUBLIC

Dan Moulthrop

There is a healthy debate among political scientists about how to save democracies and what to do to strengthen our democratic republic. There's a strong argument on one side for greater citizen engagement—a deep, deliberative form of democracy in which the means to hold elected officials accountable beyond the ballot box are available to all.

Others see that as unrealistic. For many citizens, especially those in poverty, there is no time. The resources necessary to inform oneself and fully participate are too great a hurdle to overcome. The only recourse is to leave democracy to the professionals or to rely on mini-publics—diverse groups of citizens that can stand in for the entire populace, a kind of focus group for democracy, a republic for the republic.

Political scientists are correct to worry. The idea and ideals of democracy here and abroad are under attack, sometimes willfully and sometimes through negligence, incompetence, or sheer ignorance. Of the strong and influential civil-society organizations that can help save democracies, we tend to see the press as the most important. Even today, after the weakening of legacy print media, editorial board endorsements can alter the outcome of an election, and journalistic investigations into wrongdoing and official malfeasance remain vital to public confidence in the government. But if you're not a journalist bent on afflicting the comfortable, as the saying goes, what do you do besides vent on Facebook or Twitter?

The answer may be found in the moments in our nation's history when the citizenry took notice of its collective power and used it. One such moment came at the turn of the twentieth century, when citizens across the country acted with surprising urgency and vigor to create civic institutions and practices that paved the way for reforms at the municipal, state, and national levels. The Progressive Era left us museums and orchestras to feed our minds and souls, settlement houses to meet the needs of the poor, and, perhaps most important to our nation's needs today, civic organizations that convened citizen-leaders, who coalesced around solutions to the problems facing their communities and the nation.

A handful of these organizations live on today. They are a key to strengthening democratic institutions and practices in this moment of historic stress. Among them are "city clubs." The oldest of them, the Commonwealth Club of California, was established by San Francisco's civic leaders in 1903. Cleveland, Ohio's iteration took form in 1912, and Portland, Oregon's in 1916. In those heady Progressive Era years, just about every municipality had a cohort of civic leaders interested in reforming government who came together to create a city club, citizens' league, or similar institution.

These often fulfilled dual purposes—first, to bring people together for the shared examination of vexing issues, and second, to find common cause on what to do about them. To fulfill the second purpose, city clubs would research issues, survey membership, and produce recommendations that often ended up on ballots and in lobbying efforts. This impulse for advocacy continues on the West Coast, where the Portland City Club maintains a volunteer advocacy board, passes and issues resolutions for ballot measures, and empowers members to produce research reports.

The body of research amassed by the Portland club is astonishing in its volume and breadth. Members produced more than one thousand reports over the first century of the club's life on topics ranging from greenspace conservation and water fluoridation to Oregon's Public Employee Retirement System. The influence of the reports varied, from being barely noticed to inspiring substantive legislative or policy changes to put the city on new paths.

The same impulse for advocacy animated the early years of California's Commonwealth Club. But although advocacy was often successful, it seems to have fallen off during the Great Depression and World War II. The Commonwealth Club evolved into more of a speakers' platform and convener of civic dialogue. Importantly though, the club incubated an advocacy project in 2005 that became California Forward, an organization that set out to "articulate a vision for governance reforms to break the partisan gridlock, fortify fiscal management and rebuild the relationship among the state and local governments." The club reports that its work on these goals has been "infused in decisions at the highest of levels" of state government.

Cleveland's city club distinguished itself from the outset by steering clear of advocacy. At the time of its founding, other entities—in particular the municipal association, of which many city club members were also members—were vigorous advocates, obviating the need for the city club to fill that role. The club focused on convening and dialogue. From the outset, the city club's members and speakers gave voice to diverse political views.

Although city clubs were formed all over the country during the Progressive Era, many have not survived. The City Club of St. Louis inspired Cleveland's iteration, but St. Louis no longer has a club. And while our nation's oldest and greatest city had one, New York's city club is not the convener of change agents it once was. Importantly, the Women's City Club of New York is experiencing a rebirth in this political moment, buoyed by and contributing to the rising power and influence of women in politics.

People only passingly familiar with the legacy of city clubs may disregard their influence and see them as little more than platforms for authors on book tours and professors seeking non-academic audiences. However, the surviving city clubs still generate and distribute meaningful political, cultural, and civic content that gives them influence and provides citizens with an avenue for civic participation.

One example is the role these organizations play during the early phases of presidential primaries. As candidates test the waters and their campaign messages, they often turn to city clubs to connect with voters. What happens is a bit different than the traditional chicken-dinner stop in Iowa or New Hampshire. While the basic ingredients are similar—handshakes, photo ops, stump speeches—the history of civic engagement at a city club gives dialogues with candidates more gravitas. More than that, though, there is the potential for broader impact beyond the venue itself and beyond momentary news coverage. With digital production and public media partnerships, city clubs often turn routine campaign stops into sixty-minute town halls streamed online, released as podcasts, and broadcast to tens of thousands across a given state.

For the candidate, a city club is the reason to come to a state and a community that, given our nation's quirky electoral math, might not otherwise be of interest. For the community member, it's a chance to meaningfully participate in our democracy. Citizens find themselves dialoguing with candidates who might be the next president. For the community writ large, there is an opportunity to authentically engage in sixty minutes of content, rather than sixty seconds on the news. Partnerships between city clubs and local media is a crucial part of the equation.

As much as city clubs provide platforms for freedom of speech, they also provide opportunities for exercising the final clause in the First Amendment: petitioning government for the redress of grievances. Tweed Thornton, the former director of the City Club of Chicago, tells the story of a suburban congressman who was renowned for not scheduling public town hall meetings. After a decade without them, he appeared at a city club forum, where his resistance to public engagement with his constituents became a lightening-rod issue—so much so, that he had to outrun the press after the event. There are few other venues in America where this kind of interaction is routine and, thanks to partnerships with public media, reaches tens of thousands of constituents. There are few other opportunities for a citizen to ask a mayor to explain his or her resistance to implementing immigrant-friendly policies in front of eight hundred civic and business leaders and thousands of radio listeners. Or where an elected county prosecutor can be made to fully explain how far he intends to go with bail reform.

Our republic is strengthened by this kind of work by community organizations. At any given moment, city clubs are organizing forums on local and statewide issues, from homelessness and local economic development to education reform and stormwater management in the context of national and state policy. City club audiences might come for the chance to interact with a rock-star presidential candidate or an actual rock star, but they stay for conversations that are important to the fabric of the community. Ordinary citizens and leaders develop a shared vocabulary and shared experiences that become the foundations of civic problem-solving, and that may end up in public policies, legislation, and budgets—in other words, the actual work of the republic serving its constituents.

Diane Douglas ran the Seattle City Club for more than a decade. That club's founding in 1980 is a reminder that citizens can give birth to these organizations at any time to change the dynamics of democracy. Douglas led the Seattle club to create the Washington State Debate Coalition, which manages public debates for the most important public office races in the city and state.

"There are very few institutions that have the clout to do it," Douglas said. "It required a trusted non-profit convener—one that has the bandwidth, mission and political clout to be trusted by the media, by the political parties and candidates and by other partners, in our case, colleges and universities across the state. There just aren't that many civic institutions that can pull that off and have the drive and the mission-based commitment to do that work."[1]

If we care about democracy, it is incumbent on us to ask what we can do to shore it up. While national initiatives, voter-rights lawsuits, and constitutional amendments may be the work that some organizations take on, city clubs offer places where people from across the community can simply come together to become better informed. By putting ordinary citizens directly in conversation with the leaders who are shaping the future of our communities, states, and nation, these organizations provide some of the most accessible and high-impact opportunities to strengthen our fragile democracy.

THE FUTURE OF DEMOCRACY

Mayor Ras Baraka

It was November 2016. I was in Newark, New Jersey, of which I had been elected mayor two years prior. My brother had put together a small gathering at the Robert Treat Hotel with close friends and family to watch the results of the presidential election. All of us watched in disbelief as the numbers kept coming in.

I can remember my mother being very upset, but not surprised, as almost 63 million Americans voted for a man who had made it clear that he represented some of the vilest and most backward elements in this country. He would possibly begin to roll back many of the gains she had personally sacrificed her happiness, at times, and her life for. She was one of the thousands in this country who had pushed America to be a real democracy.

She understood clearly that we were entering a dangerous time that could be likened to the period after the Civil War and Reconstruction, when slave codes and lynching became the rule of the day. Or the time after the civil rights struggles, when equal access to democracy for all Americans was met with "law and order" and pushback against the Affirmative Action and Great Society programs.

After the civil rights movement, the country began to turn away from the idea that the system was flawed and that democracy needed to be strengthened and expanded. It started blaming individuals for these systemic failures and making behavior and personal responsibility bear the burden for the shortcomings of a country founded with and enriched by the slave trade and the free labor of millions of people.

Trump represented a rollback, a push against the first black president and his family. He was a clear representative of the ideas birthed from the marriage of Reagan Democrats, social conservatives, and outright racists. They were orchestrating a transparent strategy to upend what they saw as a slow and steady push to democratize America's institutions, to color its landscape, and to make its economy responsible for the well-being of its citizens—all citizens, not just the few super wealthy.

This strategy began years before Donald Trump was elected president. This is something my mother and many others understood that evening. Donald Trump became the titular head of a movement that began well before him. He has now even become a distraction. As the country watches closely what happens to him and his associates, while we debate Russian collusion, and while we are preoccupied with his behavior and his tweets, the movement has dismantled the Voting Rights Act.[1] In fact, 2016 was the first presidential election held without the protections of the Voting Rights Act since its inception.

Today, the movement is attacking housing, welfare, and food stamps. It is rolling back criminal justice reforms, union rights, and LGBT and immigrant rights. There is a resurgence of white supremacist groups and behavior, including open home-grown terrorism and hate crimes. In several states it will be the first time in almost fifty years that a woman can be arrested for choosing to have an abortion. The fight is not and never really was about Donald Trump; it is about what American democracy meant to the millions of people who died trying to get it to actually be one.

We are now more than fifty years past the Kerner Commission report,[2] and some fifty years past the murder of Martin Luther King Jr. in Memphis, Tennessee, and yet we are still struggling to create a democracy that blankets everyone in the warmth of prosperity and visits equity into everyone's community. King, in the years before his death, organized a Poor Peoples campaign and spoke clearly about a radical redistribution of values and wealth. He understood that our problems were systemic and therefore consistent and even cultural. King knew that commissions, programs, committees, or even his eloquent words could not solve them. The problems were not just about how people treated us or about minimum wage, but about a country that purposefully locked generations of people out of prosperity and social development.

During the closing moments of King's extraordinary life, he began to see that the same people who stood with him in Mississippi against Jim Crow[3] and racist violence were not willing to travel with him to Detroit, Chicago, and Newark to fight the violence of poverty and isolation and systemic hatred. Those who went to jail so that we could eat at the same lunch counters did not stand with him to fight for the economic freedom to eat at those very restaurants.

Dr. King gave a speech at Stanford University on the topic of "The Other America," saying there were two Americas: one where dreams and prosperity were nurtured and where the blanket of American democracy kept out the chill of inequality and indifference, and another America where democracy was held back by red lines that were drawn around cities, where inequality was nurtured in our children's psyche and where poverty grew with impunity, locking people in circles of despair.

The Kerner Commission pointed out the inequality by saying there were two societies: one black and one white, separate and unequal, a legacy of the *Plessy v. Ferguson* case in 1896 that pushed America in the direction of a permanent caste system.[4]

The commission's 1967 report identified poor education, segregation, lack of housing, and poverty as key components of the civil unrest that visited Watts, Detroit, Newark, and many other cities. It implored the country to address these areas. One result was the Fair Housing Act of 1968, which targeted discrimination and intimidation in housing. But that was not enough. Just like public accommodation, the issue wasn't just about people not allowing us in their stores or their buildings because of nationality and race. There was no clear pathway to decent and affordable housing that was not run down, dilapidated, and inferior. There was no real access to homeownership.

The report even advocated that African Americans move to mostly white suburban communities to be closer to jobs and a free ride off islands of hopelessness. This was a poor prescription, as it only addressed segregation practices that still exist today and fell short of arguing for investment, development, and empowerment in neighborhoods long left out in the cold. It refused to go to the root causes of these problems. Even today in Newark there is pushback as I fight to find revenue to rebuild neglected neighborhoods and transfer some wealth for housing and development into communities where there was purposeful disinvestment. There are those who are more concerned with bringing "diversity" to their neighborhoods and are less concerned about creating opportunity and self-determination in communities that have been struggling or completely left behind for more than five decades.

Some fifty years after the Kerner Commission, our cities are languishing in relatively identical conditions. While it's not fair to say that nothing has improved in general for African Americans in this country, it is safe to say that progress is largely uneven. There exists a growing and stubborn gap of inequality between whites and blacks in this country because we have still failed to address the root causes of these issues. In fact, we have failed to have any real, consistent, and deeply meaningful discourse around race and inequality in America. It is still an uncomfortable conversation. Worse, any remedy has recently been met with serious intolerance and aggression.

In fact, during an election season with the most diverse pool of presidential candidates this country has ever seen, there is still very little space to discuss repairing the centuries of enslavement, murder, inhumanity, and disenfranchisement that were heaped upon African Americans in this country. Even some of our most "progressive" candidates cannot distinguish between the inherent inequities that exist in this system and that affect an overwhelming number of Americans, and the very clear and distinct history where this country deliberately robbed of us our humanity in every institution that purports to uphold and oversee democracy and justice.

Repairing this history is not simply about making whole the generations of people that endured this abhorrent treatment. It is to understand that we African Americans can never be fully a part of a democracy that does not recognize our humanity, as Supreme Court Justice Roger B. Taney pointed out in the Dred Scott decision.[5] It also fails to recognize that we fall and are behind not because of our lack of effort but because we were systemically left behind and still have systemic obstacles that stand in the way of our experiencing full democracy.

African Americans today are much better educated than we were fifty years ago, but we are still half as likely as whites to have college degrees. While wages have gotten better, we are still almost three times as likely to live in poverty, and the median white family has about ten times the wealth as a black family. In fact, in New Jersey, the median net worth for white families is $271,402; the median net worth for Latino families is $7,020; and the median net worth for African American families is $5,900. While African Americans work with other progressives to try to equalize

American democracy for all, a failure to address this specifically is a failure to recognize our humanity. The national unemployment rate for African Americans is higher now than it was in 1968. Our infant mortality rate, though it has gotten better, is still more than two times that of whites. Where I live, it is four times that of the state overall. One in four African American families are food insecure, and there are more African Americans in prison today than there were slaves during Dred Scott's case. We are six times more likely to be incarcerated than whites.

It wasn't until a decade or more ago that cities began demolishing high-rise projects and replacing them with low rise housing that was spread throughout the city. This did not result in access to growth but instead spread poverty throughout the city, densely populating certain communities by race and class. Though we have come a long way, there is an even longer way to travel. In America today there is a growing concentration of wealth in the hands of a few. Today a child born in the bottom fifth of incomes in this country has less of a chance to rise out of that than children do in most post-industrial nations, and certainly less than they did more than fifty years ago. A majority of Americans will be poor at some point in their lives because of job loss and lack of savings. Recently, it was said that twenty-one hedge fund managers have more wealth than all of the nation's kindergarten teachers combined, and the economic picture for African Americans is much worse. Three out of four of us will be poor at some point during our lives. African American parents who manage to move out of poverty and accumulate wealth are not a guarantee for their children.

In fact, the majority of the children born to middle-class black families will find themselves in the lower fifth of society, even as we witness $4 billion worth of development here in Newark. Even as we, like other cities around this country, work hard to make sure that our residents are not locked out of real growth. In Newark we have worked to reduce unemployment to record lows. We have implored our anchor institutions in Newark to hire Newark residents, to raise the level of local procurement and spending, and to invest in our neighborhoods. It still is not enough.

In Newark we created an inclusionary zoning ordinance to mandate affordable and low-income housing and force developers to relocate some of their monies and investments into areas outside of downtown; we still need more. As we help and promote local vendors and incubate new minority- and women-owned businesses, we still will not achieve the level of growth we need to fill the wealth gap. We have focused our efforts on trying to improve the income and opportunity gaps.

We are also working hard to promote homeownership and create opportunities for residents to purchase and develop abandoned and vacant properties. But even as we elevate our work in that area, there is so much more we need to do to make a deep impact. These issues are at the center of most urban mayors' efforts around the country, particularly in cities where the majority of residents are black and brown. Most often, we mayors seem to be on our own with no federal help and so we increasingly rely on support and ideas from each other.

Mayors are trying to expand democracy. We are looking for more ways to create jobs, opportunity, and wealth for populations that have been left behind for generations. Many mayors have begun contemplating Universal Basic Income strategies, as families are dealing with more and more economic hardships. Many are looking for ways to lessen the burden around housing and education by providing affordable, even free, pathways to college. In New Jersey, we have already begun to pilot free opportunities at community college.

Mayors are trying to attract wealth without displacing people and to build housing for multiple levels of income. Municipal governments are beginning to use local subsidies as a means to create community-benefits agreements. When developers ask for variances on zoning requirements Mayors are using this as an opportunity to require assistance with infrastructure and affordable housing and to create jobs and opportunities for their residents. They are creating land banks to organize and plan development that is city focused and not driven by speculators and giant real estate developers. Mayors are using land trusts to preserve land for affordable solutions to housing and commercial development. Many are also beginning to look at cooperatives that turn businesses over to the hands of the employees.

Most mayors want immigrants in their communities and understand the positive impact they have on local economies. We mayors look at diversity as a strength. Mayors everywhere, Newark included, have declared their cities free, open, and welcoming sanctuaries in the face of a blatant campaign to criminalize mostly immigrants of color. The Trump administration threatened to take money from cities and to push all immigrants into these sanctuary communities. Fortunately, most mayors pushed back. Some, like Philadelphia, even took the government to court and won. We mayors responded that we want more democracy, not less.

We are tackling longstanding issues around the environment and sustainability. Mayors across the country have signed on to international environmental sustainability efforts like the Paris agreement, even after the Trump administration pulled out. We are working to bring our cities to zero emissions and to find other creative ways to not add to the growing carbon footprint.

In states like New Jersey, we are challenging the concept of bail, as you might be held in jail because you are poor and can't make bail, not because you have been found guilty. Many cities are pushing for independent prosecutors and civilian oversight of police. New Jersey's governor, Phil Murphy, has enacted independent prosecutors for police-involved shootings; the city of Newark just won in the appellate division our right to have a Civilian review board with investigatory and subpoena power. In Newark we are also beginning to treat violence and crime as public-health issues and are working to center our institutions on trauma-informed care. This focus begins to demilitarize the police in our community and diverts funding to community-based initiatives that treat trauma and reduce crime and violence through alternative strategies.

For the most part as mayor, there is no real playbook and, most important, no national direction or effort to address these issues straight on. In fact, we have grown to expect no real leadership on the national side and realize that any change will come from mayors and local efforts. Even many local progressives are making the argument that our local efforts are the only thing that really matters. And while I understand that frame of thought and even agree that our work in Newark is incredibly important to the immediate outcomes of so many of our residents, I do not agree that we do not need a national thrust. The problems we have are very intractable and have their roots in longstanding policies and systems that have worked intentionally to destroy the communities that we are trying to help. Our local programs and local efforts are important, but without any real and deep commitment from national leadership to lend resources and efforts for equity, opportunity, and reparation, our fight for real democracy will continue to be elusive.

First, we need open and clear policies that seek to dismantle a system of hatred and violence that murders twelve-year-olds with BB guns in open-carry states or shoots men in the back running away at traffic stops, or chokes them to death for selling loose cigarettes. We need real federal and civilian oversight and concrete consequences for police agencies and officers that violate the law.

We need racism to be a crime and hate groups outlawed not because of their speech but because they have a history of outright violence and terror. We need serious criminal justice reforms that clearly seek to eradicate a system of uneven justice that is more about punishing people for their circumstances in life than it is about correcting outcomes. We have to demand real gun control for mothers in my city, who lose children every day because they have access to assault rifles that find their way across state lines. The homicide rates in our communities are staggering, even while getting better. We have to treat this like a public-health crisis, the same way we attack epidemic diseases. We have to attack violence in these communities through community-initiated efforts and create institutions that respond to ongoing trauma, both systemic and physical. Gun control is a part of it, along with the many social determinants that have stained this democracy for decades.

We have to stop telling the lie that there is a crisis in American education. That's just not true. More Americans graduate from high school and college now than at any other time in history, and that includes black people. The crisis lives in the cities plagued with poverty and indifference. The education crisis is in Newark's community, where when the next experiment or reform shows up the first thing we have to give away is our right to govern our own educational institutions and the policies that direct them. Our ability to have a public voice and to dictate what happens in our schools, how they are funded, and what is being taught is exchanged for the promise of a decent education. There is no education crisis. There is a crisis of poverty and segregation, fear and lack of resources.

Not just in Newark but nationally we need to invest in public education, particularly community schools, and to build a scaffold of resources around our children, including before- and after-school opportunities. We need to pay teachers more, create opportunities for parents, and direct our institutions to support public schools. We have to desegregate the curriculum and then the schools, as most students in Newark still attend segregated schools. In fact, Frederick Douglass High School, the school in Baltimore that Supreme Court Justice Thurgood Marshall attended, is still 90 percent people of color, and it is overwhelmingly poor. That is the same condition of most of the schools in Newark—segregated by both race and class. I would also venture to say this is how most schools look that are located in urban cities across America.

One of the most important things we must do is what I call an Urban Marshall Plan. In April 1947 the Marshall Plan (the European Recovery Act) gave $13 billion to war-torn Europe to rebuild roads, schools, and infrastructure and to encourage business and economic growth. Today that money would be equal to about $130 billion. This is the kind of real investment we need in the cities and communities that have been systemically and deliberately left as islands of despair. The logic used to garner support to spend billions of dollars in Europe to repair the damage done by war—the purposeful destruction of entire cities and their economies—is the same logic we should use for American cities and for people who have been in a war since we arrived here. The purposeful destruction of communities and generations of families must be repaired as deliberately as they were ravaged.

This is not just the morally sound thing to do; it is also an economically wise and prudent thing to do for this country as a whole. These resources, as in Europe, would be used to create jobs; invest in infrastructure; seed new business and development; support community and civic engagement through art, culture, and political life; promote access to capital and homeownership; develop decent and affordable housing; and create pathways to citizenship for the formerly incarcerated and immigrants in these communities. Most important, these monies should provide direct repair to millions of Americans. This can come in the form of family financial trusts, free education, direct payments, or all of the aforementioned to those who have been given a four-hundred-year disadvantage through law, policy, and practice in this country because of slavery and because of every public and private institution that benefited from the purposeful and methodical reduction of human beings to property.

These monies would also go directly to cities, not states, for infrastructure development of water and sewer, roads and bridges, transportation, schools, and hospitals. We need dollars for job training and transitional employment. We need private-sector incentives to hire the underemployed. We need monies for small-business startups. We need summer jobs for our youth and college students as well as outreach, training, and employment for those who have dropped out. We need a comprehensive job development and neighborhood stabilization plan that does not seek to drive people out but instead makes them part of society and includes community co-ops and public banking institutions.

We need resources invested in free local education, and pipelines that lead to careers, not prisons. We need money to create access to localized health care and primary care physicians that are both affordable and accessible. We need our real wages increased. We have to address a very real and growing affordable-housing crisis around this country, where people are spending 30 to 50 percent of their income on housing.

We need to invest in voter and civic education and provide more people, not fewer, with access to the ballot. We need what Dr. King called for: a radical redistribution of not only our values but also of wealth, and we need to target this redistribution in America's cities and communities that have not been able to escape, over the course of decades, an insurmountable and intractable level of poverty and isolation. We need to do this for all Americans, but with a particular opportunity to repair centuries of deliberate dehumanization and disenfranchisement of African Americans in this country.

It is my belief that this is the only thing that will move America's economy and its people forward. White supremacy is outdated, and the old machinations and designs once used to lift this economy up are the very things that are holding it back. Our failure to embrace this new, more colorful, broad, and diverse America is the obstacle that burdens us. Our inability to democratize the workforce and to make wealth accessible is limiting our imagination and creativity. Limited opportunity has limited our possibilities. If there was ever a time in America's history that we have been inextricably connected, now is that time. Our ability to do well rests on the foundation of our ability to do good. When we figure this out, we can become exceptional, and not a moment sooner.

I was born in Newark, New Jersey, a couple of years after the rebellion in 1967. I remember hearing the stories of my father being hit over the head by a police officer, who happened to be one of his former classmates from Barringer High School, from which he graduated. I saw a picture of my father chained to a wheelchair in a hospital, bleeding from his head. My mother tells stories of running through the streets of Newark looking for him. He was later charged in court, and one of his poems was read as proof of his support for the insurrectionists that were raging in the city's Third Ward. More than five decades later, I became the mayor of my city as it still struggles with the issues that Newark's first African American mayor, Kenneth A. Gibson, struggled with in 1970: our desire is to make democracy real for all of us.

My father was a thinker, an artist, an activist, and a revolutionary. He always said the struggle is about ideas. I agree—ideas have led to the death of many and the poor quality of life of generations. Ultimately, it is about people's material lives and conditions. We have to understand that it is still a privilege in this country to have the time and space to debate these ideas and concepts and to struggle about what democracy looks like. But our democracy is still in its infancy, as many have not yet figured out how to avoid going to bed hungry or spending all they have just to put a roof over their heads. Or to choose between food and medicine or to forego education for jobs that keep them in poverty in communities where your nationality and race can determine your life expectancy or flat out get you killed.

So, while the people in this country debate on social media and troll each other with tweets, Mayors have the difficult job in cities like Newark to actually figure out how to collect the garbage and fill potholes with dwindling resources, while keeping people alive at least long enough to join the debate with everyone else.

BUILDING A UNIVERSITY WHERE ALL PEOPLE MATTER

Michael M. Crow, William B. Dabars,
and Derrick M. Anderson

As Greece is the birthplace of democracy, and democracy is the chief concern of this volume, we invoke the pre-Socratic philosopher Heraclitus, who observed that all is in flux. So it is with our democratic institutions in America, where ambitions for liberty, justice, and equality are unrivaled in scale, scope, and diversity. But whether or not flux in American democracy leads to progress depends upon a number of critical factors, including the quality of our educational institutions. These institutions are central to developing and advancing democracy as both an ideal and an actuality. While the link between education and democracy is well studied and extensively theorized, renewed focus on this topic is required if we wish to successfully implement the society our founders envisioned in the eighteenth century.

America's universities have evolved over nearly four hundred years to become our most treasured and admired institutions. Replicated globally and attended by students from all nations, our universities have important roles to play in this time of continued cultural, economic, and, ultimately, sociotechnical transformation. Many see this flux leading to instability and discontinuous rapid change, while others see opportunities for enhancing American democracy and bringing it ever closer to its constitutional aspirations. The continued evolution of American democracy is as much the outcome of sociological, economic, cultural, and technological change as it is political. A dynamic such as this could never have been foreseen by philosophers, even with their abundant hubris. Now, in the early twenty-first century, we have come to a point where both democracy and education are being reshaped by these unprecedented forces.

While democracy at a grand scale continues to rely on the contributions of our universities, most long-held assumptions pertaining to higher education are in flux. This can be seen in such factors as the precipitous decline in state financial support for universities and the proliferation of elitist, hierarchical regimes to which universities gravitate in a misguided quest for legitimacy. In response to such challenges we propose to advance a vision for what we have termed the New American University, which embodies the intent of American public higher education. Accordingly, such a university builds upon the excellence of the American research university but also commits to the egalitarian notion of access that supports and advances American democracy. A New American University defines itself not by whom it excludes, but by whom it includes and how they succeed. It is a place where, in the spirit of the designers and founders of the United States, a person's birth status, family income, ethnicity, and cultural heritage are immaterial to his or her educational outcomes. This is particularly important in a society where educational attainment is the single most significant predictor of intergenerational socioeconomic mobility.

It is fitting that the notion of a New American University evolves from the ranks of our research universities. Colleges and universities endure for centuries and their evolution proceeds both within their respective types and through the emergence of new institutional types. However imperfect, America's research universities rank among the greatest producers of knowledge the world has ever known. But many looming imperfections in existing university models threaten significant consequences for our democratic institutions. Chief among these is a persistent lack of accessibility, particularly for those from families with incomes in the bottom quartile. Through exclusionary admissions practices, ever mounting costs, and a spectrum of other social and cultural barriers, our nation's leading institutions primarily serve the privileged.

To prevent our nation from becoming hopelessly divided between an affluent and highly educated upper class, a stagnant and challenged middle class, and a working class mistakenly characterized by an abandonment of aspiration, we must ensure that universities are accessible to all students and represent the intellectual and socioeconomic diversity of our nation. In fact, we may have to rethink the parameters of our universities, as was recently accomplished at Purdue University, whose president, former

Indiana governor Mitch Daniels, rightfully questioned the logic of the status of the institution as a land-grant university. He proposed that the university should become a more dynamic institution committed to broad access through online learning technologies. If the United States is to maintain its leadership and competitiveness in the globalized knowledge economy, it is imperative that it quicken the pace of discovery and innovation, not only through the conduct of research itself but also through concurrent pedagogical approaches that engage the broadest demographic possible in discovery and innovation. Inasmuch as access to knowledge underpins the societal objectives of a pluralistic democracy, broad accessibility to knowledge production must be at the core of evolving university models. This notion was expressed in the design of an American coin cast in 1792 known after the name of its designer as the Birch cent. The motto inscribed on the coin reads "Liberty is the parent of science and industry." Whereas the realization of this sentiment would require broad access to academic environments underpinned by discovery and knowledge production, the majority of American students are instead relegated to schools that merely transmit standardized knowledge. For democracy to succeed in an era driven by scientific discovery and technological innovation, millions more in our population will have to achieve greater scientific, technological, and philosophical literacy.

With this background, we propose the New American University as a new model for the American research university, which expands on and complements the existing models of colleges and universities. The objective of this model is to empower the most diverse possible student body to meet the workforce demands of an innovation-driven global economy. Without guidance from our universities, technological innovation could pose risks to our society. Inasmuch as universities are chief producers of technological innovation, they must also commit to expanding educational attainment, allowing citizens to leverage rapidly evolving technologies to empower themselves and bolster the success of the democracy. The successful implementation of the New American University model at Arizona State University suggests the extent of the potential of a subset of large-scale public universities similarly committed to expanding educational accessibility while facilitating discovery and innovation at the highest order for the benefit of society.

The Correlation Between Democracy and Knowledge

Assessment of the link between democracy and education in America should begin with the recognition that our nation was formed from thirteen agrarian colonies of Great Britain, which during the colonial era boasted only a handful of colleges. Many of the founders of our nation were college graduates and well educated in the humanities, including Thomas Jefferson, John Adams, and John Jay. Alexander Hamilton attended college. George Washington was a self-educated engineering technician and Benjamin Franklin was a self-educated scientist. The founding generation recognized that educational attainment at the highest possible level among the citizens of the new nation was critical to the success of the democratic experiment. But in retrospect we may further observe that it is highly likely that it was the educational attainment of the founders that enabled them to conceptualize American democracy. Thus, the founders articulated throughout their lives the conviction that education was an essential, if not *the* essential, ingredient to the success of democracy.

And so the imperative for citizens in a democratic society to be well educated has been integral to our collective identity and has not been, as is sometimes assessed in the twenty-first century, merely technical, transactional, instrumental, or secondary. Reaffirming the ideals of the classical Athenian democracy and inspired by the Enlightenment tenet that reason should guide human affairs, John Adams and Thomas Jefferson were representative of leaders of the early republic in their conviction that an educated citizenry is essential to a free society. Moreover, the earliest formulations of American democratic thinking express an implicit social compact in higher education. The Constitution of the Commonwealth of Massachusetts, which Adams drafted and the Commonwealth ratified in June 1780, and which served as a prototype for the Constitution of the United States, begins as follows: "Wisdom and knowledge, as well as virtue, diffused generally among the body of the people, being necessary for the preservation of their rights and liberties; and as these depend on spreading the opportunities and advantages of education in the various parts of the country, and among the different orders of the people, it shall be the duty of legislatures and magistrates, in all future periods of this commonwealth, to cherish the interests of literature and the sciences, and all seminaries of them." In this case, *seminary* can be translated to *university*, at which time there was only one in Massachusetts, known as Harvard.

The recognition among the founders that education was critical to the formation of social cohesion and the stimulation of progress set the course for the nation to pioneer novel educational frameworks, including university designs, distinct from British and European models. Consistent with its often elusive egalitarian aspirations, the United States would lead the world in the provision of primary and secondary education beginning in the mid-nineteenth century. And as expectations for a college education became the norm by the mid-twentieth century, advanced educational attainment became foundational to the success of individuals as well as the prosperity and competitiveness of the nation. Indeed, the assumption that the meritorious will succeed by means of educational attainment has shaped the core narrative arc of our democratic experience.

In his 1944 State of the Union address, President Franklin Roosevelt, a college graduate and lawyer, proposed an economic bill of rights that would include the "right to a good education." Shortly thereafter, the Truman administration's Commission on Higher Education, operating in the interests of a "fuller" American democracy in "every phase of living," tasked the American higher education system with providing a pathway for every citizen to advance their education as far as their "native capacities permit." Not some citizens, every citizen.

The consequences of this commitment to education have been unquestionably positive. Accordingly, a recent report by the National Academies concluded that "we owe our current prosperity, security, and good health to the investments of past generations, and we are obliged to renew those commitments in education, research, and innovation policies to ensure that the American people continue to benefit from the remarkable opportunities provided by the rapid development of the global economy and its not inconsiderable underpinning in science and technology." But since our continued well-being is not guaranteed, this same report cautions that without continued investments in education, the nation could lose its competitive position in the world—a prognosis that would come as a shock to most Americans.

Cognizant of the implications of this dynamic, President Barack Obama, in his first address to Congress, in February 2009, articulated a

vision for the nation to lead the world in the attainment of higher education. He outlined a goal in which half of the nation's people with a high
school diploma would gain a postsecondary certificate or degree. Nothing like this had ever been outlined in the history of our republic. In writing this chapter some ten years later, we understand that the challenges
facing American democracy are even more complex than they were then.
And the need for a renewed vision for American higher education is all
the more pressing. Since 2009 more than thirty states have articulated
goals more ambitious than those of President Obama in terms of higher
education attainment for their respective populations. As a society we
have come to realize that educational attainment is critical to the success
of both our democracy and our economy.

The Limits of Existing Models

Higher education is especially critical as a driver of human capital, the
measure of the value of the stock of knowledge, skills, and creativity that
may be acquired through investment in education and training. The benefits of educational attainment for the individual are well documented,
which apart from its intrinsic rewards begin with substantial economic
returns and significantly increased prospects for intergenerational socioeconomic mobility. These advantages are so important to our nation that
a recent report by the U.S. Department of the Treasury observed that opportunities for individuals who receive four-year degrees are not just different, but "starkly different" than they are for those who do not. It is fitting
that government agencies would underscore this point since the benefits
of broad educational attainment include aggregate economic returns from
larger pools of human capital and increased levels of civic engagement. A
more educated workforce generates greater tax revenues and influences
quality-of-place policymaking. Educated individuals are healthier,
more democratically engaged, and committed to the well-being of their
communities.

Advanced educational attainment among a greater proportion of the
population, coupled with economic growth facilitated by science-based
technological innovation in our nation's research universities following
World War II, has transformed American society. Think of the internet,
cell phones, and supercomputers. Think of companies like Google and

Amazon. Think of all the human artifacts that have improved the quality of our lives and unleashed human potential. As economists including Claudia Goldin and Lawrence Katz have shown, public-sector investment in higher education during the twentieth century produced an unmatched level of educational attainment that served as a springboard to intergenerational social and economic mobility for countless millions, and also served as a catalyst to innovation and thus national economic competitiveness. Yet, despite the success of the social compact implicit in public higher education, state investment in public colleges and universities remains well below historical levels. State funding cuts especially beginning in the wake of the Great Recession, have decreased the ability of our nation's leading universities to meet enrollment demand, compete globally in the realms of science and technology, and address the full breadth of social complexity, impeding the mobilization of the abundant dormant talent in our nation. As a result, many of the students who would most benefit from this avenue of upward mobility—those typically categorized as socioeconomically disadvantaged or historically underrepresented—cannot gain admission to highly selective universities that have grown accustomed to serving the needs of a narrowly defined, privileged student body.

Research-grade academic infrastructure in the United States still largely retains the scale of the mid-twentieth century, with some institutions expanding only nominally in recent decades despite surging enrollment demand and projections of shortfalls of highly educated participants in the workforce. Many have argued that our country has begun under-producing college graduates, especially the uniquely creative and innovative graduates that often come from research universities and that our country requires to maintain a robust pace in economic and social progress. To this point, New York Times columnist David Brooks observed, "We once had a society stratified by bloodlines, in which the Protestant Establishment was in one class, immigrants were in another, and African Americans were in another. But now we live in a society stratified by education."

Although the longstanding selectivity of our nation's top private research universities no longer surprises anyone, even our nation's leading public research universities have become increasingly exclusive, which is to say that admissions practices now routinely exclude the majority of academically qualified applicants. Despite efforts by selective schools to recruit socioeconomically disadvantaged and historically underrepresented students, admission to these institutions typically correlates more with the family's home zip code than the student's grade point average or set of SAT scores. As a consequence, reports from the Pell Institute indicate that students from families in the top income quartile are five times more likely to graduate from college with a bachelor's degree by the age of twenty-four than their peers from the bottom quartile.

Despite the historic success of the compact between society and our nation's public universities, public disinvestment in higher education exacerbates inequalities. While restoring public support is essential, institutions themselves must rethink their strategic objectives and reconceptualize their design, especially in terms of their potential to expand enrollment capacity to provide broad accessibility commensurate with the scale of population growth, enrollment demand, and the socioeconomic and intellectual diversity of our society. Intelligence is distributed throughout the population, and for many it manifests as skills, abilities, and experiences that current admissions protocols disregard. Admissions policies that merely skim from the conventionally defined top students shortchange countless gifted and creative individuals.

Despite their contributions to transformative discovery and innovation, research universities are often insufficiently concerned about societal outcomes and the equitable distribution of the benefits of research and development. Disregard of the socioeconomic challenges faced by most Americans threatens to impede the capacity of these institutions to contribute to society. The sense of this imperative is thoughtfully expressed by Richard Nelson in his 2011 reassessment of the core concern of his 1977 book, *The Moon and the Ghetto*:

> Why was it that a country that recently had accomplished the truly remarkable feat of sending a man to the moon and bringing him back to earth safely, had wiped out scourges like infantile paralysis, and more generally had achieved an historically unprecedented standard of living for the middle class, for some reason seemed unable to provide an effective education for ghetto kids, halt or significantly slow down the rising cost of medical care, keep the air and water clean, or cut down on the incidence of drug addiction and drug-related crime?

A New Model for the American Research University

Consistent with the egalitarian tenets of a democratic society, and in response to the challenges outlined here, the New American University model represents a reconceptualization of the American university based upon three foundational design components: 1) an academic platform committed to discovery and knowledge production, as with the standard model, linking teaching with research; 2) broad accessibility to students from highly diverse demographic and socioeconomic backgrounds; and 3) through its breadth of activities and functions, an institutional commitment to maximizing societal impact according to community and national needs.

Over the past seventeen years, Arizona State University (ASU) has operationalized the New American University model by dramatically expanding the size and diversity of its student body while building an academic platform of world-class knowledge production focused on societal outcomes. As the sole comprehensive research university in a metropolitan region projected to double in population by mid-century, ASU's transformation was motivated initially by the imperative for an institutional response to the region's lagging economic output and unprecedented demographic shifts. To address these economic and social dynamics, ASU redesigned many aspects of the curriculum and adopted an entirely new operational paradigm that embraces innovation and public service.

ASU articulated a charter that expresses the intent of the academic community to maximize the public value of the institution: *Arizona State University is a comprehensive public research university, measured not by whom it excludes, but by whom it includes and how they succeed; advancing research and discovery of public value; and assuming fundamental responsibility for the economic, social, cultural, and overall health of the communities it serves.* ASU's charter articulates a vision for restoring the intentions and aspirations of the historical public university model, which, building on the ideals of the Morrill Act of 1862 that established the system of land-grant universities, facilitated broad accessibility as well as engagement with society.

The demonstrable success of ASU's reconceptualization across numerous indicators substantiates the proposition that world-class knowledge production, broad accessibility, and social impact are not mutually exclusive. Universities can be scaled and diversity enhanced. The soaring enrollment growth of the new university model is accompanied by unprecedented increases in freshman persistence, degree production, learning outcomes, minority enrollment, academic success, and all measures of graduate quality. In terms of enrollment growth, ASU has been the fastest-growing research university in the United States for each of the past ten years and has succeeded in advancing both the academic rigor and diversity of its student body, which increasingly includes more students from socioeconomically disadvantaged and underrepresented backgrounds. ASU's cohort of first-generation college students reached more than 25,000 in 2019. ASU has concurrently effected robust growth in research infrastructure and sponsored project expenditures. Its research enterprise has been the fastest growing in the nation since 2004, supported by unparalleled academic accomplishment for scholars and students alike. The university has formed transdisciplinary colleges, schools, institutes, and research centers configured according to broader societal challenges rather than historically entrenched disciplines.

ASU's success has encouraged similar shifts in other research universities and led to broader adaptation of its model nationwide. For example, the University Innovation Alliance (UIA), a coalition of eleven major public universities established in September 2014, endeavors to promote educational attainment and to advance rates of graduation among historically underrepresented and socioeconomically disadvantaged students. Apart from ASU, the Alliance's member institutions include Georgia State University; Iowa State University; Michigan State University; Ohio State University; Purdue University; the University of California, Riverside; University of Central Florida; Kansas University; and the University of Texas, Austin. In the fiercely competitive arena of research-grade higher education institutions, the Alliance's universities are committed to collaboration to reshape the future of American higher education and the fabric of our society. And in their first five years, member institutions have expanded the number of Pell-eligible (socioeconomically disadvantaged) students by almost 30 percent above baseline predictions.

A still broader league of large-scale public research universities committed to this model could yet emerge. Through the integration of cutting-edge technological innovation with institutional cultures dedicated to the advancement of public value, these institutions have the potential to effect a shift toward greater social equity and equality. Building on the accomplishments of institutional predecessors, these research universities could broaden their scope and scale to accelerate knowledge production across and between the disciplines—including the arts, the humanities and social sciences, the natural sciences, and fields of technological innovations—that our pluralistic democracy will need to draw upon as the global community negotiates the complexities of the twenty-first century.

Toward a Renewed Democracy

No assessment of this moment in our society can afford to overlook the national argument that has defined our political evolution and, within that, the growing animosity directed at colleges and universities. The relationship between education and democracy stands out as an issue of concern to scholars, policy leaders, and citizens alike. Pundits proclaim a crisis in American higher education. Popular accounts of higher education emphasize disruption, dysfunction, and demise, along with widespread concern for increasing tuition and student debt. Accusations of liberal bias in the academy further reinforce skepticism toward what has increasingly been framed as a dubious enterprise. Jeremiads against higher education from diverse political and ideological vantage points have become commonplace. These criticisms often reflect that our inherently inequitable system of knowledge production is failing to respond to social needs—a phenomenon that threatens to render our democracy dysfunctional.

Many have called for rethinking and reimagining our institutions of democracy, especially our universities. Toward this end and in addition to the many other things they do, our leading universities provide essential convening functions that facilitate dialogue among citizens. Indeed, the pluralistic, multicultural, and cosmopolitan milieu of major universities constitutes a microcosm of the ideal democratic society that one might envision. As literary scholar Seth Moglen points out, universities are uniquely positioned to initiate substantive discussions regarding the complex challenges that confront our nation and the global community. We agree with the proposition that universities should explicitly proclaim democratic missions and exercise their prerogative to promote diversity and expand the public sphere with the intent to become what Moglen has rightfully termed "engines for democracy."

As de facto national policy, excluding the majority of academically qualified students from the excellence of a research-grade university education is counterproductive and ethically unacceptable. The issue of broad accessibility to research-grade academic platforms is far more urgent than policymakers realize. Our national discussion on higher education must not simply focus on the production of more college graduates for the sake of national economic competitiveness, especially when economic competitiveness is often so narrowly defined in both scale and scope. Mere access to instruction decoupled from knowledge production and discovery will not deliver the desired societal outcomes. We must ensure that far more students have access to research-grade academic platforms that deliver robust and world-class educations able to meet the demands of the knowledge economy. It is therefore imperative that new models for the American research university emerge, led by public universities responsive to the needs of society and committed to serving ever-larger student bodies that are as socioeconomically and intellectually diverse as the nation itself.

BIOPHILIA AND DIRECT DEMOCRACY

Timothy Beatley

If you were to walk around America's cities today, you would likely come across some pleasant surprises. You might find grasslands where there used to be brownfields, greenery where there once was concrete, orchards in underserved neighborhoods and mini-parks in alleys.

These are signs that you're visiting a biophilic city—a place that has learned to capture the many advantages of putting nature back into "concrete jungles."[1] Parks and gardens are nothing new in cities, but biophilic cities take renaturing to another level. The result is an array of psychological, social, and environmental benefits that cities lost in the industrial era by paving over ecosystems and destroying the services they provided, often for free.

Biophilia is a new but growing movement based on the insight of the famed biologist Edward O. Wilson that people have an "urge to affiliate with other forms of life."[2] There is no common blueprint for a biophilic city, but the common denominator is civic engagement, where residents practice direct democracy rather than relying on the officials they have elected to state and federal governments.

Today, twenty cities in the United States and around the world participate in a Biophilic Cities Network.[3] That number is likely to grow as more urban residents work to improve the quality of their neighborhoods and lives, as officials look for ways to save money on essential city services, and as more places defend themselves against the destructive and deadly impacts of global climate change.

Using Nature to Tame Nature

Although the allure of nature is strong, climate change is the most urgent driver of ecosystem restoration in metropolitan areas. In the United States, 70 percent of adults are worried about climate change because they have experienced or witnessed its impacts.[4] Sixty-five cities in the United States are among the five hundred worldwide with the largest emissions of carbon dioxide, the gas produced by burning fossil fuels, the principal cause of global warming. Three American cities—New York, Los Angeles, and Chicago—are among the world's top ten metro areas with the biggest carbon footprints.[5] Nevertheless, the U.S. government has failed to create any significant plans or programs to help cities reduce their emissions or adapt to the climate changes that are already underway.

The changes are growing more severe. The government's latest National Climate Assessment predicts that in already-hot cities like Phoenix, Arizona, the number of days over 100°F will grow significantly, from 80 today to as many as 150 by 2050. Farther north in Madison, Wisconsin, the number of days above 100°F is projected to grow from three to forty-three per year this century.[6] On average, scientists say, Madison could experience twelve days each year of "extreme heat" with a heat index above 127°F. Even with today's temperatures, there were more than eight thousand heat-related deaths in the United States from 1999 to 2010.

The biophilic solution is urban forestry and green spaces, combined with lighter-colored streets and roofs. A recent study in Dallas, Texas, found that expanding tree canopy would lower summer nighttime temperatures in that city by as much as 15°F.[7] In addition to enhancing property values, cleaning the air, absorbing carbon dioxide, and providing wildlife habitats, trees contribute to evapotranspiration that cools the air and reduces electricity demands for air conditioning. That, in turn, reduces the threat of blackouts and more carbon dioxide emissions from power plants.

Climate change also is increasing the threat of record rainfall, floods, and sea-level rise.

More than 40 million Americans live in floodplains. The last census found that 23 million Americans—nearly 40 percent of the U.S. population—live in oceanside counties vulnerable to sea-level rise and record-setting coastal storms.

The city of Houston is an example. It is naturally vulnerable to floods because it is flat and less than fifty feet above sea level. It has averaged five days of floods each year over the last twenty years. Even so, Houston was not ready for three unprecedented events that took place between 2016 and 2018. Each was a so-called "500-year" event, meaning there was only a 1 in 500 chance of it happening in any given year.

In August 2017, Hurricane Harvey dumped between twenty and forty inches of rain on nearly 29 square miles in the Houston metro area; another 3,600 square miles experienced more than forty inches of rain in one week. More than 2,000 homes were damaged or destroyed. A major problem, city officials realized, was the number of impermeable surfaces in the city—roads, roofs, and parking lots that prevented rain from being absorbed by soils and plants rather than becoming runoff. The biophilic answer is for Houston and other cities like it to use more permeable surfacing materials and to create more green spaces and rooftop gardens.

Our Many Houstons

There are many "Houstons" in the United States. Largely because of the attraction of nature, cities and villages are located near the nation's 3.5 million miles of rivers and streams, and along 95,000 miles of shoreline. Flood losses in the United States now average about $8 billion a year. On the coasts, urban development has destroyed wetlands, salt marshes, and mangrove forests—ecosystems that absorb up to five times more carbon per acre than forests while adding protection from storm surges and rising seas.[8]

In the last century, the government's response was to build flood-control structures—dams, levees, sea walls, and channelization projects. By giving developers and homebuyers the impression that floodplains were safe, more people moved into them. When a structure failed, the results were catastrophic. Failures will become more common because most of the nation's dams and levees are approaching or already past their intended lifespans. Many have been poorly maintained. Very few were designed to hold back the intense rains we see today.

In response, some communities and regions are investing in nature's way of inhibiting floods. For example, communities in the Kissimmee River Valley of Florida are restoring wetlands and the river's meander, which allow floodwaters to spread out and slow down. The Nature Conservancy has cataloged 247 coastal restoration projects in the United States involving nearly 98,000 acres and 11,165 miles of coastline.

Cities as Systems

Biophilia begins with the understanding that cities are metabolisms supported by a variety of complex ecological and resource flows and supply chains. The modification of any part of the metabolism affects the other parts in good ways or bad. Pollution from fossil fuels, for example, results in poor air quality, respiratory problems and other illnesses, higher health care costs, and lost productivity due to missed days at work and schools. But the most destructive impact of fossil fuels is that they alter the atmosphere in ways that threaten life as we know it.

To reduce or adapt to these threats, cities must make fundamental changes in how they are designed, built, powered, and grown. Biophilia does this by retrofitting cities with natural features that urban development destroyed.

For example, Los Angeles, Denver, and New York City are among several U.S. cities that have pledged to plant at least one million trees. The Arbor Day Foundation intends to plant 100 million trees by 2020 with the help of individuals, communities, and corporations. The National Forest Foundation launched a program in 2018 to plant 50 million trees in America's national forests. The foundation estimates that its tree-planting program will save more than 850 lives, remove 578,000 tons of chemical pollution from the air, and prevent 670,000 cases of acute respiratory symptoms. In Philadelphia, a grassroots group called the Philly Orchard Project is establishing community orchards in underserved neighborhoods, combining community organizing, urban greening, and food security. Neighbors come together, sometimes in pruning workshops, to care for the trees.

In a project called Greening the Bronx, the organization Trees New York planted more than eight hundred trees on City Housing Authority properties and streets. It takes only thirty-eight trees to remove the carbon dioxide equivalent of burning nearly thirty gallons of gasoline each year. Also, "urban forestry" intercepts nearly 3,800 gallons of stormwater annually.

Grassroots organizations in the South Bronx have made environmental justice a central goal for community revitalization. Cities often have located industrial facilities and infrastructure in poorer neighborhoods with less political clout. The Pratt Center for Community Development in Brooklyn helped create a greenway along the Bronx River and turned an underused expressway and an abandoned cement plant into public parks.

Impervious surfaces cover more than 70 percent of New York City, so it adopted a green infrastructure program to construct curbside gardens— also known as bioswales and stormwater green-streets—and it promotes other green infrastructure, such as permeable paving. To protect lower Manhattan from flooding and storm surges, New York City has undertaken "The Big U" project, a mix of structural and nonstructural measures along ten continuous miles of low-lying geography where 220,000 people live. The community-driven plan includes open space, parks, and other natural features with social as well as physical benefits.

In San Francisco, the roof of the Transbay Transit Center is a five-acre, half-mile-long public park with cafes, gathering places, overlooks, and an amphitheater that holds up to one thousand people. But the city is best known in the biophilia network for creating new public spaces and repurposing small spaces in its dense urban fabric.

San Francisco encourages the development of "parklets," where two or more on-street parking spaces are converted into small public parks. In San Francisco's Street Parks program, neighborhoods propose a plan for each space, and one or more designated stewards must agree to tend and look after the space over time.[9] Many of the spaces are median strips in the middle of busy roads. Each street park is unique, however, because it is created to meet the needs of the community that develops it. Some are ornamental gardens while others are dedicated to recreation, community meetings, or wildlife habitat.

The city also has a green alleyways initiative and an innovative sidewalk gardens permit that allows residents to remove some of the pavement in their neighborhoods and replace it with flowers and greenery.[10]

Growing food for personal consumption or small-scale commerce is a central feature of most biophilic cities. Permaculture gardens, community farms, yard farming, and community orchards are all examples. Urban food hubs have been created in Washington, DC, thanks to the leadership of the University of the District of Columbia's College of Agriculture, Urban Sustainability, and Environmental Studies.[11] The idea is to develop a food-growing and production center in each of the city's wards.

Milwaukee, another member of the Biophilic Cities Network, has converted parts of the city's three thousand vacant lots into neighborhood parks and gathering spaces. Fondy Park, a city-owned vacant lot that was blighted for decades, is now a beautiful community space used for yoga classes, weekly music performances, large community gatherings, and pollinator awareness classes. It also collects and retains up to seventy thousand gallons of stormwater.[12]

Biophilic cities recognize the value of wildlife in urban settings. Members of the Biophilic Cities Network are addressing this in a variety of ways, from Austin's 1.5 million Mexican Free-tailed bats to Portland's tradition of watching thousands of Vaux's Swifts roost in the chimney of the Chapman School during September.[13] San Francisco and Toronto have adopted bird-friendly design standards. Edmonton makes extensive use of wildlife passages that allow fauna to move safely through the city. In Portland, homeowners are participating in a backyard habitat certification program run by the National Audubon Society chapter there. The Vancouver Convention Center has turned its roof into a meadow that is home to birds and four hundred thousand native plants. Architect Joyce Hwang calls this "habitecture."[14]

Public health is another important benefit of natural spaces. Researchers at Colorado State University (CSU) have documented five health benefits from human interaction with nature: less stress, more energy, better brain function, recovery from mental fatigue, and even faster recovery for hospital patients. A study published in 2018 by the journal *Environmental Research*, found that "the great outdoors" produces significant reductions in diastolic blood pressure, salivary cortisol, heart rates, diabetes, and cardiovascular mortality. "Our findings should encourage practitioners and policymakers to give due regard to how they can create, maintain, and improve existing accessible greenspaces in deprived areas," the study's authors wrote.[15]

Biophilia and Democracy

As I mentioned, biophilia often involves direct democracy where citizens mobilize to solve their problems. In many cases, citizens in disaster-affected communities have held town meetings and charrettes to decide how they want their towns reconstructed. These meetings often include design professionals who serve as advisors.

A variety of technologies are available today to democratize the community-planning process, allowing citizens to vote real-time in community development options, for example, or to use virtual reality to visualize their options.

Public spaces not only result from this activism; the spaces also promote more of it. In his book *Democracy and Public Space*, John Parkinson, an associate professor of public policy at the University of Warwick, writes "Democracy depends to a surprising extent on the availability of physical, public space, even in our allegedly digital world."[16] In these spaces, we have opportunities for civility and face-to-face interactions, allowing for "all the non-verbal cues to be transmitted and received."[17]

The interdisciplinary team of Dana Fisher, Erika Svendsen, and James Connelly have conducted one of the few empirical studies of how engagement with nature can carry over into many other forms of community and civic involvement.[18] They consider ecosystem restoration to be a "clear countertrend" to the conclusion of American political scientist Robert Putnam, who argues in his book *Bowling Alone* that civic, social, and political life has collapsed in the United States.

In New York's tree-planting program, Fisher and her colleagues found that participants "were not disconnected individuals who bowl alone; they were digging together . . . For this group of volunteer stewards, [tree planting] was an essential part of their path toward more heightened democratic citizenship. . . . Digging together in the dirt planting trees for MillionTrees NYC helped to strengthen the roots of democracy by getting these New Yorkers more connected to and involved in their communities."[19]

Conclusion

Biophilia is one way that citizens are filling leadership vacuums and avoiding bureaucratic barriers in government. One indication is the more than 200 urban networks functioning today compared with 55 in 1985.[20] They range from large and well-resourced groups such as 100 Resilient Cities and C40 Cities to small programs like the nonprofit Pomegranate Center in Washington State, which coaches communities on using "creative collaboration" and "everyday democracy" to design and build public spaces.

Our future depends on these holistic civic-engagement initiatives and on our having the humility to learn from nature rather than trying to subdue it. Nature has a lot to teach us. It's the Earth's oldest laboratory, offering answers from 3.8 billion years of experimentation. With civilization pushing against the limits of a livable planet, theologian Thomas Berry counsels correctly that "reconnecting the human species with the rest of the world is the great work of the 21st century."

Urban self-determination also is a way to avoid our communities being taken over by special interests for whom urban sustainability is secondary at best. Wendell Berry writes that, destruction of our natural heritage takes place "because we have allowed ourselves to believe, and to live, a mated pair of economic lies: that nothing has a value that is not assigned to it by the market; and that the economic life of our communities can safely be handed over to the great corporations."

The late ocean explorer Jacques Cousteau pointed out that "for most of history, man has had to fight nature to survive; in this century he is beginning to realize that, in order to survive, he must protect it." To protect it, we must appreciate it, and to fully appreciate it, we must experience it. That is the ultimate mission of biophilic cities.

PURPOSE-DRIVEN CAPITALISM

Mindy Lubber

The United States is grappling with a myriad of risks. Some are consequential enough to threaten not only life as usual, but life itself. The
question is whether our capitalist democracy as it is practiced today can
overcome these threats. The evidence indicates that systemic change is
required.

That is the bad news. The good news is that corporations are showing
signs of changing their role in the economy to serve not only CEOs and
shareholders, but also the environment and society at large.

Consider two current threats: the wealth gap and global climate
change.

In 2018, the wealthiest 10 percent of Americans held 70 percent of total
household wealth, up 10 percent from 1989. Over the same thirty years, the
bottom 50 percent of households experienced no increase in wealth. Analysts say that the gains of the rich come at the expense of everyone else.[1]

An economy with a persistent wealth gap of that size can simply not
operate fairly in a democratic system. The wealthiest benefit from an
unfair and inequitable tax and regulatory system designed in their
favor. Nick Hanauer, a venture capitalist, entrepreneur, and self-described
zillionaire, affirms and warns his fellow one-percenters, "If we don't
do something to fix the glaring inequities in this economy, the pitchforks are going to come for us. No society can sustain this kind of rising
inequality."[2]

The second major threat, global climate change, is a clear and present
danger to all nations. Its adverse impacts are growing because governments and the private sector are not doing enough to mitigate them. That
includes the government of the United States, the country that is second
only to China in emitting the greenhouse gases responsible for planetary
warming. Scientists say that by the time the United States holds its next

presidential election, the world will have only ten years to make radical changes in society, energy use, and the capital flows of its economies.

Yet the world's richest oil, coal, and gas companies continue to produce carbon-based fuels and nations continue to burn them. The corporate business model is a holdover from the twentieth century, based on the extraction of resources we cannot replace and degradation of the environment in ways we cannot fix. There will be immeasurable costs to civilization and our global economy if this continues.

Realizing the liability posed by business as usual, some corporations and investors show signs of shifting to a different business model that some call "purpose-driven capitalism." There are several early adopters in the business sector (as I will point out shortly), but in August 2019, purpose-driven capitalism appeared to go mainstream. The Business Roundtable, which includes the CEOs of two hundred large companies, adopted a new "Statement on the Purpose of a Corporation" that commits to serving society and the environment in addition to shareholders.[3]

Purpose-driven capitalism has a higher mission than the accumulation and concentration of material riches. It recognizes that the well-being of business depends on the well-being of people and the environment.

In many ways, this is not a new concept. Henry **Ford** pioneered the assembly line in 1913, but the repetitive nature of the work led to high worker turnover and absenteeism. So Ford offered his employees more than double the average wage for factory workers at the time. His workforce stabilized, production surged, and the Ford Motor Company doubled its profits in less than two years. William Clay Ford, the founder's great grandson and the executive chairman of the Ford Motor Company points out today, "The purpose of any company should be to make people's lives better. Otherwise, it shouldn't exist."

Unilever, the consumer goods giant, plans to help more than a billion people improve their health and well-being by 2020. It also plans to cut its environmental footprint in half by 2030. Similar goals have been adopted by this Anglo-Dutch company, which makes Dove soap, Ben & Jerry's ice cream, and hundreds of other household products.

Nike has become a global sustainability leader while boosting revenues four-fold in the process. Nike was one of the first companies to call for climate policies and green-job efforts in the United States—a move that led to the launch of Businesses for Innovative Climate and Energy Policy (BICEP), a collaboration of leading businesses supporting climate policy.

When President Trump announced he was pulling out of the Paris Agreement in 2017, **Mars** and **Microsoft** stood with hundreds of others to launch We Are Still In, a climate action campaign now backed by more than two thousand companies and investors.

In 2018, **Danone North America** became the world's largest Certified B Corp, a status granted only to companies that meet a rigorous set of environmental, social, and governance standards. The $6 billion company, best known for its yogurt brands, is moving aggressively to eliminate waste, plastics, and carbon emissions, and has ambitious compliance programs for all of its global suppliers. The company also provides its six thousand U.S. workers with twenty-six weeks of paid parental leave and flexible time-off benefits. Employees receive free shares of stock. Meanwhile, sales and profits are thriving—especially in its healthy, plant-based product lines, which are taking off worldwide.

Interface Inc., one of the world's major flooring manufacturers, launched "Mission Zero," a program to eliminate all of the company's environmental impacts by 2020. It has lowered the carbon footprint of its manufacturing by more than 50 percent. The company has instituted carbon offsets that cover entire product lifecycles, and made its products recyclable. Today, Interface is a $1 billion company with 3,500 employees on four continents.

Opportunity or Bubble

When nearly two hundred nations approved the historic Paris Climate Agreement in 2015, they established the framework for the most substantial market opportunity in history, as well as the most significant opportunity for businesses and industries to do well by doing good.[4] The Paris Accord calls for nearly all of the world's nations to participate in the global transition to a net-zero carbon economy. That means transforming society to run on renewable energy rather than fossil fuels.

The International Energy Agency (IEA) projects that renewable energy will be the fastest-growing primary energy source over the next twenty years, capturing two-thirds of global investments in power plants.[5] Allied Market Research predicts that the renewable energy market will grow to more than $1.5 trillion in 2025.[6] The world's nearly sixty capitalist nations, including the United States, have ceded leadership in this market to China. China was responsible for almost a third of all global renewable energy investments in 2018.

The fossil energy giants must decide whether to continue fighting the transition to clean energy or whether they will become "energy transition companies." A recent study found that many of the world's oil companies are getting more active in renewable energy, particularly those with smaller oil reserves.[7] "Five out of eight oil majors have formulated an explicit renewable energy strategy, earmarked capital spending for renewables and have built dedicated renewable energy teams in their organizations," researchers found.

However, ExxonMobil and Chevron, America's two largest oil producers, are holding back. Overall, America's biggest oil and gas companies have allocated only about 1 percent of their 2018 budgets to clean energy.[8]

The conflict between these two futures surfaced in 2015 at ExxonMobil's annual meeting. After CEO Rex Tillerson talked about the company's "virtuous" role in providing cheap, reliable fossil fuels to billions of rich and poor people alike, a faith-based investor, Father Michael Crosby, challenged Tillerson for saying "not one word or syllable" about climate change. Crosby asked Tillerson why Exxon was not investing in solar energy, which is far more abundant and less expensive than oil and gas.

"Quite frankly, Father Crosby," Tillerson replied, "we choose not to lose money on purpose." He dismissed solar panels as a fool's folly. The crowd erupted with applause. Yet Tillerson's remarks made clear that Exxon is stuck in the old business model of prioritization of short-term profits that depend on finite resources and hidden externalities, the adverse impacts of oil, natural gas, and coal that ultimately are borne by taxpayers, asthmatic children, consumers, and now every living thing on the planet.

Before long, Exxon will find it can no longer compete with the declining costs and environmental benefits of renewable energy. So long as it sticks to its old business model, Exxon looks very much like a company that intends to lose money on purpose.

One indication of the energy market's new direction was that the value of the 170 companies in the Russell 3000 Energy Index, most of them in oil and gas, fell by 12 percent during President Trump's first two years in office. ExxonMobil and Kinder Morgan Inc., the pipeline and energy storage companies, each declined by 1 percent, while Peabody Energy Company, the largest private coal company in the world, fell by 4 percent. But eighty-nine major publicly traded U.S. companies with at least 10 percent of their business in clean-energy technologies experienced gains of 50 percent.

In December 2018, 415 investors with a combined $32 trillion under management called upon governments around the world to make more ambitious commitments to reduce carbon emissions.[9] A growing number of U.S. and European pension funds are aligning their portfolios with the Paris Agreement. Others are calibrating their investments to the United Nations' Sustainable Development Goals (SDGs)—a universal call "to end poverty, protect the planet, and ensure prosperity for all."

At last count, more than one thousand institutions and more than 58,000 individuals had divested nearly $10 trillion from fossil fuels, meaning they have shed stocks, bonds, and investment funds that they consider unethical or morally questionable.[10] Instead, many of these groups are investing in a green future, with clear results. California's largest public pension fund, CalPERS, is selling off its shares in coal companies and buying bigger stakes in wind and solar farms. The New York state retirement fund has invested $4 billion in a low-carbon index fund, which generated a 19 percent return in its first two years. A Canadian pension fund manager, Caisse de dépôt et placement du Québec, is earning double-digit returns by investing in solar, wind, and super-efficient buildings from North America to India.[11] In just the past six years, there has been a ten-fold jump to $12 trillion in U.S. assets invested in socially responsible ways.[12]

The world's largest asset manager, BlackRock, stewards more than $6 trillion in holdings. In his 2019 annual letter to its corporate customers, BlackRock CEO Larry Fink warned of an increasingly fragile global landscape and growing short-term behavior risks. He called for organizational leadership that embraces sustainable, long-term growth grounded in "profits and purpose."

"The world needs your leadership," he wrote. "Companies must demonstrate their commitment to the countries, regions, and communities where they operate, particularly on issues central to the world's prosperity."

Many businesses are getting the message. Nearly two hundred companies have set 100 percent renewable energy targets, including big-name manufacturers like GM, Johnson & Johnson, and Kellogg's. Apple, Microsoft, and Google have already achieved their 100 percent renewable goals. Since 2000, more than twenty countries have grown their economies without increasing their carbon emissions.[13] California—the fifth-largest economy in the world—has lowered its carbon footprint by 13 percent since 2004, even as its population has grown by several million people.

Even fossil energy groups are greening. As a result of Climate Action 100+, an investor-engagement initiative focused on the world's 165 most significant greenhouse gas emitters, oil giant Shell has set near-term greenhouse gas reduction targets, and coal giant Glencore PLC has agreed to cap coal production because of climate concerns.[14]

As companies and economies curb their emissions, the renewable energy's market share is destined to grow. The International Renewable Energy Association (IRENA) predicts that by 2020, unsubsidized onshore wind and utility-scale solar power will be consistently cheaper than any fossil fuel.[15] Renewables will gain market share not only because they cost less, but also because they are purpose-driven investments that lead to cleaner air, more stable energy prices, energy security, good jobs, and the democratization of America's energy economy, giving people a choice on where their energy comes from and the opportunity to produce their own.

But do these developments yet show that we are doing enough to further America's necessary energy transformation? The answer so far is no.

Coinciding Priorities

Purpose-driven investment is especially timely because the United States must spend trillions of dollars on repairing and modernizing its infrastructure. After analyzing the condition of our roads, bridges, airports, flood control structures, and so on in 2017, the American Society of Civil Engineers estimated that we need to spend more than $2 trillion to repair and modernize infrastructure by 2025.

The private sector currently manages $70 trillion in assets. Will investors put their money into twentieth- or twenty-first-century infrastructure? We cannot be certain because we have no national energy policy in the United States, no roadmap to a clean energy economy, and no policy consistency when elected leaders change.

However, the environment is sending some of its own signals about the best and worst investments. For example, the electricity sector's operations draw upon 41 percent of America's freshwater supplies, leading to scarcities. Water shortages already are constraining the ability of fossil and nuclear power plants to cool their equipment. Because of climate change and population growth, nearly one hundred freshwater basins in the United States are projected to suffer water shortages.[16] From 2000 to 2015, there were forty-three documented cases where power generation was affected or interrupted because of high water temperatures or water shortages.[17] The better bets are solar and wind power which, with the exception of solar thermal power plants, don't require water for cooling.

Climate change will affect businesses in many other ways. Extreme weather can cripple corporate supply chains thousands of miles away. Severe heatwaves are expected to reduce worker productivity. Businesses located along the nation's coasts are affected by sea-level rise. Four of every ten small businesses affected by floods never reopen. These vulnerabilities can all be traced back to the combustion of fossil fuels.

Bad Bets

Nevertheless, significant public and private investments are still being bet on fossil fuels. The International Monetary Fund calculates that fossil energy subsidies in the United States totaled nearly $650 billion in one recent year, second only to China when indirect as well as direct costs were counted.

Since nations approved the Paris Agreement in 2015, thirty-three global banks have invested $2 trillion in oil and gas operations, with $600 billion going to the 100 companies that are most aggressive in expanding fossil fuel production.[18]

Analysts say the United States and Canada will have to spend nearly $800 billion on new oil and natural gas infrastructure from 2018 to 2035 at current rates of production growth and consumption.[19] The U.S. is experiencing a "pipeline boom," with taxpayer support: The U.S. Department of Energy announced in April 2019 that it would spend another $40 million for research and development to improve oil and natural gas technologies.

In short, financiers, governments, and oil companies are creating what economists call "bubbles"—investments isolated from reality and unlikely to last. Several bubble-bursting forces are underway. Weather disasters intensified by climate change cost North America $415 billion over the last three years according to Morgan Stanley.[20] International scientists project that worldwide damages could grow to nearly $70 trillion by the end of this century unless we take immediate steps to mitigate climate change.[21] The bubble will burst too when distorted price signals in energy markets come to an end. Currently, fossil energy subsidies and the hidden cost of negative externalities deflate the real price of fossil fuels. There is a movement toward what Amory Lovins calls "prices that tell the truth" rather than prices that hide subsidies and externalities. One example is Congress's consideration of a tax on fossil fuels to reflect their social and environmental costs.

If we miss this opportunity to build a clean energy and disaster-resilient economy, one of two things will happen. Investments in fossil energy will be stranded as governments and markets draw down their carbon emissions, or investors will lock the world into carbon pollution for another fifty years so they obtain their full rates of return by using the infrastructure to the end of its intended life—to the detriment of life on Earth.

The United Nations considers itself an example of international democracy. The world saw it at work in 2015 at the sprawling Le Bourget complex in Paris. In the closing moments of the twenty-first year of climate-action negotiations among nations, it seemed the world had turned the corner on climate change. As the gavel came down to signal the adoption of the deal, delegates from 196 nations rose to their feet, cheering and applauding. Joining them were hundreds of companies and investors who had traveled to Paris to voice their support for a strong climate accord that would provide an essential market signal about the low-carbon future.

It was an exciting and hopeful moment. All of us—governments, capitalists, civil society groups—thought we had just witnessed the beginning of a clean economic transformation that would protect the planet and future generations while generating millions of new jobs.

But we are not yet firmly on the path to a net–zero carbon world. Government upheavals, entrenched fossil fuel interests, and myopic lending practices around the world have bogged us down. After a three-year pause, global CO_2 emissions jumped 2.7 percent in 2018, with nearly all countries contributing to the increase, including the United States, China, and India. Atmospheric concentrations of carbon dioxide, which will determine the ultimate extent of warming, rose to 415 parts per million (ppm) early in 2019, the highest level in human history and far greater than the 350 ppm that scientists consider relatively safe.

At World Economic Forum 2019, political, business, and other national leaders agreed that "the world is clearly sleepwalking into catastrophe." We are far off course from staying below the 1.5°C warming limit (compared to pre-industrial temperatures) that scientists now recommend. If we exceed it, tens of millions more people worldwide will be exposed to life-threatening heat waves, water shortages, and coastal flooding. Exceeding 1.5°C would create enormous and destructive economic ripples, including significantly higher losses in marine fisheries, crop yields, and country-by-country GDP.

We already see the devastating effects of one degree of warming, including a sharp increase in billion-dollar disasters in the United States, as a result of more extreme weather. Paying for record-setting floods, wildfires, and hurricanes has caused a five-fold jump[22] in federal disaster relief spending compared to twenty-five years ago—costs that are borne primarily by taxpayers.

In warmer, poorer countries around the world, hotter temperatures are suffocating economic growth with reduced crop yields, water scarcity, and excessive heat. A 2019 Stanford University study found that from 1961 to 2010, global warming decreased per capita GDP in India, Nigeria, and Brazil by 31 percent, 29 percent, and 25 percent, respectively.[23]

Unfortunately, the United States is the prime example of the ambition gap between the goals of the Paris Accord and what nations are actually doing. When it polled Americans in June 2019, Reuters found that nearly 70 percent of Americans, including a majority of Republicans, wanted the United States to take aggressive action against climate change.[24] But the current U.S. president denies that climate change is real, and Congress has done nothing. In short, we are stuck in a failure of representative democracy.

What will it take to restore Americans' faith in democracy as a problem solver in the public's interest? How can we sustain capitalism that supports democracy, and democratic principles that encourage purpose-driven capitalism? Here is my prescription.

The Promise for More—and How to Get There

Many Americans believe that government has the most influence on our future, but capital markets have as much or more potential to fix the world's problems. Businesses are trusted far more than governments— 80 percent of Americans say companies should take the lead in solving global problems. Businesses have a unique power over the global economy. By some measures, the one thousand largest firms control 70 percent of global GDP.

Business leaders also have considerable influence on public policies, and lately the public is encouraging greater use of that influence on moral grounds, particularly amongst younger generations. For instance, millennials are credited with influencing corporations to sign the World Business Council's new purpose statement. When millennial workers were asked in a 2018 Deloitte survey what the primary purpose of businesses should be, 63 percent said "improving society" rather than "generating profit."

So, now comes the big question: how do we achieve a better form of capitalism that is accountable to shareholders *and* the public good?

The answer is that companies must integrate purpose and values across their entire enterprise—from priority-setting and governance to stakeholder engagement, accountability, and compensation. This is what it looks like, starting at the top:

- Companies redefine their charters to include broader goals focused on sustainability and *all* major stakeholders, not just shareholders.
- Each company's purpose is reflected in time-bound deadlines for improving performance on greenhouse gas emissions, water use, waste, and human capital management.
- C-suite executives and boards of directors prioritize critical environmental and social issues, including climate change, that pose "material" risks and opportunities.
- Corporate boards oversee key sustainability issues and recruit diverse, independent members with expertise on these issues.
- Energy companies with significant exposure to climate issues consider adding climate experts to their boards.
- Product innovation, including R&D spending, aligns with global sustainability trends, such as the growing demand for low-carbon products.
- Executive compensation is focused more on sustainable, long-term growth and less on short-term metrics, such as quarterly earnings and share price.

Companies should open their doors to diverse stakeholders—both within and outside the business—who can deepen their understanding of environmental and social challenges and offer innovative opportunities for dealing with them. Employees, communities, and suppliers are key stakeholders, but engaging with government policymakers is also critical.

Supporting environmental and social goals but failing to reinforce those values on the policy front is not good enough. While more companies are speaking out in support of strong climate policies, more corporate voices are needed, especially those of CEOs. For democracy to prevail, for purpose-driven capitalism to flourish, leadership is urgently needed to fight for policies that ensure a sustainable future.

For their part, **investors** must recognize that their long-term returns will only be as sustainable as the world in which they invest. They can start by doing the following:

- Aligning their portfolios with global environmental and social goals, including carbon-reducing targets established under the Paris Agreement or the UN SDGs.
- Reallocating capital across various asset classes to generate positive impacts and solid market-rate returns. Green bonds and climate bonds,

for example, are good options for fixed-income assets. Green bond issuances have grown fifteen-fold in just the past five years, to $168 billion in 2018, but they still account for only a tiny fraction of bond issuances worldwide.

- Boosting interactions with companies to better understand how they manage social and environmental issues like climate change, water scarcity, and workplace discrimination.
- Calling on companies to eschew short-term metrics and focus more on sustainable long-term growth. Powerhouse investors like Warren Buffett and JP Morgan's Jamie Dimon have called for ending quarterly earnings guidance, saying it "often leads to an unhealthy focus on short-term profits at the expense of long-term strategy, growth, and sustainability."
- Engaging in direct advocacy for government policies that ensure a sustainable future. If Wall Street's most prominent financial leaders are earnest about systemic risks like climate change, they should be spending more time in Washington trying to fix it.

Capital markets, which are governed by policymakers as well as regulators like stock exchanges, the Federal Reserve Board, accounting boards, and the federal Securities and Exchange Commission (SEC), should reshape the rules and incentives that drive business activity, investments, and the overall global economy. They should reflect the true systemic and portfolio risks in their mandates.

We cannot solve the problems that confront us without changing market signals. Simply put, we need signals that encourage beneficial business activities and discourage damaging ones. Capital markets can start by doing the following:

- Eliminating economic policies that promote short-sighted corporate practices at the expense of sustainable, long-lasting business models. During the Reagan presidency, tax and security laws created overly generous compensation for shareholders and executives, such as lower federal income and capital gains taxes. This has morphed into the vast income inequality between the top 1 percent and the rest of the country. Changing these rules would discourage powerful activist investors who push public companies to cut costs and forego long-term investments in order to return more cash to shareholders.

- Instituting tighter accounting systems for measuring long-term economic impacts on issues like climate change, biodiversity, and human capital. Current accounting tools, which evolved during a period of natural abundance and low population, are overly focused on measuring growth—as evidenced by our global obsession with GDP.
- Improving transparency. As climate disruption escalates, it is increasingly important that companies fully disclose their potential risks, whether physical or regulatory. Investors, credit-rating agencies, and even stock exchanges are clamoring for this information, but the breadth and quality of disclosures are lacking.

The next president and Congress must realign the **government**'s fiscal policies to support what makes the nation stronger rather than weaker. Fossil energy subsidies should be shifted to clean energy. Congress should appropriate sufficient funds for a comprehensive public/private R&D initiative to speed the development of more efficient wind turbines and solar panels, better energy storage, direct-air carbon capture, and other technologies communities and companies need to achieve their 100 percent carbon-free goals.

There are limits to nature's ability to absorb abuse without push-back, and we have reached them through our current capitalist system's structuring. Through the lens of history, capitalism has been an enormous success. It has been incredibly effective in catalyzing innovation and global economic growth. It has lifted hundreds of millions of people out of poverty—results that other economic systems did not deliver. Our capitalist democracy has also shown an ability to evolve and self-correct. When sweeping air and water pollution laws were enacted by Congress a half-century ago, for example, the capital markets responded, and the economy flourished. We can accomplish greater economic growth and global stability by employing similar principles on a larger scale.

As the 116th Congress began in January 2019, the Green New Deal, a resolution that framed an agenda for achieving climate stability and social justice, was announced. It contained more goals than specific solutions, but it was the first congressional proposal with the bold scope necessary to match the scale of our environmental and social challenges.

It laid out a ten-year blueprint for achieving 100 percent clean energy, millions of new jobs, and a more equitable economy in the United States.

Public opinion research shows that an overwhelming majority of Americans support objectives like those in the Green New Deal. Climate change has become an existential test for representative government and for capitalism, and time is running for both to pass the test.

RESTORING DEMOCRACY: NATURE'S TRUST, HUMAN SURVIVAL, AND CONSTITUTIONAL FIDUCIARY GOVERNANCE

Mary Christina Wood

While Americans cherish and champion democracy, they rarely associate it with ecology. The overlooked truth is that democracy and ecological health are co-dependent. When the government mismanages vital natural resources, it impoverishes society and drains power from the people. The national context shifts slowly, almost imperceptibly—but steadily nonetheless—toward environmental tyranny. As President Theodore Roosevelt proclaimed, "conservation of all our natural resources [is] essentially democratic in spirit, purpose and method."

The United States has codified more environmental laws than any other country in the world. Laws such as the Clean Air Act, the Clean Water Act, the Endangered Species Act, and the National Environmental Policy Act were passed nearly half a century ago, when 20 million Americans took to the streets on Earth Day to protest environmental destruction. However, those statutes obscure a dirty little secret today. The agencies implementing them too often have stopped serving the public and instead use their permitting authority to legalize the destruction the statutes were designed to prevent.

Congress gave environmental agencies breathtaking discretion in administering environmental statutes on the assumption that officials would act on behalf of the public interest. Industries lobby the agencies intensively to issue permits to bend the law in their favor. Fully "captured" agencies serve the industries they are supposed to regulate. Campaign contributions vastly exacerbate the problem. Presidents and governors often appoint agency heads with loyalty to the industries that fund their campaigns. These political appointees view the industries, rather than the public, as their clients. Politics end up circumventing the law.

Now entire planetary life-support systems are unraveling, and the impacts are striking communities with horrifying frequency and intensity. With climate change, for example, warnings of tipping points, irreversible losses, and unpredictable cataclysmic planetary changes are issued by the scientific community in growing alarm. Yet corporations continue to devour our nation's most essential resources, dump pollution into the atmosphere, and destroy the planet's vital carbon cycle—all pursuant to permits issued by agencies. Elizabeth Kolbert writes in *Field Notes from a Catastrophe*, "It may seem impossible to imagine that a technologically advanced society could choose, in essence, to destroy itself, but that is what we are now in the process of doing."

Environmental disruptions—including the loss of biodiversity, soil degradation and deforestation—are so pervasive that small mitigation measures are futile. We need a new era of environmental law and policy framed by the bedrock principles of the government's ecological obligations. Agency powers, expertise and revenues must be directed away from destroying resources to building a regenerative economy, or, as Hunter Lovins calls it, "an economy in service to life."[1] We must impose strict obligations on governmental actors so that protection, not destruction, becomes the default mode of regulation.

The principle to guide this transformation is already embedded in American law. It is the public trust doctrine. Far older and more comprehensive than any statute, the doctrine is rooted in Roman law and has informed legal systems worldwide. It designates the government as a trustee of natural resources, including air, streams, wildlife, the sea, and seashores—indeed all resources of "public concern"—with a strict fiduciary responsibility to protect them for all citizens throughout time. The trust remains the primary legal mechanism to carry out the Constitution's promise to "secure the Blessings of Liberty to ourselves and our *Posterity*"— that is, our descendants. President Roosevelt invoked the trust principle when he said, "Our duty to the whole, including the unborn generations, begs us to restrain an unprincipled present-day minority from wasting the heritage of these unborn generations." The public trust governs for the endurance, rather than the expiration, of the nation.

The principle is so fundamental that scholars have called it "the law's DNA." However, although it has existed in the American legal system since the nation's beginning, the doctrine has slipped into legal dormancy, buried by an avalanche of modern environmental regulations. Most agency regulators have never heard of the public trust and remain unaware of their fiduciary obligations to protect public ecological assets. Now, lawyers, citizens, judges, and regulators are unearthing these principles and applying them to environmental controversies. The principles *still exist in the law*, ready to be called to action against environmentally destructive regimes.

Reframing Government: Nature's Trust for the New Ecological Age

George Lakoff, the cognitive linguist who has written about the power of mental frameworks, notes "Reframing is changing the way the public sees the world. It is changing what counts as common sense."[2] We must reframe nature as an irreplaceable ecological endowment, belonging in trust to all citizens throughout time. This framing draws upon common property rights tracing back to Roman law's *Institutes of Justinian*, which declared: "By the law of nature these things are common to mankind— the air, running water, the sea, and consequently the shores of the sea."

In American jurisprudence, such anciently recognized common ownership evolved into a trust concept that limits the government's ability to privatize crucial resources. A trust is a unique form of property that splits the ownership of wealth between a trustee and a beneficiary. The trustee controls the assets, but must manage them for the *exclusive and singular* benefit of the beneficiary. In a public trust, courts designate the government, the only enduring institution of society, as the trustee of crucial natural resources.

The trust protects against the consumption of the commonwealth by securing a perpetual *public property right* in crucial natural resources. In the landmark U.S. public trust case, *Illinois Central Railroad v. Illinois*, the U.S. Supreme Court held that a state legislature did not have the power to convey the shoreline of Lake Michigan to a private railroad company. The court ruled that the shoreline was a resource of great "public concern" that must be held in trust for the people as a whole to serve public interests (recognized then as fishing, navigation, and commerce). Conveying such an important resource to a private party would "be a grievance which never could be long borne by a free people." To enforce this principle, courts prevent one set of legislators from wielding so much power over ecology as to cripple future legislatures in meeting their citizens' needs.

This is in marked contrast to the current social framework, which conceals the public-property character of ecological resources, obscures the sovereign's obligation to manage them, and lulls the public into complacency. The government's administration of environmental law might serve a den of thieves, but the public perceives no theft because it perceives that nature is not really owned by anyone. When the public ends up on the losing side of environmental disputes, agencies explain it away as "political reality." The "political reality" delivers a potent tranquilizer to the public—after all, who will argue with reality?—and becomes a self-serving truism defined and perpetuated by those in power.

President Roosevelt invoked the public trust again when he stood at the rim of the Grand Canyon in 1903 and declared: "We have gotten past the stage, my fellow citizens, when we are to be pardoned if we treat any part of our country as something to be skinned for two or three years for the use of the present generation, whether it is the forest, the water, the scenery. Whatever it is, handle it so that your children's children will get the benefit of it." The trust is a twin of democracy itself, based on the simple premise that people grant power to their government, not the reverse. Citizens would never give the government or private interests the power to impair resources crucial to their survival and welfare, so they implicitly reserve unto themselves common property rights to these vital assets. Because the social compact authorizing government incorporates this understanding, the public trust is widely deemed an "attribute of sovereignty," a constitutive principle that government cannot shed or abdicate. In the words of one federal court: "The trust is of such a nature that it can be held only by the sovereign, and can only be destroyed by the destruction of the sovereign."[3]

The Trust Requirements

The Supreme Court emphasized in an early public trust case: "The power or control lodged in the state, resulting from this common ownership, is to be exercised, like all other powers of government, *as a trust for the benefit of the people*, and not as a prerogative for the advantage of the government as distinct from the people, or for the benefit of private individuals as distinguished from the public good."[4] Any trust enshrines a set of strict legally enforceable fiduciary obligations owed to the beneficiaries. They create a coherent framework of government accountability in managing ecology.[5] These duties are to:

Protect the Resources

Again, the quintessential fiduciary duty requires trustees to protect vital ecology. Adopting a practical rather than purist construction, courts define the threshold of impermissible damage as "substantial impairment" of the resource. The fiduciary duty of protection remains active, not passive, so a trustee may not sit idle and allow the trust property to "fall into ruin on his watch." As trustees, government agents may not abet privateers poised to destroy or degrade the public's resources.

Conserve the Natural Inheritance of Future Generations

An ages-old waste prohibition of trust law prohibits trustees from diminishing the wealth available to future beneficiaries. The waste injunction presents a powerful counterweight to the government's political impulse to overindulge the living generation (people who vote and make campaign contributions) by raiding the trust inheritance needed by unborn citizens, who have no present political clout.

Maximize the Societal Value of Natural Resources

Government trustees must manage trust resources to maximize their benefits to the people. The current regulatory system utterly misses this step, handing out permits to destroy public resources without asking whether any public purpose justifies the harm. Not unlike the Once-ler in *The Lorax* who cut down the magnificent Truffula trees to produce massive amounts of unnecessary "thneeds," corporations produce billions of marginally useful products that leave ravaged ecosystems behind. Many polluting uses of air, water, and soil would fail under a trust approach. Usually, a corporation pollutes these valuable resources to capitalize on a free repository for waste disposal—minimizing, rather than maximizing, the societal value of the resource.

Scrutiny of Private Use

Government trustees may not manage public natural commonwealth primarily to serve private ends. Captive agencies violate this fundamental principle when they issue permits primarily to benefit their allied industries. The trust does not altogether prohibit private use of public trust resources, but rather aims to harness private enterprise to promote the public good. A trustee may privatize public trust assets only when doing so (1) clearly aids a public trust purpose; and (2) does not cause "substantial impairment" to the public's interest in the remaining lands and waters.

Restore the Trust

A trustee must restore a trust asset that has been damaged. This basic principle seeks to return the beneficiaries to their rightful position by making the trust whole again. Trustees have an affirmative obligation to recoup monetary damages against third parties that harm or destroy trust assets. In the public trust context, for example, the duty demands the recovery of natural resource damages from oil companies that cause spills in the ocean.

Phase Out the Permit System

Collectively, these fiduciary duties would force a phase-out of the broad-scale pollution permitting system. They would also compel government trustees to weigh the cataclysmic outcome of continued fossil fuel extraction against the viable, safer alternatives of renewable energy. The restoration duty would oblige agencies to seek damages from industries that have destroyed vital resources. Disgorgement of fossil fuel industry profits could fund the cleanup of the carbon dioxide dump in the sky through investment in natural methods of carbon drawdown and sequestration. In short, a trust framework would redirect government resources toward replenishing the Earth's endowment rather than bankrupting it.

The Duty of Loyalty

The trust demands steadfast, undivided loyalty toward the designated beneficiaries. It prohibits flirtations that could engender even the possibility of self-dealing by the trustee. This exacting and rigorous duty of loyalty is "not the duty to resist temptation, but to eliminate temptation, as the former is assumed to be impossible." Courts regularly invalidate trust transactions tainted by conflicts of interest.

This duty would confront the political putrefaction subsuming environmental law: the corruptive influence of campaign contributions by industries that stand to benefit from government decisions on environmental issues. Campaign financing creates exactly the kind of temptation that the trust abhors; the political actor will serve the industry through legislative votes and executive agency decisions rather than risk alienating a key campaign funder.

The problem is not that this corruption goes unrecognized, but that it has become institutionalized. The U.S. Supreme Court's *Citizens United* decision, allowing corporations to make massive donations to political campaigns, created an oligarch's marketplace for the purchase of elected American leaders. Rather than govern for the public interest, many legislators on the state and federal levels tend to vote in wicked symmetry with their political campaign funding, even when that results in asymmetry with their voters' best interests.

Despite its appalling consequences for democracy, *Citizens United* remains difficult to legally dislodge because the court categorically held that corporations have constitutionally protected First Amendment rights to make campaign contributions. The public trust's duty of loyalty delegitimizes this political behavior, not by invalidating the corporation's act of making campaign contributions, but by constraining the ability of officials to make decisions tainted by the contributions. The fiduciary duty of loyalty would require lawmakers to recuse themselves from decisions in which a corporate-affiliated campaign donor has a significant interest.[6]

Nature's Trust

In sum, the public trust repositions all players in their relationship to ecology. It conceives of government officials as fiduciary trustees rather than as political actors, and it bears no tolerance toward disloyal public servants. It presents nature as a priceless endowment comprising tangible and quantifiable assets, instead of a vague "environment" with amorphous value. The citizens stand as beneficiaries holding a clear public property interest in crucial natural resources, rather than as weakened political constituents with increasingly desperate appeals to bring to their public officials. At a time when the government acts as the accomplice of profiteers engaged in permanent resource loss, the trust must be rebuilt and the people's natural wealth restored. However, this paradigm requires rigorous enforcement of fiduciary obligations, or it is not a trust at all.

The Judicial Role Enforcing the Trust in the Face
of Climate Emergency

To prevent a despotic ruler, the founders carefully devised three branches of government with significant checks and balances. The role of the judiciary is vital to enforcing the trust obligations of the other branches. But just as a bow string loses its force when not taut, democracy loses its essential vitality when legal and political tension between the three branches becomes slack.

For most of the nation's history, courts sculpted fundamental principles of sovereign duty toward ecology, applying the public trust derived from England to the blank slate of new America. Towering opinions such as *Illinois Central* emerged from a canvas of common sense. Judges molded the common law to unprecedented circumstances and protected citizens against the monarchical impulses of legislatures inclined to hand over vital public resources to their industry allies. With constitutional force, the public trust helped check aggrandized legislature power.

However, today's courts often take a posture of undue deference toward agencies, uncritically presuming that agencies will faithfully carry out their statutory duties. Invoking this "deference doctrine," many courts take a self-appointed wallflower role in statutory cases. Their opinions are often technical and narrow in scope, bland in justice, and overstuffed with process. Characteristically brittle, they steadily ossify an area of law that demands agility as society confronts environmental threats. One federal appellate judge announced a "Wake Up Call for Judges," objecting that an "enfeebled" judicial branch contributes to a "wholesale failure of the legal system to protect humanity from the collapse of finite natural resources by the uncontrolled pursuit of short-term profits."[7]

The most urgent judicial role today is the courts' intervention in the climate emergency. An inexorable promotion of fossil fuels by the executive branch and Congress—across administrations—in the face of increasingly dire warnings by scientists has brought humanity to an unthinkable moment when global climate disaster threatens to result in a fundamentally "different planet" hostile to human life.[8] Federal energy policy includes massive subsidies, regulatory permits, approvals of export proposals, and the leasing, exploration, drilling, and mining of public lands and offshore areas. All of these actions are carried out and/or authorized by federal agencies under "environmental" law.

Meantime, international scientists warn that the world's carbon emissions must be cut about 45 percent by 2030 on the path to net-zero carbon economies by mid-century. A U.S. president's ability to expand America's fossil fuel production and exports effectively vests Donald Trump with god-like power unimagined by the founders when they created America's three-branch system of government. The question is, will a court force the government to pull the emergency brake before the president plunges the nation and the world over the climate precipice?

Legal action by young Americans could compel swift reversal of this disastrous energy course. American youth have sued the government in an unprecedented litigation strategy to confront the existential climate threat by invoking their fundamental rights under the public trust doctrine.

A campaign known as Atmospheric Trust Litigation (ATL) began in 2011, when the nonprofit, Our Children's Trust, spearheaded lawsuits or administrative petitions on behalf of youth against every state government, and against the federal government. The youth have asked the courts to require that the government develop enforceable plans to lower carbon emissions according to a prescription developed by leading climate scientists. A scientists' brief supporting the youth declared, "Failure to act with all deliberate speed in the face of the clear scientific evidence of the danger functionally becomes a decision to eliminate the option of preserving a *habitable climate system.*"[9]

Some judges dismissed early ATL cases reasoning that the courts should have no role in the climate crisis. To their thinking, climate was a "political question" for the other branches of government. As Professor Douglas Kysar and Henry Weaver put it, by "denying [their] own expansive power, [these courts] cowered before catastrophe."[10]

The tide began to turn for ATL when a Washington court judge found a state constitutional public trust right to a protected atmosphere.[11] Declaring that the children's "very survival depends upon the will of their elders to act now, decisively and unequivocally," the court ordered the state to promulgate science-based emissions-reduction rules. Courts in other countries also delivered victories for citizens in climate cases, holding their governments accountable for hard emissions reduction. Several of these courts characterize climate stability as a matter of fundamental rights and intergenerational equity, squarely rejecting portrayals of climate as a political question.

Then, in 2015, twenty-one youth across America sued the Obama administration in the federal district court of Oregon, challenging the entire fossil fuel policy of the United States. Known by many as "the biggest case on the planet," an early procedural win inspired a growing wave of new ATL cases.

The principal case, *Juliana v. United States,* persists against the Trump administration. The youth plaintiffs assert their public trust rights to a stable atmosphere as well as a due process right to be free from the government's affirmative action endangering their lives, liberty, and property. Documents compiled by Our Children's Trust lawyers show that the government has known about the climate danger for decades and yet intensified the crisis through its affirmative fossil fuel policy.[12] The youths' complaint alleges, "Defendants have acted with deliberate indifference to the peril they knowingly created."

In November 2016, federal district court judge Ann Aiken issued a groundbreaking decision affirming the legal basis of the youths' claims. Characterizing the case as a civil rights action and "no ordinary lawsuit," the court denied the government's motions to throw out the case. Judge Aiken wrote, "I have no doubt that the right to a climate system capable of sustaining human life is fundamental to a free and ordered society."

The *Juliana* case may be the last legal maneuver that can stop a catastrophic energy policy from breaching climate tipping points. In February 2019, lawyers for the youths made the extraordinary attempt to stop one hundred federal fossil energy projects poised for release by the Trump administration. The monumental nature of the case provoked government lawyers to double down on their efforts to derail it from going to trial. As I write this, the case is awaiting a decision in the Ninth Circuit.

As the nation's former chief climate scientist, Dr. James Hansen, has declared in support of the youths, "[judicial relief] may be the best, the last, and, at this late stage, the only real chance to preserve a habitable planet for young people and future generations."[13]

The ATL cases could produce unparalleled legal leverage to confront the climate emergency. A public trust remedy can scale to the systemic causes of harm—the fossil fuel energy system—obviating the traditional statutory "whack-a-mole" approach that would require challenging the many thousands of scattered actions under the government's energy policy. While a court will not devise the pathways to decarbonization, it can force the other branches to do so. By supervising, but not devising, the policy, the courts would perform their constitutionally appointed role.

The courts have multiple powers to affect federal action. They could compel the other branches of government to address the crisis with all deliberate speed. They can issue swift and urgent "backstop" injunctions to prevent further injury to the climate system. Courts are situated to stop on-shore and offshore drilling, fracking, permits for coal-fired plants, and proposals for export facilities.

Importantly, atmospheric trust litigation brings a rigorous fact-finding process to the climate emergency. Investigators have exposed documents indicating that some industry executives and high government officials were warned long ago about the probable climate impacts of fossil fuels but manipulated the American public by spreading misinformation about climate science.[14] Unlike the other two branches, courts have a time-tested adversarial process that relies on evidence and standards of proof. As lead attorney Julia Olson notes, in a court of law, "alternative facts are considered perjury."

Last, courts bring a singular type of integrity to the prospect of climate action. Judges cannot be personally lobbied in the sense that legislatures can, and federal judges are not allowed to engage in political causes. Citizens have a distinctive platform to make their interests known. Organizations, elected leaders, and uniquely situated individuals and groups can submit amicus "friend of the court" briefs to the court. The *Juliana* case drew several high-visibility amicus briefs, including one filed on behalf of youths worldwide that drew more than 36,000 signatures within several days.

If the planet remains habitable at the end of the century, it may well be because extraordinary jurists across the world fulfilled their constitutional role and enforced the rights of young people as beneficiaries of the atmospheric trust—and did so before climate tipping points rendered the law altogether moot. Atmospheric Trust Litigation was conceived for precisely this moment.

Nature's Trust: Fiduciary Governance and Ecological Legacy

In sum, environmental law came unmoored from the expectations that once anchored it. Through the permitting system, modern agencies use the statutes to legalize the very harm they were designed to prevent. Statutes

Components	Political model	Trust model
Congress/state legislatures	Politicians	Trustees
Agency staffers	Politicized bureaucrats	Agents of the trustees
Citizens	Political constituents	Trust beneficiaries
Natural resources	Diffused, intangible parts of the environment	Quantifiable, valuable assets

remain necessary as administrative tools, but time-tested fiduciary principles enforceable against government agencies must define the boundaries of right and wrong. The trust approach steers the government away from oligarchy and back toward democracy by imposing a basic duty to serve the citizen.

The primordial rights instilled by the trust have surfaced at epic times in history. They forced the Magna Carta on the English monarchy in 1215 and propelled Mahatma Gandhi's great Salt March to the sea in 1930. Americans must assert those rights again in defense of democracy, humanity, and all generations to come.

Beyond the legal and civic realm, the trust evokes a moral language. It taps a wellspring of human understanding that remains instinctive, passion-bound, and deeply shared among citizens of distant cultures. The same trust principles that flow through a judge's pen can be preached from a pulpit or spoken as the last words from a grandmother to her grandchildren anywhere in the world—because the trust encompasses a moral instruction to protect our children's rightful legacy. This expectation transcends all governments, cultures, and peoples on Earth.

Our moment in human history carries unfathomable importance. Actions taken over the past few decades will reverberate far into the future as the consequences of an ill-considered past. Guiding humanity to a safe ecological path becomes the most urgent call on Earth, for it will determine how well—or even whether—humanity will survive on the planet. The current generation's work of protecting Earth's ecological endowment must revive the everlasting covenant that protects humanity's future in trust.

CONCLUSION: ACHIEVING DEMOCRACY

Ganesh Sitaraman

The essays in *Democracy Unchained* offer a kaleidoscopic set of answers to a single question: what will it take for democracy to survive? Some of the authors focus on diagnosing the current crisis of democracy, others on how government no longer seems responsive to popular preferences. Some focus on institutional challenges at every level—states, bureaucracies, political parties, educational institutions, philanthropy—and others on challenges at the level of core social and political values. At times, these individual analyses and the collective impact of *Democracy Unchained* might leave many with a daunting, uncomfortable feeling: democracy might not make it.

But the title of the volume, *Democracy Unchained*, isn't simply a warning about populism run amok, about the fears of an unregulated democracy that worried the ancient Greeks and the American founders. The title indicates a chance, an opportunity, to think about what might happen when our democracy is unchained from what currently restricts its movement—from economic inequality and social fracturing, from structural racism and institutional pathologies. What would it mean to let democracy break free—to achieve democracy?

If we are going to achieve democracy, however, we need to know what preconditions are needed for democracy to work. Across these chapters, three elements rise to the top: political democracy, economic democracy, and a united democracy. Many of the essays illustrate how unrepresentative our political democracy has become. On issue after issue, majorities of the American people want action, and yet nothing happens. Climate change, gun control, Social Security, wages, health care—on these issues, and on others, majority preferences have little sway. This crisis in representation has been well documented by political scientists in recent years. Studies show that elected representatives are more responsive to the views of wealthy people and corporations than to those of ordinary Americans.

The wealthy are more likely to vote, contribute to campaigns, reach out to their members of Congress, and volunteer. They are more likely to run for office themselves. And they are better represented by lobbyists in Washington. It is no surprise that studies of policy outcomes have concluded that ordinary people have effectively no influence over public policy—and that the views of the wealthy matter a great deal.

In Congress, the executive branch, and the courts, our system allows moneyed interests to gain disproportionate influence. Congress is beset by lobbyists for big corporations and wealthy individuals, while ordinary families have few lobbyists advocating for their interests. In the executive branch, high-level appointees roll back and forth from government into the precise firms and industries they are supposed to be regulating. The last four Democratic secretaries of the treasury, for example, worked in finance before or after (or both before *and* after) their service. Despite his stated aim to "drain the swamp," President Donald Trump has appointed more than 180 lobbyists to government positions. The courts have always been unrepresentative by design—a legal check on politics—but they too are captured. Most federal judges come from private practice representing corporate clients; only a small handful have worked in nonprofits or had experience in consumer protection or similar areas.

Of course, our constitutional system was built to constrain majority preferences and protect minority interests—but not like this. Our system of government does build in veto-gates that make it hard to pass legislation. Among other things, we have a bicameral legislature, the presidential veto, Supreme Court review, committees in Congress, the filibuster, and federalism. The authors in this book have gone further and showed how current political dynamics have given these institutional features even more bite than was intended. For example, Jacob Hacker and Paul Pierson argue that asymmetric polarization combined with an anti-government ideology has meant that Congress is largely at the mercy of an extreme faction of the Republican Party that uses institutional rules to play power politics.

But although it is important to protect minority interests from the tyranny of the majority, the problem we face today is the *tyranny of the minority*. Majority preferences are almost never passed into law, and if the only minority interests being protected are those of the wealthy and well connected, that is hardly democratic. The problem, of course, goes even deeper because our system has never quite achieved the ideal of representative democracy. For starters, African Americans and women were locked out of representative government in America for generations. And today, voting practices like Tuesday voting and onerous registration requirements make it hard for everyone to have voice in the political system at a basic level.

One of the central tasks today, then, is structurally reforming the basic institutions of political democracy so our representative democracy can truly be representative of all the people. This will mean changes to our electoral institutions, from rules on gerrymandering to voter registration to the practice of voting. It will mean changes to our basic structures of government, to stop the revolving door and root out corruption from lobbying. And it will mean reforming campaign finance laws so that members of Congress can focus on representing their constituents instead of the wealthy.

A second set of chapters describe the economic crisis facing America and gesture at its relationship to democracy: the disproportionate influence of big money in politics, the effect on workers and families of neoliberalism's deregulatory approach to the economy, the unregulated big tech companies and the rise of surveillance capitalism, and the outsized and unchecked power of philanthropy. While these chapters discuss a variety of sectors, at their core is a common theme: concentrated economic power is incompatible with democracy.

The reasons why have been well understood from at least the time of the ancient Greeks and Romans. Economic power can be exerted against people directly to threaten their livelihoods and reduce their freedom. Intrusions on privacy, serf-like labor contracts, and horrible working conditions are all examples of economic power being used as a tool for dominating individuals. Economic power can also be used to influence and capture government, thereby allowing the economically powerful to rig the rules to further serve their interests. Lobbying, the revolving door, and a campaign finance system based on raising money from the rich are the most prominent vectors of influence in this category. And although it would be a big step forward, simply banning any of these practices will not be enough because of what scholars call the "hydraulic problem." Money is like water; it will always find a crack through which to flow.

What is needed to achieve democracy, then, is relative economic equality. Without it, the rich will find a way to oppress the poor, or the poor will revolt and overthrow the rich—and neither oligarchy nor instability are desirable fates. For generations of Americans past, the lesson was that democracy required a measure of economic equality. As Noah Webster, the author of the first American dictionary, once wrote, an "equality of property is the very soul of a republic." Or as President Theodore Roosevelt put it, "There can be no real political democracy unless there is something approaching an economic democracy."

Today, achieving economic democracy has two components: relative economic equality and an economy in which no person or corporation is so powerful that it can dominate government or the economy. Let's start with relative economic equality. Over the last generation, the United States has become more and more unequal. The top 1 percent of people in the country now take home more than 15 percent of the nation's income. Meanwhile, for many families, wages have been stagnant, and the only way to make ends meet is to take on mountains of debt.

Corporations have also gained in power. Sector after sector of the economy has become increasingly concentrated, with a small number of firms capturing the dominant market share. Pick your favorite area: airlines, cable/internet, prescription drugs, beer, rental cars. The new era of monopoly power means higher prices and less competition, more difficult entry for startups and small businesses, and, perhaps most important, the chance for the biggest players to lobby and capture the government to preserve their dominant positions in the market.

If, as centuries of statesmen have posited, political democracy requires economic democracy, then the current situation cannot stand. Americans must reassert democratic control over the economy. This would include policies to help address economic inequality at the personal and family levels—from increasing wages to strengthening labor unions, from raising tax rates on the wealthiest people to investing in universal public goods that expand opportunity for everyone.

It also requires addressing economic power at the firm level. Here, Americans have long pursued two different, but often interconnected, strategies: antitrust and regulation. Under the antitrust approach, economic democracy is maintained by breaking up big corporations into smaller ones so that no entity has too much power. With a regulatory approach, economic democracy is preserved when the government regulates firms. Some of these regulations, like safe workplaces or environmental regulations, apply to all firms. In some sectors, however, firms are regulated as public utilities; they remain in place as effective monopolies, but are constrained so they act in the public interest. Achieving economic democracy today will require reinvigorating both antitrust and regulation.

At its core, democracy is a government in which we the people decide our fate together. That requires a shared vision for the future, at least in some very basic sense. As a result, one of the great threats to democracy is social fracturing—the increasingly fundamental divisions in our values and ambitions as a society. Extreme political tribalism, economic divisions between rich and poor, structural racism, and geographic divisions all place considerable strain on the central premise of democracy: that we the people can come together to determine our country's future.

Historically, the solution to the challenge of achieving a relatively united democracy was to have democracies operate in small geographic areas. Political philosophers called this the "small republic thesis." For a republic to work, it had to be small, so that people shared the same beliefs and feelings and could deliberate together about their common good. Of course, the United States has always been a large and expansive country, so from the beginning the small republic thesis posed a problem. In *Federalist 10*, however, James Madison offered an alternative to the small republic thesis. He argued that in an extended republic, there would be so many different and dynamic views on different topics that entrenched factions would never coalesce. These different interests would clash, and, as a result, representatives would be able to focus on pursuing the public good.

Madison's theory is ingenious. But the extended republic thesis rested on a few critical assumptions: there would be many different interests in society, there would be a basic set of shared norms that operated as a foundation below those interests, and there would be elected representatives who were above the clash of interests and felt duty-bound to act in the public interest. The challenge now, as some of the chapters in this volume point out, is that we are in an era of severe asymmetric polarization, that technology puts us in "filter bubbles" where we interact with like-minded people almost exclusively, and that our shared social values are sometimes contested at the level of first principles. Structural racism also persists, and individual racists are now bolder and more open than they have been in recent years. This fraying in our social fabric has placed the extended republic thesis under great strain.

But the situation is not hopeless. Throughout American history there have always been active efforts, albeit incomplete, to stitch together our country's social fabric. Public schools and land-grant colleges brought people from different walks of life together to gain an education, including in civics. The military draft brought men from different regions, nationalities, and ultimately races together, placed them in the greatest of dangers, and in the process turned them into a band of brothers. Economic policies—from the postal service offering free rural delivery to regulated industries in telecommunications and transportation—connected cities, small towns, and rural areas. Martin Luther King Jr.'s Poor People's Movement sought to unite poor people across races to achieve economic and racial justice simultaneously. This is not to say that there were not mighty divisions throughout American history. There were. But at important junctures, Americans advanced policies that attempted to forge one nation from many. *E pluribus unum*. Americans today need to embrace policy choices that will stitch together a country with deep divisions.

Political democracy, economic democracy, and a united democracy: achieving all three of these preconditions for democracy is a Herculean task. But the magnitude of the challenge also illustrates the majesty of democracy. Democracy is not something that is easy to achieve, nor is it inevitable. It is fragile and elusive. The historian Arthur Schlesinger Jr. once wrote that the American project has often been seen both as an experiment and as destiny. Throughout our history, our greatest statesmen and observers have ebbed and flowed between these two views—the need for citizens to make the fragile democratic experiment succeed and the faith of citizens who knew a glorious future was secure.

These two views, however, are not in such stark opposition. Because the American democratic experiment has, in a sense, always been about destiny. In a democracy, the people themselves choose their destiny. And from the start, the core of the American experiment has been trying to figure out whether that proposition is a viable one. As Alexander Hamilton noted in the very first of the *Federalist Papers*, Americans would "decide the important question, whether societies of men are really capable or not of establishing good government from reflection and choice, or whether they are forever destined to depend for their political constitutions on accident and force."

Democracy, with its political, economic, and social preconditions, cannot be achieved in the sense of reaching a permanent, static, final outcome. Achieving democracy means embracing the experiment, it means striving constantly, actively, persistently to adapt as conditions change over time. This today is the task—to unchain democracy from what holds it back and to unchain ourselves from the feeling that we have lost control over our politics, economy, and society. We must once again grasp the fact that in a democracy, it is we the people who determine our destiny.

ACKNOWLEDGMENTS

This book grew from a conference on The State of American Democracy in 2017. The success of both that event and this book owes a great deal to the remarkable competence of my colleagues, Jane Mathison, Julie Min, Dan Moulthrop, Kaia Diringer, and Ginny O'Dell. Their considerable skill, deep commitment, personal graciousness, and dedication to the cause of a humane and robust democracy was essential to making this book a reality.

The same is true of my co-editors and colleagues, Bill Becker, Andrew Gumbel, and Bakari Kitwana. Their editorial skill, sound judgment on matters large and small, and great dedication is evident throughout the book. We, in turn, thank Carl Bromley at The New Press for encouraging and facilitating the evolution of a proposal into a book.

Democracy Unchained is a part of a larger effort to expand and deepen the conversation about restoring the promise of democracy in our time. For their advice and wisdom, we thank the members of the advisory committee: Carmen Ambar, the Reverend Dr. Andrew Barnett, Conyers Davis, Stephen Heintz, Bakari Kitwana, Marvin Krislov, Nancy MacLean, Dan Moulthrop, Grant Oliphant, John Powers, Nick Rathod, Vikki Spruill, and Mary Evelyn Tucker.

Thanks to those whose generosity helped to launch the State of American Democracy Project, particularly Charlotte and Chuck Fowler and Adam and Melony Lewis, Chip Haus, and Debbie Gruelle. We are grateful to Stephen Heintz and the staff at the Pocantico Center of The Rockefeller Brothers Fund for their warm hospitality and support for an important meeting of the contributors. Finally, heartfelt thanks to John Powers, a longtime friend and unsung hero in the movement to build a durable, resilient, and democratic future. This book is dedicated to him.

NOTES

Dedication

1. Lao Tzu, *Tao Te Ching*, trans. Stephen Mitchell (New York: Harper, 1988).

Foreword

1. David Frum, "How to Build an Autocracy," *The Atlantic*, March 2017, 59.

Introduction

1. Reinhold Niebuhr, *The Irony of American History* (New York: Scribner, 1952), 174.

2. Charles Lindblom, *Politics and Markets* (New York: Basic Books, 1977), 356.

3. Ganesh Sitaraman, *The Crisis of the Middle-Class Constitution* (New York: Knopf, 2017).

4. Edwin Black, *IBM and the Holocaust* (New York: Three Rivers Press, 2002).

5. Adam Smith, *The Wealth of Nations* (New York: The Modern Library, 1937/1776), 128.

6. Thomas Piketty, *Capitalism in the Twenty-First Century* (Cambridge, MA: Harvard University Press, 2014); Walter Scheidel, *The Great Leveler* (Princeton, NJ: Princeton University Press, 2017).

7. Quoted in Greg Grandin, *The End of the Myth* (New York: Metropolitan Books, 2019), 195; "Report by the Policy Planning Staff," February 24, 1948, history.state.gov /historicaldocuments/frus1948v01p2d4.

8. Grandin, *The End of the Myth*; Daniel Immerwahr, *How to Hide an Empire* (New York: Farrar, Straus and Giroux, 2019).

9. "Speech at the Federal Convention, June 29, 1787," in *James Madison Writings*, ed. Jack N. Rakove (New York: The Library of America, 1999), 116.

10. Grandin, *The End of the Myth*; Richard Falk, *Power Shift* (London: ZED Books, 2016); Chalmers Johnson, *The Sorrows of EMPIRE* (New York: Metropolitan Books, 2004); John Dower, *The Violent American Century* (Chicago: Haymarket Books, 2017); Tom Engelhardt, *A Nation Unmade by War* (Chicago: Haymarket Books, 2018); Andrew Bacevich, *Twilight of the American Century* (Notre Dame, IN: Notre Dame University Press, 2018).

11. Shoshana Zuboff, *The Age of Surveillance Capitalism* (New York: Public Affairs, 2019).

12. Oliver Sacks, "The Machine Stops," *New Yorker,* February 11, 2019, 28–29.

13. Zuboff, *Age of Surveillance,* 513.

14. Sheldon Wolin calls this "inverted democracy" in *Democracy Incorporated* (Princeton, NJ: Princeton University Press, 2008/2017).

15. Steven Levitsky and Daniel Ziblatt, *How Democracies Die* (New York: Crown, 2018), 222–23; Thomas Mann, a Democrat, and Norman Ornstein, a Republican, go further, writing "the Republican Party, has become an insurgent outlier—ideologically extreme; contemptuous of the inherited social and economic policy regime; scornful of compromise; unpersuaded by conventional understanding of facts, evidence, and science; and dismissive of the legitimacy of its political opposition" in *It's Even Worse Than It Looks* (New York: Basic Books, 2012). Jacob Hacker and Paul Pierson note further that "the GOP has learned how to win politically by fostering dysfunction, to achieve its policy goals not by brokering agreement but by breaking government" in *American Amnesia* (New York: Simon & Schuster, 2016), 166; Sahil Chinoy, "What Happened to America's Political Center of Gravity?" *New York Times*, June 26, 2019.

16. Lest we forget our history, assaults on government go back to the anti-Federalists and to John C. Calhoun's nullification fight, and the battles over states' rights and slavery. The Reagan presidency revived the war on government with the neoliberal faith in the infallibility of unregulated markets. Deregulated markets are supposedly more efficient than government at a lower cost. No matter how many times the theory fails in practice, it rises again to terrorize the poor and the powerless, like Jason in multiple sequels of *Friday the Thirteenth*. For reasons of greed and less obvious reasons buried in the human psyche, the true believers of neo-liberalism aimed all along to render the government incapable of solving even the most basic of problems. The predictable results are a festering accumulation of structural failures, public disrepair, growing public anger, and partisan animosity.

17. Michael Lewis, *The Fifth Risk* (New York: Norton, 2018).

18. Jane Mayer, "Trump TV," *New Yorker*, March 11, 2019; see also Theda Skocpol and Vanessa Williamson, *The Tea Party and the Remaking of Republican Conservatism* (New York: Oxford University Press, 2012).

19. Lewis, *The Fifth Risk*.

20. Levitsky and Ziblatt, *How Democracies Die*, 146. The "erosion of democratic norms," they write, "began in the 1980s and 1990s and accelerated in the 2000s," p. 9.

21. Tim Wu, "What the Public Wants, It Doesn't Get," *New York Times*, March 5, 2019.

22. Benjamin Page and Martin Gilens, *Democracy in America?* (Chicago: University of Chicago Press, 2017), 68.

23. Zuboff, *Age of Surveillance*, 519.

24. *Federalist Paper* 51.

25. C.S. Lewis, *Present Concerns* (New York: Harcourt Brace Jovanovich, 1986), 17–20.

26. Mayer, "Trump TV," 40; Jonathan Mahler and Jim Rutenberg, "How Murdoch's Empire of Influence Remade the World," *New York Times*, April 4, 2019; Skocpol and Williamson, *The Tea Party*, 202.

27. Marvin Kalb, *Enemy of the People* (Washington, DC: Brookings, 2018), 7.

28. Benjamin Barber, *Strong Democracy* (Berkeley: University of California Press, 1984); Frances Moore Lappé and Adam Eichen, *Daring Democracy* (Boston: Beacon Press, 2017); and the classic defense of politics by Bernard Crick, *In Defence of Politics* (New York: Penguin Books, 1983).

29. Andrew Gumbel, *Down for the Count* (New York: New Press, 2016); Ari Berman, *Give Us the Ballot* (New York: Farrar, Straus and Giroux, 2015); David Daley, *Ratf**ked** (New York: Liveright, 2016).

30. John Dryzek, et.al., "The Crisis of Democracy and the Science of Deliberation," *Science* 363, no. 6432 (March 15, 2019): 1144–6; Ilya Somin's perspective to the contrary in *Democracy and Political Ignorance,* 2d. ed. (Stanford, CA: Stanford University Press, 2016), 58–62.

Populism and Democracy, Yascha Mounk

1. "Freedom in the World 2019: Democracy in Retreat," Freedom House, freedomhouse.org/report/freedom-world/freedom-world-2019/democracy-in-retreat.

2. See Freedom House report, "Freedom in the World 2019."

3. Yascha Mounk and Jordan Kyle, "What Populists Do to Democracy," *The Atlantic*, December 26, 2018.

4. "I Have a Dream" speech by the Reverend Martin Luther King Jr. at the Lincoln Memorial for the March on Washington for Jobs and Freedom, August 28, 1963, Stanford University Martin Luther King, Jr. Research and Education Institute, kinginstitute.stanford.edu/king-papers/documents/i-have-dream-address-delivered-march-washington-jobs-and-freedom.

5. "A More Perfect Union" speech by Senator Barack Obama at the Constitution Center on March 18, 2008, constitutioncenter.org/amoreperfectunion.

Reconstructing Our Constitutional Democracy, K. Sabeel Rahman

1. *Federalist Paper* 10.

2. "Debunking the Voter Fraud Myth," Brennan Center for Justice, January 2017, www.brennancenter.org/analysis/debunking-voter-fraud-myth.

3. See, for example, "Written Testimony of Chiraag Bains to the House of Representatives on H.R.1, the For the People Act," Demos, February 2019, www.demos

.org/testimony-and-public-comment/written-testimony-chiraag-bains-house-hr-1
-people-act#footnoteref6_9ntid3x.

4. See Phoebe Henninger, Marc Meredith, and Michael Morse, "Who Votes With-out Identification? Using Affidavits from Michigan to Learn About the Potential Impact of Strict Photo Voter Identification Laws," July 2018, esra.wisc.edu/papers /HMM.pdf.; Bernard Fraga and Michael Miller, "Who Does Voter ID Legislation Keep from Voting?" December 2018, www.dropbox.com/s/lz7zvtyxxfe5if8 /FragaMiller_TXID_2018.pdf?dl=0.

5. Erick Trickey, "Where Did the Term Gerrymander Come From?" *Smithsonian Magazine*, July 20, 2017, www.smithsonianmag.com/history/where-did-term -gerrymander-come-180964118.

6. Sam Wang, "Gerrymanders, Part 1: Busting the Both-Sides Do It Myth," Princeton Election Consortium, December 30, 2012, election.princeton.edu/2012/12 /30/gerrymanders-part-1-busting-the-both-sides-do-it-myth.

7. *Gill v. Whitford*, 138 S. Ct. 1916, 1923 (2018).

8. For example, see *Shaw v. Reno*, 509 U.S. 630 (1993); *Shaw v. Hunt*, 517 U.S. 899 (1996).

9. *Rucho v. Common Cause*, 588 U.S. ___ (2019).

10. Rick Hasen, "The Gerrymandering Decision Drags the Supreme Court Further into the Mud," *New York Times,* June 27, 2019.

11. 424 U.S. 1 (1976).

12. *Citizens United v. FEC*, 558 U.S. 310 (2010).

13. *McCutcheon v. FEC*, 572 U.S. 185 (2014).

14. Ashley Balcerzak, "Study: Most Americans Want to Kill 'Citizens United' with Constitutional Amendment," Center for Public Integrity, Public Radio International, May 10, 2018, www.pri.org/stories/2018-05-10/study-most-americans-want -kill-citizens-united-constitutional-amendment.

15. Joshua Cohen, "Democracy v. Citizens United?" University of Chicago Law School, April 20, 2011, www.law.uchicago.edu/recordings/joshua-cohen-democracy -v-citizens-united.

16. Robert Post, *Citizens Divided: Campaign Finance Reform and the Constitution* (Cambridge, MA: Harvard University Press, 2016).

17. See Zephyr Teachout, *Corruption in America: From Benjamin Franklin's Snuff Box to Citizens United* (Cambridge, MA: Harvard University Press, 2014); Lawrence Lessig, *Republic Lost, How Money Corrupts Congress—and a Plan to Stop It* (New York: Twelve Publishing, 2011).

18. "Outside Spending," Open Secrets, Center for Responsive Politics, www .opensecrets.org/outsidespending.

19. See generally, Martin Gilens, *Affluence and Influence: Economic Inequality and Political Power in America* (Princeton, NJ: Princeton University Press, 2012). For

an in-depth case study corroborating those general findings in a large American city, see Laura Williamson, "Big Money in the Charm City," Demos, March 6, 2019, www.demos.org/sites/default/files/2019-03/Big%20Money%20in%20Charm%20City.pdf.

20. "Automatic Voter Registration and Modernization in the States," Brennan Center for Justice, March 29, 2019, www.brennancenter.org/analysis/voter-regis tration-modernization-states.

21. "Automatic Voter Registration," Brennan Center.

22. Automatic Voter Registration Act, H.R. 2840, 115th Cong. § 1 (2017).

23. For the People Act of 2019, H.R. 1, 116th Cong. § 1 (2019).

24. "Independent Redistricting Commissions," *Ballotpedia*, ballotpedia.org /Independent_redistricting_commissions.

25. "Number of States Using Redistricting Commissions Growing," *Associated Press*, March 21, 2019, www.apnews.com/4d2e2aea7e224549af61699e51c955dd.

26. For the People Act of 2019, *supra* note 23.

27. For the People Act of 2019, *supra* note 23.

28. 369 U.S. 186 (1962).

29. 377 U.S. 533 (1964).

30. Jamelle Bouie, "The Senate Is as Much a Problem as Trump," *New York Times*, May 10, 2019.

31. See, generally, Bill Bishop, *The Big Sort: Why the Clustering of Like-Minded America Is Tearing Us Apart* (New York: Houghton Mifflin, 2008). See also Richard Florida, "America's 'Big Sort' Is Only Getting Bigger," *CityLab*, October 25, 2016, www .citylab.com/equity/2016/10/the-big-sort-revisited.

32. *White v. Regester*, 412 U.S. 755, 765 (1973).

33. Lani Guinier, *The Tyranny of the Majority: Fundamental Fairness in Repre-sentative Democracy* (New York: Free Press, 1994), 55.

34. See, for example, Richard John, *Network Nation: Inventing American Tele-communications* (Cambridge, MA: Belknap Press, 2010).

35. C. Thi Nguyen, "Echo Chambers and Epistemic Bubbles," *Episteme* (2018): 1–21.

36. See, for example, Zeynep Tufecki, "It's the (Democracy-Poisoning) Golden Era of Free Speech," *Wired*, January 2018; Tim Wu, *Attention Merchants: The Epic Scramble to Get Inside Our Heads* (New York: Knopf, 2017); Mostafa M. El-Bermaway, "Your Filter Bubble Is Destroying Democracy," *Wired*, November 18, 2016.

37. See, for example, Thomas Piketty, *Capital in the Twenty-First Century* (2013) (homing our interest on wealth disparities and differential rates of return to labor and capital); Joseph Stiglitz, *The Price of Inequality: How Today's Divided Society Endangers Our Future* (New York: W.W. Norton & Co., 2012) (focusing on the inter-play between political and economic inequality); Robert J. Gordon, *The Rise and Fall of American Growth: The U.S. Standard of Living Since the Civil War* (Princeton, NJ:

Princeton University Press, 2016) (providing a *longue durée* account of American economic growth and providing a pessimistic view of growth in the near future).

38. See, for example, Larry Bartels, *Unequal Democracy: The Political Democracy of the New Gilded Age*, 2d. ed. (Princeton, NJ: Princeton University Press, 2016); Martin Gilens, *Affluence and Influence: Economic Inequality and Political Power in America* (Princeton University Press, 2014); Jacob Hacker and Paul Pierson, *Winner-Take-All Politics: How Washington Made the Rich Richer—And Turned Its Back on the Middle Class* (New York: Simon & Schuster, 2011). See also Martin Gilens & Benjamin I. Page, "Testing Theories of American Politics: Elites, Interest Groups, and Average Citizens," *Perspectives on Politics* 12, no. 3 (2014): 564.

39. See David Weil, *The Fissured Workplace: Why Work Became So Bad for So Many and What Can Be Done to Improve It* (Cambridge, MA: Harvard University Press, 2014).

40. See, for example, *Janus v. AFSCME*, 138 S. Ct. 2448 (2018), *Epic Systems Corp. v. Lewis*, 138 S. Ct. 1612 (2018); Jed Purdy, "Beyond the Bosses' Constitution: The First Amendment and Class Entrenchment," *Columbia Law Review* 118, no.7 (2018): 2161.

41. See Kate Andrias, "The New Labor Law," *Yale Law Journal* 126, no. 1 (2016), 46–47.

42. See, for example, Matt Stoller, *Goliath: The 100-Year War Between Monopoly Power and Democracy* (New York: Simon & Schuster, 2019); Zephyr Teachout, "Target Monopolies!" *Democracy Journal*, no. 45 (Summer 2017); Tim Wu, *The Curse of Bigness: Antitrust in the New Gilded Age* (New York: Columbia Global Reports, 2018).

43. Richard Rothstein, *The Color of Law: A Forgotten History of How Our Government Segregated America* (New York: Liveright Publishing: 2017).

44. Patrick Sharkey, *Stuck in Place: Urban Neighborhoods and the End of Progress Toward Racial Equality* (Chicago: University of Chicago Press: 2013).

45. See, for example, Kathryn J. Edin and H. Luke Shaefer, *$2.00 A Day: Living on Almost Nothing in America* (New York: Houghton Mifflin Harcourt, 2016), 32; Daniel L. Hatcher, *The Poverty Industry: The Exploitation of America's Most Vulnerable Citizens* (New York: New York University Press, 2016), 22–24; Michael B. Katz, *The Undeserving Poor: America's Enduring Confrontation with Poverty* (New York: Pantheon Books, 1989).

46. William J. Novak, "Law and the Social Control of American Capitalism," *Emory Law Journal* 60, no. 2 (2010): 377, 393–97; K. Sabeel Rahman, *Democracy Against Domination* (New York: Oxford University Press, 2016).

47. Gillian Metzger, "Administrative Constitutionalism," *Texas Law Review* 91 (2013): 1897; K. Sabeel Rahman, "Constructing Citizenship," *Columbia Law Review* 118 (2019): 2447.

48. Sophia Z. Lee, "Race, Sex, and Rulemaking: Administrative Constitutionalism and the Workplace, 1960 to the Present," *Virginia Law Review* 96 (2010): 799; Sophia Z. Lee, *The Workplace Constitution from the New Deal to the New Right* (New York: Cambridge University Press, 2014).

49. Karen Tani, *States of Dependency: Welfare, Rights, and American Governance 1935–72* (New York: Cambridge University Press, 2016); Karen Tani, "Administrative Equal Protection: Federalism, the Fourteenth Amendment, and the Rights of the Poor," *Cornell Law Review* 100 (2015): 825.

50. See David Barton Smith, *The Power to Heal: Civil Rights, Medicare, and the Struggle to Transform America's Healthcare System* (Nashville, TN: Vanderbilt University Press, 2016); Olatunde Johnson, "Beyond the Private Attorney General: Equality Directives in American Law," *New York University Law Review* 87, no. 5 (November 2012).

51. See, for example, Kim Phillips-Fein, *Invisible Hands* (New York: W.W. Norton & Co., 2009); Gillian Metzger, "1930s Redux: The Administrative State Under Siege," *Harvard Law Review*, 131 (November 2017): 2–4.

52. See, for example, Nancy Maclean, *Democracy in Chains: The Deep History of the Radical Right's Stealth Plan for America* (New York: Penguin Random House, 2017).

53. See, for example, *Kisor v. Wilkie*, 588 U.S. ___ (2019); *Gundy v. United States*, 588 U.S. ___ (2019).

54. Amanda Shanor, "The New Lochner," *Wisconsin Law Review* 133 (2016); Amanda Shanor and Robert L. Post, "Adam Smith's First Amendment," *Harvard Law Review Forum* 128, no. 165 (2015); Jeremy Kessler and David Pozen, "The Search for an Egalitarian First Amendment," *Columbia Law Review* 118, no. 7 (2018): 1953; Amy Kapczynski, "The Lochnerized First Amendment and the FDA: Toward a More Democratic Political Economy," *Columbia Law Review* 118, no. 7 (2018): 179.

Restoring Healthy Party Competition, Jacob S. Hacker and Paul Pierson

1. Paul Pierson and Eric Schickler, *Madison's Constitution Under Stress: A Developmental Analysis of Political Polarization*, unpublished manuscript (2019).

2. Thomas E. Mann and Norman J. Ornstein, *It's Even Worse Than It Looks: How the American Constitutional System Collided with the New Politics of Extremism* (New York: Basic Books, 2012), xiv.

3. Jacob S. Hacker and Paul Pierson, "Confronting Asymmetric Polarization," in *Solutions to Political Polarization in America*, ed. Nathaniel Persily (New York: Cambridge University Press, 2015), 59–72; Jacob S. Hacker and Paul Pierson, *American Amnesia: How the War on Government Led Us to Forget What Made America Prosper* (New York: Simon & Schuster, 2016).

4. Jacob M. Grumbach, "From Backwaters to Major Policymakers: Policy Polarization in the States, 1970–2014," *Perspectives on Politics* 16, no. 2 (June 2018): 416–435.

5. Mark Tushnet, "Constitutional Hardball," *John Marshall Law Review* 37, no. 2 (2004): 523–553; Joseph Fishkin and David E. Pozen, "Asymmetric Constitutional Hardball," *Columbia Law Review* 118, no. 3 (2018): 915–982.

6. Steven Levitsky and Daniel Ziblatt, *How Democracies Die* (New York: Crown, 2018).

7. Marty Cohen et al., *The Party Decides: Presidential Nominations Before and After Reform* (Chicago: University of Chicago Press, 2008).

8. Jacob S. Hacker and Paul Pierson, *Winner-Take-All Politics: How Washington Made the Rich Richer—and Turned Its Back on the Middle Class* (New York: Simon & Schuster, 2010); Hacker and Pierson, *American Amnesia*.

9. Facundo Alvaredo et al., "The Top 1 Percent in International and Historical Perspective," *Journal of Economic Perspectives* 27, no. 3 (2013): 3–20.

10. Adam Bonica et al., "Why Hasn't Democracy Slowed Rising Inequality?" *Journal of Economic Perspectives* 27, no. 3 (Summer 2013): 103–124. Data for 2018 from Adam Bonica, Twitter post, 4 June 2019, 5:31 pm, twitter.com/adam_bonica/status /1136067959858712576.

11. Theda Skocpol and Alexander Hertel-Fernandez, "The Koch Network and Republican Party Extremism," *Perspectives on Politics* 14, no. 2 (September 2016): 681–699.

12. Hacker and Pierson, *American Amnesia*, 213–227.

13. Jeffrey M. Berry and Sarah Sobieraj, *The Outrage Industry: Political Opinion Media and the New Incivility* (New York: Oxford University Press, 2013).

14. Theda Skocpol and Vanessa Williamson, *The Tea Party and the Remaking of Republican Conservativism* (New York: Oxford University Press, 2012); Matt Grossman and David A. Hopkins, *Asymmetric Politics: Ideological Republicans and Group Interest Democrats* (New York: Oxford University Press, 2016).

15. Jonathan A. Rodden, *Why Cities Lose: The Deep Roots of the Urban-Rural Political Divide* (New York: Basic Books, 2019).

16. Mann and Ornstein, *It's Even Worse Than It Looks*; Hacker and Pierson, *American Amnesia*.

17. Geoffrey Kabaservice, *Rule and Ruin: The Downfall of Moderation and the Destruction of the Republican Party, from Eisenhower to the Tea Party* (New York: Oxford University Press, 2012).

18. Hacker and Pierson, *American Amnesia*, 201–227.

19. Robert Mickey and Lucan Way, "Can American Democracy Survive the Loss of 'White' Dominance," paper presented at 2019 Successful Societies Program Meeting on European and American Populism and Group Boundaries, Banff, Alberta, Canada, May 10, 2019.

When Democracy Becomes Something Else: The Problem of Elections and What to Do About It, Andrew Gumbel

1. Quoted in Ed Pilkington, "US voter suppression: Why this Texas woman is facing five years' prison," *The Guardian*, August 28, 2018.

2. See Mark Niesse, "Black Senior Citizens Ordered Off Georgia Bus Taking Them to Vote," *Atlanta Journal-Constitution*, October 16, 2018.

3. Zachary Roth and Wendy R. Weiser, "This Is the Worst Voter Suppression We've Seen in the Modern Era," Brennan Center blog, November 2, 2018.

4. See Brennan Center for Justice, "Voting Laws Roundup 2017," www .brennancenter.org/analysis/voting-laws-roundup-2017.

5. The National Conference of State Legislatures keeps useful tabs on the number and variety of voter ID laws. See www.ncsl.org/research/elections-and-campaigns /voter-id.aspx.

6. GAO, *Issues Related to State Voter Identification Laws* (September 2014, revised February 27, 2015).

7. Martin Wiskcol, "Armey Wants to Transform Congressional GOP," *Orange County Register*, September 2, 2010.

8. David Wright and Eugene Scott, "GOP Congressman: Voter ID Law Will Help Republican Presidential Candidate," *CNN*, April 6, 2016.

9. Commission on Federal Election Reform, *Building Confidence in U.S. Elections* (Washington, DC: Center for Democracy and Election Management, 2005).

10. See Jennifer Rubin, "GOP Autopsy Goes Bold," *Washington Post*, March 18, 2013.

11. For an account of how the Tea Party in Texas used voter ID to beat out the moderates, even before there was a law on the books, see Andrew Gumbel, *Down for the Count: Dirty Elections and the Rotten History of Democracy in America* (New York: The New Press, 2016), 215–18.

12. For more on Kobach, see Andrew Gumbel, "Trump's 'Election Integrity' Group Is Waging War on the Right to Vote," *The Guardian*, September 17, 2017.

13. Quoted in Griffin Connolly, "Georgia Gov. Brian Kemp Brushes Off House Investigation of Voter Suppression," *Roll Call*, March 6, 2019.

14. On the popularity of making Election Day a holiday, see, for example, e.g. Julia Manchester, "Majority Says Election Day Should Be a Federal Holiday, Poll Finds," *The Hill*, November 6, 2018. On McConnell, see Felicia Sonmez, "McConnell Says Bill That Would Make Election Day a Federal Holiday Is a 'Power Grab' by Democrats," *Washington Post*, January 30, 2019.

15. The consultant was Tom Hofeller, the GOP's district mapmaker extraordinaire best known for flipping North Carolina's congressional delegation, after the 2010 Census, from a 7–6 split favoring the Democrats to a 9–4 split favoring the Republicans, with no significant shift in voting patterns. His secret study was uncovered

after his death. See Michael Wines, "Deceased G.O.P. Strategist's Hard Drives Reveal New Details on the Census Citizenship Question," *New York Times*, May 30, 2019.

16. National Association of Secretaries of State NASS statement, January 17, 2017.

17. The commissioner was Hans von Spakovsky. See John Wagner, "Trump Voting Fraud Panel Member Lamented Adding Democrats, 'Mainstream' Republicans," *Washington Post*, September 13, 2017.

18. See David Becker of the Center for Election Innovation and Research, quoted in Andrew Gumbel, "Why US Elections Remain 'Dangerously Vulnerable' to Cyber-Attacks," *The Guardian*, August 13, 2018.

19. The paper stock rule was introduced in Ohio in 2004 under the Republican secretary of state Kenneth Blackwell and was later rescinded. The Georgia legislature considered abolishing Sunday early voting in 2018, but the initiative ultimately failed.

20. The Texas case is *Veasey v. Perry*, later renamed *Veasey v. Abbott*. Judge Nelva Gonzales-Ramos's opinion was delivered on October 9, 2014, and was initially upheld on appeal. After the law was watered down under court supervision for the 2016 election, the Texas Senate softened some of its provisions. Judge Ramos did not find this sufficient, but the appeals court, ruling in April 2018, did.

21. See Patricia Mazzei, "Floridians Gave Ex-Felons the Right to Vote. Lawmakers Just Put a Big Obstacle in Their Way," *New York Times*, May 3, 2019.

22. The grassroots organizing group RepresentUs (www.represent.us) has helped sponsor a number of successful anti-corruption, campaign finance reform, and anti-gerrymandering ballot initiatives in North Dakota, Missouri, Colorado, New Jersey, and elsewhere. The advocacy group FairVote.org has been tirelessly promoting ranked choice voting for years. It was passed in Maine in 2016 (and, as noted, introduced to voters in 2018) and is on the ballot in New York for 2020.

The Best Answer to Money in Politics After *Citizens United*: Public Campaign Financing in the Empire State and Beyond, Chisun Lee

1. Chisun Lee is senior counsel at the Brennan Center for Justice at NYU School of Law. Hazel Millard, research and program associate at the Brennan Center, provided excellent research assistance.

2. Aída Chávez, "Small-Dollar Donors Are Playing a Growing Role in Congressional Campaigns," *The Intercept*, March 6, 2019, theintercept.com/2019/03/06/house-democrats-small-dollar-donations.

3. Moreland Commission to Investigate Public Corruption, *Preliminary Report*, December 2, 2013, 30, publiccorruption.moreland.ny.gov/sites/default/files/moreland_report_final.pdf.

4. Brennan Center for Justice, *The Case for Small Donor Public Financing in New York State*, February 26, 2019, 3, www.brennancenter.org/sites/default/files/publications /CaseforPublicFinancingNY_0.pdf.

5. Brennan Center, *Case for Small Donor Public Financing*, 2.

6. *Arizona Free Enter. Club PAC v. Bennett*, 564 U.S. 721, 754 (2011) ("We have said that governments 'may engage in public financing of election campaigns' and that doing so can further 'significant governmental interest[s],' such as the state interest in preventing corruption.") (quoting *Buckley v. Valeo*, 424 U.S. 1, 57 n.65, 92–93, 96 (1976)); *Buckley*, 424 U.S. at 93, 108 (upholding constitutionality of presidential public financing system and stating that public financing "furthers, not abridges, pertinent First Amendment values").

7. In New York City, which leans heavily toward one party, the real electoral competition tends to happen at the primary stage. In the last citywide elections in 2017, the available data show that 84 percent of primary candidates participated in the city's match program. In the general election, 64 percent of candidates participated in the match. New York City Campaign Finance Board, *Keeping Democracy Strong: New York City's Campaign Finance Program in the 2017 Citywide Elections*, August 2018, 3, www.nyccfb.info/pdf/2017_Post-Election_Report_2.pdf.

8. Elisabeth Genn, Sundeep Iyer, Michael Malbin, and Brendan Glavin, *Donor Diversity Through Public Matching Funds*, Brennan Center for Justice, May 14, 2012, 4–5, www.brennancenter.org/sites/default/files/legacy/publications/DonorDiversityRe port_WEB.PDF.

9. Brennan Center, *Case for Small Donor Public Financing*, 2; Martin Austermuhle, "Bowser Signs Bill Creating Public Financing Program for Political Campaigns—and Will Fund It," *WAMU American University Radio*, March 13, 2018, wamu.org/story/18/03/13/bowser-signs-bill-creating-public-financing-program -political-campaigns-will-fund; David M. Schwartz, "Suffolk Legislature OKs Public Financing of County Campaigns," *Newsday*, December 19, 2017, www.newsday .com/long-island/politics/suffolk-public-financing-1.15523881.

10. Bill Mahoney, "Democrats Capture State Senate with Biggest Majority Since 1912," *Politico*, November 7, 2018, www.politico.com/states/new-york/albany/story /2018/11/07/democrats-capture-state-senate-with-biggest-majority-since-1912-685748.

11. Vivian Wang, "How 3 Little Letters (I.D.C.) Are Riling Up New York Progressives," *New York Times*, September 11, 2018, www.nytimes.com/2018/09/11 /nyregion/independent-democratic-conference.html.

12. Kenneth Lovett, "Exclusive: Prominent Unions Pushing for New York State to Enact Public Campaign Financing System," *New York Daily News*, November 26, 2018, www.nydailynews.com/news/politics/ny-pol-unions-cwa-32bj-public-finacing -20181125-story.html.

13. "About Fair Elections for New York," Fair Elections for New York, fairelectionsny.org/about.

14. Hazel Millard, "Another Election Winner—Public Financing," Brennan Center for Justice, November 12, 2018, www.brennancenter.org/blog/another-election-winner-%E2%80%94public-financing.

15. Nancy Pelosi and John Sarbanes, "The Democratic Majority's First Order of Business: Restore Democracy," *Washington Post*, November 25, 2018, www.washingtonpost.com/opinions/the-democratic-majoritys-first-order-of-business-restore-democracy/2018/11/25/9aeb3dbe-ece2-11e8-96d4-0d23f2aaad09_story.html.

16. Peter Overby, "House Democrats Introduce Anti-Corruption Bill as Symbolic 1st Act," *NPR*, January 5, 2019, www.npr.org/2019/01/05/682286587/house-democrats-introduce-anti-corruption-bill-as-symbolic-first-act; Ella Nilsen, "House Democrats Just Passed a Slate of Significant Reforms to Get Money Out of Politics," *Vox*, March 8, 2019, www.vox.com/2019/3/8/18253609/hr-1-pelosi-house-democrats-anti-corruption-mcconnell.

17. Mitch McConnell, "Behold the Democrat Politician Protection Act," *Washington Post*, January 17, 2019, www.washingtonpost.com/opinions/call-hr-1-what-it-is-the-democrat-politician-protection-act/2019/01/17/dcc957be-19cb-11e9-9ebf-c5fed1b7a081_story.html.

18. Harry Enten, "Ranking the States from Most to Least Corrupt," *FiveThirtyEight*, January 23, 2015, fivethirtyeight.com/features/ranking-the-states-from-most-to-least-corrupt.

19. Ian Vandewalker and Lawrence Norden, "Small Donors Still Aren't as Important as Wealthy Ones," *The Atlantic*, October 18, 2016, www.theatlantic.com/politics/archive/2016/10/campaign-finance-fundraising-citizens-united/504425.

20. Chisun Lee, Katherine Valde, Benjamin Brickner, Douglas Keith, *Secret Spending in the States*, Brennan Center for Justice, June 26, 2016, 1–4, www.brennancenter.org/sites/default/files/analysis/Secret_Spending_in_the_States.pdf.

21. Martin Gilens and Benjamin I. Page, "Testing Theories of American Politics: Elites, Interest Groups, and Average Citizens," *Perspectives on Politics* 12, no. 3 (2014): 572, 575, scholar.princeton.edu/sites/default/files/mgilens/files/gilens_and_page_2014_-testing_theories_of_american_politics.doc.pdf; Peter K. Enns, Nathan J. Kelly, Jana Morgan, and Christopher Witko, "The Power of Economic Interests and the Congressional Economic Policy Agenda," *Scholars Strategy Network* (2016): 9, 15, scholars.org/sites/scholars/files/witko_the_power_of_economic_interests_and_the_congressional_economic_policy_agenda.pdf; Michael J. Barber, "Representing the Preferences of Donors, Partisans, and Voters in the US Senate," *Public Opinion Quarterly* 80, no. 1 (2016): 12, static1.squarespace.com/static/51841c73e4b04fc5ce6e8f15/t/56e97017b09f951532074016/1458139160759/POQ_Early_Access.pdf; David E. Broockman and Joshua L. Kalla, "Campaign Contributions Facilitate Access to Congressio-

nal Officials: A Randomized Field Experiment," *American Journal of Political Science* 60, no. 3 (2016): 553, onlinelibrary.wiley.com/doi/epdf/10.1111/ajps.12180.

22. Lawrence Norden, Brent Ferguson, and Douglas Keith, *Five to Four*, Brennan Center for Justice, January 13, 2016, 1, www.brennancenter.org/sites/default/files /publications/Five_to_Four_Final.pdf.

23. End Citizens United, *End Citizens United Action Fund: Clean Elections Battleground Survey Findings*, August 2018, 8, endcitizensunited.org/wp-content/uploads /2016/04/ECU-Clean-Elections-Deck.pdf.

24. Bradley Jones, "Most Americans Want to Limit Campaign Spending, Say Big Donors Have Greater Political Influence," Pew Research Center, May 8, 2018, www .pewresearch.org/fact-tank/2018/05/08/most-americans-want-to-limit-campaign -spending-say-big-donors-have-greater-political-influence.

25. "The Democracy Project Report," Democracy Project, June 26, 2018, www .democracyprojectreport.org/report.

26. Richard Briffault, "Reforming Campaign Finance Reform: The Future of Public Financing," in *Democracy by the People: Reforming Campaign Finance in America*, ed. Eugene D. Mazo and Timothy K. Kuhner (Cambridge: Cambridge University Press, 2019), 104.

27. Frances Dinkelspiel, "Public Financing Is Being Used for the 1st Time in Berkeley Election; How's It Going So Far?" *Berkeleyside*, August 8, 2018, www .berkeleyside.com/2018/08/08/campaign-notebook-how-public-financing-of-city -council-elections-is-working.

28. Martin Austermuhle, "Candidates Are Using D.C.'s New Public Financing Program to Challenge Powerful Incumbents," *DCist*, August 9, 2019, dcist.com/story /19/08/09/candidates-are-using-d-c-s-new-public-financing-program-to-challenge -powerful-incumbents.

29. Briffault provides a full overview of the different systems of public financing and the jurisdictions in which each has been used. Briffault, "Reforming Campaign Finance Reform," 107–10.

30. "Political Power," Movement for Black Lives, accessed June 19, 2019, policy .m4bl.org/political-power.

31. Monifa Bandele and Richard Wallace, "Public Financing of Elections Is a Matter of Racial Justice," *Gotham Gazette*, March 20, 2019, www.gothamgazette.com /opinion/8370-public-financing-of-elections-is-a-matter-of-racial-justice.

32. FY 2019 New York State Executive Budget: Good Government and Ethics Reform Article VII Legislation, Part F (N.Y. 2018), www.budget.ny.gov/pubs/archive /fy19/exec/fy19artVIIs/GGERArticleVII.pdf; FY 2018 New York State Executive Budget: Good Government and Ethics Reform Article VII Legislation, Part D (N.Y. 2017), www.budget.ny.gov/pubs/archive/fy18archive/exec/fy18artVIIbills/GGERArticleVII .pdf; 2016–17 New York State Executive Budget: Good Government and Ethics Reform

Article VII Legislation, Part C (N.Y. 2016), www.budget.ny.gov/pubs/archive /fy17archive/eBudget1617/fy1617artVIIbills/GGER.pdf; 2015–16 New York State Executive Budget: Public Protection and General Government Article VII Legislation, Part E (N.Y. 2015), www.budget.ny.gov/pubs/archive/fy1516archive/eBudget1516 /fy1516artVIIbills/PPGGArticleVII.pdf.

33. Overby, "House Democrats Introduce Anti-Corruption Bill as Symbolic 1st Act," January 5, 2019.

34. Jimmy Vielkind, "State Street: Albany Lawmakers Eye Campaign Finance Reform, but Activists Want More," *Wall Street Journal*, January 13, 2019, www.wsj .com/articles/state-street-albany-lawmakers-eye-campaign-finance-reform-but -activists-want-more-11547398800.

35. Andrew Cuomo, "2019 State of the State Address" (speech, Albany, New York, January 15, 2019), www.governor.ny.gov/news/video-audio-photos-rush-transcript -governor-cuomo-outlines-2019-justice-agenda-time-now.

36. For example, in 2015, former Assembly Speaker Sheldon Silver and former Senate Majority Leader Dean Skelos both stepped down due to corruption scandals involving major donors. The two legislative leaders were convicted on their respective corruption charges in 2018. Benjamin Weiser, "Sheldon Silver, Ex-New York Assembly Speaker, Gets 7-Year Prison Sentence," *New York Times*, July 27, 2018, www .nytimes.com/2018/07/27/nyregion/sheldon-silver-sentencing-prison-corruption .html; Vivian Wang, "Guilty, Again: Dean Skelos, Former Senate Leader, Is Convicted of Corruption in Retrial," *New York Times*, July 17, 2018, www.nytimes.com/2018/07 /17/nyregion/dean-skelos-corruption-son-senate-ny.html. In its preliminary report on public corruption in New York state, the Moreland Commission also provided several examples of Albany's pay-to-play culture, uncovered by the commission through its investigations. Moreland Commission, *Preliminary Report*, 33–34.

37. Chisun Lee and Nirali Vyas, "Analysis: New York's Big Donor Problem & Why Small Donor Public Financing Is an Effective Solution for Constituents and Candidates," Brennan Center for Justice, January 28, 2019, www.brennancenter.org/analysis/nypf.

38. Brennan Center, *Case for Small Donor Public Financing*, 2.

39. Brennan Center, *Case for Small Donor Public Financing*, 3.

40. Gilens and Page, "Testing Theories of American Politics," 572, 575; Enns et al., "The Power of Economic Interests," 9, 15; Barber, "Representing the Preferences of Donors," 12; Broockman and Kalla, "Campaign Contributions Facilitate Access," 553.

41. "The Brennan Center's Money in Politics Toolkit," Brennan Center for Justice, updated May 14, 2018, www.brennancenter.org/brennan-centers-money-politics -toolkit.

42. Michael J. Malbin, Peter W. Brusoe, and Brendan Glavin, "Small Donors, Big Democracy: New York City's Matching Funds as a Model for the Nation and States," *Election Law Journal* 11, no. 1 (2012): 16–17, www.cfinst.org/pdf/state/nyc-as-a-model _elj_as-published_march2012.pdf.

43. Malbin, Brusoe, and Glavin, "Small Donors, Big Democracy: New York City's Matching Funds as a Model for the Nation and States," 17.

44. Public Hearing, Before the New York City Charter Revision Commission, June 14, 2018 (statement of Michael Malbin, executive director of the Campaign Finance Institute), www1.nyc.gov/assets/charter/downloads/pdf/06-14-18-NYCCharter-PublicHearing.pdf.

45. Brennan Center, *Case for Small Donor Public Financing*, 8–9.

46. Spencer A. Overton, "The Participation Interest," *Georgetown Law Journal* 100 (2012): 1279, scholarship.law.gwu.edu/cgi/viewcontent.cgi?article=1167&context=faculty_publications.

47. Briffault, "Reforming Campaign Finance Reform," 109.

48. The Brennan Center analyzed profiles of small donors to New York City Council candidates in 2017 and to New York State Assembly candidates in 2018, using data from the New York State Board of Elections and the New York City Campaign Finance Board via datasets produced by the Campaign Finance Institute and the National Institute on Money in Politics. From this analysis, we determined that, in the city's poorest regions, City Council candidates received donations from 3,604 residents, while Assembly candidates received donations from only 522 residents.

49. The Brennan Center analyzed profiles of small donors to New York City Council candidates in 2017 and to New York State Assembly candidates in 2018, using data from the New York State Board of Elections and the New York City Campaign Finance Board via datasets produced by the Campaign Finance Institute and the National Institute on Money in Politics. From this analysis, we determined that, in the city's poorest regions, residents gave $167,407 in small-dollar private funds to City Council candidates, while donors to Assembly candidates only gave $36,274.

50. The Brennan Center analyzed profiles of small donors to New York City Council candidates in 2017 and to New York State Assembly candidates in 2018, using data from the New York State Board of Elections and the New York City Campaign Finance Board via datasets produced by the Campaign Finance Institute and the National Institute on Money in Politics. When public matching funds are included, small donors from New York City's poorest neighborhoods contributed $973,541 to City Council candidates. This represents 3.7 percent of total public and private funds raised by all City Council candidates ($26,251,299) during the 2017 election cycle. Small donations from these neighborhoods to Assembly candidates were $36,274 and represented 1.1 percent of funds raised by all Assembly candidates ($3,288,705) during the 2018 election cycle.

51. Malbin, Brusoe, and Glavin, "Small Donors, Big Democracy," 9.

52. Brennan Center, *Case for Small Donor Public Financing*, 9–10.

53. Samar Khurshid, "After Making History, James Seeks Change," *Gotham Gazette*, March 22, 2015, www.gothamgazette.com/government/5631-after-making-history-james-seeks-change.

54. Letitia James, "Public Financing" (speech, Unrig the System Summit, New Orleans, Louisiana, February 2–4, 2018), https://www.youtube.com/watch?v =MWxzfB2L_ks.

55. Russell Berman, "The Battle to Be Trump's Javert in New York," *The Atlantic*, August 6, 2018, www.theatlantic.com/politics/archive/2018/08/trump-teachout -attorney-general-new-york/566819; Brennan Center, *Case for Small Donor Public Financing*, 4.

56. Michael G. Miller, *Subsidizing Democracy: How Public Funding Changes Elections and How It Can Work in the Future* (Ithaca, NY: Cornell University Press, 2014), 63.

57. Michael J. Malbin and Brendan Glavin, *Small-Donor Matching Funds for New York State Elections: A Policy Analysis of the Potential Impact and Cost*, Campaign Finance Institute, February 2019, 10, www.cfinst.org/pdf/State/NY/Policy-Analysis _Public-Financing-in-NY-State_Feb2019_wAppendix.pdf.

58. Op-eds are listed on NY LEAD's news pages. "New York," NY LEAD, nylead .org/category/new-york-news.

59. Samar Khurshid, "Advocates and Senators Refute Assembly Democrats' Concerns with Campaign Finance Reform," *Gotham Gazette*, March 21, 2019, www .gothamgazette.com/state/8376-advocates-and-senators-refute-assembly -democrats-concerns-with-campaign-finance-reform.

60. Malbin and Glavin, *Small-Donor Matching Funds*, 12.

61. For the People Act of 2019, H.R. 1, 116th Cong. §§ 541(b)(1), 5114 (2019).

62. Brian Lehrer, "Assembly Speaker Heastie on Democratic Control," *WNYC*, January 30, 2019, www.wnyc.org/story/assembly-speaker-heastie-democratic -control.

63. Malbin and Glavin, *Small-Donor Matching Funds*, 10.

64. Research suggests that public financing programs may increase competition, having reduced the number of uncontested elections in certain jurisdictions where it is available to candidates. Kenneth Mayer, "Public Election Funding: An Assessment of What We Would Like to Know," *The Forum* 11, no. 3 (October 2013): 370–74, doi-org.proxy.library.nyu.edu/10.1515/for-2013-0049.

65. Act of April 1, 2019, ch. 59, Part XXX, § 1(a) (N.Y. 2019).

66. Lawrence Norden and Chisun Lee, "A Small-Donor Matching Public Campaign Finance System Is in Reach in New York," *New York Daily News*, April 8, 2019, www.nydailynews.com/opinion/ny-oped-campaign-finance-reform-in-reach-in -new-york-20190408-kj4ffkbfffeylbvdqjpltenfue-story.html.

Remaking the Presidency After Trump, Jeremi Suri

1. Alexis de Tocqueville, *Democracy in America*, trans., Arthur Goldhammer (New York: Library of America, 2004), 363–64.

2. Abraham Lincoln, First Inaugural Address, March 4, 1861, available at avalon .law.yale.edu/19th_century/lincoln1.asp.

3. See winstonchurchill.org/resources/quotes/the-worst-form-of-government.

4. See, among many others, Richard Neustadt, *Presidential Power* (New York: John Wiley, 1960); Clinton Rossiter, *The American Presidency* (Boston: Harcourt, 1960); Jeremi Suri, *The Impossible Presidency: The Rise and Fall of America's Highest Office* (New York: Basic Books, 2017).

5. See Stephen Skowronek, *The Politics Presidents Make: Leadership from John Adams to Bill Clinton* (Cambridge, MA: Harvard University Press, 1997); William G. Howell, *Thinking About the Presidency: The Primacy of Power* (Princeton, NJ: Princeton University Press, 2013); Suri, *The Impossible Presidency*.

6. For some of the best information about progressive millennial politics, and evidence of demographic and policy shifts in this direction, see the website for the Millennial Action Project: www.millennialaction.org.

7. There is a large body of literature on this topic in the field of "American Political Development." See, among others, Joanna L. Grisinger, *The Unwieldy State: Administrative Politics Since the New Deal* (New York: Cambridge University Press, 2012); Brian Balogh, *The Associational State: American Governance in the Twentieth Century* (Philadelphia: University of Pennsylvania Press, 2015); Karen Orren and Stephen Skowronek, *The Policy State: An American Predicament* (Cambridge, MA: Harvard University Press, 2017).

8. See Arthur Schlesinger Jr., *The Imperial Presidency* (Boston: Houghton Mifflin, 1973).

9. On this point, see Jack N. Rakove, *Original Meanings: Politics and Ideas in the Making of the Constitution* (New York: Alfred Knopf, 1996), 244–87; Suri, *The Impossible Presidency*, 3–22.

10. Jeffrey K. Tulis, *The Rhetorical Presidency* (Princeton, NJ: Princeton University Press, 1987).

Renewing the American Democratic Faith, Steven C. Rockefeller

1. *Federalist Paper* 45.

2. As quoted in Gordon S. Wood, *The Radicalism of the American Revolution* (New York: Alfred Knopf, 1992), 221. I have relied on Jill Lepore, *These Truths: A History of the United States* (New York: W.W. Norton & Company, 2018) for an account of the founding and basic information on American history.

3. Sidney Ahlstrom, *A Religious History of the American People* (New Haven: Yale University Press, 1972), 124.

4. Philip Gorsky, *American Covenant: A History of Civil Religion From the Puritans to the Present* (Princeton: Princeton University Press, 2017), 13–19.

5. Wood, *Radicalism*, 95–109.

6. Gorski, *American Covenant*, 23–26; Wood, *Radicalism*, 104.

7. Wood, *Radicalism*, 229–43.

8. Michael Sandel, *Democracy and Its Discontents: America in Search of a Public Philosophy* (Cambridge, MA: Harvard University Press, 1963), 3.

9. See "A Call to Civil Society: Why Democracy Needs Moral Truths," a joint project of the Institute for American Values and the University of Chicago Divinity School. The council's report was issued in 1998, but the moral decline it describes has only worsened, and its recommendations remain as relevant as when first released.

10. David Brooks, *The Second Mountain: The Quest for a Moral Life* (New York: Random House, 2019), 3–11.

11. Paul Mendes-Flohr, *Martin Buber: A Life of Faith and Doubt* (New Haven, CT: Yale University Press, 2019), 13.

12. For an example of a broad, ethical vision that integrates democratic and eco-logical values, see the Earth Charter. www.earthcharter.org.

13. Michael Sandel, *Justice: What's the Right Thing to Do?* (New York: Farrar, Strauss and Giroux, 2009), 261–69.

14. For information on the Collaborative for Spirituality in Education and the National Council, see www.spiritualityineducation.org.

American Land, American Democracy, Eric Freyfogle

1. I take up the cultural roots of our misuses of nature in various writings, includ-ing *A Good That Transcends: How U.S. Culture Undermines Environmental Reform* (Chicago: University of Chicago Press, 2017). My thoughts on how we distinguish good land use from bad also appear in various places, including most fully *Our Oldest Task: Making Sense of Our Place in Nature* (Chicago: University of Chicago Press, 2017).

2. I expand considerably on the comments here about private property and its overdue reform in *The Land We Share: Private Property and the Common Good* (Washington, DC: Island Press, 2003) and *On Private Property: Finding Common Ground on the Ownership of Land* (Boston: Beacon Press, 2007). My critique of the presumed public–private dichotomy in land ownership appears in *Agrarianism and the Good Society: Land, Culture, Conflict, and Hope* (Lexington: University Press of Kentucky, 2007), 83–106.

What Black Women Teach Us About Democracy, Andra Gillespie and Nadia E. Brown

1. Andra Gillespie and Nadia Brown published the expanded and more schol-arly version of this essay with data in "#BlackGirlMagic Demystified: Black Women as Voters, Partisans and Political Actors," *Phylon* (Winter 2019).

2. A gender gap can also be defined as the percentage of women voting for the winning candidate (regardless of party) minus the percentage of men voting for the

same candidate. M. Margaret Conway (2008) traces the gender gap back to 1964 using American National Election Study data. Howell and Day (2000) noticed the black gender gap. While they suspected that the source of the black gender gap differed from the source of the white gender gap, they acknowledged that this had not been sufficiently studied to offer a good explanation for the difference. See Margaret M. Conway "The Gender Gap: A Comparison Across Racial and Ethnic Groups," in *Voting the Gender Gap*, edited by Lois Duke Whitaker (Urbana-Champaign University: University of Illinois Press: 2008), 170–183; and Susan E. Howell and Christine L. Day, "Complexities of the Gender Gap," *The Journal of Politics* 62, no. 2 (2000): 858–874.

3. Barbara Norrander, "The History of the Gender Gaps" in *Voting the Gender Gap*, edited by Lois Duke Whitaker (Urbana-Champaign: University of Illinois Press: 2008), 10–12.

4. Wendy Smooth, "Intersectionality in Electoral Politics: A Mess Worth Making," *Politics and Gender* 2, no. 3 (2006): 405.

5. National Partnership for Women & Families, "Fact Sheet: Black Women and the Wage Gap," April 2019, nationalpartnership.org/our-work/resources/workplace/fair-pay/african-american-women-wage-gap.pdf.

6. Nadia Brown and Sarah Gershon, "Intersectional Presentations: An Exploratory Study of Minority Congresswomen's Websites; Biographies," *Du Bois Review* 13, no. 1 (2016).

7. Alvin B. Tillery, "Tweeting Racial Representation: How the Congressional Black Caucus Used Twitter in the 113th Congress," *Politics, Groups, and Identities* (June 18, 2019): 1–20. doi.org/10.1080/21565503.2019.1629308.

8. See Edith J. Barrett, "The Policy Priorities of African American Women in State Legislatures." *Legislative Studies Quarterly* 20, no. 2 (1995): 223–47; Kathleen Bratton, Kerry Haynie, and Beth Reingold, "Agenda Setting and African American Women in State Legislatures," *Journal of Women, Politics, Policy* 28, no. 3 (2007): 71–96; Bryon D'Andra Orey, Wendy Smooth, Kimberly S. Adams, and Kisah Harris-Clark, "Race and Gender Matter: Refining Models of Legislative Policy Making in State Legislatures," *Journal of Women, Politics & Policy* 28, no. 3/4 (2006): 97–119; and Nadia Brown, *Sisters in the Statehouse: Black Women and Legislative Decision Making* (New York, NY: Oxford University Press, 2014).

Civic and Environmental Education: Protecting the Planet and Our Democracy, Judy Braus

1. Thanks to all my many brilliant colleagues for their insights that helped shape this article, including Kei Kawashima-Ginsberg, John Flicker, John Dedrick, Bora Simmons, Katie Navin, Jonathan Adams, John Carey, Kevin Colye, Christy Merrick, Martha Monroe, Kristen Kunkle, Jon Shields, and Kathy McGlauflin.

2. "Freedom in the World 2019: Democracy in Retreat," Freedom House, February 5, 2019, freedomhouse.org/report/freedom-world/freedom-world-2019/demo
cracy-in-retreat.

3. Kei Kawashima-Ginsberg, Presentation, Kettering Foundation, February 2019.

4. "Americans Are Poorly Informed About Basic Constitutional Provisions," The Annenberg Public Policy Center of the University of Pennsylvania, September 18, 2017, www.annenbergpublicpolicycenter.org/americans-are-poorly-informed-about
-basic-constitutional-provisions; Amanda Robert, "16% of Americans Think Clarence Thomas Is Chief Justice, ABA Civics Survey Finds," *ABA Journal*, May 1, 2019, www.abajournal.com/web/article/aba-survey-reveals-gaps-in-americans-civic
-knowledge; Alex Vandermaas-Peeler, Daniel Cox, Maxine Najle, Molly Fisch-Friedman, Rob Griffin, and Robert P. Jones, "American Democracy in Crisis: Civic Engagement, Young Adult Activism, and the 2018 Midterm Elections," *PRRI*, October 11, 2018, www.prri.org/research/american-democracy-in-crisis-civic-engagement
-young-adult-activism-and-the-2018-midterm-elections.

5. Mathew Shaw, "Civic Illiteracy in America," *Harvard Political Review*, May 25, 2017.

6. Lorien Nesbitt, Michael J. Meitner, Cynthia Girling, Stephen R.J. Sheppard, and Yuhao Lu. "Who Has Access to Urban Vegetation? A Spatial Analysis of Distributional Green Equity in 10 US Cities," *Landscape and Urban Planning* 181 (January 2019): 51–79, doi:10.1016/j.landurbplan.2018.08.007.

7. Heather Buskirk, "Our Students—and Our Teachers—Need True Project-Based Learning," RealClearEducation, April 18, 2019, www.realcleareducation.com
/articles/2019/04/18/our_students__and_our_teachers__need_true_project-based
_learning_110322.html.

8. Nicole Ardoin and Christy Merrick, *Environmental Education: A Brief Guide for U.S. Grantmakers*, a joint publication by Cedar Tree Foundation, North American Association for Environmental Education, Stanford Woods Institute for the Environment, and Environmental Education Collaborative (2013), nmardoin.people
.stanford.edu/sites/g/files/sbiybj4916/f/Grantmakers%2010.6.pdf.

9. Louise Dubé, "Can Civics Education Repair a Failing Democracy?" *Yale Insights*, June 5, 2019, insights.som.yale.edu/insights/can-civics-education-repair
-failing-democracy.

10. National Science Teachers Association (NSTA), "NSTA Position Statement: The Teaching of Climate Science," www.nsta.org/about/positions/climatescience
.aspx.

11. *Developing a Framework for Assessing Environmental Literacy*, NAAEE report (2011), naaee.org/our-work/programs/environmental-literacy-framework.

12. "The Benefits of Environmental Education for K–12 Students," NAAEE (2019), naaee.org/eepro/research/eeworks/student-outcomes.

The Supreme Court's Legitimacy Crisis and Constitutional Democracy's Future, Dawn Johnsen

1. The published version of this chapter is lightly endnoted due to space constraints, but the online version includes extensive notes.

2. Sanford Levinson and Jack M. Balkin, *Democracy and Dysfunction* (Chicago: University of Chicago Press, 2019): 77–80; Jack M. Balkin, "The Recent Unpleasantness: Understanding the Cycles of Constitutional Time," *Indiana Law Journal* 94, no. 1 (2019): 253–296.

3. Thomas Edsall, "The Fight Over How Trump Fits In with the Other 44 Presidents," *New York Times*, May 15, 2019.

4. Thomas E. Mann and Norman Ornstein, *It's Even Worse Than It Looks: How the American Constitutional System Collided with the New Politics of Extremism* (New York: Basic Books, 2d ed. 2012).

5. Daniel Epps and Ganesh Sitaraman, "How to Save the Supreme Court," *Yale Law Journal* (forthcoming 2019).

6. Paul D. Carrington and Roger C. Cramton, eds., *Reforming the Court: Term Limits for Supreme Court Justices* (Durham, NC: Carolina Academic, 2006).

7. Marty Lederman, "The Vicious Entrenchment Cycle," *Balkinization*, October 6, 2018, https://balkin.blogspot.com/2018/10/the-vicious-entrenchment-circle.html.

8. Office of Legal Policy, U.S. Department of Justice, Report to the Attorney General, "The Constitution in the Year 2000: Choices Ahead in Constitutional Interpretation" (1988); Office of Legal Policy, U.S. Department of Justice, "Guidelines on Constitutional Litigation" (1988); Dawn Johnsen, "Ronald Reagan and the Rehnquist Court on Congressional Power: Presidential Influences on Constitutional Change," *Indiana Law Journal* 78, no. 1 (2003): 363–412.

9. Ethan Bonner, *Battle for Justice: How the Bork Nomination Shook America* (New York: Union Square Press, 2d ed. 2007), 230.

10. Joseph Fishkin and David E. Pozen, "Asymmetric Constitutional Hardball," *Columbia Law Review* 118, no. 3 (2018): 915–82; Mark Tushnet, "Constitutional Hardball," *Journal of Marshall Law Review* 37 (2004): 523–53.

11. Jack M. Balkin, "From Off the Wall to On the Wall: How the Mandate Challenge Went Mainstream," *The Atlantic*, June 4, 2012.

12. Michael J. Graetz and Linda Greenhouse, *The Burger Court and the Rise of the Judicial Right* (New York: Simon & Schuster, 2016); Goodwin Liu, Pamela S. Karlan, and Christopher H. Schroeder, *Keeping Faith with the Constitution* (Washington, DC: American Constitution Society, 2009); Laurence H. Tribe, *God Save This Honorable Court: How the Choice of Supreme Court Justices Shapes Our History* (Minneapolis: University of Minnesota Law School, 1985).

13. Dawn Johnsen, "Windsor, Shelby County, and the Demise of Originalism," *Indiana Law Journal* 89, no. 3 (2014): 3–25.

14. Robert O'Harrow Jr. and Shawn Boburg, "A Conservative Activist's Behind-the-Scenes Campaign to Remake the Nation's Courts," *Washington Post*, May 21, 2019.

15. Dawn Johnsen and Walter Dellinger, "The Constitutionality of a National Wealth Tax," *Indiana Law Journal* 93, no. 1 (2018): 111–137.

16. *New York Times*, June 21, 2019.

17. Brian Frazelle, "A Banner Year for Business as the Supreme Court's Majority Is Restored," Constitutional Accountability Center, July 17, 2018, www.theuscon stitution.org/think_tank/a-banner-year-for-business-as-the-supreme-courts -conservative-majority-is-restored.

18. Linda Greenhouse, "Abortion Cases: A Conservative Judicial Agenda?" *New York Times*, April 1, 2019.

Can Democracy Survive the Internet? David Hickton

1. Erik Brynjolfsson and Andrew McAfee, *The Second Machine Age: Work, Progress, and Prosperity in a Time of Brilliant Technologies* (New York: Norton, 2016).

2. Jameel Jaffer, "Digital Journalism and the New Public Square—Or' Emet Lecture," *Just Security*, November 13, 2018.

3. Craig Silverman, "This Analysis Shows How Viral Fake Election News Stories Outperformed Real News on Facebook," *BuzzFeed News*, November 16, 2016.

4. Jennifer Kavanagh and Michael D. Rich, *Truth Decay: An Initial Exploration of Facts and Analysis in American Public Life* (Santa Monica, CA: RAND Corporation, 2018).

5. See Tim Wu, *The Attention Merchants: The Epic Scramble to Get Inside Our Heads* (New York: Vintage Books, 2017) and Jaron Lanier, *Ten Arguments for Deleting Your Social Media Accounts Right Now* (New York: Henry Holt and Company, 2018).

6. Timothy Snyder, "What Turing Told Us About the Digital Threat to a Human Future," *New York Review of Books Daily*, May 6, 2019.

7. See Christian Zilles, "The #MeToo Movement Shows the Power of Social Media," *SocialMedia HQ*, May 3, 2018.

8. See Dave Cullen, *Parkland* (New York: HarperCollins, 2019).

9. Thomas L. Friedman, *The World Is Flat: A Brief History of the Twenty-First Century* (New York: Farrar, Straus and Giroux, 2005).

10. See, for example, Jessi Hempel, "Social Media Made the Arab Spring, But Couldn't Save It," *Wired*, January 26, 2016. Cutting access to internet services did not always have the intended consequences. In Egypt, for example, President Hosni Mubarak's decision to cut access at the start of the Tahrir Square protests in 2011 backfired, sending more protesters into the streets and accelerating his downfall. Egypt's military government became more adept at online censorship after 2013.

11. Fred Hu and Michael A. Spence, "Preventing the Balkanization of the Internet," *Project Syndicate*, March 28, 2018.

First Understand Why They're Winning: How to Save Democracy from the Anti-Immigrant Far Right, Sasha Polakow-Suransky

1. "Hillary Clinton: Europe Must Curb Immigration to Stop Rightwing Populists," *The Guardian*, November 22, 2018.

2. Nick Cohen, *What's Left? How the Left Lost Its Way*, updated ed. (London: Harper Perennial, 2007), 196.

3. Yascha Mounk and Martin Eiermann, "2017 Was the Year of False Promise in the Fight Against Populism," *Foreign Policy*, December 29, 2017.

4. Dara Lind, "Watch: Sanders Town Hall Audience Surprises Bret Baier with How Much They Like Bernie's Health Care Plan," *Vox*, April 15, 2019; Alex Thompson, "Trump Backers Applaud Warren in Heart of MAGA Country," *Politico*, May 11, 2019.

5. Cas Mudde, "Why Copying the Populist Right Isn't Going to Save the Left," *The Guardian*, May 14, 2019.

6. Maggie Haberman, "Furious Gay Rights Advocates See Trump's 'True Colors,'" *New York Times*, July 26, 2017.

7. Kenan Malik, *From Fatwa to Jihad* (London: Atlantic Books, 2009), 140.

8. "Murder and Extremism in the United States in 2018," Anti-Defamation League: ADL Center on Extremism, January 2019.

9. Renaud Camus, *Le grand remplacement*, 3d ed. (Plieux, France: Chateau de Plieux, 2015), Kindle locations 4162–81.

10. Bharat Ganesh, "Jihadis Go to Jail, White Supremacists Go Free," *Foreign Policy*, May 15, 2019.

11. Robert P. Jones, "Trump Crowds See the Passing of White Christian America," *New York Times* (Room for Debate), August 9, 2016.

12. Sam Levin, "'It's a Small Group of People': Trump Again Denies White Nationalism Is Rising Threat," *The Guardian*, March 15, 2019.

13. Alexander Betts, "Let Refugees Fly to Europe," *New York Times*, September 24, 2015.

14. "Horst Seehofer: Islam Does Not Belong to Germany, Says New Minister," *BBC News*, March 16, 2018.

15. Carla Herreria, "Alexandria Ocasio-Cortez 'Astonished' by Trump Supporter Who Backs Her, Too," *Huffington Post*, May 11, 2019.

16. Kanta Kumari Rigaud, Alex de Sherbinin, Bryan Jones, Jonas Bergmann, Viviane Clement, Kayly Ober, Jacob Schewe, Susana Adamo, Brent McCusker, Silke Heuser, and Amelia Midgley, *Groundswell: Preparing for Internal Climate Migration* (Washington, DC: The World Bank, 2018).

17. Reihan Salam, *Melting Pot or Civil War?* (New York: Penguin Random House, 2018).

18. Oli Khan, "I Swallowed the Brexit Lies. Now I Regret Telling Curry House Workers to Vote Leave," *The Guardian*, February 15, 2019.

19. John B. Judis and Ruy Teixeira, *The Emerging Democratic Majority* (New York: Simon & Schuster, 2002); John B. Judis, "Why Identity Politics Couldn't Clinch a Clinton Win," *Washington Post*, November 11, 2016.

20. Reihan Salam, "The Next Populist Revolution Will Be Latino," *The Atlantic*, September 2018.

21. John Henley, "GreenLeft proves to be big winner in Dutch election," *The Guardian*, March 16, 2017.

22. Saim Saeed, "France's Socialists Put Paris Headquarters Up for Sale," *Politico EU*, September 20, 2017.

23. Matthew Goodwin, "The Party Is Over," *Foreign Policy*, October 24, 2018.

24. Gonzalo Fanjul, "Spain Rescued a Ship. It Won't Rescue Europe," *Foreign Policy*, July 2, 2018.

Powering Democracy Through Clean Energy, Denise G. Fairchild

1. Sean Sweeney, *Resist, Reclaim, Restructure: Unions and the Struggle for Energy Democracy* (New York: The Worker Institute, Cornell University, 2012).

2. Statista Research Department, *Largest Gas and Electric Utilities in the U.S. as of April 2019 Based on Market Value (in Billion U.S. Dollars)* (Statista, May 2019).

3. Ben Geman, "What Oil and Power CEOs Really Make," *Axios*, July 26, 2018.

4. Sasha Ingbur, "31 Percent of U.S. Households Have Trouble Paying Energy Bills," NPR, September 19, 2018.

5. Nathan Taft, "What Subsidies Do Oil Companies Receive?" *Fuel Freedom Foundation*, June 26, 2018.

6. Darryl Fear, "For Gulf Oil Spill, No End in Sight," *Washington Post*, October 22, 2018.

7. David Hasemyer, "Enbridge Fined for Failing to Fully Inspect Pipelines After Kalamazoo Oil Spill," *Climate News*, May 3, 2018.

8. Stephanie Sadowski, "5 Significant Natural Gas Explosions in Pennsylvania in the Past Decade," *Penn Live*, July 2, 2017.

9. Nora Caplan-Bricker, "The Human and Community Toll When a Pipeline Bursts in a Suburban Neighborhood in Arkansas," *New Republic*, November 18, 2013.

10. "Coal Blooded: Putting Profits Before People," report by NAACP, Indigenous Environmental Network, and Little Village Environmental Justice Network (Baltimore, April 2016).

11. See, for example, Gallup's polling on energy questions, available at Gallup .com.

12. Zoya Tierstein, "How Big Oil Is Trying to Change Its Image," *Grist*, March 22, 2019.

13. Denise Fairchild and Al Weinrub, eds., *Energy Democracy Advancing Equity in Clean Energy Solutions* (Washington, DC: Island Press, 2017).

14. Michelle Mascarenhas-Swan, "The Case for a Just Transition," in *Energy Democracy: Equity Solutions in Clean Energy Solutions*, ed. Denise Fairchild and Al Weinrub (Washington, DC: Island Press, 2017), 37–56.

15. "The Cooperative Human," *Nature Human Behavior* 2, (2018): 427–28.

16. See Jefferson's letter to George Logan, November 12, 1816.

17. Lynn Benander, Diego Angarita Horowitz, and Isaac Baker, "New Economy Energy Cooperatives Bring Power to the People," in *Energy Democracy: Equity Solutions in Clean Energy Solutions, ed.* Denise Fairchild and Al Weinrub (Washington, DC: Island Press, 2017), 195–217.

The Long Crisis: American Foreign Policy Before and After Trump, Jessica Tuchman Mathews

1. R. Chetty, D. Grusky, M. Hell, N. Hendren, R. Manduca, and J. Narang, "The Fading American Dream: Trends in Absolute Income Mobility since 1940," National Bureau of Economic Research, 2016.

2. Robert Gates speech at Kansas State University, November 26, 2007.

3. A comprehensive accounting finds eighty-one interventions in foreign elections by the United States between 1946 and 2000. See D. Levin, "Partisan Electoral Interventions by the Great Powers: Introducing the PEIG Dataset," *Conflict Management and Peace Science*, 2016.

The Case for Strong Government, William S. Becker

1. The United States is the world leader in international sales of the weapons of war. It accounted for 40 percent of the intergovernmental arms trade in 2018, far ahead of the second-place country, Britain, at 19 percent. U.S. arms exports totaled nearly $56 billion in fiscal year 2018, 33 percent more than the year before. The increase is attributed to President Trump's focus on boosting arms sales to create manufacturing jobs in the United States. Trump has made this a priority in U.S. foreign policy. Even so, the record year for U.S. arms sales was in 2012, during the Obama administration, when there was nearly $70 billion in arms exports.

2. Symonds Public Affairs based on EIA data. See shorturl.at/eGJNY.

3. Nace, Plant and Browning, "The New Gas Boom: Tracking Global LNG Infrastructure," June 2019.

4. Gilens and Page, American Political Science Association, "Testing Theories of American Politics: Elites, Interest Groups and Average Citizens," 2014.

5. See the Center for Responsive Politics' website OpenSecrets.org.

6. Kari Paul, Market Watch, "Young People Blame Climate Change for Their Small 401(k) Balances," August 4, 2019.

7. Jarvensivu et al., "Governance of Economic Transition," Global Sustainable Development Report 2019, August 14, 2018.

8. David Spratt and Ion Dunlop, "Existential Climate-Related Security Risk: A Scenario Approach," Breakthrough—National Centre for Climate Restoration, May 2019. The authors emphasize that this is not a projection. Rather it is a scenario that could occur.

9. United States Army War College, "Implications of Climate Change for the U.S. Army," August 9, 2019.

10. Externalized costs are those paid by others than the manufacturer or consumer of a product. It is common practice for businesses to improve their cost-competitiveness by externalizing as much as possible of a product's actual costs to the economy, environment, and society. As historian and social critic Noam Chomsky puts it, a basic principle of modern capitalism is to socialize costs and risks while privatizing profits.

11. Jacob S. Hacker and Paul Pierson, "The Republican Devolution: Partisanship and the Decline of American Governance," *Foreign Affairs*, July/August 2019.

The States, Nick Rathod

1. Tyler Blackmon contributed to the research of this essay. He is a progressive advocate currently based out of Minnesota, where he has worked in various capacities to advance progressive values in state legislatures—both in the halls of the State Capitol and on the campaign trail.

Democracy in a Struggling Swing State, Amy Hanauer

1. Rich Exner, "Ohio Democrats Nearly Match Republicans in Statehouse Votes, but Will Remain in the Deep Minority; What's Ahead for Gerrymandering," Cleveland.com, November 15, 2018, expo.cleveland.com/news/erry-2018/11/0f32e7624 11182/ohio-democrats-outpolled-repub.html.

2. "Overhaul: A Plan to Rebalance Ohio's Income Tax," *Policy Matters Ohio*, June 25, 2018, www.policymattersohio.org/research-policy/quality-ohio/revenue -budget/tax-policy/overhaul-a-plan-to-rebalance-ohios-income-tax.

3. "Overhaul," *Policy Matters Ohio*.

4. "Working for Less: Too Many Jobs Still Pay Too Little, 2019," *Policy Matters Ohio*, May 1, 2019, www.policymattersohio.org/research-policy/fair-economy/work -wages/minimum-wage/working-for-less-too-many-jobs-still-pay-too-little-2019.

5. National Institute for Early Education Research, "The State of Preschool 2018," 2019, http://nieer.org/wp-content/uploads/2019/04/YB2018_Full-ReportR2 .pdf, 134.

6. Mark Urycki, "Ohio School Funding Unequal 20 Years After Supreme Court Case," *Ideastream*, April 25, 2017, www.ideastream.org/stateimpact/2017/04/25/ohio-school-funding-unequal-20-years-after-supreme-court-case.

7. "Revenue & Budget," A Quality Ohio, *Policy Matters Ohio*, www.policymat tersohio.org/research-policy/quality-ohio/revenue-budget/budget-policy/building-better-need-based-aid-in-ohio.

8. "2019 Health Value Dashboard Snapshot," Health Policy Institute of Ohio, www.healthpolicyohio.org/wp-content/uploads/2019/04/2019HealthValueDash board_Snapshot_posted.pdf.

9. "Dying Waiting for Treatment: The Opioid Use Disorder Treatment Gap and the Need for Funding," report by the Democratic Staff of the Senate Committee on Finance, October 10, 2016, www.finance.senate.gov/imo/media/doc/101116%20 Opioid%20Treatment%20Gap%20Report%20Final.pdf, 2.

10. "Infant Mortality Rates by State," National Center for Health Statistics, Centers for Disease Control and Prevention, www.cdc.gov/nchs/pressroom/sosmap /infant_mortality_rates/infant_mortality.htm.

11. Kaitlin Schroeder and Laura Bischoff, "Gov. Mike DeWine on Ohio's Infant Deaths: 'This Must Stop,'" *Dayton Daily News*, March 10, 2019, www.daytondailynews .com/news/gov-mike-dewine-ohio-infant-deaths-this-must-stop/gQDQfSbt40heI koxhujC8I.

12. Wendy Patton, "State Cuts Sting Ohio Localities," *Policy Matters Ohio*, January 2017, www.policymattersohio.org/wp-content/uploads/2017/01/Local-Gov-1-3 -2017-2.pdf.

13. "Sentencing Reform Through a Stronger SB 3," *Policy Matters Ohio*, May 13, 2019, www.policymattersohio.org/research-policy/quality-ohio/corrections/senten cing-reform-through-a-stronger-sb-3.

14. Jeremy Pelzer, "Ohio House Passes Bill to Bail Out Nuclear Plants, Gut Green-Energy Mandates," Cleveland.com, May 29, 2019, www.cleveland.com/open/2019 /05/ohio-house-passes-bill-to-bail-out-nuclear-plants-gut-green-energy-mandates .html.

Can Independent Voters Save American Democracy? Why 42 Percent of American Voters Are Independent, and How They Can Transform Our Political System, Jaqueline Salit and Thom Reilly

1. In 2018, IndependentVoting.org conducted a survey of five thousand independent voters across fifty states. Sixty-six percent said that they had become independents because they believe "the two major parties are failing our country and put the interests of their own party ahead of the interests of the American people."

2. The gender-neutral term for Latino/Latina, a person of Latin American descent.

3. Morning Consult, "To Weigh the Chances of a Third Party, Look to the 2016 Voters Who Feel Adrift," February 14, 2019.

4. Walter Karp, *Indispensable Enemies: The Politics of Misrule in America* (New York: Franklin Square Press, 1993), 22.

5. Jeremy Gruber, Michael Hardy, and Harry Kresky, "Let All Voters Vote: Independents and the Expansion of Voting Rights in the United States," *Touro Law Review* 35 (2019): 649.

6. Katherine M. Gehl and Michael E. Porter, September 2017, Harvard Business School.

7. Pew Research Center, "Political Independents: Who They Are, What They Think," March 14, 2019.

8. Matthew Sheffield, "Most Favor Policies to Improve Environment, but Are Divided Over Paying for It," *The Hill*, from Hill-HarrisX survey, January 25, 2019.

9. Eric Hedberg, Thom Reilly, David Daugherty, and Joseph Garcia, "Voters, Media & Social Networks," ASU Morrison Institute, April 2017.

10. Michael Barthel, "The Modern News Consumer," Pew Research Center, July 7, 2016.

11. Pew Research Center, "Millennials Increasingly Identify as Political Independents," March 5, 2014.

12. Omar Ali, Stephanie Orosco, Brittany Rodman, Mariah Hunt, and Rachel Cooley, "College Independents Poll: The Emergence of a Non-Partisan Politics?" The University of North Carolina at Greensboro, 2013.

13. University of Chicago, "Gen Forward,"(May 2019), 31.

Philanthropy and Democracy, Stephen B. Heintz

1. Christopher Ingraham, "Wealth Concentration Returning to 'Levels Last Seen During the Roaring Twenties,' According to New Research," *Washington Post*, February 8, 2018.

2. John Fraher and Nico Grant, "Dell CEO Joins Davos Debate on 70% Tax Rate: 'Not Supportive,'" *Bloomberg*, January 23, 2019.

3. Dylan Matthews, "Meet the Folk Hero of Davos: The Writer Who Told the Rich to Stop Dodging Taxes," *Vox*, January 30, 2019.

4. Anand Giridharadas, *Winners Take All* (New York: Knopf, 2018), 11.

5. Giridharadas, *Winners Take All*, 8.

6. Robert Kuttner, *Can Democracy Survive Global Capitalism?* (New York: W.W. Norton & Co., 2018), 27.

7. *Public Trust in Government: 1958–2017*, Pew Research Center, 2017.

8. Drew Desilver, "For Most U.S. Workers, Real Wages Have Barely Budged In Decades," Pew Research Center, August 7, 2018.

9. *Public Trust in Government: 1958–2017*, Pew Research Center, 2017.

10. *Giving USA 2018: The Annual Report on Philanthropy for the Year 2017*, Giving USA, 2018.

11. Loulla-Mae Eleftheriou-Smith, "America, New Zealand and Canada Top List of World's Most Generous Nations," *Independent*, February 2, 2016.

12. Rob Reich, *Just Giving* (Princeton, NJ: Princeton University Press, 2018), 73.

13. Alexis de Tocqueville, *Democracy in America*, trans. George Lawrence (New York: Harper & Row, 1966), 513.

14. Robert Putnam, *Bowling Alone* (New York: Simon & Schuster, 2001).

15. Thomas Mann, *The Coming Victory of Democracy* (New York: Knopf, 1938).

16. *Foundation Funding for U.S. Democracy*, Foundation Center, https://democracy.candid.org.

17. Stephen Heintz, "How Philanthropy Can Turn Dark Realities into Hope," *The Chronicle of Philanthropy*, January 8, 2019.

18. James A. Smith, *The Idea Brokers* (New York: Free Press, 1993), xiii.

19. David Callahan, "Gara LaMarche: A Practitioner, and Critic, of Big Philanthropy Embraces the Irony," *Inside Philanthropy*, December 4, 2014.

20. Miles Rapoport and Cecily Hines, "A New Playing Field for Democracy Reform," *The American Prospect*, December 24, 2018.

21. *America Goes to the Polls 2018*, Nonprofit Vote (Report forthcoming in mid-March).

22. Olivier Zunz, *Philanthropy in America* (Princeton, NJ: Princeton University Press, 2014), 209–211.

23. John Dewey, *The Ethics of Democracy* (Andrews & Company Publishers, 1888), 18.

Keeping the Republic, Dan Moulthrop

1. Interview with the author.

The Future of Democracy, Mayor Ras Baraka

1. The Voting Rights Act of 1965 prohibits racial discrimination in voting. In June 2013, the U.S. Supreme Court struck down what was widely considered the heart of the act: its requirement that states with a history of discrimination, mostly in the South, could not change their election rules without federal approval.

2. After urban rioting in the 1960s, President Lyndon Johnson commissioned a National Advisory Commission on Civil Disorders, generally known as the Kerner Commission. The Commission issued its report in March 1968, concluding that riots were caused by poor conditions in urban neighborhoods and limited job opportunities for African Americans resulting from racism and rampant discrimination in housing and labor markets.

3. Jim Crow refers to a period in which state and local laws in the American South enforced racial discrimination. They were enacted in the late nineteenth and early twentieth centuries by white state legislatures after the Reconstruction period. They were upheld by the Supreme Court in 1896 and were enforced until 1965.

4. In *Plessy v. Ferguson*, the Supreme Court ruled in 1896 that racial segregation was constitutional. It established the "separate but equal" doctrine that was reflected in Jim Crow legislation and the separation of public accommodations.

5. In 1857, the Supreme Court affirmed the right of slave owners to take slaves into the Western territories of the United States. The case involved Dred Scott, a slave who sued to gain his freedom, arguing that he had lived in states where slavery was not practiced. The court ruled that Scott was not considered a person under the U.S. Constitution, that he was the property of his owner, and that he could not be taken from his owner without due process.

Biophilia and Direct Democracy, Timothy Beatley

1. See Timothy Beatley, *Biophilic Cities: Integrating Nature into Urban Design and Planning* (Washington DC: Island Press, 2011) and Timothy Beatley, *Handbook of Biophilic City Planning and Design* (Washington, DC: Island Press, 2017).

2. E.O. Wilson, *Biophilia* (Cambridge, MA: Harvard University Press,1984); Stephen Kellert, Judith Heerwagen, and Martin Mador, eds., *Biophilic Design: The Theory, Science and Practice of Bringing Buildings to Life* (New York: Wiley, 2011).

3. See BiophilicCities.org

4. See Umair Irfan, "Americans Are Worried About Climate Change—but Don't Want to Pay Much to Fix It," *Vox*, January 28, 2019, https://www.vox.com/2019/1/28/18197262/climate-change-poll-public-opinion-carbon-tax.

5. Maya Miller, "Here's How Much Cities Contribute to the World's Carbon Footprint," *Scientific American*, June 2018.

6. See Union of Concerned Scientists, "Killer Heat Interactive Tool," https://www.ucsusa.org/global-warming/global-warming-impacts/extreme-heat-interactive-tool?location=madison<-><-->wi.

7. Urban Climate Lab, "Dallas Urban Heat Island Management Study," 2017, with Texas Trees Foundation.

8. See The Royal Society, "The Role of Land Carbon Sinks in Mitigating Global Climate Change," July 9, 2001, https://royalsociety.org/topics-policy/publications/2001/land-carbon-sinks.

9. See San Francisco Parks Alliance, "Street Parks," https://www.sfparksalliance.org/our-work/programs/street-parks.

10. See Beatley, *Biophilic Cities* and Beatley, *Handbook of Biophilic City Planning and Design*.

11. Urban Food Hubs, https://www.udc.edu/causes/urban-food-hubs.

12. See Biophilic Cities, "Milwaukee, Wisconsin," https://www.biophiliccities.org /Milwaukee.

13. See Biophilic Cities, "Swift Roost at Chapman Elementary School, Portland Oregon," YouTube, https://www.youtube.com/watch?v=T5OPqdcFyMk.

14. Joyce Hwang, "Towards an Architecture for Urban Wildlife Advocacy," *Biophilic Cities Journal*, 2017, https://issuu.com/biophiliccities/docs/biophiliccitiesjournal2 .29jdb.

15. C. Twohig-Bennett and A. Jones, "The Health Benefits of the Great Outdoors: A Systematic Review and Meta-Analysis of Greenspace Exposure and Health Outcomes," Environmental Research 166 (October 2018): 628–637, https://www.ncbi.nlm .nih.gov/pubmed/29982151.

16. John R. Parkinson, *Democracy and Public Space: The Physical Sites of Democratic Performance* (Oxford: Oxford University Press, 2012), 2.

17. Parkinson, *Democracy and Public Space*, 204.

18. Dana R. Fisher, Erica S. Svendsen, and James Connelly, *Urban Environmental Stewardship and Civic Engagement: How Planting Trees Strengthens the Roots of Democracy* (Routledge, 2015).

19. Fisher et al, *Urban Environmental Stewardship and Civic Engagement*, 59.

20. Acuto, Michele, "Give Cities a Seat at the Top Table," *Nature*, September 28, 2016.

Purpose-Driven Capitalism, Mindy Lubber

1. Batty, Michael, Jesse Bricker, Joseph Briggs, Elizabeth Holmquist, Susan McIntosh, Kevin Moore, Eric Nielsen, Sarah Reber, Molly Shatto, Kamila Sommer, Tom Sweeney, and Alice Henriques Volz, "Introducing the Distributional Financial Accounts of the United States," *Finance and Economics Discussion Series* 2019-017, Washington: Board of Governors of the Federal Reserve System, 2019, https://doi.org /10.17016/FEDS.2019.017.

2. "The Pitchforks Are Coming . . . for Us Plutocrats," Nick Hanauer, *Politico*, July/August 2014.

3. See Business Roundtable, "Our Commitment," https://opportunity.business roundtable.org/ourcommitment.

4. United Nations, "Summary of the Paris Climate Agreement," undated.

5. International Energy Agency "World Energy Outlook, Power Capacity Additions by Fuel from 2017 to 2040," 2018.

6. "Renewable Energy Market by Type (Hydroelectric Power, Wind Power, Bioenergy, Solar Energy, and Geothermal Energy), and End-use (Residential, Commercial, Industrial, and Others): Global Opportunity Analysis and Industry Forecast, 2018–2025," Allied Market Research, May 2019.

7. "Renewable Energy Market by Type."

8. "Big Oil Spends 1 Percent on Green Energy in 2018," Reuters, November 11, 2018,

9. "The Investor Agenda: Accelerating Action for a Low-Carbon World," UNEP Finance Initiative, December 10, 2018.

10. "1000+ Divestment Commitments," Gofossilfree.org/divestment/commit ments.

11. "How to Do Sustainable Investing Right, According to a Pension Fund Manager," *Barron's*, January 10, 2019.

12. "Socially Responsible Investing Movement Is Hot and There Are No Signs of It Cooling Off," CNBC, May 13, 2019.

13. "The Roads to Decoupling: 21 Countries Are Reducing Carbon Emissions While Growing GDP," World Resources Institute, April 5, 2016.

14. "Climate Group with $32 Trillion Pushes Companies for Transparency," *Bloomberg Businessweek*, April 11, 2019; "Glencore, the King of Coal, Bows to Investor Pressure Over Climate," *Wall Street Journal*, February 20, 2019.

15. International Renewable Energy Agency, "Renewable Power Generation Costs in 2018," 2019.

16. Brown Mahat and Ramirez, "Adaptation to Future Water Shortages in the United States Caused by Population Growth and Climate Change," *Earth's Future*, October 2018.

17. McCall, Macknick, and Hillman, National Renewable Energy Laboratory, "Water-Related Power Plant Curtailments: An Overview of Incidents and Contributing Factors," December 2016.

18. Banking on Climate Change, "Fossil Fuel Finance Report Card 2019—Summary Version," March 2019.

19. "U.S., Canada to Require $800 Billion in Natural Gas, Oil, and NGL Infrastructure Investment," INGAA Foundation, June 18, 2018.

20. Tom DiChristopher, "Climate Disasters Cost the World $650 Billion over Three Years—Americans Are Bearing the Brunt: Morgan Stanley," CNBC, February 14, 2019.

21. Marco Bindi et al., "Impact of 1.5°C of Global Warming on Natural and Human Systems," International Panel on Climate Change. The damage estimated here is based on 2°C of warming. For more estimates of the cost of inaction, see the Union of Concerned Scientists' fact sheet at https://www.ucsusa.org/sites/default/files /legacy/assets/documents/global_warming/climate-costs-of-inaction.pdf.

22. "The Budgetary Impact of Climate Change," House Committee on the Budget, November 27, 2018.

23. "Climate Change Has Worsened Global Economic Inequality, Stanford Study Shows," Stanford News Service, April 22, 2019.

24. "Americans Demand Climate Action (as Long as It Doesn't Cost Much)," Reuters, June 29, 2019.

Restoring Democracy: Nature's Trust, Human Survival, and Constitutional Fiduciary Governance, Mary Christina Wood

1. L. Hunter Lovins, Stewart Wallis, Anders Wijkman, John Fullerton, *A Finer Future: Creating an Economy in Service to Life* (Gabriola Island, BC: New Society Publishers, 2018).

2. George Lakoff, *Don't Think of an Elephant! Know Your Values and Frame the Debate* (White River Junction, VT: Chelsea Green Publishing, 2004).

3. United States v. 1.58 Acres of Land Situated in the City of Boston, Suffolk Cy, Mass., 523 F.Supp. 120, 124 (D. Mass. 1981).

4. Geer v. Connecticut, 161 U.S. 519, 529 (1896) (emphasis added).

5. For references and citations, see Mary Christina Wood, *Nature's Trust: Environmental Law for a New Ecological Age*, chapters 8, 9 (New York: Cambridge University Press, 2014).

6. See John C. Nagle, "The Recusal Alternative to Campaign Finance Legislation," *Harvard Journal on Legislation* 37 (2000): 69 (discussing recusal apart from trust duty of loyalty).

7. Alfred T. Goodwin, "A Wakeup Call for Judges," *Wisconsin Law Review* no. 4 (2015): 785.

8. See, for example, James Hansen, "Failure to act with all deliberate speed functionally becomes a decision to eliminate the option of preserving a habitable climate system." Brief for Dr. James Hansen as Amici Curiae Supporting Plaintiffs-Appellants at 7, Alec L. v. Jackson, No. C–11–2203 EMC, 2011 WL 8583134 (N.D. Cal. Nov. 14, 2011); Will Steffen et al., "Trajectories of the Earth System in the Anthropocene," PNAS (August 14, 2018); Doyle Rice, "Hothouse Earth: Runaway Global Warming Threatens 'Habitability of the Planet for Humans,'" *USA Today*, August 6, 2018 (discussing PNAS study); Gus Speth, (the world "won't be fit to live in" by mid-century under current business-as-usual emissions trajectory); *Foster v. Washington*, Foster II, No. 14-2-25295-1 SEA, at 4–5 (Wash. Super. Ct. Nov. 19, 2015) ("In fact, as [youth] Petitioners assert and this court finds, their very survival depends upon the will of their elders to act now, decisively and unequivocally, to stem the tide of global warming by accelerating the reduction of emissions of GHGs before doing so becomes first too costly and then too late."). For broad descriptions, see David Wallace-Wells, *The Uninhabitable Earth: Life After Warming* (New York: Tim Duggan Books, 2019); David Wallace-Wells, "The Uninhabitable Earth," *New York* magazine, July 2017; Bill McKibben, "This Is How Human Extinction Could Play Out," *Rolling Stone*, April 9, 2019.

9. Brief for Dr. James Hansen as Amici Curiae Supporting Plaintiffs-Appellants at 7, Alec L. v. Jackson, No. C–11–2203 EMC, 2011 WL 8583134 (N.D. Cal. Nov. 14, 2011).

10. R. Henry Weaver & Douglas A. Kysar, "Courting Disaster: Climate Change and the Adjudication of Catastrophe," *Notre Dame Law Review* 93 (2017): 295, 329.

11. For further discussion of cases and citations, see Michael C. Blumm and Mary Christina Wood, "No Ordinary Lawsuit," *American U. L. Review* 1 (2017).

12. The historic record shows that presidents as far back as Lyndon Johnson have known about the climate crisis.

13. Hansen, supra note 9, at 7.

14. See Naomi Oreshkes and Erik M. Conway, *Merchants of Doubt: How a Handful of Scientists Obscured the Truth on Issues from Tobacco Smoke to Global Warming* (New York: Bloomsbury Press, 2010); Union of Concerned Scientists, "Holding Major Fossil Fuel Companies Accountable for Nearly 40 Years of Climate Deception and Harm," https://www.ucsusa.org/global-warming/fossil-fuel-companies-knew -about-global-warming.

CONTRIBUTOR BIOGRAPHIES

Derrick M. Anderson is associate professor in the School of Public Affairs and advisor to the president at Arizona State University.

Ras Baraka is the fortieth mayor of Newark, New Jersey. He is author of *Black Girls Learn Love Hard* (2006) and co-author of *In the Tradition: An Anthology of Young Black Writers* (1992).

Timothy Beatley is the Teresa Heinz Professor of Sustainable Communities in the School of Architecture at the University of Virginia, where he also directs the Biophilic Cities Project.

William S. Becker is executive director of the Presidential Climate Action Project. He previously served as a senior official at the U.S. Department of Energy, and remains an advisor to several policy organizations and think tanks.

Judy Braus is executive director of the North American Association for Environmental Education. She previously managed the education and outreach departments at the National Audubon Society, World Wildlife Fund, and the National Wildlife Federation, and has developed widely used educational materials and leadership programs for national and international audiences.

Nadia E. Brown is a university scholar and associate professor of political science and African American studies at Purdue University. She is author of *Sisters in the Statehouse: Black Women and Legislative Decision Making* (2014).

Michael M. Crow is the sixteenth president of Arizona State University and professor of public administration and policy. He was previously executive vice provost and professor of science and technology policy at Columbia University.

William B. Dabars is senior director of research for the New American University in the Office of the President and an associate research professor in the School for the Future of Innovation in Society at Arizona State University.

Michael Eric Dyson is a professor of sociology at Georgetown University, a *New York Times* contributing opinion writer, and a contributing editor of the *New Republic*. He is the author of numerous books, including *Tears We Cannot Stop: A Sermon to White America* (2017).

Denise G. Fairchild is the president and CEO of Emerald Cities Collaborative. She previously served as executive director of LISC-LA and is founder and past director of the Community and Economic Development Department at Los Angeles Trade-Technical College.

Eric Freyfogle is research professor and Swanlund Chair Emeritus at the University of Illinois at Urbana-Champaign. His writings include *Our Oldest Task: Making Sense of Our Place in Nature* (2017) and *Why Conservation Is Failing and How It Can Regain Ground* (2006).

Andra Gillespie is associate professor of political science and director of the James Weldon Johnson Institute at Emory University. She is author of *The New Black Politician: Cory Booker, Newark and Post-Racial America* (2012) and *Race and the Obama Administration: Substance, Symbols and Hope* (2019).

Andrew Gumbel has worked as a foreign correspondent around the world and has won awards as an investigative reporter, political columnist, and feature writer. His books include a forthcoming book about an underdog southern university that is rewriting the rules of social mobility and graduating unprecedented numbers of lower-income students.

Jacob S. Hacker is Stanley Resor Professor of Political Science and director of the Institution for Social and Policy Studies at Yale University. He and Paul Pierson have co-authored several books, including *American Amnesia: How the War on Government Led Us to Forget What Made America Prosper* (2016).

Amy Hanauer is executive director of Citizens for Tax Justice and Institute on Taxation and Economic Policy. She is on the board of *The American Prospect* magazine. For twenty years, Hanauer ran the think tank Policy Matters Ohio, before shifting to national-level tax justice work.

Stephen B. Heintz is president of the Rockefeller Brothers Fund. Prior to this, he was founding president of Demos and executive vice president and chief operating officer of the EastWest Institute. He devoted the first fifteen years of his career to politics and government service.

David Hickton is the founding director of the University of Pittsburgh Institute for Cyber Law, Policy, and Security, and the former U.S. attorney for the Western District of Pennsylvania. He is also the co-chair of the Blue Ribbon Commission on Pennsylvania's Election Security.

Maria Hinojosa is an award-winning news anchor and journalist, contributing to PBS, CBS, WNBC, CNN, NPR, Frontline, and CBS Radio. In 2010, she created the Futuro Media Group and is the anchor and executive producer of the Peabody Award–winning show, *Latino USA*.

Dawn Johnsen is the Walter W. Foskett Professor of Law at the Indiana University Maurer School of Law. She served in the U.S. Department of Justice and on the transition teams for President Bill Clinton and President Barack Obama.

Robert Kuttner is the co-founder and co-editor of *The American Prospect* and professor at Brandeis University's Heller School. He is author of twelve books, most recently *The Stakes: 2020 and the Future of American Democracy* (2019).

Chisun Lee is senior counsel in the democracy program at the Brennan Center for Justice at NYU Law School. She previously practiced federal criminal law in New York City and covered legal issues as a staff reporter for *ProPublica*.

Mindy Lubber is CEO and president of Ceres, a leading sustainability nonprofit working with investors and companies to drive solutions throughout the economy. A recognized thought leader, she has received numerous awards for her leadership in helping build a sustainable future.

Jessica Tuchman Mathews is a distinguished fellow at the Carnegie Endowment for Internal Peace, where she served as president for eighteen years. She was deputy to the undersecretary of state for global affairs and served on the National Security Council. She has held senior positions at the Council on Foreign Relations and the World Resources Institute and was a member of the *Washington Post*'s editorial board.

Bill McKibben is co-founder and senior advisor of 350.org, an international climate campaign that works in 188 countries around the world. He is the author of *The End of Nature* (1989), widely regarded as the first book for a general audience about climate change. He was awarded the Right Livelihood Prize, also called the "alternative Nobel."

Dan Moulthrop is the CEO of the City Club of Cleveland. He is co-author of the best-selling book *Teachers Have It Easy: The Big Sacrifices and Small Salaries of America's Teachers* (2005).

Yascha Mounk is an associate professor at Johns Hopkins University, a contributing editor at *The Atlantic*, a senior fellow at the German Marshall Fund, and a senior advisor at Protect Democracy. His latest book is *The People vs Democracy* (2018).

David W. Orr is Paul Sears Distinguished Professor of Environmental Studies and Politics Emeritus at Oberlin College. He is author of eight books, including *Dangerous Years: Climate Change and the Long Emergency* (2016) and co-editor of three others.

Paul Pierson is the John Gross Professor of Political Science at the University of California, Berkeley. He and Jacob Hacker have co-authored several books, including *American Amnesia: How the War on Government Led Us to Forget What Made America Prosper* (2016).

Sasha Polakow-Suransky is a deputy editor at *Foreign Policy*. He was a 2015–2016 Open Society Foundations fellow and previously an op-ed editor at the *New York Times* and senior editor at *Foreign Affairs*.

K. Sabeel Rahman is president of Demos, a think-and-do tank focused on democracy, racial justice, and economic inequality. He is also an associate professor at Brooklyn Law School and a faculty co-director of the Law and Political Economy Project.

Nick Rathod is the founder and former executive director of the State Innovation Exchange and previously served as special assistant to the president and deputy director for intergovernmental affairs in the Obama White House. He has spent his career working in state and local politics.

Thom Reilly is chancellor of the Nevada System of Higher Education, former director of the Morrison Institute for Public Policy, and professor at Arizona State University. Previously, he was the county manager for Clark County, Nevada (the Las Vegas valley).

Rashad Robinson is president of Color Of Change, a leading racial justice organization building power for Black communities. He previously held leadership roles at the Gay and Lesbian Alliance Against Defamation, Right To Vote Campaign, and FairVote.

Steven C. Rockefeller is professor emeritus of religion at Middlebury College, where he also served as dean. He has served on numerous boards and commissions, including the National Commission on the Environment, the National Audubon Society, and the Rockefeller Brothers Fund, which he chaired from 1998 to 2006. He is author of *John Dewey: Religious Faith and Democratic Humanism* (1991).

Jacqueline Salit is president of IndependentVoting.org. She has built the largest network of independent leaders and activists in the country and is the author of *Independents Rising: Outsider Movements, Third Parties and the Struggle for a Post-Partisan America* (2012).

Ganesh Sitaraman is chancellor's faculty fellow, professor of law, and director of the program on law and government at Vanderbilt Law School. He is the author of several books, most recently *The Great Democracy: How to Fix Our Politics, Unrig the Economy, and Unite America* (2019).

Stephen Skowronek is the Pelatiah Perit Professor of Political and Social Science at Yale University. His most recent book, *The Policy State: An American Predicament*, was published in 2017.

Jeremi Suri is the Mack Brown Distinguished Chair for Leadership in Global Affairs at the University of Texas at Austin. He is the author or editor of nine books, including *The Impossible Presidency: The Rise and Fall of America's Highest Office* (2017).

Mary Christina Wood is the Philip H. Knight Professor of Law at the University of Oregon and the faculty director of the law school's Environmental and National Resources Law Center. She is the co-author of leading textbooks on public trust law and natural resources law.

INDEX OF NAMES

ABOUT THE EDITORS

William S. Becker is executive director of the Presidential Climate Action Project, a nonpartisan initiative launched in 2007 to advise the president of the United States on using executive authorities to fight climate change and expedite America's transition to a clean energy economy. He served for fifteen years as a senior official at the U.S. Department of Energy, and remains an advisor to several policy organizations and think tanks dealing with clean energy and climate change. A former journalist with the Associated Press and a widely distributed blogger, Bill is also the author of *The 100-Day Action Plan to Save the Planet*.

Andrew Gumbel is a British-born journalist who has worked as a foreign correspondent around the world and won awards as an investigative reporter, political columnist, and feature writer. He has written extensively about democratization and voting rights and is the author of *Down for the Count: Dirty Elections and the Rotten History of Democracy in America* (The New Press), as well as *Oklahoma City: What the Investigation Missed—And Why It Still Matters* and another forthcoming book for The New Press, about an underdog southern university that is rewriting the rules of social mobility and graduating unprecedented numbers of lower-income students. He is also a regular contributor to *The Guardian*.

Bakari Kitwana is a journalist, activist and thought leader in the area of hip-hop and black youth political engagement who has provided commentary on CNN, FOX News, CSPAN, PBS, and NPR. The founder and executive director of Rap Sessions, which conducts town hall meetings on difficult dialogues facing the hip-hop and millennial generations, he's been editor-in-chief of *The Source* magazine and editorial director of Third World Press. Kitwana has taught in the political science department at the University of Chicago and is author of the groundbreaking *The Hip-Hop Generation: Young Blacks and the Crisis in African American Culture.*

David W. Orr is the Paul Sears Distinguished Professor of Environmental Studies and Politics Emeritus at Oberlin College and a founding editor of the journal *Solutions*. He is the author of eight books, including *Dangerous Years: Climate Change, the Long Emergency, and the Way Forward* and *Down to the Wire: Confronting Climate Collapse,* and co-editor of three others. He has been nationally recognized for his pioneering work on environmental literacy and ecological design.

PUBLISHING IN THE PUBLIC INTEREST

Thank you for reading this book published by The New Press. The New Press is a nonprofit, public interest publisher. New Press books and authors play a crucial role in sparking conversations about the key political and social issues of our day.

We hope you enjoyed this book and that you will stay in touch with The New Press. Here are a few ways to stay up to date with our books, events, and the issues we cover:

- Sign up at www.thenewpress.com/subscribe to receive updates on New Press authors and issues and to be notified about local events
- Like us on Facebook: www.facebook.com/newpressbooks
- Follow us on Twitter: www.twitter.com/thenewpress

Please consider buying New Press books for yourself; for friends and family; or to donate to schools, libraries, community centers, prison libraries, and other organizations involved with the issues our authors write about.

The New Press is a 501(c)(3) nonprofit organization. You can also support our work with a tax-deductible gift by visiting www.thenewpress.com /donate.